Assessment of Higher Order Thinking Skills

A volume in
Current Perspectives on Cognition,
Learning, and Instruction

Series Editors:
Daniel R. Robinson, *The University of Texas at Austin*
Gregory Schraw, *University of Nevada, Las Vegas*

Current Perspectives On Cognition, Learning, and Instruction

Daniel R. Robinson and Gregory Schraw, Editors

Mathematical Cognition (2003)
edited by James M. Royer

The Cognitive Revolution on Educational Psychology (2006)
edited by James M. Royer

*Transfer of Learning from a
Modern Multidisciplinary Perspective* (2006)
edited by Jose P. Mestre

*Recent Innovations in Educational Technology
that Facilitate Student Learning* (2008)
edited by Daniel H. Robinson and Gregory Schraw

Assessment of Higher Order Thinking Skills (2011)
edited by Gregory Schraw and Daniel R. Robinson

Assessment of Higher Order Thinking Skills

edited by

Gregory Schraw
University of Nevada

and

Daniel R. Robinson
The University of Texas at Austin

Information Age Publishing, Inc.
Charlotte, North Carolina • www.infoagepub.com

Library of Congress Cataloging-in-Publication Data

Assessment of higher order thinking skills / edited by Gregory Schraw and Daniel R. Robinson.
p. cm. -- (Current perspectives on cognition, learning, and instruction)
Includes bibliographical references.
ISBN 978-1-61735-505-9 (pbk.) -- ISBN 978-1-61735-506-6 (hc) --
ISBN 978-1-61735-507-3 (e-book)
1. Thought and thinking. 2. Cognitive learning. 3. Educational tests and measurements.
I. University of Texas at Austin.
  LB1590.3.A778 2011
  370.15'2--dc23

2011020342

Printed in the United States of America

ACC LIBRARY SERVICES AUSTIN, TX

CONTENTS

1. Conceptualizing and Assessing Higher Order Thinking Skills
   Gregory Schraw and Daniel R. Robinson *1*

PART I: CONCEPTUAL APPROACHES TO UNDERSTANDING
HIGHER ORDER THINKING SKILLS

2. An Overview of Thinking Skills
   Gregory Schraw, Matthew T. McCrudden,
   Stephen Lehman, and Bobby Hoffman *19*

3. Higher Order Thinking and Knowledge: Domain-General and
   Domain-Specific Trends and Future Directions
   Patricia A. Alexander, Daniel L. Dinsmore, Emily Fox
   Emily M. Grossnickle, Sandra M. Loughlin, Liliana Maggioni
   Meghan M. Parkinson, and Fielding I. Winters *47*

4. Designing Assessments of Self-Regulated Learning
   Philip H. Winne, Mingming Zhou, and Rylan Egan *89*

PART II: COGNITIVE ASSESSMENT MODELS

5. Test Design With Higher Order Cognition in Mind
   Joanna S. Gorin and Dubravka Svetina *121*

6. A Cognitive Model for the Assessment of
   Higher Order Thinking in Students
   Jacqueline P. Leighton *151*

PART III: HIGHER ORDER THINKING IN CONTENT DOMAINS

7. The Assessment of Higher Order Thinking in Reading
   Peter Afflerbach, Byeong-Young Cho, and Jong-Yun Kim *185*

8. Assessing Learning From Inquiry Science Instruction
   Stephanie B. Corliss and Marcia C. Linn 219

9. Assessment of Higher Order Thinking:
   the Case of Historical Thinking
   Kadriye Ercikan and Peter Seixas 245

PART IV: PRACTICAL ISSUES IN THE ASSESSMENT OF HIGHER ORDER THINKING SKILLS

10. Issues in the Design and Scoring of
    Performance Assessments That
    Assess Complex Thinking Skills
    Suzanne Lane 265

11. Incorporating Cognitive Demand in
    Credentialing Examinations
    Susan L. Davis and Chad W. Buckendahl. 303

12. Strategies for Constructing Assessments of
    Higher Order Thinking Skill
    Susan M. Brookhart and Anthony J. Nitko 327

13. Critical Thinking in the Classroom:
    Teachers' Beliefs and Practices in
    Instruction and Assessment
    Bruce Torff 361

14. Aligned by Design: A Process for
    Systematic Alignment of Assessments to
    Educational Domains
    William D. Schafer 395

CHAPTER 1

CONCEPTUALIZING AND ASSESSING HIGHER ORDER THINKING SKILLS

Gregory Schraw and Daniel R. Robinson

The present volume examines the assessment of higher order thinking skills in educational contexts. We do so for two reasons. One is that the topic continues to be highly underserved in the educational community, perhaps because it lies at the intersection of disciplines such as cognitive psychology, psychometrics, and pedagogy. We believe it is essential to develop a better understanding (i.e., a conceptual and pedagogical theory) of the nature of higher order thinking, as well as the measurement and assessment of these skills.

A second reason is that recent accountability initiatives such as No Child Left Behind (NCLB) have raised the assessment stakes in education much higher, even though some have argued that they have lowered the higher order thinking skills bar by creating a scenario in which teachers teach to minimal competency (i.e., meeting standards) rather than exceeding standards (Baker, 2007a; Wiliam, 2010; Zvoch, 2006). NCLB likewise has reopened discussions of levels of processing related to higher order thinking, as well as depth of knowledge related to content and per-

Assessment of Higher Order Thinking Skills, pp. 1–15
Copyright © 2011 by Information Age Publishing
All rights of reproduction in any form reserved.

1

formance benchmarks when creating standards and assessments aligned to those standards (Porter, 2002; Schafer, this volume; Webb, 1999, 2007).

PURPOSE

The purpose of this volume is to provide a variety of contemporary views on the structure and assessment of higher order thinking skills (HOTS). Although there are a number of ways in which one might define HOTS, we define them in the present context as *skills that enhance the construction of deeper, conceptually-driven understanding*. We asked experts in a variety of disciplines to discuss the meaning and measurement of HOTS within their disciplines. We believe that all of the contributors would consider themselves experts in cognition and instruction, psychometrics, or both. The selection of participants was intentional on our part in the hope of exploring recent innovations that span the domains of human cognition and psychometrics. In particular, we hoped to receive chapters that explored the span of human cognition related to HOTS, theoretical models that probed the intersection of cognition and psychometric theory, as well as chapters that offered practical solutions to defining, teaching, and assessing HOTS.

We are delighted with the chapters we received, which fall naturally into four general topic areas. The first three chapters may be classified as *cognitive perspectives on higher order thinking skills*. Each of these chapters focuses on key cognitive issues such as definition of skills, the relationship of one type of thinking to another, the extent to which skills are domain-specific, and how these skills might be assessed using a variety of different methods.

The chapters by Leighton (this volume) and Gorin and Svetina (this volume) address what we refer to as *cognitive-psychometric assessment models* in that they translate current cognitive models of information processing into assessment models in which outcome measures are selected and validated based on cognitive criteria. We strongly support the ongoing development and use of these "hybrid" models, which incorporate the best of thinking and 30 years of research in two otherwise disparate domains—human cognition and test development. It is our belief, consistent with the motivation for this volume, that cross-fertilization of domains leads to better understanding, instruction, and assessment of learning skills.

The third set of chapters address the *assessment of HOTS in the specific content domains*, including reading, science, and historical reasoning. The chapters by Afflerbach, Cho and Kim (this volume), Corliss and Linn (this volume), and Ercikan and Seixas (this volume) address two critical issues. One is the extent to which each domain requires specific thinking skills and how those skills might be enhanced instructionally. Their arguments are consistent with previous research by Ericsson (2003) and Lehman, Lempert, and Nesbitt (1988) who found that higher order thinking is typically domain-specific and the end result of extensive instruction and practice using specific reasoning skills for a specific purpose within a domain. A second issue is that some domains may require either more or better assessment strategies for "high-traffic" thinking skills.

The fourth and final set of chapters address a variety of practical assessment issues in a variety of contexts, including traditional classrooms, distance learning, online evaluation, licensure, and national accountability programs such as No Child Left Behind (NCLB) and the National Assessment of Educational Progress (NAEP) initiatives. These chapters discuss a wide variety of assessment strategies that include traditional multiple-choice tests, performance assessments, as well as guidelines for building and aligning assessments to standards.

AN OVERVIEW OF THE CHAPTERS

Schraw, McCrudden, Hoffman, and Lehman (this volume) provide a conceptual overview of different types of higher order thinking skills, as well as a brief review of past research, the development of thinking, assessment issues, and teaching higher order thinking. They begin by providing several diverse definitions of thinking skills and provide a taxonomic summary of different skills such as inference making, constructing mental models, use of evidence to support arguments, problem-solving skills, and metacognition. They next consider the development of thinking skills from two different vantage points. The first is how individuals think at multiple levels of complexity, whereas the second is how thinking develops over time due to experience and the acquisition of expert knowledge. They conclude with a discussion of issues in the assessment and instruction of different types of thinking skills.

Alexander et al. (this volume) examine higher order thinking within and across academic domains. They review a variety of conceptions of higher order thinking within cognitive psychology that focus on a variety of sophisticated processing skills such as generating inferences and logical reasoning, yet move beyond these definitions in two extended ways. One extension is the notion that higher order thinking actively transforms information in a context-relevant, constructivist manner. A second extension is that higher order thinking takes place with in the context of personal epistemological assumption on the part of the thinker, especially internal standards that are used to set goals for understanding and monitor progress toward those goals. The bulk of their chapter focuses on a discussion higher order thinking with respect to four dimensions of learning, referred to as the who, what, when, and where of learning. The *what* dimension refers to the ideas that one thinks about and actively transform vis-à-vis the learner's goals for learning. The *who* refers to refers to all the characteristics of the learner that may influence the process and products of learning, including prior knowledge, motivations, intellectual positions, and epistemological perspective. The *where* dimension refers to the physical, social, and cultural milieu where learning occurs. The *when* considers how learning exists in relation to both the immediate and long-term effects that constrain its process and products. They suggest that experienced learners are more likely to think deeply than those who are younger or inexperienced because age and experience bring with them ability to think with greater complexity. Collectively, Alexander et al. examine the extent to which each of these dimensions may facilitate higher order thinking, either in conjunction, or separate from intellectual ability.

This chapter provides invaluable insights into higher order thinking because it argues that such thinking is less a matter of underlying intellectual ability or use of "thinking skills," and more a matter of the broad context in which thinking occurs and the goals and exigencies that motivate thinking. Furthermore, they argue that because thinking occurs within a reciprocal environment, thinking within different domains such as science and history reflects different types and degrees of critical thinking in order to meet different goals and purposes.

Winne, Zhou and Egan (this volume) examine the assessment of self-regulated learning, which can be defined as a learner's ability to control and regulate her own study and monitoring behavior. To do so, each self-regulated learner must employ a variety of higher order thinking skills that support planning, strategy implementation, inference construction, and self-monitoring.

Winne et al. begin with a summary of major conclusions from previous research on the assessment of self-regulated learning, and review the strengths and weaknesses of current assessment strategies. Foremost, they argue that there is no gold standard for measuring self-regulation and higher order thinking skills, adopting instead, the position that higher order thinking requires a variety of sophisticated skills that can best be measured using an integrated sets of assessment strategies. In addition, they argue that self-regulation and higher order thinking differ from domain to domain and person to person based on a number of important constraints such as prior knowledge, task expertise, motivation, and personal beliefs about learning.

Winne et al. distinguish between two approaches for assessing self-regulated thinking and learning. The first is asking individuals to describe states and processes related to their learning using surveys, diaries, or think-aloud methods. The second is to assess performance using ongoing *traces* such as reading time, eye tracking, navigational choices while studying, recall, or other measures of understanding. The bulk of their chapter features a discussion of methods that can be used to assess eight different aspects of self-regulated learning, including goal-setting, use of study tactics, making predictions, and justifying one's learning strategies.

Leighton (this volume) presents a model of higher order thinking skills in which she traces the 50-year history of taxonomies that attempt to define levels of higher order thinking. She reviews definition in which higher order thinking beginning with Benjamin Bloom and continuing to recent work, including a revision of Bloom's taxonomy (Krathwohl, 2002) and work by cognitive psychologists in thinking, reasoning, and decision making (Anderson et al., 2001; Kuhn, 2001, 2005). She argues that higher order thinking includes a variety of skills and processes that span declarative, conceptual, procedural, and metacognitive types of knowledge. In addition to cognitive and self-regulatory aspects of thinking, she also discusses dispositional factors such as personal beliefs and self-efficacy that affect thinking and cognition at all levels.

Leighton presents a detailed model for the assessment of higher order thinking skills based on Kuhn's (2001) model of knowing. She uses this model to explain how selected-response and constructed-response items may be used to assess different types of thinking at different levels of complexity. She also provides guidelines based on recent research for scoring criteria for constructed-response items, including a helpful discuss of strategies for assessing the reliability of constructed-response measures such as essays and performances.

This chapter makes a valuable contribution to the literature by articulating a model which relates different types of thinking to well-defined cognitive processes (e.g., generating inferences, analysis of arguments, hypothesis testing), as well as criteria for assessing and scoring higher level cognitive processes. It also provides comprehensive discussion of taxonomies of knowledge, how these types of knowledge relate to higher order thinking, and assessment strategies they offer effective ways to assess this knowledge.

Gorin and Svetina (this volume) explore the design of tests with higher order thinking in mind. They provide a brief review of current models, including the National Research Council's report titled *Knowing What Students Know: The Science and Design of Educational Assessment* (KWSN; NRC, 2001). They also consider Embretson's cognitive design system (CDS; Embretson, 1993, 1998) and Mislevy's evidence-centered design (ECD; Mislevy, 1994; Mislevy, Steinberg, & Almond, 2003). Both models propose an integrated cognitive framework for that guides item development based on multilevel assessments of declarative and procedural knowledge.

The authors provide a number of interesting examples to illustrate how these models can be used to plan, build, implement and evaluate assessments of higher order thinking skills. They also discuss several related issues such as appraisal of latent traits embedded within the cognitive measurement model, computation and use of classical and modern (i.e., IRT) item and test parameters, confirmatory modeling to determine the dimensionality of the model, and building an evidence-based validity argument (Kane, 1992, 2006; Messick, 1989, 1995). Of special interest, they discuss the utility of formative and summative evidence used to construct a comprehensive validity argument.

Gorin and Svetina conclude with a discussion of how cognitively-based assessment design improves reliability and validity (Kane, 2006; Mislevy, 2007). They summarize six reasons based on Embretson and Gorin (2001), including improved construct definition, how models can be used as an empirical basis for selecting items based on the relationship between characteristics of items and cognitive components to be measured, increased accuracy of item parameters, using models to implement automated scoring of complex item types, and providing algorithms for item generation and scoring.

Afflerbach, Cho, and Kim (this volume) focus on how to conceptualize higher order thinking skills in the context of reading and how to develop assessments that measure these skills. They argue that with respect to reading processes, Bloom's (1956) taxonomy distinguishes between basic thinking at the knowledge and comprehension levels versus higher order thinking at the application, analysis, synthesis and evaluation levels. In their view, the two lower levels represent important thinking even though they are frequently algorithmic and automated in good readers, while the higher levels are increasingly constructive and metacognitive. They also link this division to the Construction-Integration model of reading proposed by Kintsch (1998), which distinguishes between microlevel skills sounds as decoding versus macrolevel skills such as inference generation and the construction of situation models of a text.

Afflerbach et al. devote the bulk of their chapter to describing characteristics of effective formative and summative reading assessments in the context of an eighth-grade classroom. Formative assessments may be used to promote higher order thinking during reading, whereas summative assessments may be used to determine whether higher order thinking processes have been applied to a text to construct meaning, evaluate, and articulate critical arguments. Their approach focuses on objective and performance-based assessments that span basic to higher order thinking. Basic thinking can be measured using multiple-choice and short constructed-response questions, while higher order thinking can be assessed using an "arc of questions" that necessitate increasingly sophisticated reading processes and understanding. These questions focus on the "argument structure" of a text, which is constructed and evaluated using a variety of critical reading and reasoning skills, culminating in metacognitive monitoring of their understanding.

Corliss and Linn (this volume) discuss the assessment of higher order thinking in the context of science inquiry learning. The basis for science inquiry is to develop research questions, form hypotheses, design investigations, analyze and interpret data, and form and evaluate scientific explanations (Linn & Eylon, 2006). In contrast, they argue that traditional science assessments do not measure the type of complex thinking that is promoted in inquiry instruction, but focus on factual recall. Corliss and Linn describe a *knowledge integration framework* based on four integrated learning components, in which educators make science accessible, make thinking visible, help students learn from each other, and promote lifelong learning (Linn, Clark, & Slotta, 2003; Linn & Hsi, 2000).

A variety of summer workshops are described that help practicing teachers develop assessments to evaluate the four components of the knowledge integration framework. In these workshops, teachers work collaboratively to construct knowledge integration rubrics for embedded formative assessment items that can be used to provide assessment in face-to-face as well as distance-education settings. The workshops also help educators to align curriculum, professional development, and assessment in a manner that increases student learning. Manu of the rubrics developed in these workshops are presented in the chapter to illustrate assessment- development guidelines and practices.

Ercikan and Seixas (this volume) consider how to assess the progression of disciplinary expertise in historical thinking and reasoning. They argue that effective assessment practices not only capture the development of declarative and procedural skills, but promote these skills by emphasizing the use and refinement of higher order thinking skills. To do so, assessments must capture the rich content within a domain, the interconnectedness of higher order thinking with domain-specific declarative knowledge, and the cognitive complexity of thinking skills used in that domain.

Ercikan and Seixas propose an evidence centered assessment design based on the work of Mislevy and colleagues (Mislevy, Steinberg, & Almond, 2002; Mislevy, Wilson, Ercikan, & Chudowky, 2002). This framework includes three main components, referred to as the *cognition and learning model, the task model,* and *the evidence model.* The cognition and learning model consists of elements of knowledge, competencies and higher order thinking that are the targets for the assessment; the task model describes procedural activities that evoke student responses and products that provide evidence of students' levels in the learning progression; while the evidence model describes criteria for what should be measured (e.g., declarative and procedural processes) as well as how it can be scored (e.g., rubric development).

The authors illustrate the evidence centered assessment model using a progression based on six elements of historical thinking. They argue the model facilitates valid assessment by linking cognitive processes to a detailed task and evidence model, and in addition, promotes higher order thinking by specifying the skills and learning progressions that are best suited for the students being evaluated.

Lane (this volume) addresses the design of complex performance based assessments. She argues that performance assessment are well suited, and perhaps even better suited, to assess complex thinking skills multiple choice items because they mirror the performance conditions under which complex thinking occurs and allow for richer scoring. Guidelines are provided based on Baker (2007b) and Baxter and Glazer (1998) for identifying relevant content, distinguishing essential processes, and defining multiple levels of task-complexity for content and processes across a developmental learning progression. In addition, she provides an excellent summary of recent advances in computer-based assessment of performance skills, which include automated scoring. These technologies have been used successfully in large-scale assessments such as licensure examinations in medicine, architecture and accountancy, which make it possible to assess problem solving and complex reasoning skills with a high degree of reliability and validity. The use of computer-based testing environments greatly expands the possibility of administering complex, performance-based items that otherwise are time consuming to administer and score.

The design and use of scoring rubrics is discussed in detail, including guidelines for aligning to-be-assessed content and cognitive processes to multiple levels of task complexity in a flexible manner that allows the test planner to use the same rubric for difference performance assessments. Lane also provides an example taken from recent research on the scoring of automated writing performance in which she considers how different aspects (e.g., grammar, spelling, composition) of performance may be weighted based on the cognitive complexity of the task.

Lane concludes with a discussion of the validity and generalizability of performance assessments, given they often are based on a small number of items. Perhaps the single most important aspect of validity is construct representativeness. She argues that performance assessments are advantageous in that they allow examinees to demonstrate both conceptual knowledge and procedural skills across a wide span of cognitive complexity; thus, they provide better indicators of the full breadth of the construct. Ideally, breadth and depth of coverage increase the usefulness of the score as an indicator of current achievement, but also enhance the generalizability of scores. She also argues that performance assessments provide excellent measures of instructional sensitivity because that assesses knowledge and procedural skills under conditions that may be more closely related to real-life situations.

Brookhart and Nitko (this volume) present some practical strategies for constructing assessment items and scoring schemes for higher-order thinking skills. They propose three general guidelines for constructing assessments, which include specifying the kind of content and thinking for which you wish to see evidence, designing a task or test item that requires the use of this kind of thinking, and deciding what constitutes evidence for that kind of thinking. They also describe 16 different assessment tasks for assessing higher order thinking, provide examples of each task, and discuss how the task might be used to elicit relevant student behavior and outcome data to evaluate performance on the task. The tasks can be further subsumed under three broad types of thinking, including reasoning, problem solving, and critical judgment. Typically, each of the 16 strategies (e.g., analyzing arguments) is broken down into finer-grained component skills, which include seven individual substeps.

For each of the 16 strategies, the authors also provide three general criteria that can be used to evaluate performance. The first of these is accuracy of assumption, data, or to-be- evaluated information. The intent of this criterion is to assure that the student has a clear and accurate grasp of the information that is central to the higher order thinking skill. The second criterion is quality of reasoning, which can be assessed in most instances using the same rubric for each of the 16 different strategies. The third criterion is appropriateness of evidence, which refers to whether the student selects the right evidence and determines whether or not it is germane to the task and dependable. Brookhart and Nitko also recommend that each of the three criteria subsumed under the 16 strategies be evaluated using a 4-point rubric that spans incomplete and inaccurate performance on the dimension to complete and accurate performance. Guidelines and examples for constructing rubrics are provided, as are the pros and cons of different test item formats.

Davis and Buckendahl (this volume) consider the role of cognitive demand (i.e., the depth to which areas of content should be measured) in test development in the context of credentialing examinations. They discuss three main topics related to cognitive demand, including 10-component framework for test validity, a definition of cognitive demand, and strategies for creating assessments that span multiple levels of cognitive demand. They view cognitive demand as a continuum which can be operationally defined as a system of levels or dimensions such as those described by Bloom (1956). They also distinguish between the difficulty of a test item, which refers to the *amount* of knowledge or processing required, versus cognitive demand, which refers to the *type* of knowledge or processing required. Fundamentally, they argue that test validity depends on the ability of the test developer to identify, exemplify, and integrate cognitive demand in the exam development process.

Davis and Buckendahl suggest that cognitive demand is especially relevant to content domain analysis, content development, content review, and standard setting. However, test developers must first select a taxonomy of cognitive demand and train subject matter experts to use it. They recommend the use of a two-level (i.e., met vs. not met) system derived from Anderson et al. (2001). Training typically includes an overview of the cognitive demand levels, (2) a description of how and where cognitive demand will be used at different stages of the exam development process, (3) an example of each level of cognitive demand, and (4) examples of how each level of cognitive demand can be targeted to the given participants.

Torff (this volume) explores teachers' beliefs about higher order thinking, specifically *critical thinking*, and how these beliefs affect curricular and pedagogical choices in classrooms. Torff defines critical thinking (CT) as purposeful, goal-directed thinking that helps one reach desired goals. He also distinguishes between two strands of critical thinking research, including *instruction* and *assessment*, arguing that both dimensions are necessary for a school-based critical thinking program to succeed (Ritchhart & Perkins, 2005; Zohar, 2008).

Of special interest, Torff discusses the role of student socioeconomic status in access to and relative success of CT programs. He reviews research literature which shows that schools frequently reserve CT programs for high-achieving students, which in turn leads to a self-fulfilling prophecy where the highest achieving students widen the gap between themselves and lower-achieving students. In contrast, he argues that studies have already demonstrated that low-achieving students benefit as much or more form CT programs as high-achieving students (Brookhart & Nitko, this volume; Pogrow, 1990, 1994, 2006; Torff, 2003, 2005; Zohar & Dori, 2003).

Torff also describes the development of an instrument called the *Critical Thinking Belief Appraisal* (CTBA) which can be used to assess teachers' beliefs about the usefulness of CT programs for high- and low-advantage students. A number of validation studies are discussed that suggest high reliability, excellent construct validity, as well as good convergent and discriminant validity with other relevant instruments. The CTBA subsequently was used to examine in-service teachers' beliefs about high-CT and low-CT activities for different student populations (Torff, 2005, 2006; Warburton & Torff, 2005). These studies revealed an "advantage effect" in which in-service teachers rated both high-CT and low-CT activities better suited for high-achievement students. In contrast, expert teachers were significantly more likely than in-service teachers to support use of high-CT activities in the classroom for low-achieving students, though neither group differed with respect to high-achieving students.

Subsequent qualitative interview studies revealed three variables that were associated with significant preferences for high-CT activities over low-CT ones when teaching low-advantage students, including high-stakes tests, influence of administrators, and the nature of the subject area. Teachers believed that high-CT activities enhanced performance on tests, were supported by administrators, and were highly beneficial in subject areas that required construction of conceptual models.

Schafer (this volume) discusses the role of alignment test items to standards in which he argues for an integrated assessment system that addresses the role of curriculum, instruction, and assessment so that students and teachers understanding the rationale for what is being taught and tested. He focuses on the role of alignment in test development with regard to content specifications and depth of cognitive processes. Content may be defined in terms of factual, conceptual and procedural knowledge, while the cognition dimension refers to levels of the complexity of thinking such as the such levels described by Anderson and Krathwohl (2001) (i.e., remembering, understanding, applying, analyzing, evaluating, and creating).

Schafer also describes four commonly used criteria for revaluating alignment developed by Webb (2005). These criteria include categorical concurrence, depth of knowledge consistency, range of knowledge, and balance of representation. Categorical concurrence examines whether there are sufficient items on the assessment to support all categories of knowledge. Depth of knowledge addresses the cognitive demand of test items. Range of coverage refers to the total number of content strand indicators within a standard that are matched to test items The balance of representation criterion evaluates the even-ness of coverage of the indicators for those that are represented within the outcomes. Guidelines are provided as well for determining the extent to which test items and standards are satisfactorily aligned using the four Webb criteria. Schafer concludes with an excellent 10-step procedural checklist for conducting high-quality alignment studies.

FIVE EMERGENT THEMES

We believe the chapters in this volume address five emergent themes. One is that surprisingly little has changed over the last 50 years with respect to conceptualizing higher order thinking. Indeed, most authors based their working definition of higher order thinking, as well as the hypothesized levels of thinking, on the classic taxonomy proposed by Benjamin Bloom (1956), especially Anderson et al. (2010) and Krathwohl (2002). Indeed, most of the chapters in this volume draw heavily upon contemporary revisions of the classic Bloom's taxonomy. We attribute the longevity of this model to the fact that Bloom conceptualized both content and cognitive processes in a manner that spanned a broad spectrum of sophisticated skills

A second theme is that models of cognitive processing have become increasingly sophisticated since the development of the Bloom's 1956 taxonomy, as have models of cognitive assessment (Baker, 2007b; Mislevy, 1994, 2007). These models are especially impressive with respect to the cross-fertilization between cognitive psychology and psychometrics (Gorin & Svetina, this volume; Leighton, this volume; Zohar, 2008), accounting for multiple levels of content and cognitive processing in terms of multifaceted measurement schemes, as well as complex assessment models such as item response theory.

A third theme is the effort by authors to situate higher order thinking within a specific domain, time, and place. In essence, many of the contributors to this volume argue that thinking is higher order due to expertise and deliberate practice rather than raw intellectual ability that cuts across a variety of domains (Ericsson, 2003). Consistent with evolving models of situated cognition and domain-specific expertise, it seems reasonable to conceptualize performance as contingent upon both domain-general and domain-specific knowledge and reasoning skills. One extremely important implication of this view is that higher order thinking is cultivated within a specific setting through practice and coaching rather than attributable to domain-general abilities per se.

A fourth theme is the growing realization that assessment of higher order thinking requires a broad array of methods and occasions, including the increased use of qualitative methods (interviews) performance assessments necessary at higher levels, as well as online "traces." Using multiple types of assessments to establish convergent evidence of student understanding and performance is perhaps the most dependable way to increase the reliability and validity of assessments (Kane, 1992, 2006).

A fifth theme is that assessments in the future increasingly will be electronic in nature. We view this as a very positive step forward for several reasons. One is that electronic administration and scoring saves time and money. A second is that computer-administered tests, and especially adaptive tests that match items to a particular examinee, decrease fatigue and increase reliability. Third, electronic scoring enables test developers to create much more sophisticated test questions or problem simulations, that in turn, provide richer information about the examinee's skills, ability, and current achievement level.

SUMMARY

We believe this volume brings together a diverse group of experts who are uniquely qualified to provide state of the art update about the assessment of higher order thinking skills. They provide compelling models of human cognition linked to current measurement theory, as well as many suggestions for designing, implementing, and evaluating assessments in a number of domains and at a variety of levels of cognitive processing. We thank the authors for their diligence and hope that each of the following chapters helps the reader to develop a better conceptual and applied approach to assessment and higher order thinking.

REFERENCES

Anderson, L. W., & Krathwohl, D. R. (2001). *A taxonomy for learning, teaching, and assessing*. New York, NY: Longman.

Anderson, L. W., Krathwohl, D. R., Airasian, P. W., Cruikshank, K. A., Mayer, R. E., Pintrich, et al. (2001). *A taxonomy for learning, teaching, and assessing: A revision of Bloom's taxonomy of educational objectives*. New York, NY: Longman.

Baker, E. L. (2007a). The end(s) of testing. *Educational Researcher, 36*, 309-317.

Baker, E. L. (2007b). Model-based assessments to support learning and accountability: The evolution of CRESST's research on multiple-purpose measures. *Educational Assessment, 12*(3&4), 179-194.

Baxter, G. P., & Glaser, R. (1998). Investigating the cognitive complexity of science assessments. *Educational Measurement: Issues and Practice, 17*(3), 37-45.

Bloom, B. S. (1956). Taxonomy of educational objectives. *Handbook 1: Cognitive Domain*. New York, NY: McKay.

Embretson, S. E. (1993). Construct validity: Construct representation versus nomothetic span. *Psychological Bulletin, 93*, 179-197.

Embretson, S. E. (1998). A cognitive design system approach to generating valid tests: Application to abstract reasoning. *Psychological Methods, 3*, 380-396.

Embretson, S. E., & Gorin, J. S. (2001). Improving construct validity with cognitive psychology principles. *Journal of Educational Measurement, 38*(4), 343-368.

Ericsson, K. A. (2003). The acquisition of expert performance as problem solving: Construction and modification of mediating mechanisms through deliberate practice. In J. E. Davidson & R. J. Sternberg (Eds.), *The psychology of problem solving* (pp. 31-83). Cambridge, England: Cambridge University Press.

Kane, M. T. (1992). An argument-based approach to validation. *Psychological Bulletin, 112*, 527-535.

Kane, M. T. (2006). Validation. In R. L. Brennan (Ed.). *Educational measurement* (4th ed.). Washington, DC: American Council on Education/Praeger.

Kintsch, W. (1998) *Comprehension: A paradigm for cognition.* New York, NY: Cambridge University Press.

Krathwohl, D. R. (2002). A revision of Bloom's taxonomy: An overview. *Theory into Practice, 41,* 212-218.

Kuhn, D. (2001). How do people know? *Psychological Science, 12,* 1–8.

Kuhn, D. (2005). *Education for thinking.* Cambridge, MA: Harvard University Press.

Lehman, D. R., Lempert, R. O., & Nisbett, R. E. (1988). The effects of graduate training on reasoning. *American Psychologist, 43,* 431-442.

Leighton, J. P. (this volume). A cognitive model for the assessment of higher order thinking in students. In G. Schraw & D. H. Robinson (Eds.), *Assessment of higher order thinking skills* (pp. xx-xx). Charlotte, NC: Information Age Publishing.

Linn, M. C., Clark, D., & Slotta, J. D. (2003). WISE design for knowledge integration. *Science Education, 87*(4), 517-538.

Linn, M. C., & Eylon, B. -S. (2006). Science Education: Integrating Views of Learning and Instruction. In P. A. Alexander & P. H. Winne (Eds.), *Handbook of Educational Psychology (2nd Ed.,* pp. 511-544). Mahwah, NJ: Erlbaum.

Linn, M. C., & Hsi, S. (2000). *Computers, teachers, peers: Science learning partners.* Mahwah, NJ: Erlbaum.

Messick, S. (1989). Meaning and values in test validation: The science and ethics of assessment. *Educational Researcher, 18*(2), 5-11.

Messick, S. (1995). Validity of psychological assessment: Validation of inferences from persons' responses and performances as scientific inquiry into score meaning. *American Psychologist, 50,* 741-749.

Mislevy, R. J. (1994). Evidence and inference in educational assessment. *Psychometrika, 59,* 439-483.

Mislevy, R. J. (2007). Validity by design. *Educational Researcher, 36*(8), 463-469.

Mislevy, R. J., Almond, R. G., & Lukas, J. F. (2003). A Brief Introduction to Evidence Centered Design. (Technical Report RR-03-16). Princeton, NJ: Educational Testing Service.

Mislevy, R. J., Steinberg, L. S., & Almond, R. G. (2002). On the structure of educational assessments. *Measurement: Interdisciplinary Research and Perspectives, 1,* 3-63.

Mislevy, R., Wilson, M., Ercikan, K., & Chudowsky, N. (2002). Psychometric principles in student evaluation. In D. Nevo & D. Stufflebeam (Eds.), *International Handbook of Educational Evaluation* (pp. 478-520). Dordrecht, the Netherlands: Kluwer Academic Press.

National Research Council. (2001). *Knowing what students know: The science and design of educational assessment.* Washington, DC: National Academy Press.

Pogrow, S. (1990). Challenging at-risk learners: findings from the HOTS program. *Phi Delta Kappan, 71,* 389-397.

Pogrow, S. (1994). Helping learners who "just don't understand." *Educational Leadership, 52,* 62-66.

Pogrow, S. (2006). Restructuring high-poverty elementary schools for success: A description of the high-perform school design. *Phi Delta Kappan, 88,* 223-229.

Porter, A. (2002). Measuring the content of instruction: Uses in research and practice. *Educational Researcher, 31*, 3-14.

Ritchhart, R., & Perkins, D. N. (2005). Learning to think: The challenges of teaching thinking. In K. Holyoak & R. Morrison (Eds.), *The Cambridge handbook of thinking and reasoning* (pp. 775-802). Cambridge, England: Cambridge University Press.

Torff, B. (2003). Developmental changes in teachers' use of higher-order thinking and content knowledge. *Journal of Educational Psychology, 95*, 563-569.

Torff, B. (2005). Developmental changes in teachers' beliefs about critical-thinking activities. *Journal of Educational Psychology, 97*, 13-22.

Torff, B. (2006). Expert teachers' beliefs about critical-thinking activities. *Teacher Education Quarterly, 33*, 37-52.

Warburton, E. C., & Torff, B. (2005). The effect of perceived learner advantages on teachers' beliefs about critical-thinking activities. *Journal of Teacher Education, 56*, 24-33.

Webb, N. L. (1999). *Alignment of science and mathematics standards and assessments in four states.* Washington, DC: Council of Chief State School Officers.

Webb, N. L. (2005, April). *Issues related to judging the alignment of curriculum standards and assessment.* Presented at the American Educational Research Association Annual Meeting, Montreal.

Webb, N. L. (2007). Issues related to judging the alignment of curriculum standards and assessments. *Applied Measurement in Education, 20*, 7-25.

Wiliam, D. (2010). Standardized testing and school accountability. *Educational Psychologist, 2*, 107-122.

Zohar, A. (2008). Teaching thinking on a national scale: Israel's pedagogical horizons. *Thinking Skills and Creativity, 3*, 77-81.

Zohar, A., & Dori, J. (2003). Higher order thinking and low-achieving students: Are they mutually exclusive? *The Journal of the Learning Sciences, 12*, 145-182.

Zvoch, K. (2006). The challenge of assessing students and evaluating schools in the era of high-stakes accountability. *Measurement, 4*, 267-270.

PART 1

CONCEPTUAL APPROACHES TO UNDERSTANING HIGHER ORDER THINKING SKILLS

CHAPTER 2

AN OVERVIEW OF THINKING SKILLS

**Gregory Schraw, Matthew T. McCrudden,
Stephen Lehman, and Bobby Hoffman**

This chapter provides an overview of different types of thinking skills, as well as a summary of recent research on the development, teaching, and assessment of thinking skills. Terms such as thinking, critical thinking, higher order thinking, and reflective thinking are used often, but rarely defined because there are a myriad of cognitive skills that contribute to sophisticated thinking. Similarly, much of the available research focuses on some specific aspect of thinking such as planning, strategy selection and implementation, and metacognitive monitoring, rather than thinking as an integrated cognitive activity. We believe there is a large, systematic literature on a variety of reasoning and thinking skills that promote higher order thinking. Moreover, although these skills have been studied in a wide variety of domains, there is strong reason to believe that they affect thinking in similar ways across domains in a manner that allows researchers and teachers to discuss these skills in a domain-general fashion (Leighton & Sternberg, 2004).

Issues related to thought and thinking has been of interest to philosophers and educators for 2,000 years. Nevertheless, learning theorists did

Assessment of Higher Order Thinking Skills, pp. 19–45
Copyright © 2011 by Information Age Publishing
All rights of reproduction in any form reserved.

not turn their full attention to the study of thinking and cognition until the advent of cognitive psychology in the 1950s. Since then there have been major advancements in the study of thinking (Baron, 2008; Halpern, 2003), problem solving, expertise (Ericsson, 2003; Mayer & Wittrock, 2006), argumentation (Kuhn, 1991), and critical thinking (Ennis, 1987, 1997). A great deal is now known about specific aspects of thinking such as deductive and inductive reasoning, decision making, constructing inferences and mental models, as well as memory processes that support thinking.

This chapter is divided into five sections to provide a review and update of thinking skills based on recent research. The first section compares definitions of thinking skills and considers what constitutes higher order thinking. Section two presents a cross-section of four different types of thinking skills that includes reasoning, argumentation, problem-solving and critical thinking, and metacognition. Section three summarizes issues related to teaching thinking skills, including five challenges to teaching thinking as well as a summary of recent stand-alone programs. Section four overviews the assessment of higher order thinking. Section five provides a summary of the main ideas presented in this chapter.

DEFINITIONS AND PRACTICAL ISSUES IN THINKING

Thinking is a difficult term to define because it connotes a variety of meanings. To illustrate the complexity of the term, *Webster's Encyclopedic Unabridged Dictionary* (2001) provides 27 related definitions of thinking that include the following mental activities: hold in consciousness, remembering, making rational decisions, evaluating information, to conceive an idea, to make a plan, to evaluate actions, and to challenge the intellect. Given the complexity of the mental activity that we call thinking, perhaps a single definition is impossible. However, we believe that the terms *thinking* and *critical thinking* draw on a set of core activities that enable researchers to provide general definitions. Table 2.1 provides definitions of reasoning, thinking, or critical thinking taken from recent volumes on the topics of reasoning, thinking and human cognition. These definitions provide general definitions that offer different views of thinking and some of the different purposes for thinking.

The definitions in Table 2.1 and the skills described in section two of this paper suggest that thinking consists of several nonmutually exclusive skills and processes. That is, thinking is componential in that it utilizes multiple skills in a flexible sequence to accomplish potentially different outcomes such as evaluate information, reason, solve problems, analyze arguments, make a decision, or self-regulate one's learning. Not surprisingly, section two of this chapter summarizes four types of cognitive skills which are described in most models of critical and reflective thinking (Ennis, 1989; Halonen, 1991; King & Kitchner, 1994; Kuhn, 1991; Schon, 1983). These skills include reasoning, constructing and evaluating arguments, problem-solving and critical thinking, and metacognition.

One common attribute of the definitions in Table 2.1 is that thinking, and human cognition in general, is a goal-directed activity. We think to accomplish some intellectual end or to achieve a desired outcome (Ennis, 1989; Halpern, 2003; Holyoak & Morrison, 2005). A second common attribute is to gather and evaluate information that is relevant to one's goal (McCrudden & Schraw, 2007; Yanchar, Slife, & Warne, 2008). Typically, we are asked to process more information than is feasible or possible, especially when a task is complex; thus, there may be an evolutionary mandate that prompts us to select information that is most relevant to our current goals, while simultaneously reducing the processing demands of less-relevant information (Mayer & Wittrock, 2006; Wilson & Sperber,

Table 2.1.   Six Definitions of Thinking

Source	Term	Definition	Purpose of Thinking
Halpern (2003, p. 6)	Critical thinking	The use of cognitive skills or strategies that increase the probability of a desired outcome.	The use of cognitive skills to set and reach goals.
Mayer & Wittrock (2006, p. 288)	Critical thinking	Evaluation of ideas that could be used to solve a problem.	Evaluate information to solve problems
Holyoak & Morrison (2005, p. 2)	Thinking	The systematic transformation of mental representations of knowledge to characterize actual or possible states of the world, often in service to goals.	Construct mental representations of the world.
Webster's Encyclopedic Unabridged Dictionary (2001, p. 1971)	Thinking	To employ one's mind rationally and objectively in evaluating or dealing with a situation.	Analysis of events or problems.
Ennis (1989, p. 5)	Critical thinking	Reflective thinking that is focused on deciding what to believe or do.	Strategic decision making.
Leighton (2004, p. 3)	Reasoning	The process of drawing conclusions.	A process that mediates knowledge and cognitive outcomes.

2004). A third important attribute is to construct meaning and conceptual representations that can be used to analyze events around us. A fourth attribute is to engage in strategic decision making and judgments that enhance our ability to self-regulate and prosper. For example, Ennis (1989) provided a detailed list of 13 separate critical thinking skills that may be used to self-regulate thinking in an environmentally adaptive fashion. Finally, there is the definition proposed by Leighton (2004) which views thinking and reasoning as a fundamental cognitive tool that promotes adaptation and successful intellectual and behavioral outcomes.

Notwithstanding the somewhat different nature of these definitions, we believe there are four dimensions of thinking that everyone agrees on. One is that thinking is goal-directed to achieve a specific purpose, or perhaps multiple purposes. A second is that thinking is intentional, often with the intent to articulate a problem, select a problem-solving solution, analyze relevant information, and choose some course of action. A third is that thinking is nonautomated, meaning it requires some portion of our limited processing resources that may impose enormous cognitive load on the information processing system (Mayer & Wittrock, 2006). A fourth dimension is that thinking is reflective and constructive in that the intellectual outcome of conscious, reflective activities is new knowledge or understanding (King & Kitchener, 1991; Kuhn, 1991).

TYPES OF THINKING SKILLS

We believe that definitions and models of thinking must take into account a wide variety of cognitive skills. Figure 2.1 presents a taxonomy of thinking skills that partitions a wide variety of separate cognitive skills into four broad, nonmutually exclusive categories based on four core cognitive activities: reasoning, evaluating evidence and arguments, problem-solving and critical thinking, and metacognitive processes (i.e., thinking about thinking). Some tasks may be so complex (e.g., complex decision making) that they require all of these thinking skills. It is important to note that other types of sophisticated thinking skills exist that could be included in a more comprehensive taxonomy, including scientific and legal reasoning (Dunbar & Fugelsang; Ellsworth, 2005), hypothesis testing, logic and probability (Baron, 2008), as well as moral reasoning and creativity (Halpern, 2003).

Reasoning skills include deductive and inductive processes. Deductive reasoning uses facts, claims, or evidence to support a conclusion. Consider the following the following premises: Susan is a physicist and all physicists are well-educated. Based on this evidence, we may conclude that Susan is well educated. However, for a deductive conclusion to be

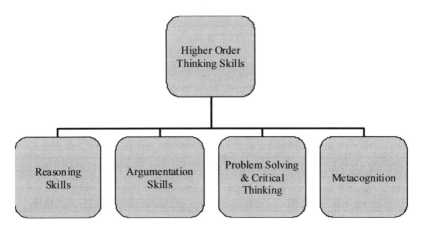

Figure 2.1.   Four components of higher order thinking.

true, its claims or premises must be true as well. If the conclusion follows logically from the premises, then the conclusion is valid. Deduction moves logically from specific evidence to a more general type of claim that may or may not be true.

In contrast, inductive reasoning is a process in which a verifiable conclusion is generalized to a new case. For example, if all humans you have met have five fingers, you may infer that all humans you will meet in the future will have five fingers. The inference may be disproven given new evidence. This type of reasoning moves logically from general claim that that is assumed to be true to make an inference or conjecture about an unknown case. Thus, while deductive reasoning cannot go beyond given information, inductive reasoning does so by generalizing unknown instances.

Both deductive and inductive processes are essential to higher order thinking, especially drawing valid conclusions based on evidence and generalizing conclusions to new cases. These skills are essential components of logical, legal, moral, and probabilistic reasoning as well. Deduction is important because it allows us to use evidence from one's physical environment or evidence in memory to draw conclusions. In addition, deduction allows us to construct complex mental models of the world and psychological phenomena based on incremental, valid conclusions (Johnson-Laird, 2004). Induction is important because it allows us to make credible inferences about the unknown based on what we do know to be true or assume to be true.

Researchers also have studied heuristic reasoning, which refers to shortcuts or "rules of thumb" in the reasoning process that often save the individual time and effort (Kahneman & Frederick, 2005; Stanovich, 2003). Roberts (2004) describes a variety of heuristics intended to reduce cognitive load (i.e., effort devoted to moment-by-moment information processing or maintenance of information in memory) by restricting one's attention to relevant or important information (McCrudden & Schraw, 2007), restricting what is represented in memory such as key facts rather than a veridical representation of many facts, limiting the search for all viable solutions in problem solving, and restricting the number of inferences or conclusions drawn about a problem. Needless to say, limiting online processing may save time, but also may decrease precision and introduce reasoning errors.

A second general type of thinking skill includes generating and evaluating evidence and arguments (Inch & Warnick, 1998). An argument in its simplest form is a claim that supports a premise using credible evidence. For example, one might argue that global warming (i.e., a premise) leads to changes in weather across the planet (i.e., a claim). One might support this claim with evidence and qualify the evidence as well. Argumentation is an important thinking skill that helps individuals make assertions, gather and evaluate evidence, and integrate multiple sources of evidence to support a claim, or to refute or counterargue a claim (Andrews, 2005, 2007).

Premises and claims may take several different forms. For example, Inch and Warnick (1998) distinguished between factual, value, and policy-based claims. Similarly, evidence may take several forms, including pseudo, correlational, and causal evidence that differs in terms of one's ability to marshal compelling and irrefutable evidence in support of a claim (Kuhn, 1991). There is strong evidence that argumentation skills develop slowly during adolescence and early adulthood. Formal education is related to the sophistication of arguments and the construction of counterarguments in particular (Halpern, 2003). Beliefs about the importance and relevance of arguments and counterargument are important as well (Kuhn & Udell, 2007).

Arguments vary from simple to extremely complex, but there are at least four different types (Inch & Warnick, 1998). A *simple argument* uses a single premise and a single claim. A *complex argument* uses a multiple premises and a single claim. A *chain argument* involves one premise that leads to a second premise that leads to a claim. These arguments often involve causal chains in reasoning. For example, one might argue that global warming causes icecaps to melt which is causing ocean levels to rise which is damaging coastal marshlands. Many experimental research projects postulate some type of causal relationship in which there are multiple causal steps that link one premise to another and eventually to a claim.

Finally, a *compound argument* incorporates multiple premises and claims that may involve multiple chains as well.

A third major type of thinking skill is problem-solving and critical thinking. Researchers sometimes distinguish between *well-defined* and *ill-defined* problems. The former has only one correct solution and a guaranteed method for finding it. Solving a quadratic equation by using the quadratic formula in an algebra class is a good example of a well-defined problem because there is not only a unique solution but also a guaranteed means of obtaining it. In contrast, an ill-defined problem may have multiple solutions and no clear path to the solution.

Research on problem-solving suggests a general 5-stage strategy that includes: (1) identifying the problem, (2) representing the problem, (3) selecting an appropriate strategy, (4) implementing the strategy, and (5) evaluating solutions. This general process is used across all domains and intellectual disciplines with equal success (Lovett, 2002; Novick & Bassok, 2005; Pretz, Naples, & Sternberg, 2003). Experts who study problem solving have noted that people's ability to solve a problem depends on two crucial factors: one is the amount of domain-specific knowledge at our disposal; another is the amount of experience we have in trying to solve a particular class of problems (Mayer & Wittrock, 2006). Indeed, the development of expert problem-solving often takes 5-10 years or 10,000 hours of deliberate practice to develop true expertise in a domain regardless of intellectual aptitude (Alexander, 2003; Ericsson, 2003; Lajoie, 2003).

Five characteristics of experts have been shown to facilitate problem-solving. These include a high degree of domain knowledge, a comprehensive organized framework for that knowledge, a repertoire of automated problem-solving skills, more up-front planning time, and effective comprehension monitoring. Collectively, characteristics explain why experts are faster, more efficient, and more reflective problem-solvers than novices. These differences can be attributed to the depth and breadth of an expert's knowledge.

A similar argument can be made for critical thinking, which can be defined as reflective thinking focused on deciding what to believe or do (Ennis, 1987). Ennis has proposed the most comprehensive set of skills thus far in which he distinguishes between two major classes of critical thinking activities: *dispositions* and *abilities*. The former refers to affective and dispositional traits that each person brings to a thinking task, such as open-mindedness; an attempt to be well-informed; and sensitivity to others' beliefs, feelings, and knowledge. The latter refers to the actual cognitive abilities necessary to think critically, including focusing, analyzing, and judging. These skills include focusing on the question, analyzing arguments, asking questions, evaluating evidence, defining terms, identifying assumptions, and comparing possible outcomes. A similar set of skills has been proposed by Halpern (2003).

Programs designed to improve problem-solving and critical thinking skills fall into one of two categories: stand-alone and embedded programs. Stand-alone programs focus on the development of thinking skills independent of content area material. Embedded programs focus on improving thinking skills within the context of a particular content area, such as history or science. Most experts suggest that thinking skills be embedded in specific content areas at least some of the time (Ritchhart & Perkins, 2005; Swartz & Perkins, 1990). One reason is that content material may increase students' interest in learning and their ability to transfer those skills in a way that is not possible with stand-alone programs. A second reason is that scant evidence suggests that learning thinking skills is made more difficult when students are asked to learn new content material as well. In addition, programs should include at least three steps: (1) identifying appropriate skills, (2) implementing instruction, and (3) evaluating the program. We consider each of these steps in more detail later in this chapter.

A fourth general type of thinking skill is metacognition, which refers to *thinking about and regulating one's thinking* (McCormick, 2003; Pressley & Harris, 2006). Metacognition generally includes two main subcomponents referred to as knowledge of cognition and regulation of cognition (Schraw, 2006). Knowledge of cognition refers to what we know about our cognition, and may be considered to include three subcomponents. The first, declarative knowledge, includes knowledge about ourselves as learners and what factors influence our performance. For example, most adult learners know the limitations of their memory system and can plan accordingly. Procedural knowledge, in contrast, refers to knowledge about strategies and other procedures. For instance, most adults possess a basic repertoire of useful strategies such as note-taking, slowing down for important information, skimming unimportant information, using mnemonics, summarizing main ideas, and periodic self-testing. Finally, conditional knowledge, includes knowledge of why and when to use a particular strategy. Individuals with a high degree of conditional knowledge are better able to assess the demands of a specific learning situation and, in turn, select strategies that are most appropriate for that situation.

Regulation of cognition includes at least three components: planning, monitoring, and evaluation. Planning involves the selection of appropriate strategies and the allocation of resources. Planning includes goal-setting, activating relevant background knowledge, and budgeting time. Previous research suggests that experts are more self-regulated than novices largely due to their use of effective planning, particularly global planning that occurs prior to beginning a task. Monitoring includes the self-testing skills necessary to control learning. Research indicates that adults monitor at both the local (i.e., an individual test item) and global levels (i.e., all items on a test). Research also suggests that even skilled adult learners may monitor poorly under certain conditions (Veenman, Van Hout-Walters, & Afflerbach, 2006). Evaluation refers to appraising the products and regulatory processes of one's learning. Typical examples include reevaluating one's goals, revising predictions, and consolidating intellectual gains. Skilled learners engage in all of these activities during learning (White & Frederiksen, 2005).

ISSUES IN TEACHING THINKING SKILLS

Cognitive psychologists and educators have invested a great deal of time and effort into conceptualizing instructional models that are designed to promote thinking skills. Their attempts have been successful in a number of ways, yet unsuccessful in others, due in part to time and resources. Ritchhart and Perkins (2005) identified five major challenges related to teaching thinking, which we summarize below in a slightly different order of presentation compared to theirs. They include what to teach, the role of dispositions to think, the learning culture in which teaching thinking occurs, whether thinking skills transfer across domains, and whether instruction in thinking skills yields noticeable effects. To these we would add a sixth challenge; namely, how to assess the outcomes of programs that purport to improve thinking skills. These challenges provide a means for asking important questions that encompass thinking skills programs. We summarize these challenges below, as well as recent research on different instructional strategies. We turn to a more detailed discussion of assessment issues in the following section.

Five Challenges to Teaching Thinking Skills

One challenge is defining what is meant by good thinking and translating this definition into standards and a functional curriculum. Good thinking pertains to a variety of skills that cannot be taught in a short time span; thus, one issue is whether to teach traditional thinking skills such as those in Figure 2.1, or focus on situated thinking that is useful to individuals in a particular context. A related issue is whether to teach thinking skills in a stand-alone fashion in which skills are taught independent of content or in an embedded program in which they are linked directly to the type of content being taught. Research generally supports the conclusion that thinking skills instruction is most effective when it focuses on a context-relevant set of skills that are taught in an embedded learning context (Lehman, Lempert, & Nisbett, 1988; Novick & Bassok, 2005).

A second critical challenge is how individual dispositions affect thinking and teaching thinking (Braten, Stromso, & Samuelstuen, 2008; Hofer, 2004; Kuhn, 1991; Perry, 1970). Although most models of thinking focus on student abilities and thinking skills, personal dispositions are well known to affect one's predisposition to think, as well as the quality of thinking one engages in. For example, *need for cognition* assesses one's inclination to engage in deep and effortful cognition (Macpherson & Stanovich, 2007). Research shows that individuals who demonstrate a high need for cognition are more inclined to generate better arguments and evidence, generate more counterarguments, and reach solutions that are characterized as rich, thoughtful, and inclusive of multiperspectives. Similarly, epistemological beliefs (i.e., beliefs about the acquisition and structure of knowledge) have a strong effect on reasoning, learning, and classroom teaching (Kuhn, 1991; Maggioni, & Parkinson, 2008). The disposition to think, and to value the process of learning to think, also has been linked to the role of emotions in thinking (Mayer, Salovey, & Caruso, 2008) and motivational factors such as mastery goal (Dweck & Leggett, 1988) and self-efficacy (Anderman & Wolters, 2006; Bandura, 1997). Ironically, research suggests that it may be easier to change thinking skills through instruction than it is to change the underlying beliefs that support thinking (Hofer, 2004; Ozgun-Koca & Sen, 2006; White, 2000).

A third challenge is how to best promote an intellectual culture that values and promotes thinking. Previous research has explored ways to promote a culture of thinking in the classroom, using direct instruction, modeling, and various forms of written and verbal reflection on beliefs (Ennis, 1987, 1996; King & Kitchener, 1994; Kuhn, 1999; O'Donnell, 2006; Schon, 1983; Tishman, Perkins, & Jay, 1995). These strategies have been successful with older stuents, especially at the university level, but less successful with younger students. Researchers also have used conceptual change strategies in an attempt to change beliefs and create a positive culture for thinking (Gill, Ashton, & Algina, 2004). Unfortunately, research suggests that changing beliefs may be far more complicated than people assume. One reason is that beliefs are formed on the basis of cognitive and affective information (Murphy & Mason, 2006). In this view, cognitive appraisal of information is objective and rational; affective appraisal is subjective and based on emotional reactions to an object. Whether beliefs are changeable may depend, in large part, on how beliefs initially were formed. Those formed on the basis of affective responses may be resistant to change by cognitive means; those formed on the basis of cognitive responses may be resistant to affective means of persuasion.

A fourth challenge is how to promote transfer of existing or new thinking skills across domains. One truism of education and learning is that knowledge and procedural skills tend to be inert; that is, they rarely transfer spontaneously to new settings. Studies of expertise show that learning typically is domain-specific and usually underwritten by considerable domain-knowledge and automatized procedural skills that take years to develop (Ericsson, 2003). Indeed, some researchers believe that transfer occurs very rarely, if ever, because expertise and expert problem-solving skills are *welded* to specific domains (Detterman, 1993), and students may be unmotivated to persist until knowledge and skills transfer (Pugh & Bergin, 2006). Although these skills do not transfer spontaneously, instructional strategies such as *transfer appropriate processing* (Ritchhart & Perkins, 2005) play an important role in promoting transfer. In addition, Halpern (2003) and Mayer and Wittrock (2006) suggest that problem-solving skills may transfer, provided educators help students use these skills in a variety of settings, and promote the use of metacognition and self-regulation. Some instructional methods appear to work better than others in this regard. One of the most useful is to provide structured practice that promotes automated problem solving. Automated skills appear easier to transfer than nonautomated skills. A second strategy is to relate problem-solving skills in one domain to those in a new domain by using analogies. A third strategy is to provide students with detailed worked-out examples and feedback. Other methods, such as unstructured discovery, appear to be less productive, although several recent studies indicate that structured discovery promotes deeper learning as well as spontaneous transfer between different types of problems.

A fifth challenge concerns whether instructional programs designed to improve thinking skills are beneficial. Cognitive psychology has a rich tradition spanning 30 years of teaching problem-solving and critical thinking (Ackerman, & Lohman, 2006; Alexander, 2003; DeCorte & Masui, 2004; Hmelo-Silver, 2004). These programs generally report a high degree of success when teaching domain-specific problem-solving skills such as mathematical problem solving. However, programs that attempt to teach generic problem-solving skills are less successful, due in part to constraints on instructional time, class size and funding, and to the scope and complexity of the typical thinking skills curriculum (Pithers & Soden, 2000).

Programs Designed to Promote Thinking Skills

Successful thinking skills programs focus on three main goals, including identifying appropriate skills, implementing instruction, and evaluating the program. Regarding the identification of skills, program design should begin with questions about the kind of model that will guide instruction (Halpern, 2003). *Descriptive models* explain how good thinking actually happens (Baron, 2008). Often, good thinkers use sophisticated rules, strategies, and heuristics to evaluate information and reach decisions. This does not mean that such thinking is free of errors or is the best way to think in a particular setting. Rather, it describes what good thinkers actually do. *Prescriptive models* explain how good thinking ought to happen. They presume that some forms of thinking are better than others. Educators sometimes design instruction based on a prescriptive model that is too complicated or time-consuming to be used in most everyday settings.

In practice, most programs adopt a a descriptive perspective, emphasizing how good thinkers solve problems and reach decisions in everyday life even if their thinking is less than optimal. Instructors in these programs must first decide what kinds of thinking skills they wish to include in their program, such as those in Figure 2.1, or skills related to particular aspects of a program or curriculum (e.g., legal reasoning). In addition, instructors must consider whether *direct* or *indirect* instruction will be used. The former refers to teacher-directed instruction that focuses on clearly identified rules for good thinking. The latter refers to a student-directed approach to instruction that emphasizes the discovery of meaningful criteria for good thinking. Direct instruction appears to be most effective in situations in which an easy-to-identify strategy exists and problem solutions are limited. Indirect instruction may be most useful when attempting to develop guidelines for thinking about ill-defined problems, such as moral and ethical dilemmas faced in everyday life.

Regarding implementation, teachers must present thinking skills in a clear and meaningful sequence. Instructors should identify this sequence and model it for students. Several general rules are helpful when considering sequencing. One rule is to start broadly, even in embedded programs. A second rule is to provide ample time to teach the thinking-skill sequence. In general, planning on a 6-month to 1-year time frame seems most reasonable. A third rule is to use what Swartz and Perkins (1990) refer to as *bridging*, which involves grafting a skill previously used in a stand-alone program onto a regular content class, such as history or biology. In essence, bridging refers to embedding previously isolated thinking skills. Bridging is important because eventually students should be able to transfer general thinking skills to a variety of settings and in a variety of content areas. A fourth rule is that effective instruction also must provide varied, extensive practice. The idea of practice as a means for developing automaticity is an important one. Researchers know that automaticity develops faster if a skill is practiced regularly, over a long period of time, and in a variety of settings.

Planning evaluation may be the most challenge part of the program. Experts agree that thinking-skills programs are underevaluated rather than overevaluated (Barrel, 1991; DeCorte & Masui, 2004; Tishman, Perkins, & Jay, 1995). Unfortunately, common problems can undermine the evaluation process. One frequent problem is that teachers encounter resistance to teaching "thinking skills," as opposed to teaching "content." A second problem is that very few tests reliably measure improvements in thinking. A third problem is that successful thinking-skills programs may take years to achieve their aims.

Instructors should evaluate three aspects of every program (Norris & Ennis, 1989; Zohar, 2006, 2008). One aspect is the design adequacy of the program *before* it is implemented. Questions to ask at this stage include the following: (1) Does the program include the kind of skills you want to improve? (2) Is the program sustainable for long enough to achieve its goals? (3) Are support systems available? (4) Will the criterion skills transfer to new domains? and (5) Does it provide plenty of opportunities to practice the new skills?

A second aspect is the need to evaluate the program *during* implementation. Questions to ask at this stage include the following: (1) Are the criterion skills being mastered? (2) Are the new skills being used inside and outside the classroom? (3) Do the new skills seem to make a difference in students' thinking? (4) Does the program provide sufficient feedback to students? and (5) Does the instructor have access to evaluative feedback? DeCorte and Masui (2004) emphasized the importance of establishing baseline knowledge and skills prior to instruction they refer to as *competence skills*, which segments instruction into four stages. Stage one includes a preparatory phase in which the learner masters essential skills and knowledge to think critically within a domain. The second stage focuses on creating an environment in which effective critical thinking may occur, including student collaboration, opportunity for reflection, a focus on learning goals, and use of metacognitive skills. The third stage provides an intervention that helps develop necessary thinking and self-regulation skills. The fourth stage provides regular formative and summative assessment of instructional quality and students' use of newly developed skills. Awareness of these four stages can improve one's ability to ask questions targeting the specific stage of instruction being evaluated.

A third aspect is the need for evaluation *after* the program has been implemented. Questions to ask at this stage include the following: (1) Has the program achieved its goals? (2) Did the program improve students' thinking? (3) Was this improvement seen in other areas of thinking or across the curriculum? (4) Are provisions made for maintaining the progress made in the program? and (5) Was the program the most effective use of the students' time?

Instructional Strategies Within Programs

A wide variety of thinking skills programs have been evaluated over the past 40 years. Some of these focus on specific skills such as drawing inferences, which Ritchhart and Perkins (2005) refer to as *micrological*, while others focus on a large, integrated set of competencies referred to as *macrological*, sometimes based on an overarching model of thinking skills (Ennis, 1987; Halonen, 1991; Kerr, Serdikoff, Zinn, & Baker, 2008; Kuhn, 1999). Both types of programs report success. Interventions focusing on micrological skills usually have infused one to three general thinking skills into a specific course or content area with positive results. For example, Davies (2006) reported the infusion of a general diagramming program that was used to create visual maps and diagrams of students' reasoning processes as used in college classes. Pre-posttest gains over a 12-week period yielded a one standard deviation gain in critical reasoning scores. Several studies have examined distance education instruction of critical thinking skills that focus on analyzing arguments, selecting and using evidence, and drawing conclusions (Astleitner, 2002; Huff, 2000). These studies reported significant increases in critical thinking over a 12-week period using standardized and teacher-developed assessments of critical thinking. A number of studies also examined critical thinking pedagogy in a cooperative learning setting in which students participated in small-group discussion with critical reflection or peer tutoring. These studies reported better reasoning in the form of more complete argument and use of evidence (Burbach, Matkin, & Fritz, 2004; Dam & Volman, 2004; McKinstery & Topping, 2003; O'Donnell, 2006; Topping & Bryce, 2004).

Typical examples of macrological programs include the Productive Thinking Program (Covington, Crutchfield, Davies, & Olton, 1974), the CoRT Thinking Materials (de Bono, 1973), the Feuerstein Instrumental Enrichment (FIE) Program (Feuerstein, Rand, Hoffman, & Miller, 1980), the *Jasper Woodbury* series (Cognition and Technology Group at Vanderbilt, 2000); and the CLIA program (DeCorte, Verschaffel, & Masui, 2004). The Productive Thinking Program includes a set of 15 lessons designed to teach general problem-solving skills to upper level elementary school children. Each lesson describes two children who face "mystery" situations requiring detective-like activities. The CoRT Thinking Materials (Cognitive Research Trust) materials consist of a 2-year course for improving thinking skills (de Bono, 1973). The lessons include not only problem-solving skills but also the development of interpersonal skills and creative thinking. The Feuerstein Instrumental Enrichment Program system centers on what Feuerstein (Feuerstein et al., 1980) calls *mediated-learning experiences* (MLEs). Mediated-learning experiences provide activities that teach learners to interpret their experience. MLEs are deliberate interventions, by teachers, parents, or others, designed to help learners interpret and organize events. The stories *The Jasper Woodbury* series are intended to promote active and cooperative learning and discussion in small groups while solving real world problems (Cognition and Technology Group at Vanderbilt, 2000). The CLIA program described earlier focuses on the development of self-regulatory competency skills. Evaluation of these programs suggests that students of differing abilities all show improvement on measures of problem-solving skill compared with comparable control groups. In addition, programs also report modest gains for self-regulation skills (often the focus of the programs), as well as transfer of skills across different learning contexts (Hanley, 1995; Pithers & Soden, 2000).

Several other studies used existing critical thinking programs, designed either as stand-alone programs or based on existing textbooks, to promote thinking skills. For example, Penningroth, Despain, and Gray (2007) developed a psychological science course based on critical thinking principles described in Lawson (1999) and Stanovich (2003), which emphasized psychology-specific reasoning skills such as understanding researcher bias, the role of causation in justifying experimental claims, evaluating multiple causal explanations for an outcome, and the use of control groups. Students met 1 hour each week for 13 weeks and worked in small groups of four to six students. Pre-posttest test results showed significant gains in critical thinking scores for the treatment group, as well as significant gains compared to a control group with equivalent pretest scores. These results were typical of programs that enacted a 10 to 15-week critical thinking skills program on college (Penningroth et al., 2007), high school students (Lizarraga, Baquedano, Mangado, & Cardelle-Elwar, 2009), and middle school students (Burke & Williams, 2008). In general, best results were achieved when skills were infused into an existing class via scaffolded, modeled instruction with ample opportunity for student collaboration and interaction (Buskist & Irons, 2008). The most effective programs embedded a variety of core skills (e.g., generating inferences, evaluation evidence, justify conclusions, diagramming conceptual models, generating and testing hypotheses) within the to-be-learned content and utilized extensive collaboration among students. Studies that included a follow-up phase also indicated that results persisted over time (e.g., 1 year). Zohar (2008) has argued that successful programs include three components comprised of (a) standards, curriculum and learning materials designed to promote higher order thinking, (b) professional development that prepares educators to use the curriculum and innovative pedagogy to promote higher order thinking, and (c) a diverse assessment program that evaluates multiple aspects of higher order thinking using a repertoire of objective and performance-based assessments.

Overall, studies have reported significant increase in thinking skills as a result of 1- to 12-week interventions. Gains usually range from an effect size of .30 to .75, with longer instructional programs producing more gain. There does not appear to be any important differences as a function of scope of program, number of skills taught, or type of skills, although we were unable to locate a meta-analytic comparison. Intelligence and skill level do not appear to be important constraining variables either in that even lower-skill students benefited significantly from thinking skills interventions (Macpherson & Stanovich, 2007; Zohar & Dori, 2003; Zohar, Degani, & Vaaknin, 2001). In contrast, some student dispositions such as *openness to experience* appear to be related to more and better types of critical thinking (Clifford, Boufal, & Kurtz, 2004). Personal beliefs, especially epistemological beliefs, constrain critical thinking as well (Bendixen & Rule, 2004; Edman, 2008; Perry, 1970). Fortunately, observed gains did not appear to necessitate a great deal of additional teacher preparation or instructional time. Rather, skills typically were infused into regular classroom instruction with little added time or effort.

ISSUES IN ASSESSING THINKING SKILLS

Interest in educational assessment has increased dramatically in the past decade due to accountability-based programs such as No Child Left Behind (Schraw, 2010). Regarding thinking skills, it is important to distinguish between assessment models versus assessment practices, where models address *what* to assess and practices address *how* to assess. Two chapters in this volume describe psychometrically-oriented assessment models (Gorin & Svetina, this volume; Leighton, this volume) that complement other models described in the literature (Mislevy & Haertel, 2006). In contrast, this section summarizes assessment practices that focus on knowledge, procedural skills and attitudes related to students' thinking skills.

Instructional programs designed to promote thinking skills vary substantially in terms of the skills they teach and outcomes they assess. However, outcomes may be classified into three discrete categories we refer to as *knowledge, procedures,* and *attitudes and dispositions*, and a strong argument can be made that each of the three types of assessment is necessary, as well as a variety of subtypes within each of the three categories (Ku,

2009). A comprehensive review of measures is beyond the scope of this chapter; thus, we focus on typical outcome measures used in the literature for each of the three categories. Knowledge outcomes refer to the assessment of facts, concepts, or mental models related to the content being taught. It should be noted that stand-alone instructional programs geared for promoting general skills may not focus on course-relevant content per se (Barrel, 1991; Hanley, 1995; Lizarraga et al., 2009), whereas embedded approaches which teach skills within the context of a particular content area such an introductory psychology research methods class (Penningroth et al., 2007) are more likely to focus on specific types of content knowledge. Procedural outcomes refer to the assessment of specific thinking skills and strategies (e.g., generating inferences), self-regulatory processes (e.g. metacognitive monitoring), or content-based procedural skills (e.g., selecting the appropriate statistical analysis). In this case, the assessment could focus on declarative knowledge about the procedure or the student's ability to apply or use the skill. Attitudinal outcomes refer to attitudes about thinking skills instruction or skill-implementation, or dispositions that predispose student to learn and use skills. Halonen (2008) provides an engaging discussion of assessment strategies in which she emphasizes the importance of assessing multiple thinking skills, using multiple measures of each skill to the fullest extent possible.

Knowledge Outcomes

Virtually all programs that are designed to teach thinking skills within a specific content area include some type of multiple-choice format assessment of relevant content knowledge. Multiple-choice tests are ideally designed to assess abroad array of facts and concepts in a quick and reliable manner. Pre- and posttest assessments are a common format for evaluating the effectiveness of thinking skills instruction. In addition, researchers may be interested in assessing the extent to which the learner had constructed a mental model of the domain or comprehensive understanding of a complex process (Schraw, 2006). A number of researchers have assessed mental models (Johnson-Laird, 2004) and systematic conceptual understanding using concurrent think-aloud reports (Beyer, 1997; Ericsson, 2003; Kuhn, 1991) or essays and interviews that follow instruction (Boekaerts & Corno, 2005; Falk, Ort, & Moirs, 2007). Interviews typically are structured and scored analytically using criteria and scoring rubrics constructed in advance. Written responses usually are scored analytically using rubrics that focus on the implementation of learning skills (see procedural outcomes below), but also the degree to which important concepts are described, integrated, and synthesized into a holistic conceptual model. In addition, researchers have measured conceptual knowledge and synthesis by asking learners to generate or fill in summary matrices that demonstrate how main concepts may be organized into interrelated categories (Patz, 2006). Yet another approach is to assess the extent to which learners can transfer conceptual principles to an analogous problem of learning situation (Baker, 2007; Mayer & Wittrock, 2006). For example, Baker suggests instruction and associated curriculum that is rich in worked-examples that students can use to think-aloud with peers or teachers. Teachers also may be trained to evaluate student think-alouds and provide cognitive feedback that promotes better self-regulation and instantiation of general principles that are likely to cut across different academic domains.

Procedural Outcomes

Teaching and assessing procedural learning is at the heart of all attempts to teach thinking skills. At least two aspects of procedural competence must be assessed, including the use of individual thinking skills and strategies, and the use of self-regulatory skills use to manage and evaluate ongoing learning. Researchers typically assess skills included in instruction, which we refer to as first-order thinking skills. Researchers also may assess these skills using frequency-of-use checklists of generic problem-solving tests that evaluate general thinking skills such as generating inferences and drawing conclusions. In addition, it may be helpful to assess self-regulatory skills that we refer to as second-order thinking skills, because their primary purpose is to manage first-order thinking skills.

Many instructional programs focus on teaching first-order thinking skills. These skills can be measured in a variety of ways, including observation of how a student uses a skill, inferences made about use of the skill in a complex assessment environment, scores from standardized thinking skills tests, or self-reported use of strategies using think-alouds or checklists. First-order thinking skills often may be observed directly. For example, Halonen (2008) provided templates for computational and problem-solving worksheets that can be used to evaluate application of thinking skills, as well as rubrics for assessing student problem-solving, analysis, evaluation, and creativity while engaged in critical thinking and problem solving. Tal (2005) also provided a critical review of observation-based problem-solving that can be scored with rubrics created to assess a variety of thinking skills at different levels of proficiency. Observational methods have been used successfully as well while evaluating demonstrations in which a more-advanced student models thinking skills for a novice student.

A variety of researchers have examined how to assess the use of thinking skills during real-time problem solving. One approach has been to use *learning traces*, which include observable records of an individual's ongoing learning that can be used to make inferences about self-regulation behaviors. The amount of time individuals spend on a task (e.g., reading a passage) or on specific information within a passage (e.g., a diagram or pictorial model) often provides valuable information about duration, and perhaps intensity, of engagement. Eye tracking devices also provide useful information about what individuals attend to and how long they do so (Winne & Perry, 2000). Other examples of traces include underlining, external notes, and diaries (see Boekaerts & Corno, 2005).

Real-time problem-solving has been studied using think-aloud and reflection as well during simulated problems (Apple, Serdikoff, Reis-Bergan & Barron, 2008; Kuhn, 1991; Schon, 1983). Think-alouds provide extremely rich data about online processes (e.g., construction of mental models), even though they are time intensive and may interfere with online activities. Another approach is to examine note-taking using e-logs, which provides a wealth of data regarding what learners perceive to be important (Schraw, 2010). The structure of notes also may reveal how deeply a learner understands information. A third strategy is to examine intereactions between a learner and computer-based tutor that provides feedback and assessments. This type of data is especially helpful when considering the effectiveness of competing auto-tutoring programs.

A host of measures have been developed in the past 40 years that assess a variety of specific thinking skills under the general heading of *critical thinking*. These assessments often include an array of multiple-choice type items that provide an overall score of critical thinking ability (see Facione & Facione, 2007; Halonen, 2008; and Wagner & Harvey, 2006 for examples), and may be helpful for two reasons; one is that they are easy to administer, while a second is that they have readily available norms by which a researcher might compare a specific sample to other potential similar samples. Some assessments focus on domain-general thinking skills, whereas others focus on domain-specific applications of skills. Research suggests that both types are important, but that domain-specific tests may yield a larger effect size due to instruction (Renaud & Murray, 2008).

Finally, a researcher may assess the type or number of thinking skills an individual uses via checklist or self-report. Checklists typically include strategies and skills that were included within an instructional invention. In this case, the individual simple indicates whether she used the skill and how often the skill was used (Halonen, 2008). An alternative approach is for students to record or describe their strategy use as they work (Boekaerts & Corno, 2005). This approach is very useful for understanding online processing and regulation of learning. Another alternative is to use self-report inventories that assess the skills and self-regulatory strategies used during learning (Pintrich, 2003; Schraw & Dennison, 1994).

Attitude and Dispositional Outcomes

Researchers have devoted increasing attention to the role that is played by beliefs, attitudes, and dispositions on thinking outcomes. For example, it is well known that high self-efficacy within a domain has a strong positive relationship between engagement, persistence, and performance on any task (Bandura, 1997). Indeed, self-efficacy often is a better predictor of future performance than intellectual ability and current achievement. Other attitudinal measures, such as the need for cognition (i.e., one's propensity to engage in challenging cognition), provide predictors of engagement and performance (Macpherson & Stanovich, 2007). In addition, questionnaires that measure metacognitive knowledge (Hanley, 1995; Schraw & Dennison, 1994) or self-regulation (Pintrich, 2003) may be significantly related to performance as well.

Another important line of research has been the extent to which motivational dispositions are related to the use of thinking skills, as well as performance outcomes. Although beyond the scope of this chapter, researchers have found that beliefs in mastery orientations, attributions, personal epistemology and ontology are important predictors of the development and use of thinking and self-regulatory skills (Anderman & Wolters, 2006; Kuhn, 1991; Tishman et al., 1995).

SUMMARY AND CONCLUSIONS

This chapter provided an overview of thinking skills. We argued that no single definition of thinking is sufficient to cover the range of skills and activities that individuals engage in while thinking. Rather, we suggested that thinking includes several key components, characterized by goal-directed activity that is used to gather and evaluate information that is relevant to one's goal, instruction geared toward helping students construct meaning and conceptual representations, and to encourage learners to use thinking skills to plan and adapt to new situations.

We identified four general types of thinking skills, including reasoning, evaluating evidence and arguments, problem-solving and critical thinking, and metacognitive processes (i.e., thinking about thinking). We described five challenges to designing and implementing thinking skills programs and summarized two generic types of programs. Stand-alone programs focus on the development of thinking skills independent of content area material, whereas embedded programs focus on improving thinking skills within the context of a particular content area, such as history or science. Both types of programs have been successful, although embedded programs appear to be the more successful of the two. Successful programs have at least five characteristics in common, including: (a) they focus on planning and assessment before, during, and after implenetation, (b) they span 4 to 12 weeks of instruction, (c) they provide a core set of skills and strategies, (d) they provide scaled, model instructiion with feedback, and (e) they offer regular assessment opportunites using a variety of assessments.

We also reviewed different types of assessment strategies, focusing on measures of knowledge, procedural skills, and attitudes. Knowledge outcomes refer to the assessment of facts, concepts, or mental models related to the content being taught. Procedural outcomes refer to the assessment of specific thinking skills and strategies (e.g., generating inferences), self-regulatory processes (e.g. metacognitive monitoring), or content-based procedural skills (e.g., selecting the appropriate statistical analysis). Attitudinal outcomes refer to attitudes about thinking skills instruction or skill-implementation, or dispositions that predispose student to learn and use skills.

Overall, our review indicates that there is a large body of research that addresses a wide variety of thinking skills. All of these skills are necessary components of learning and all are teachable. A large number of instructional program suggest that skills may be taught quite effectively when limited to a corset of skills that are taught with an embedded class or content area (e.g., a unit on scientific hypothesis testing). Skill acquisition is related positively to improved attitudes and learning. In addition, embedded instruction increases across-domain transfer, provided this is one of the goals of the program.

REFERENCES

Ackerman, P. L., & Lohman, D. F. (2006). Individual differences in cognitive function. In P. A. Alexander & P. H. Winne (Eds.), *Handbook of Educational Psychology* (2nd ed., pp. 139-162). Mahwah, NJ: Erlbaum.

Alexander, P. A. (2003). The development of expertise: The journey from acclimation to proficiency. *Educational Researcher, 32*, 10-14.

Anderman, E. M., & Wolters, C. A. (2006). Goals, values, and affect: Influences on student motivation. In P. A. Alexander & P. H. Winne (Eds.), *Handbook of Educational Psychology* (2nd ed., pp. 369-390). Mahwah, NJ: Erlbaum.

Andrews, R. (2005). Models of argumentation in educational discourse. *Text, 25*, 107–127.

Andrews, R. (2007). Argumentation, critical thinking and the postgraduate dissertation. *Educational Review, 59,* 1-18.

Apple, K. J., Serdikoff, S. L., Reis-Bergan, M., & Barron, K. E. (2008). Programmatic assessment of critical thinking. In D. Dunn, J. S. Halonen & R. A. Smith (Eds), *Teaching critical thinking in psychology: A handbook of best practices* (pp. 77-88). Chichester, England: Wiley-Blackwell.

Astleitner, H. (2002). Teaching critical thinking online. *Journal of Instructional Psychology, 29,* 53-76.

Baker, E. (2007). Model-based assessment to support learning and accountability: The evolution of CRESST's research on multiple-purpose measures. *Educational Assessment, 3-4,* 179-194.

Bandura, A. (1997). *Self-efficacy: The exercise of control.* New York, NY: Freeman

Baron, J. (2008). *Thinking and deciding* (4th ed.). New York, NY: Cambridge University Press.

Barrel, J. (1991). *Teaching for thoughtfulness.* New York, NY: Longman.

Bendixen, L. D., & Rule, D. C. (2004). An integrative approach to personal epistemology: A guiding model. *Educational Psychologist, 39,* 69-80.

Beyer, B. K. (1997). *Improving student thinking: A comprehensive approach.* Boston, MA: Allyn & Bacon.

Boekaerts, M., & Corno, L. (2005). Self-regulation in the classroom: A perspective on assessment and intervention. *Applied Psychology: An International Review, 54,* 199-231.

Braten, I., Stromso, H., & Samuelstuen, M. (2008).Are sophisticated students always better? The role of topic-specific personal epistemology in the understanding of multiple expository texts, *Contemporary Educational Psychology, 33,* 814-840.

Burbach, M., Matkin, G. S., & Fritz, S. (2004). Teaching critical thinking skills in an introductory leadership course utilizing active learning strategies. *College Student Development, 38,* 482-493.

Burke, L. A., & Williams, J. M. (2008). Developing young thinkers: An intervention aimed to enhance children's thinking skills. *Thinking Skills and Creativity, 4,* 104-124.

Buskist, W., & Irons, J. G. (2008). Simple strategies for teaching your students to think critically. In D. Dunn, J. S. Halonen & R. A. Smith (Eds.), *Teaching critical thinking in psychology: A handbook of best practices* (pp. 49-57). Chichester, England: Wiley-Blackwell.

Clifford, J. S., Boufal, M. M., & Kurtz, J. E. (2004). Personality traits and critical thinking in college students: Empirical test of a two-factor theory. *Assessment, 11,* 169-181.

Cognition and Technology Group at Vanderbilt. (2000), Adventures in anchored instruction: Lessons from beyond the ivory tower. In R. Glaser (Ed.), *Advances in instructional psychology. Volume 5: Educational design and cognitive science* (pp. 35-99). Mahwah, NJ: Erlbaum.

Covington, M. C., Crutchfield, R. S., Davies, L. B., & Olton, R. M. (1974). *The Productive Thinking program: A course in learning to think.* New York, NY: Merrill.

Dam, G. T., & Volman, M. 2004). Critical thinking as a citizenship competence: Teaching strategies. *Learning and Instruction, 14,* 359-379.

Davies, W. M. (2006). An infusion approach to critical thinking: Moore on the critical thinking debate. *Higher Education Research and Development, 2,* 179-193.

De Bono, E. (1973). *CoRT thinking materials.* London, England: Direct Education Services.

De Corte, E., Verschaffel, L., & Masui, C. (2004). The CLIA-model: A framework for designing powerful learning environments for thinking and problem solving. *European Journal of Psychology of Education, 20,* 365-384.

Detterman, D. K. (1993). The case for the prosecution: Transfer as an epiphenomenon. In D. K. Detterman & R. J. Sternberg (Eds.), *Transfer on trial: Intelligence, cognition and instruction* (pp. 1-24). Norwood, NJ: Ablex.

Dunbar, K., & Fugelsang, J. (2005). Scientific reasoning and thinking. In K. Holyoak & R. Morrison (Eds.), *The Cambridge handbook of thinking and reasoning* (pp. 705-726). Cambridge, England: Cambridge University Press.

Dweck, C. S., & Leggett, E. S. (1988). A social-cognitive approach to motivation and personality. *Psychological Review, 95,* 256–273. (This review article presents Dweck and Leggett's influential theory in a highly readable fashion.)

Edman, L. R. (2008). Are they ready yet? Developmental issues in teaching thinking. In D. Dunn, J. S. Halonen & R. A. Smith (Eds.), *Teaching critical thinking in psychology: A handbook of best practices* (pp. 35-48). Chichester, England: Wiley-Blackwell.

Ellsworth, P. C. (2005). Legal reasoning. In K. Holyoak & R. Morrison (Eds.), *The Cambridge handbook of thinking and reasoning* (pp. 685-704). Cambridge, England: Cambridge University Press.

Ennis, R. H. (1987). A taxonomy of critical thinking dispositions and abilities. In J. Baron & R. Sternberg (Eds.), *Teaching thinking skills: Theory and practice.* New York, NY: W. H. Freeman.

Ennis, R. H. (1989). Critical thinking and subject specificity: Clarification and needed research. *Educational Researcher, 18,* 13-16.

Ennis, R. H. (1997). Incorporating critical thinking in the curriculum: An introduction to some basic issues. *Inquiry, 16,* 1-9.

Ericsson, K. A. (2003). The acquisition of expert performance as problem solving: Construction and modification of mediating mechanisms through deliberate practice. In J. E. Davidson & R. J. Sternberg (Eds.), *The psychology of problem solving* (pp. 31-83). Cambridge, England: Cambridge University Press.

Facione, P. A., & Facione, N. C. (2007). California critical thinking inventory (2007 ed.). Millbrae, CA: Insight Assessment.

Falk, B., Ort, S. W., & Moirs, K. (2007). Keeping the focus on the child: Supporting and reporting on teaching and learning with a classroom-based performance assessment system. *Educational Assessment, 12,* 47-75.

Feuerstein, R., Rand, Y., Hoffman, M. B., & Miller. R. (1980). *Instructional enrichment: An intervention program for cognitive modifiability.* Baltimore, MD: University Park Press.

Gill, M. G., Ashton, P. T., & Algina, J. (2004). Changing preservice teachers' epistemological beliefs about teaching and learning in mathematics: An intervention study. *Contemporary Educational Psychology, 29,* 164-185.

Hanley, G. L. (1995). Teaching critical thinking: Focusing on metacognitive skills and problem solving. *Teaching of Psychology, 22,* 68-72.

Halpern, D. F. (2003). *Thought and knowledge: An introduction to critical thinking* (4th ed.). Mahwah, NJ: Erlbaum.

Hmelo-Silver, C. E. (2004). Problem-based learning: What and how do students learn? *Educational Psychology Review, 16*, 235-266.

Hofer, B. (2004). Introduction: Paradigmatic approaches to personal epistemology. *Educational Psychologist, 39*, 1-3.

Holyoak, K. J., & Morrison, R. G. (2005). Thinking and reasoning: A reader's guide. In K. J. Holyoak & R. G. Morrison (Eds.), *The Cambridge handbook of thinking and reasoning* (pp. 1-9). Cambridge, England: Cambridge University Press.

Halonen, J. S. (1991). Demystifying critical thinking. *Teaching of Psychology, 22*, 80.

Halonen, J. S. (2008). Measure for measure: The challenge of assessing critical thinking. In D. Dunn, J. S. Halonen & R. A. Smith (Eds.), *Teaching critical thinking in psychology: A handbook of best practices* (pp. 61-75). Chichester, England: Wiley-Blackwell.

Huff, M. T. (2000). A comparison study of live instruction versus interactive television for teaching students. *Research on Social Work Practice, 10*, 400-416.

Inch, E. S., & Warnick, B. (1998). *Critical thinking and communication: The use of reason in argument* (3rd ed.). Boston, MA: Allyn & Bacon.

Johnson-Laird, P. N. (2004). Mental models and reasoning. In J. Leighton & R. Sternberg (Eds.), *The nature of reasoning* (pp. 169-201). Cambridge, England: Cambridge University Press.

Kahneman, D., & Frederick, S. (2005). A model of heuristic judgment. In K. Holyoak & R. Morrison (Eds.), *The Cambridge handbook of thinking and reasoning* (pp. 267-294). Cambridge, England: Cambridge University Press.

Kerr, N. K., Serdikoff, S. L., Zinn, T. E., & Baker, S. C. (2008). Have we demystified critical thinking? In D. Dunn, J. S. Halonen & R. A. Smith (Eds.), *Teaching critical thinking in psychology: A handbook of best practices* (pp. 23-33). Chichester, England: Wiley-Blackwell.

King, P. M., & Kitchener, K. S. (1994). *Developing reflective judgment*. San Francisco, CA: Jossey-Bass.

Ku, K. Y. (2009). Assessing students' critical thinking performance: Urging for measurements using multi-response formats. *Thinking Skills and Creativity, 4*, 70-76.

Kuhn, D. (1991). *The skills of argument*. New York, NY: Cambridge University Press.

Kuhn, D. (1999). A developmental model of critical thinking. *Educational Researcher, 28*, 16-25.

Kuhn, D., & Udell, W. (2007). Coordinating own and other perspectives in argument. *Thinking and Reasoning, 13*, 90-104.

Lajoie, S. P. (2003). Transitions and trajectories for studies of expertise. *Educational Researcher, 32*, 21-25.

Lawson, T. J. (1999). Assessing psychological critical thinking as a learning outcome for psychology majors. *Teaching of Psychology, 26*, 13-17.

Lehman, D. R., Lempert, R. O., & Nisbett, R. E. (1988). The effects of graduate training on reasoning. *American Psychologist, 43*, 431-442.

Leighton, J. P. (2004). Defining and describing reason. In J. Leighton & R. Sternberg (Eds.), *The nature of reasoning* (pp. 3-11). Cambridge, England: Cambridge University Press.

Lizarraga, M. L., Baquedano, M. T., Mangado, T., G., & Cardelle-Elwar, M. (2009). Enhancement of thinking skills: Effects of two intervention methods. *Thinking Skills and Creativity, 4,* 30-43.

Lovett, (2002). Problem solving. In D. Medin (Ed.), S*tevens' handbook of experimental psychology: Vol. 2 Memory and cognitive processes* (3rd ed., pp. 317-362). New York, NY: Wiley.

Macpherson, R., & Stanovich, K. (2007). Cognitive ability, thinking dispositions, and instructional set as predictors if critical thinking. *Learning and Individual Differences, 17,* 115-127.

Maggioni, L., & Parkinson, M. (2008) The role of teacher epistemic cognition, epistemic beliefs, and calibration in instruction. *Educational Psychology Review, 20*(4), 445-461.

Mayer, R. E., & Wittrock, M. C. (2006). Problem solving. In P. A. Alexander & P. H. Winne (Eds.), *Handbook of Educational Psychology* (2nd ed., pp. 287-304)). Mahwah, NJ: Erlbaum.

Mayer, J. D., Salovey, P., & Caruso, D. R. (2008). Emotional Intelligence: New ability or eclectic traits, *American Psychologist, 63,* 503-517.

McCormick, C. B. (2003). Metacognition and learning. In W. M. Reynolds & G. E. Miller (Eds.), *Handbook of psychology: Educational psychology* (pp. 79-102). Hoboken, NJ: Wiley.

McCrudden, M. T., & Schraw, G. (2007). Relevance and goal-focusing in text processing. *Educational Psychology Review, 19,* 113-139.

McKinstery, J., & Topping, K. J. (2003). Cross-age peer tutoring of thinking skills in the high school. *Educational Psychology in Practice, 19,* 199-219.

Mislevy, R. J., & Haertel, G. D. (2006). Implications of evidence-centered design for educational testing. *Educational Measurement: Issues and Practices, 25,* 6-20.

Murphy, P. K., & Mason, L. (2006). Changing knowledge and beliefs. In P. A. Alexander & P. H. Winne (Eds.), *Handbook of Educational Psychology* (2nd ed., pp. 305-325). Mahwah, NJ: Erlbaum.

Norris, S. P., & Ennis, R. H. (1989). *Evaluating critical thinking.* Pacific Grove, CA: Critical Thinking Books and Software.

Novick, L. R., & Bassok, M. (2005). Problem solving. In K. Holyoak & R. Morrison (Eds.), *The Cambridge handbook of thinking and reasoning* (pp. 321-350). Cambridge, England: Cambridge University Press.

O'Donnell, A. (2006). The role of peer and group learning. In P. A. Alexander & P. H. Winne (Eds.), *Handbook of Educational Psychology* (2nd ed., pp. 781-802). Mahwah, NJ: Erlbaum.

Ozgun-Koca, S., & Sen, A. (2006). The beliefs and perceptions of pre-service teachers enrolled in a subject-area dominant teacher education program about "effective education." *Teaching and Teacher Education, 22,* 946-960.

Patz, R. J. (2006). Building NCLB science assessments: Psychometric and practical considerations. *Measurement, 4,* 199-239.

Penningroth, S. L., Despain, L. H., & Gray, M. J. (2007). A course designed to improve psychological critical thinking. *Teaching of Psychology, 34,* 153-157.

Perry, W. G., Jr. (1970). *Forms of intellectual and ethical development in the college years*. New York, NY: Academic Press.

Pintrich, P. R. (2003). Motivation and classroom learning. In W. M. Reynolds & G. E. Miller (Eds.), *Handbook of Psychology: Educational Psychology* (p. 7). Hoboken, NJ: Wiley.

Pithers, R. T., & Soden, R. (2000). Critical thinking in education: A review. *Educational Research, 42*, 237-249.

Pressley, M., & Harris, K. R. (2006). Cognitive strategy instruction: from basic research to classroom instruction. In P. Alexander & P. Winne (Eds.), *Handbook of educational psychology* (2nd ed., pp. 265-286). San Diego, CA: Academic Press.

Pretz, J. E., Naples, A. J., & Sternberg, R. J. (2003). Recognizing, defining, and representing problems. In J. E. Davidson & R. J. Sternberg (Eds.), *The psychology of problem solving* (pp. 3-30). Cambridge, England: Cambridge University Press.

Pugh, K. J., & Bergin, D. A. (2006). Motivational issues on transfer. *Educational Psychologist, 41*, 147-160.

Renaud, R. D., & Murray, H. G. (2008). A comparison of a subject-specific and general measure of critical thinking. *Thinking Skills and Creativity, 3*, 85-93.

Ritchhart, R., & Perkins, D. N. (2005). Learning to think: The challenges of teaching thinking. In K. J. Holyoak & R. G. Morrison (Eds.), *The Cambridge handbook of thinking and reasoning* (pp. 775-802). Cambridge, England: Cambridge University Press.

Roberts, M. J. (2004). Heuristics and reasoning: Making deduction simple. In J. Leighton & R. Sternberg (Eds.), *The nature of reasoning* (pp. 234-271). Cambridge, England: Cambridge University Press.

Schon, D. A. (1983). *The reflective practitioner*. New York, NY: Basic Books.

Schraw, G. (2006). Knowledge: Structures and processes. In P. Alexander & P. Winne (Eds.), *Handbook of educational psychology* (2nd ed., pp. 245-264). San Diego, CA: Academic Press.

Schraw, G. (2010). No school left behind. *Educational Psychologist, 45*, 1-6.

Schraw, G., & Dennison, R. S. (1994). Assessing metacognitive awareness. *Contemporary Educational Psychology, 19*, 460-475.

Stanovich, K. E. (2003). The fundamental computational biases of human cognition: Heuristics that (sometimes) impair decision making and problem solving. In J. E. Davidson & R. J. Sternberg (Eds.), *The psychology of problem solving* (pp. 291-342). Cambridge, England: Cambridge University press.

Swartz, R. J., & Perkins, D. N. (1990). *Teaching thinking: Issues and approaches*. Pacific Grove, CA: Midwest.

Tal, T. (2005). Implementing multiple assessment modes in an interdisciplinary environmental education course. *Environmental Education Research, 11*, 575-601.

Tishman, S., Perkins, D. N., & Jay, E. (1995). *The thinking classroom*. Boston, MA: Allyn & Bacon.

Topping, K. J., & Bryce, A.(2004). Cross-age peer tutoring of reading and thinking: Influence on thinking skills. *Educational Psychology, 24*, 595-621.

Veenman, M., V. J., Van Hout-Walters, B. H. A., & Afflerbach, P. (2006). Metacognition and learning: Conceptual and methodological considerations. *Metacognition and Learning, 1,* 3-14.

Wagner, T. A., & Harvey, R. J. (2006). Development of a new critical thinking test using item response theory. *Psychological Assessment, 18,* 100-105.

Webster's encyclopedic unabridged dictionary. (2001). San Diego, CA: Thunder Bay Press.

White, B. (2000). Pre-service teachers' epistemology viewed through the perspectives on problematic classroom situations. *Journal of Education for Teaching, 26*(3), 279-306.

White, B., & Frederiksen, J. (2005). A theoretical framework and approach for fostering metacognitive development. *Educational Psychologist, 40,* 211-223.

Wilson, D., & Sperber, D. (2004). Relevance theory. In L. Horn & G. Ward (Eds.), *Handbook of pragmatics* (pp. 607–632). Oxford, England: Blackwell.

Winne, P. H., & Perry, N.E. (2000). Measuring self-regulated learning. In M. Boekaerts, P. Pintrich, & M. Zeidner (Eds.), *Handbook of self-regulation* (pp. 531-566). San Diego, CA: Academic Press.

Yanchar, S. C., Slife, B. D., & Warne, R. (2008). Critical thinking as a disciplinary practice. *Review of General Psychology, 12,* 265-281.

Zohar, A. (2006). The Nature and Development of teachers' metastrategic knowledge in the context of teaching higher order thinking. *The Journal of the Learning Sciences, 15,* 331-377.

Zohar, A. (2008). Teaching thinking on a national scale: Israel's pedagogical horizons. *Thinking Skills and Creativity, 3,* 77-81.

Zohar, A., & Dori, Y. J. (2003). Higher order thinking skills and low-achieving students: Are they mutually exclusive? *Journal of the Learning Sciences, 12,* 145-181.

Zohar, A., Degani, A., & Vaaknin, E. (2001). Teachers' beliefs about low-achieving students and higher order thinking. *Teaching and Teacher Education, 17,* 469-485.

CHAPTER 3

HIGHER ORDER THINKING AND KNOWLEDGE

Domain-General and Domain-Specific Trends and Future Directions

Patricia A. Alexander, Daniel L. Dinsmore, Emily Fox, Emily M. Grossnickle, Sandra M. Loughlin, Liliana Maggioni, Meghan M. Parkinson, and Fielding I. Winters[1]

In the development of intelligence there is a great principle which is often forgotten. In order to acquire learning, we must first shake ourselves free of it. We must grasp the topic in the rough before we smooth it out and shape it.

—Alfred North Whitehead (*Modes of Thought*, 1938, p. 6)

In a series of lectures delivered at Wellesley College toward the end of his career, Alfred North Whitehead (1938), renowned philosopher and mathematician, railed against the dominant approaches to teaching formal logic that led to what he regarded as inert knowledge, or "the slow descent of accepted thought towards the inactive commonplace" (p. 174).

Assessment of Higher Order Thinking Skills, pp. 47–88
Copyright © 2011 by Information Age Publishing
All rights of reproduction in any form reserved.

Rather, he set out to argue for the complexity and multiplicity of human thought. Yet, Whitehead understood that in order to alter current frames of mind regarding the nature of thinking, we must first "shake ourselves free" of the notions and practices we have dutifully acquired (p. 6). Within the pages that follow, we commit ourselves to Whitehead's mission of re-thinking thinking, and set forth to shake ourselves (and perhaps others) free of conceptions of higher order thinking that have dominated educa-tional research and practice for more than 50 years. Our ambitious goal is to replace that prevailing view with an alternative mode of thought that illuminates the intricate relation that exists between higher order think-ing and knowledge.

For those who have devoted much of their professional lives to the study of academic development in some manner or form, as we have, it may seem strange that we should be called upon to examine the relations between higher order thinking and knowledge. In what way is it possible to comprehend or investigate one of these foundational constructs in the absence of the other? Can one think in a *higher order* way about nothing? Is it conceivable to have or acquire knowledge without ever engaging in higher order thought? However, even a cursory examination of the educa-tional literature suggests that what we regard as an inherent association between higher order thinking and knowledge has not been subjected to careful scrutiny. Moreover, what we have discerned from the literature suggests that a reframing of the very concept of *higher order thinking* seems warranted in light of the burgeoning literatures in epistemic beliefs, expertise, and academic development (Alexander, 2003; Murphy & Mason, 2006).

In our judgment, this reframing would consequently promote a recon-sideration of the marriage between higher order thinking and knowledge as it unfolds both across domains and within domains. The context of this marriage is framed by ways of acting and believing that must be acquired and nurtured over time, and that demand effort and reflection in execu-tion. In framing this issue we first articulate key principles, issues, and processes that merit discussion and use this frame to forward a definition of higher order thinking. We then position those principles, issues, and processes in the domains of reading, history, and science. Our choice of these three domains was compelled in part by our expertise and empirical histories, but also because we assert that these are exemplars of well-researched and core domains that serve to highlight significant similari-ties and differences in the relation between higher order thinking and knowledge. We consider multiple domains here to closely examine how the marriage between higher order thinking and knowledge may con-verge and diverge in these different domains. Finally, we consider the future for the orchestrated pursuit of higher order thinking empirically and in educational contexts.

WHAT IS HIGHER ORDER THINKING?

Conceptions in Historical Literature

From an historical standpoint, the phrase *higher order thinking* or some iteration (e.g., critical or creative thinking) has populated the philosophical and psychological literatures for centuries. From the dialogues of Plato to the critiques of Kant and the principles of James, there has been the concerted effort to specify the nature and characteristics of human thought and, further, to ascribe to that thinking particular qualities or features that are regarded as nonpedestrian or unconventional. Still, the document most associated with the idea of higher order thinking within the contemporary educational literature remains the *Taxonomy of Educational Objectives* penned by Benjamin Bloom and colleagues (1956).

Although the phrase *higher order thinking* is not explicitly defined within the pages of *Taxonomy of Educational Objectives*, much of the writing on higher order thinking that followed referenced this landmark volume that set forth a category of educational objectives in the cognitive domain. New lines of inquiry into higher order thinking have subsequently been shaped and guided in both terminology and practice by that now famous listing of six ordered classifications for the cognitive domain (i.e., knowledge, comprehension, application, analysis, synthesis, and evaluation). Among the enduring legacies of that cognitive ordering has been the prevailing perception that (a) the movement from knowledge to evaluation signifies the movement from lower order to higher order thinking; (b) that lower order and higher order thinking can best be understood as particular mental processes or procedures for dealing with information; and (c) that there is something more valuable or desirable about higher order than lower order thinking.

We describe these interpretations of Bloom et al. (1956) as a prevailing perception for two reasons. First, as mentioned, the phase *higher order thinking* does not expressly appear in this volume; rather these authors refer to higher and lower levels of educational objectives. Nonetheless, this phraseology has consistently been attributed to Bloom et al. (e.g., Schrire, 2004; Smythe & Halonen, 2009). Additionally, Bloom and colleagues shaped their discussion so as to avoid the interpretation that the movement from knowledge to evaluation signified a strictly hierarchical relation. Specifically, Bloom et al. discussed at length their decision to apply an Aristotelian categorization method in their taxonomy. The choice was significant, because an Aristotelian method creates distinct, bounded categories ordered by complexity without the hierarchical assumption that higher-level categories always entail instantiation of those lower in the taxonomy (e.g., when evaluating, it is not always necessary to first apply and synthesize). Moreover, Aristotelian categorization emphasizes that these groupings are closely related and difficult to tease apart. This theoretical interrelation was supported by research in the 1970s on the correlational structure of the taxonomy, further challenging the interpretation of a dichotomy between higher and lower levels (e.g., R. B. Smith, 1970). Despite the original frame forwarded by Bloom and colleagues, however, the division of the taxonomy of educational objectives into classes representing lower order (i.e., knowledge, comprehension, and application) and higher order thinking (i.e., analysis, synthesis, and evaluation) has prevailed in research (e.g., Wimer, Ridenour, Thomas, & Place, 2001; Zohar & Dori, 2003).

Of course, not all scholars conceptualize higher order thinking as Bloom et al. did. For instance, 3 decades after the publication of Bloom et al.'s (1956) taxonomy, Lauren Resnick (1987) forwarded premises about the nature of higher order thinking meant to counter certain long-held notions. Those premises were as follows:

- Higher order thinking is difficult to define but easy to recognize when it occurs;
- Higher order thinking has always been a major goal of elite educational institutions. The current challenge is to find ways to teach higher order thinking within institutions committed to educating the entire population;
- Higher order thinking is the hallmark of successful learning at all levels—not only the more advanced;
- Good thinking depends on specific knowledge, but many aspects of powerful thinking are shared across disciplines and situations. (pp. 44-45)

While our perspective on the relation between higher order thinking and knowledge resonates with Resnick's (1987) premises to a certain extent, we still find this depiction constrained and incomplete on several grounds. For one, from the standpoint of assessment and intervention, we do not agree that higher order thinking is as readily identifiable as Resnick contended. Part of the difficulty we witness in the thinking and performance of learners across grades and across domains is that they manifest problem-solving behaviors that those guiding their instruction may regard as facilitative for higher order thinking, but which we and others would consider to be inhibitive. Oftentimes, heuristics intended to facilitate higher order thinking transform an ill-structured task ripe for higher order thinking into a well-structured task executed via routinized procedures.

In her premises, Resnick (1987) also asserted that higher order thinking is the hallmark of successful learning at all levels. What we seek to demonstrate, based largely on the research in expertise and academic development, is that the characteristics of the learner (the *who*), the focus of the learning (the *what*), and the temporal and sociocultural contexts (the *when* and *where*) have a significant role to play in determining whether higher order thinking is warranted and whether it is likely to be manifest. It is precisely these conditional elements that illuminate the relation between higher order thinking and knowledge that is the focus of this chapter. Resnick's final proposition that "many aspects of powerful thinking are shared across disciplines and situations" (p. 45), highlights the historical tendency to conceptualize the processes of higher order thinking in a domain-general manner, with specific knowledge as the variant. Through our examination of higher order thinking across the domains of reading, history, and science, we aim to expound upon the nature of higher order thinking in accordance with the *who, what, where,* and *when* conditions specific to each of these academic domains.

As noted, we hold that the interpretation of higher order thinking that Resnick offered, while meritorious, remains incomplete and, thus, problematic. Specifically, where Resnick's (1987) perspective mirrors that of Bloom et al. (1956) (as well as many other theorists and researchers; Bransford, Brown, & Cocking, 1999; Halpern, 1996; Mayer, 1983; Sternberg, 1985) is in conceptualizing higher order thinking as "a cluster of elaborative mental processes requiring nuanced judgment and analysis" (Resnick, 1987, p. 44). Even though those mental processes vary within the thinking, reasoning, and problem solving literature, they are the constituent element in the conceptual or operational definitions of higher order thinking or the family of related terms. For instance, while Mayer (1983) and Sternberg (1985) discuss creative thinking in regard to inductive and deductive reasoning, Halpern (1996) considers the nature of critical thinking in regard to the use of cohesive and logical reasoning. Yet, despite these differences in focus and terminology, these scholars long associated with higher order thinking retain the process-oriented view of higher order (and lower-order) thinking articulated by Bloom et al. (1956) and reiterated in Resnick (1987).

We do not discount that there is a procedural dimension to higher order thinking, quite to the contrary. Much of our own theoretical and empirical work has centered on cognitive and metacognitive strategies and their influence in learning and development (e.g., Dinsmore, Loughlin, & Parkinson, 2009; Fox, Dinsmore, Maggioni, & Alexander, 2009; Parkinson, 2009). We also have engaged in the categorization of these strategies in a manner that suggests discernible levels by dealing with what we refer to as deep-processing or surface-level strategies (Alexander, 2004). Further, we do not dispute that those thinking processes have both a domain-general and domain-specific character. In fact, we have explored such processes across a range of academic domains (e.g., Alexander, Murphy, Woods, & Duhon, 1997; Alexander, Sperl, Buehl, Fives, & Chiu, 2004). What we *do* seek to counter is the judgment that higher order thinking can be relegated solely to such processes, however liberally or carefully delineated those processes may be. In our view, considering higher order thinking without regard to an epistemic orientation may lead to interventions that focus on heuristics (e.g., the sandwich model) while ignoring the learner's underlying epistemic beliefs, thereby not accomplishing stable, enduring change within the learner.

We find hints of an epistemic orientation in the language of Resnick (1987) and others (e.g., Bransford et al., 1999; Mayer, 1983), as when Resnick talked about uncertainty, effort, and complexity as key features of higher order thinking or when Halpern (1996) depicted critical thinking as purposeful and goal directed. Marton and Säljö (1976) similarly conceptualized deep versus surface approaches to learning in the form of actions and goals. Deep processors intended to understand meaning, question the author, justify evidence, and relate material to personal experience, while the surface processors memorized details pertinent to posttests in a rote fashion. Although such characterizations have epistemic overtones, they are more often regarded as conditions of the problem-solving act and not as relatively stable beliefs held by the learner. There is some mention of dispositions toward problem solving in the literature (e.g., Oliver & Hannafin, 2000) or personality characteristics that appear related to nonroutine or unconventional thinking (e.g., Matthews & Burnett, 1989). Yet, even these more stable learner characteristics are not directly tied to individuals' beliefs about knowledge and knowing; beliefs that we regard as part and parcel of higher order thinking.

Conceptions in Current Literature

Before we move to a more detailed analysis of the alternative conception of higher order thinking we espouse, we wanted to explore whether the views of this construct voiced by such renowned scholars as Bloom, Resnick, Bransford, Halpern, Mayer, and Sternberg into the late 1990s have carried into the recent empirical research that purports to investigate some form of nonconventional, complex, or nuanced thinking. Our approach to this survey was to physically examine the volumes of several leading journals for the last 5 years (i.e., *American Educational Research Journal*, *Contemporary Educational Psychology*, *Instructional Science*, *Journal of Educational Psychology*, and *Learning and Instruction*). This perusal had several outcomes of import to this exploration of higher order thinking and knowledge.

First, it became apparent that the rich empirical literature on higher order thinking that emerged in the 1980s has not been sustained. We did find ample evidence of studies that explored problem-solving procedures. In fact, the interest in cognitive and metacognitive strategies and self-regulation remains strong (Dinsmore, Alexander, & Loughlin, 2008). Yet, this interest in strategies and self-regulation was infrequently tied explicitly to higher order thinking or its variants (i.e., critical and creative thinking). Second, among the identified works that targeted higher order (critical or creative) thinking, a relatively limited number contained either explicit or implicit definitions of those thinking terms and many referred to the foundational writings of Bloom et al. (1956) or Resnick (1987) to undergird their conceptualizations. Third, much of the recent empirical activity concerns comprehension and argumentation (e.g., Dori, Tal, & Tsaushu, 2003) or mathematical problem solving (e.g., Hay & Booker, 2006). Finally, as with the classic works previously described, the perception of higher order thinking populating these empirical studies is the demonstration of nonroutine, deep, and effortful procedures (e.g., Brown, 2007; Zydney, 2008).

Reconception of Higher Order Thinking

The conceptualization of higher order thinking we proffer thus has a dual aspect encompassing both the transformational character of the intellectual activity involved as well as an epistemic orientation toward knowledge and knowing that is characteristically reflective and analytic:

> Higher order thinking is the mental engagement with ideas, objects, and situations in an analogical, elaborative, inductive, deductive, and otherwise transformational manner that is indicative of an orientation toward knowing as a complex, effortful, generative, evidence-seeking, and reflective enterprise.

These dual aspects, the learner's intellectual activity and epistemic orientation, characterize higher order thinking regardless of the task or domain under consideration. However, higher order thinking also exhibits distinctive qualities arising from the nature of the domain within which the task or activity is situated. The nature of the domain gives rise to characteristics of what is to be known (the *what*) as well to the circumstances under which it is encountered (the *when* and the *where* and by *whom*). These dimensions influence both the features of the intellectual activity that will be appropriate for engaging with an object, idea, or situation within that domain and the manner in which the learner views the nature and the justification of the knowledge that can be expected to result from such engagement.

Thus, within our three chosen domains of reading, history, and science, there are both broad and subtle differences in the types of intellectual activity and epistemic orientations that are associated with what is considered to be higher order thinking. Moreover, there has been considerable research attention given to investigation of the types of intellectual activity that are involved in domain-specific engagement, particularly when viewed as strategic processes or problem solving. In the reading literature, for instance, higher order thinking is typically described as critical, reflective, analytical, or evaluative (Brown & Campione, 1990). Strategic activities associated with such thinking in reading include: generating a purpose for reading; reading selectively; constructing provisional hypotheses regarding global meaning; making knowledge-based elaborations; questioning the author; and using background knowledge of the topic, of the domain, or of domain discourse to evaluate the accuracy, coherence, or quality of the text or of its argument (Pressley & Afflerbach, 1995).

In history, the literature does not usually refer explicitly to higher order thinking. Rather, it describes the thinking necessary to build understanding about the past (or historical thinking) as critical, argumentative, grounded in evidence, respectful of different perspectives, and capable of empathy (Stearns, Seixas, & Wineburg, 2000). Given the often textual nature of historical sources, strategic activities associated with historical thinking overlap somewhat with those associated with reading and include: generating researchable questions about the past; selecting evidence from the remnants of the past; interrogating historical sources in order to gain understanding about specific aspects of the past; evaluating authors; corroborating and contextualizing sources; using evidence and background knowledge about the topic, the domain, and the domain discourse to build contextualized and provisional interpretations; testing and revising interpretations in light of additional evidence; and identifying causation (Donovan & Bransford, 2005).

In science, higher order thinking is often synonymous with scientific inquiry and scientific reasoning and problem solving (e.g., Barak & Shakhman, 2008; National Science Teachers Association [NSTA], 2003). Deep-processing skills associated with higher order thinking in science include: designing and using complex procedures to address a specific question; construction of, and reasoning with, analog models; evaluating, coordinating, and resolving (sometimes conflicting) results from multiple sources; building multiple forms of argument; and constructing theories that postulate mechanisms with unobservable variables (Dunbar & Fugelsang, 2005; Zimmerman, 2007; Zohar & Dori, 2003). At its highest formulation, higher order thinking in science is characterized by creativity and ingenuity in the formulation, design, and evaluation of an investigation.

Within the domains of reading, history and science, less attention has been given to the learner's domain-specific orientation toward knowing (i.e., the learner's epistemic orientation). This orientation takes the form in any given learning situation of learning goals, the standards used to monitor progress toward those goals, and therefore also of the behaviors that aim toward achievement of the active goals (Marton & Säljö, 1997). In reading, which has the overarching goal of learning from text, the reader can be oriented toward remembering, understanding, and evaluating text (Fox, 2009). In pursuit of these goals and subgoals, the reader enacts specific behaviors, such as: connecting to relevant background knowledge; attending to the "big picture" instead of details; constructing, testing, and revising provisional interpretations, predictions, and conclusions; and evaluating consistency and accuracy of content and quality and appropriateness of the author's presentation of the content (Pressley & Afflerbach, 1995).

In history, the overarching goal of learning about the past can be pursued by the learner by reading or generating critical accounts of the past. Acknowledgment that accounts are not best viewed as absolute, but rather with reference to specific questions, perspectives, and assumptions is usually associated with the behaviors of manifestation of empathy, avoidance of presentism, tolerance for disagreement, and careful consideration of evidence (Stearns et al., 2000). In science, the overarching goal of understanding phenomena of the physical, biological, psychological, and social worlds is met with an orientation that acknowledges that scientific knowledge can be characterized as durable yet changeable, and that while the world is understandable, not all questions about it can be answered by science (American Association for the Advancement of Science [AAAS], 1989). In pursuit of their goal, scientists engage in constructing, testing, and revising provisional interpretations, predictions, and conclusions in light of evidence (Klahr & Dunbar, 1988; Kuhn, 1989; Schauble, 1996).

For each of these domains, we see that the nature of the domain distinctively shapes the characterization of higher order thinking, the types of intellectual activities that are seen as associated with higher order thinking, and the grounding of the pursuit of knowledge that is undertaken in the domain. This initial domain-specific application of the general definition of higher order thinking serves as an initial laying out of the territory which we will explore in a more focused way in the discussion that follows of the four principles associated with the dimensions of the *what, who, where,* and *when*.

A PRINCIPLED EXAMINATION OF THE INTERFACE OF KNOWLEDGE AND HIGHER ORDER THINKING

In their theoretical exploration of the construct of learning, Alexander, Schallert, and Reynolds (2009) sought to grapple with this immense and complex terrain via a topographical analysis. Four dimensions were chosen to frame that analysis, the *what*, the *who*, the *where*, and the *when*. The *what* dimension represents the act, object, idea, or situation that is the focus of learning, whereas the *who* refers to all the characteristics of the learner that may influence the process and products of learning. In their mapping, Alexander et al. further conceptualized the *where* dimension as the ecological context (i.e., the social and cultural milieu) in which learning occurs, while the *when* acknowledges the temporal nature to all learning in relation to both the immediate and long-term effects of time in shaping its process and products. We regard these same dimensions as effective organizing principles for unraveling the intricate relation between higher order thinking and knowledge in that this relation is a critical feature of learning's landscape and cannot be well understood outside this context.

In the discussion that follows, we overview each of the four dimensions and consider its potential influence on the landscape marked by the intersection of higher order thinking and knowledge. To initiate this discussion, we pose general principles about the *what, who, where,* and *when* and justify those principles with reference to the theoretical and empirical research on human learning and development. Of course, it is important to recognize that these four dimensions do not exist in isolation but are in continual interplay (Alexander et al., 2009). Therefore, even as we highlight one or the other dimension, we pay homage explicitly or implicitly to the others. Following the general introduction of each dimension, we examine how its principle is instantiated within the domains of reading, history, and science, not only to demonstrate the generalizability of the principles but also to illuminate their iterative nature.

The What Dimension

> Although any act, object, idea, or situation may become the target of higher order thinking, such thinking is more apt to occur when the inherent or perceived complexity of that act, object, idea, or situation invites such thought.

When humans engage in thought of any sort, there is inevitably some focal point. We think of *something* or we think about *something*. Thus, there is always a *what* that is being pondered in the act of thought, and that *something* can take many forms; from a physical act or concrete entity, to an abstract, amorphous notion or phenomenological experience. Further, as we witnessed in the classical and contemporary writings on higher order thinking, there is ample evidence that the acts, objects, ideas, or situations that constitute the *what*s of thought can be distinguished and classified (e.g., Brown & Conley, 2007; Torff, 2003). And, the bases for those distinctions and classifications are significant to the process of thinking that unfolds, as well as to the products of thought that arise.

In light of this essential role played by the *what*s of thinking, we find it disconcerting that either so little regard has been afforded to the reciprocal nature of the *what* and the process and products of thought or that their nature has been treated in overly simplistic or misguided ways. For instance, within the educational literature, there is the presumption that "higher order" questions or tasks will inherently result in higher order thinking. Such a presumption appears to nest the level of thought directly in the act, object, idea, or situation as though such mental processes or products were inherent in that act, object, idea, or situation. Conversely, there are programs or interventions aimed at promoting higher order thinking that center almost exclusively on the procedures or strategies to be learned and demonstrated; so much so that the role of the act, object, idea, or situation under thought seems to matter little. As we seek to establish herein, neither of these positions appropriately acknowledges the synergy between thinking and the *what* of thought.

As the wording of our guiding principle suggests, we do not discount that the inherent or perceived complexity of an act, object, idea, or situation may *invite* effortful and unconventional thought. When an act is reflexive or habituated versus provocative or demanding, an object is perceived as highly familiar versus novel, an idea is judged as commonplace versus intriguing or enigmatic, or a situation is interpreted as routine versus unconventional or surprising, there would appear to be little cause to engage in higher order thinking. Conversely, if ways of thinking that are indicative of higher order thought (e.g., elaborative or generative processing) are not themselves developed or honed, then whatever invitation an act, object, idea, or situation might present might well be overlooked, misinterpreted, or ignored.

We recognize the complexity of the principle we present in that it eliminates any simple mechanism for classifying or cataloguing the *what*s of higher order thinking; thinking that potentially rests on individuals' perceptions as much as on any inherent nature of act, object, idea, or situation. Moreover, we appreciate the pragmatics of forwarding some system of classification that allows for the formulation of educational experiences and environments. However, we hold that it is possible to regard given acts, objects, ideas, or situations as more or less likely to invite higher order thinking among certain individuals under certain conditions. Thus, classifications or categorization schemes that remain somewhat conditional with regard to the *who, when,* and *where* dimensions and do not intentionally or unintentionally reify the level of status of any act, object, idea, or situation might be constructed.

For instance, Alexander et al. (2009) proposed one such classification system in which the *whats* of learning were represented as three levels: acquired habits and conditioned responses; spontaneous concepts and action sequences; and scientific concepts. These levels were further formed from the interplay of factors that could systemically vary in degree (e.g., intensity, frequency, or magnitude), including the degree to which enculturation into a particular social practice was required, the degree to which conscious effort was needed, and the degree of abstraction or complexity involved. Consequently, we would assume that the invitation to engage in higher order thinking would be stronger as one moved away from acquired habits and conditioned responses toward scientific concepts and as the degree of requisite enculturation, effort, and complexity was increased.

Having discussed the *what* principle as framed, that is, in its broadest form as applying to any possible *what* of learning, we now turn to focus more specifically on how this principle takes shape with regard to the specific *whats* of learning of our chosen academic domains: reading, history, and science. Having different *whats* of learning is, in fact, the core distinction between different academic domains (Alexander, Kulikowich, & Jetton, 1994). The domain of the *what* informs the nature of the potential inherent or perceived complexity that can become the matter for the learner's generative, elaborative, transformational activity. What learners are invited to do or perceive themselves as being invited to do in the way of engagement in higher order thinking will thus differ depending on the domain with which the given *what* is associated or in which it is perceived to belong.

For reading, the *what* of learning, in the most basic sense, is the text. The critical, reflective, evaluative, or analytical engagement with the text that is higher order thinking in reading will be more or less invited depending on the degree to which the reader is aware or is made aware of the text as the communication of an author (Graesser, Millis, & Zwaan, 1997; T. Shanahan, 1992), and as belonging as well to a larger discursive context (Geisler, 1994). The complexity of the *whats* of reading emerges as an invitation and a challenge for the reader who approaches reading as a participatory, communicative, and principled activity or who encounters texts that evoke such an approach. Examples of potentially evocative texts include texts with an explicit author presence (e.g., Paxton, 1997, 2002), controversial or deliberately ambiguous texts (e.g., Afflerbach, 1990; Charney, 1993), or texts that are overtly nested in a particular stream of argumentative or knowledge-building discourse (e.g. Chambliss, 1995; Wyatt, Pressley, El-Dinary, Stein, Evans, & Brown, 1993).

From the reader's point of view, the text can be seen to call for more or less participatory, constructive activity from the reader. However, merely being an active reader does not necessarily guarantee that the activity will be generative, transformational, or even relevant (Fox, 2009). It is also essential that the text be viewed as a message crafted according to an author's purpose, and thus as evoking conversational, critical, or argumentative interaction (Haas & Flower, 1988; Olson, Duffy, & Mack, 1984). The text can further be seen as framed within a set of specific principles and discourse conventions, and thus subject to evaluative criteria and standards (Geisler, 1994). The reader's view of the text essentially determines the nature of the reader's activity and learning outcomes from that activity. And the reader's view of the text, that is, what the *what* of reading is taken to be, will depend in any given reading situation on both the text and the reader.

This reciprocal dependence between the *what* and the *who* characterizes also the history domain, although philosophers and historians have differently envisioned the nature of this relation (Gadamer, 1975; Marrou, 1954; Novick, 1988; Popper, 1968; White, 1973). Though, in a general sense, the past is the *what* of historical knowledge, history is more than the chronicle of past events. From its very origins with Herodotus and Thucydides, whether to celebrate it or to learn from it, historians have been prompted to investigate the past in order to achieve a better understanding of the human experience. Thus, the questions pursued by historians certainly play a key role in deciding *what* past will become history. At the same time, in offering those remnants of the past that can address historians' investigations, the archive both shapes and sometimes changes those very questions that historians set out to answer, and places a constraint on the legitimacy of historians' reconstructions. The interplay of these aspects of historical knowledge evokes an approach that is critical, since fruitful questions usually spring from the careful evaluation of prior knowledge; argumentative, because these initial questions act as hypotheses that guide the historian's search and structure the historical account that will follow; and grounded in evidence, because knowledge of the past is mediated by availability of its remnants. Thus, historical accounts that make the voice of the historian and the evidentiary traces clearly discernible (Wineburg, 1999) and pedagogical practices that expose the *nature* of historical knowledge through the analysis of multiple accounts and multiple sources, may favor the emergence of higher order thinking (Bain, 2005; VanSledright, 2002).

In addition, while learners cannot but start from the present in which they are immersed, the *what* of historical knowledge is situated in a past which is profoundly "other" in respect to the point of entrance of the *who* and that "should be encountered as simultaneously bizarre and wonderful" (Lowenthal, 2000, p. 79). On one hand, it is the sharing in the human experience that enables learners to understand the past, and thus it would be detrimental to try severing the link with one's present point of view (beside being impossible); on the other hand, the inevitable and often astonishing otherness of past human experience constitutes a formidable challenge for contemporary understanding. It is this tension between the familiar and the foreign that especially invites higher order thinking in the form of a capacity for empathy with past experiences (Lee, Dickinson, & Ashby, 1997).

In the domain of science, the *what* of higher order thinking is the natural world. Scientists seek to understand and explain phenomena and processes associated with biological, physical, chemical, social and other aspects of this world. However, as with the domains of reading and history, the degree to which higher order thinking is invited by the world depends on the *who* engaging with it. The creative and transformational nature of higher order thinking in science will only be manifested by a person who views the natural world as complex, but explainable and knowable in a principled manner. In fact, when engaged in authentic scientific inquiry, scientists are working towards building incrementally justified conclusions based on evidence, with a recognition that such understandings must be considered probably partial and open to refutation. Only with such a mindset will the complexity of the natural world encourage a scientist to view his or her investigations as ill-structured, knowledge-rich, and with potentially multiple conflicting outcomes (NSTA, 2003). In contrast, explorations of the world in the form of simple experiments with set conclusions, general observations devoid of a clear purpose, or illustrations of well established laws (often called "inquiry" activities in educational settings) are often knowledge-lean, are rarely ill-structured, and—in their relation to the natural world—do not invite higher order thinking (Chinn & Malhotra, 2002).

The Who Dimension

Learners' knowledge, interests, motivations toward the act, object, idea, or situation under thought, their propensity to be reflective, and their comfort in dealing with complexity, ambiguity, and uncertainty enhance their likelihood of engagement in higher order thinking.

Perhaps one of the most provocative aspects of this discussion of the marriage of higher order thinking and knowledge is the perspective on the thinker that we posit as critical to that association. Consideration of the learner in the literature on higher order thinking is certainly not new. Individuals' background knowledge (Anderson, Reynolds, Schallert, & Goetz, 1977; Bransford & Johnson, 1973), expertise (Ackerman, 2003), metacognitive or self-regulatory behaviors (Boekaerts, Pintrich, & Zeidner, 2001), general cognitive capability (Sweller, van Merrienboer, & Paas, 1998), and their goal orientations (Elliot & Harackiewicz, 1996) are some of the person variables that have been linked to higher order thinking. Within this literature, it has been argued that those with more relevant knowledge or experience and who report or demonstrate more metacognitive or self-regulatory behaviors, or who are more cognitively (e.g., greater working memory) or developmentally (e.g., formal reasoning) advanced are more apt to engage in higher order thinking. We acknowledge these well-established learner characteristics as correlated with higher order thinking as it has typically been studied. For our purposes, however, we want to extend consideration of the *who* dimension to facets that have not been systematically linked to the process and products of higher order thinking. Those facets include the individuals' intentions or motives; their deep-seated interests; and their orientations toward knowledge and knowing.

Not only is higher order thinking, as we have defined it, predicated on individuals' perceptions of any given act, object, idea, or situation, but also on individuals' particular intentions with regard to those *what*s. Precisely because higher order thinking, as we and others have defined it, requires effortful and unconventional processing, it will not occur unless individuals intend to engage mentally at the requisite level. Thus, any conception of higher order thinking must accept the necessary willingness of the individual to think deeply, analytically, and in an otherwise nonroutine manner. Of course, it is conceivable that the *invitation* issued by some act, object, idea, or situation is almost too strong to resist or that the sociocultural milieu almost compels the individual to reflect deeply or unconventionally. Yet, these characteristics, which pertain to the construct of situational interest, only serve to facilitate learners' intentions to engage in higher order thinking and cannot circumvent the need for those intentions.

However, interest need not be fleeting or tied to the immediate situation or context, as in the case of situational interest. Interest can be a more enduring person characteristic; an individual's deep-seated investment in or passion for some act, object, idea, or situation (i.e., individual or personal interest). When these enduring interests form, they guide individuals' perceptions of the *whats*, enhance judgments of personal relevance, and increase the probability that higher order thinking will be manifest. One explanation for the catalytic nature of individual interest offered by Dewey and James rests in the perception of lessened effort or labor being committed to the process or products of higher order thinking.

> The root idea of the term [interest] seems to be that of being engaged, engrossed, or entirely taken up with some activity because of its recognized worth. The etymology of the term inter-esse, "to be between," points in the same direction. Interest marks the annihilation of the distance between the person and the materials and results of his action; it is the sign of their organic union. (Dewey, 1913, p. 17)

Thus, when individuals perceive some manner of interest in the focus of their thought, there may be greater likelihood that they will engage more deeply and reflectively. Moreover, when that interest arises from the perception of an enduring link between person and the object of thought, that likelihood becomes greater or more predictable.

The consideration of interest as an enticer of higher order thinking centers on the transitory or on the enduring value attributed to the act, object, idea, or situation. However, one core aspect of our definition of higher order thinking transcends the value ascribed to any specific *what* and focuses, instead, on valuing of the habits of mind associated with reflective, analytic, and unconventional thought. Because of our investment in a conceptualization of higher order thinking as a more predictable or stable engagement, we posit that individuals who manifest a propensity toward reflection and are comfortable in dealing with complexity, ambiguity, and uncertainty are more apt to engage in higher order thinking beyond the sporadic or isolated occurrence.

The aforementioned attributes (e.g., propensity toward reflection) are associated with epistemic orientations toward knowledge and knowing deemed more conducive to deeper and transformational learning (e.g., Mason, Gava, & Boldrin, 2008). In some instances, those orientations have been explored at a general level of human thinking, whereas, in other cases, such habits of mind have been investigated in particular domains or disciplines (e.g., Schraw & Sinatra, 2004). Whether domain-general or domain-specific in character, however, it has been repeatedly argued that certain epistemic orientations make one more disposed to engagement in the processes associated with higher order thinking. More than merely representing correlates with higher order thinking as it has been previously conceptualized, we regard these propensities and epistemic orientations as salient characteristics of those who manifest deep reflection and effortful processing with some regularity.

There is, perhaps, a stronger theoretical rationale supporting the existence of the type of learner who manifests deep reflection and effortful processing across domains than there is direct empirical evidence. Such a learner, who has been labeled an "intelligent novice" (Brown & Campione, 1990; Mathan & Koedinger, 2005) or someone who has "learned how to learn" (Brown, Campione, & Day, 1981; Hofer & Yu, 2003), would be one who is drawn to actively contemplate and flexibly adapt the nature of his or her own learning activity as such. Research investigating the learning of a specific subject-matter is unlikely to target successfully the behaviors associated with this metacognitive focus, while metacognition itself is notoriously difficult to capture in a reliable and nonintrusive way (Meijer, Veenman, & van Hout-Wolters, 2006; Schraw, 2000). Within domains, there is considerably more evidence that learners can bring with them a more or less consistent approach to knowledge-building activities in relation to a given subject matter that can be more or less driven by individual interest, intention to invest effort, and readiness to grapple with complexity and ambiguity (e.g., Bereiter & Scardamalia, 1993; Murphy & Alexander, 2002; Ramsden, 1997). Consideration of our three chosen domains, reading, history, and science, positions us to address the role of the *who* in higher order thinking both at the level of connection to a specific subject matter of learning and at the level of particular modes of learning that span across domains, and thus can offer the broader perspective of learning to learn: learning from text and learning as inquiry.

With regard to reading, the likelihood that an individual reader will engage in critical, reflective, evaluative, or analytical engagement with the text on a specific reading occasion can be viewed as arising from his or her grounding in terms of knowledge, interest, and motivations toward the particular subject matter addressed by the text, along with his or her conception of that subject matter as open for ambiguity, complexity, and uncertainty. The greater knowledge, stronger individual interest, intention to build knowledge, and willingness to grapple in an effortful, reflective, and evidence-building way that we associate with higher order thinking in this case are linked to the reader's conception of the *what* about which he or she is reading (Alexander, 1997; Scardamalia & Bereiter, 1991). However, as bound to that particular *what* they represent an encapsulated instantiation of factors promoting higher order thinking in reading. Higher order thinking might not be manifested by the same reader in an encounter with a text regarding a different *what*. Or higher order thinking could be manifested by means of a perceived or constructed analogy to the *what* to which the factors promoting higher order thinking are linked for that reader (e.g., Graves, 2001; Roth & Bowen, 2003).

Another way of viewing the reader's likelihood of engaging in higher order thinking during reading is to consider the reader's relation to the *what* of reading as the text itself. In this case, the reader's knowledge, interest, intentions and propensities concern text as text and the activity of reading viewed as more or less participatory, communicative, and principled. Here the issue is the learner's beliefs about the nature of reading and learning from text, his or her knowledge about reading, interest in reading as an activity, and proclivity for coming to reading with a particular suite of intentions and motivations (Alexander, 2006; Chall, 1983; Gray & Rogers, 1956). A reader whose profile on these factors suggested an openness and attraction to higher order thinking would be expected to evince a readiness to engage in higher order thinking when reading across subject-matters, to the degree that the reading situation allowed. Once the reader has arrived at an awareness of text as inviting participatory, communicative, and principled activity by its nature as text, that awareness does not seem likely to turn on and off. But the awareness of the subject-matter of the text as inviting such activity, on the contrary, could vary from text to text. Therefore, those attributes of the *who* or reader that we have identified as associated with higher order thinking can form the seat of both a general propensity to higher order thinking when reading and learning from text or a more specific inclination, depending on the *what* involved.

The dual aspects of learning, as learning from text and learning as inquiry, well illustrate the modes that most commonly favor the development of historical knowledge. Learners' first encounter with history is usually in the form of listening to, watching, or reading narratives of past events. The knowledge that will result from such encounters strongly depends on the conceptualization that the learner has of a historical text (Rouet, Marron, Perfetti, & Favart, 1998; Wineburg, 1998, 2000, 2001): is the text a chronicle of past events or is it the result of the interpretive work of its author? If the former, the appropriate role of the *who* resembles that of a faithful recorder, but the space and the appropriateness of higher order thinking is hardly present. Whether a narrative written by a historian or a primary document analyzed during some form of historical inquiry, it is only when the text is perceived as a communication of an author that spaces for higher order thinking open up, and the *who* usually manifests those critical, argumentative, and empathetic traits that we posed as characterizing historical thinking.

Which of these traits are more or less desirable and central for the development of historical knowledge depends on how the *what* of history is conceptualized; hence, it has been matter of debate among different schools of thought and is at the root of various historiographic traditions (Seixas, 2004). Conceived as a remarkable occasion of encountering the "other," history highlights the capacity of learners to be aware of their positionality while, at the same time, cultivating an attentive and sympathetic openness to anything that can refine their developing understanding (VanSledright, 2001). It is in this context that heuristics such as sourcing, contextualization, corroboration, and evaluation come to characterize historical thinking without degrading into a set of skills that miss the mark of higher order thinking (Wineburg, 2007). To be sure, a variety of cognitive abilities and understandings may support higher order thinking; among these we note general reading strategies, the ability to think chronologically, the decentration necessary for empathy, school experiences fostering the development of first- and second-order concepts, and a broader knowledge base about topics, text types, and text structures. Yet, these attributes may not suffice unless coupled with the epistemic and affective traits described above (Lee, 2005; Wineburg, 2001).

Learning as inquiry is at the heart of higher order thinking in science. However, the likelihood that a learner will engage routinely in higher order thinking, increases to the degree that he or she holds particular beliefs about the *what*—the domain and knowledge—of science. In particular, the learner must hold the view that the natural world is far more complex than our knowledge of it can grasp; that the processes we utilize to understand the natural world produce only an estimation of the actual object under consideration; that we can only "know" the natural world to the extent that we have accumulated justified evidence; and that even then our knowledge is subject to alteration based on future evidence (AAAS, 1989) This epistemic stance is fostered in part by an increase in the person's relevant prior knowledge and growing appreciation that scientific knowledge is to some degree socially-constructed (Driver, Asoko, Leach, Mortimer, & Scott, 1994). Further, a learner will be more inclined to engage in higher order thinking while inquiring about the natural world if he or she views scientific knowledge as a coherent system of ideas, rather than a collection of facts and problem-solving methods (Schauble, 1996).

The Where Dimension

> Higher order thinking is more apt to occur when the physical, educational, social, and cultural context is supportive of such reflective and unconventional engagement and when learners are exposed to explicit or implicit models of such engagement.

As Alexander and Murphy (1998) stated, learning never occurs in a vacuum but transpires in situ. The same can be said for thinking. Thinking—higher order or otherwise—inevitably has a place, a *where*. Moreover, while the physical elements of context are influential to the thinking that occurs, context also refers to more abstract and less tangible dimensions of *place*, including the educational, social, and cultural.

We do not wish to imply that thoughts are determined by the context in which they arise. Indeed, there is ample evidence that one's thoughts can be dramatically removed or abstracted from the immediate physical surroundings. In essence, the *where* of thought is not synonymous with the physical environment. In his moving volume, *Man's Search for Meaning*, for instance, Victor Frankl (1985) described his ability to survive the horrors of the Nazi concentration camps by keeping his thoughts intensely focused on reasons for living, such as his loving wife and their life together. As he wrote, "Man can preserve a vestige of spiritual freedom, of independence of mind, even in such terrible conditions of psychic and physical stress" (p. 86).

We find this quote by Frankl (1985) compelling for several reasons. For one, it serves as a powerful reminder that there can be forces within the context that motivate thoughts, which evoke strong emotions or affect in the thinker. Thus, thoughts are not cognitive emanations devoid of human emotion. For another, Frankl's words demonstrate that "place" is not tantamount to the physical context. Nonetheless, it is our contention that, as functioning human beings, we cannot consistently separate mind from the environment and therefore cannot sustain thought of either conventional or unconventional form without coming into touch with physical, educational, social, and cultural surroundings. For example, it could be argued that it was the very adversity and horrors that Frankl faced that drove him to preserve the spiritual freedom and independence of mind so actively and effortfully.

When it comes to recurring, transformational processing and complex, reflective orientation toward knowing that we regard as higher order thinking, this relation between thought and place becomes even more significant. For one, the nature of that context can support effortful and unconventional thought, or likewise hinder it. That positive support can come in the form of questions or tasks that are sufficiently challenging, novel, or personally-relevant to provoke higher order thinking. Likewise, we could surmise that contexts that are cognitively arid, that rely on routine or unexamined acts, that reward conformity, or that seek to stifle novel, creative, or critical demonstrations will be less welcoming to the reflective, critical, analytical, or transformational mind.

Of course, we grant that there are learners who, as a consequence of their predispositions, intentions, or expertise may *typically* require more or less contextual support than others who do not share those attributes. Even the unwelcoming conditions we depicted will not prevent the outbreak of higher order thinking from time to time or for certain learners.

Such learners may simply find great pleasure in complicating the simple, questioning the status quo, or strategically maneuvering around impediments to reflection or critical analysis. However, the nature of the physical, educational, social, and cultural context can still serve to facilitate or inhibit reflective or unconventional processing under given circumstances. Moreover, the need for such support can fluctuate in time and over time as the attributes of the *who* interact with characteristics of the *what* under thought.

The nature of oral or written exchanges within the context may also encourage reflection, probing, examination, or justification of the acts, objects, ideas, or situations under consideration. Murphy, Wilkinson, Souter, Hennessey, and Alexander (2009) would characterize these discourse communities as critical-analytic in nature. However, it is not just the inducement to such cognitive engagement that matters in the manifestation of higher order thinking. As Garner (1990) reminds us, such environments also allow the time required for effortful and planful processing and incorporate explicit or implicit rewards for the display of unconventional, reflective, and transformation processing. If such features are not evident, then verbal encouragements will not routinely or easily translate into occasions of higher order thinking.

As just discussed, supportive contexts for higher order thinking solicit the unconventional or transformational cognitive processes and the complex, effortful, generative, evidence-seeking orientations toward knowing that are the components of higher order thinking. Further, these supportive contexts either draw well on the knowledge and experiences that individuals already possess relative to the acts, objects, ideas, or situation under thought or introduce pertinent knowledge or experiences into the context. They do so by providing the basics of the *what*s that are to be pondered and by including explicit or implicit models that *demonstrate* these processes and orientations. In essence, the notion of "supportive" is not inherent in the context but derives from its congruency with the *who* and the *what*.

This mutual congruency suggests that the makeup of a supportive or inhibitive context for learning, the *where*, will depend in important ways on the nature of the domain being studied, which has already been seen to be woven into the *what* and the *who* of learning. When we turn to consider how the general *where* principle articulated above carries through into the specific domains of reading, history, and science, it might at first appear that, as academic domains, they share the same context: the school setting. However, even within the school setting, a reading classroom differs essentially as a physical, educational, social, and cultural context from a history classroom or a science classroom (Stevens, Wineburg, Herrenkohl, & Bell, 2005), although they may take place in the same location and involve the same pupils instructed by the same teacher. What students are asked to do in the classroom, their own actions, expectations and values and those of the individual teacher, of the school authority structure, and of the inhabitants of other elements of their ecosystems will be patterned differently for different domains (Bronfenbrenner & Ceci, 1994; Fisher & Frey, 2007). In addition, any given academic domain will project differently into the learner's nonacademic life; history or science or reading will clearly have different roles in the learner's out-of-school interests, activities, and needs. So, although there is a sense in which any school contexts are similar in being just that, school contexts, there is also a sense in which they differ in critical ways as contexts for learning, which means that, depending on the domain, there will be different nexuses of supportive or inhibitory factors both in-school and out-of-school.

With regard to reading, the classroom environment at all levels of schooling can offer situations that both promote and inhibit readers' engagement in higher order thinking, and in so doing it can foster or stunt their capacity and propensity to engage in higher order thinking on their own. Elements of the classroom context that would be likely to inhibit readers from reflective, analytical, critical, and evaluative thinking, and that would tend to engender a passive and rigid stance toward reading include an exclusive reliance on textbooks and other forms of author-less text, where no one has responsibility for the authoritative and unquestioned content being dispensed, and the identification of reading and learning from reading with preselected and predigested texts, unrealistic or irrelevant tasks, and mechanically-applied skills (Bereiter & Scardamalia, 1986, 1993). Another set of inhibitory contextual factors include a view of the function of reading as enabling either regurgitation or recognition of what has been pointed out at important content by someone else (Perry, 1959), and the subordination of the time-consuming enterprise of learning from reading in a critical, analytical, reflective, and evaluative manner to the time-constrained goal of performance on tests, particularly high-stakes tests (Ivey & Fisher, 2005).

On the other hand, elements of the classroom context that might be expected to promote the capacity and propensity to approach reading as participatory, communicative, and principled include increased experience with texts presented as domain discourse and as having an author (Paxton, 1997, 2002; C. Shanahan, 2009). In addition, higher order thinking in reading is supported by contexts that ensure development of a base of relevant knowledge and mastery, but not primacy, of lower-level reading skills (Alexander, 2006; Chall, 1983). Finally, both in and out of school, readers will be more likely to engage with what they are reading in a critical, reflective, and elaborative way when their reading is motivated by a genuine need to learn, communicate, and evaluate (Chall, 1983). A key feature of a supportive *where* of learning consists of precisely this tendency to present the learner with genuinely motivating and appropriate tasks and goals; such tasks and goals in reading could include: gaining a better understanding of oneself and one's situation; supporting the pursuit of a personal interest in a particular academic or nonacademic topic, issue, or activity; and broadening one's perspective by learning about otherwise unencountered real or fictional times, cultures, lifestyles, or points of view.

In history, these facilitating conditions for engaging in higher order thinking take on the additional features of an increased experience and sensitivity to the characteristics of the historical texts (conceived as medium of domain discourse), explicit discussion and modeling of heuristics typical of the domain, exposure to historical inquiry, and development of a knowledge base that can facilitate contextualization. Conversely, the drive to master a specific narrative and a focus on regurgitation and recognitions of decontextualized events or uncritically accepted accounts do not favor historical thinking (Bain, 2000; Britt, Perfetti, Van Dyke, & Gabrys, 2000; Rosenzweig, 2000; VanSledright, 2002).

From a broader perspective, the *where*, as the sociocultural environment in which the development of knowledge takes place, assumes a unique role in the history domain, influencing both the *who* and the *what* of history. Perhaps the most superficial (in a sense) but more visible effect of context lies in the very choice of the narrative conveyed by the school curriculum. In deciding about what and how to teach about the past, schools also decide about the perspective that, in the present, makes those issues and accounts significant (Seixas, 1997; VanSledright, 1997). The battles between different constituencies, often resulting in ever-expanding textbooks and curricula, amply testify to the relevance of this broader context; and it may well be that this state of affair is connatural to the discipline of history, since, in looking at the past, we cannot but start from the present and we look at the past, because we believe that it has some relevance for the present.

However, although the contemporary *where* may well be the point of departure for the development of historical knowledge, it does not follow that it also has to be its final destination. The difference between a context teaching heritage and one teaching history lies in the choice made in regard to this final goal and whether it favors learning about the "other," with all that it implies in terms of the learner's attitudes, or promoting unquestioned allegiance to "our-self." Thus, the deeper influence of the *where* depends, in our view, on the choice between fostering the acquisition of a specific narrative (liberal, conservative, or something else), promoting a generalized, sterile criticism for any account, or favoring the encounter with the past by introducing the learner to the nature of history and to the methods for justifying historical claims and the higher order thinking that such an approach requires (Seixas, 2000; Wineburg, 2007).

Similar to the domains of reading and history, contexts that hinder and discourage development of higher order thinking in science focus on recall and recognition of inert knowledge. These contexts typically employ well-structured, straightforward tasks, which are often isolated from a larger body of scientific knowledge. In such contexts, the learner's epistemological development is not supported. Inquiry becomes merely a progression of steps a learner must rigidly follow in order to "do science," and scientific knowledge becomes a collection of facts and disconnected processes. Learners in these contexts, such as the traditional high-school laboratory, spend much time replicating set experiments by following a series of very specific instructions. Reasoning, justification, and argumentation are not part of the process. The outcome is predetermined by the lab manual or instructor, and the ability to follow steps and record observations becomes the important focus of learning, rather than the application of the process to the development of new knowledge.

In contrast, contexts that give the learner opportunities to explore the complexities of the natural world and uncertainties of authentic inquiry into natural phenomena support the learner's beliefs that science is an ill-structured, but coherent, system of ideas; that doing science is about applying a process to transform or create knowledge and thus expand, however incrementally, the field under investigation. These contexts may also support higher order thinking by encouraging discussion about the nature of science (Chinn & Malhorta, 2002). A learner who consistently engages with the *what* in such contexts will develop an epistemological stance towards scientific knowledge that will increase the likelihood of his or her engagement in higher order thinking and the transformation and creation of scientific knowledge.

The When Dimension

Even though higher order thinking might be evidenced by learners of any age or expertise, the recurrent manifestation of such reflective and unconventional engagement requires a particular level of maturation and experience.

Within the developmental psychological literature, there is ample evidence that age—or more precisely the neuropsychological maturation and life experiences that come with age—can have significant effects on mental processing (e.g., Luna, Garver, Urban, Lazar, & Sweeney, 2004). In essence, older or more experienced learners have a higher possibility of pondering and reflecting in depth with regularity than those who are younger or inexperienced. That is because with age typically comes the ability to handle abstraction, complexity, and ambiguity with greater comfort and facility, as well as the ability to perceive regularities, discrepancies, or anomalies in informational arrays (Joseph, Liversedge, Blythe, White, Gathercole, & Rayner, 2008; Kato, Kamii, Ozaki, & Nagahiro, 2002). Older and more experienced thinkers likely have available to them a multitude of induced and deduced patterns at multiple levels of organization to fit to the perceptual and cognitive data confronting them. In this way, creative, multidimensional, and reflective forms of reasoning (e.g., analogical reasoning) may more readily come to mind in questioning and explaining phenomena encountered. However, such ready availability could also promote automaticity or routinized thinking. Consequently, for older thinkers as well, consideration of the learner's orientation toward knowledge continues to be essential in gauging the likelihood of engagement in higher order thinking.

Moreover, age may provide one with a broader vista on what might be regarded as "traditional" or "conventional" responses to given acts, objects, ideas, or situations, aiding in the effortful pursuit of the unconventional or transformational thoughts regarded as "higher order." What this consideration of development also illuminates is the critical relation between the *who* and the *when* dimensions, in that it is the change to the individual that comes with the passage of time that enhances the probability of higher order thinking.

Although we would expect higher order thinking, as we have defined it, to be more characteristic of learners with greater age or experience engaged in tasks for which they are somewhat competent, we do not intend to preclude such processing for younger or novice learners. To the contrary, learners of almost any age or level of expertise can display transformational thought with the right task or under the right circumstances, especially if appropriate cognitive tools are made available to them. Vygotsky's (1978) zone of proximal development and the empirical research that it has spawned (Tzuriel, 2000) have sought to illustrate how the presence of a more "knowledgeable other" can provoke a higher level of thought or instigate a higher level of performance than one might typically demonstrate. From a developmental perspective, it is not simply the capacity to engage in higher order thinking that is in question. Rather, it is the recurrent manifestation of such reflective and unconventional engagement that gives credence to the developmental and expertise-related influences that we address.

The developmental advantage noted above, however, is not indiscriminate, but also tends to become associated with given contexts or with particular fields or venues over time. In essence, with the passage of time, individuals have repeated experiences within similar contexts that may begin to instantiate certain frames of mind that contribute to or constrain higher order thinking. Thus, K-12 students who perceive formal education as largely a test-preparation experience—a perception that gets repeatedly reinforced over time—may be less primed or less inclined to think deeply and transformationally when such manner of thoughts seems unnecessary or even detrimental to test performance. In contrast, students who are placed in instructional contexts that provoke reflection or offer repeated opportunities for reflection or nontraditional thinking may over time manifest a greater inclination toward higher order thinking. In these cases, the *where* and the *when* interact to create conditions that influence the occurrence of higher order thinking.

Moreover, individuals tend to become more goal-directed and focused in their interests and more targeted in the experiences they pursue with the passage of time (Alexander, Johnson, Leibham, & Kelley, 2008). Thus, the knowledge, skills, and strategies individuals acquire and the beliefs and orientations toward knowledge they form can vary greatly from one domain to another, affecting how they conceptualize the *what* that characterizes specific domains. That is why the research on expertise is especially invaluable to understanding the relation between higher order thinking and knowledge. Much of our theoretical and empirical research in the past decade has been devoted to the study of individuals' development in particular academic domains (e.g., Alexander et al., 2004). Through this extensive program of inquiry, we have come to recognize that the nature of mental processing differs markedly depending on whether one is functioning as a novice and or as an expert or as somewhere in between these extremes. Expertise development, in essence, captures the essential interplay of the *who*, *what*, *where*, and *when* dimensions of higher order thinking. That is because expertise is by definition a characterization of the individual (*who*) that is nested in a particular context (*where*) and involves certain orientations to domain-specific acts, objects, ideas, or situations (*what*) that arise over an extended period of time (*when*).

Turning to consideration of the *when* dimension as related to each of our chosen domains of reading, history, and science, it is apparent, first, that there is a relatively well-defined developmental trajectory for learners in each domain, with higher order thinking likely, as outlined above, to emerge as learners are farther along in that developmental trajectory. This domain-specific progressive development is a matter both of the accumulation of individual experiences of interacting with the *what* (as framed by a particular *where*) and also of the evolution of the nature of those experiences. One feature of such evolution is the mastery of certain threshold-level skills and familiarity with certain threshold-level knowledge pertinent to the given domain. Although these developmental mechanisms of accumulation and evolution are domain-general, what they involve in terms of the character of appropriate experiences and requisite threshold skills and knowledge will be bound up with both the nature of the *what* that constitutes the domain and the learner's perception of and orientation toward the *what* as inviting higher order thinking.

Learners' development as readers proceeds along two distinct developmental paths, the interaction of which remains relatively unexplored territory and which are often commingled in theories of reading development (Chall, 1983; Scardamalia & Bereiter, 1991). Looking down the first path, we see that as learners become more knowledgeable, experienced, and focused in their interest in a particular domain, they are also likely to become more expert in the reading they do related to their learning in that domain (Alexander, 1997; Scardamalia & Bereiter, 1991), with a consequent increased likelihood of consistent engagement in higher order thinking when doing such reading. They will have mastered the threshold-level skills and knowledge required to navigate the demands of making sense of domain-specific reading, including domain-specific vocabulary. Through extensive exposure to domain-related texts in which they are reading to address their own strong domain-related purposes and interests, they will become familiar with the features of the domain discourse, and become more open to and capable of responding to the text in a participatory and principled way. They will be positioned to question, argue with, reflect on, elaborate upon, and evaluate what they are reading in the text and will have standards and criteria available to support these effortful and generative reading activities (Geisler, 1994). In addition, their awareness of the text as a communication of an author's message will be fostered by the likelihood that they have themselves become authors and attempted to communicate their own domain-related messages to readers (Scardamalia & Bereiter, 1991).

The second developmental path in reading is that taken by the reader as a reader. Movement down this path involves increasing knowledge, experience and interest related to reading itself (Alexander, 2006). It is likely to be supported as well by experience with writing, insofar as such experience fosters greater awareness of the role of an author in crafting a text with a purpose and with attention to the reader as audience. Becoming an expert reader in this sense requires extensive exposure to a wide variety of text types, the development of strong meaning-making skills, and comfort and confidence in taking up any text as an invitation to principled, participatory discourse (Alexander, 2006; Chall, 1983; Gray & Rogers, 1956). As Chall noted about those few readers who achieve the highest stage of reading development in her stage theory, Stage 5 readers need knowledge, confidence, and humility, but "above all, the reader needs a feeling of entitlement" (p. 51). Expert readers come to any text already assuming that they are entitled to criticize, argue, evaluate, and selectively integrate what they read; they may not do this on every occasion or with equivalent rigor or effort with every text, but it is always a possibility. It is this feeling of entitlement that underlies the consistent and recurrent manifestation of higher order reasoning in reading, whether across or within domains; this feeling is undergirded by the accumulation of extended and intensive experiences with reading and by the evolution of the reader's understanding of those experiences as participatory discourse.

Research on the development of historical thinking suggests several instances of overlapping with the reading developmental path, although the specific features of the journey are expressed in terms of the *what* of the domain (VanSledright, 2004). In terms of threshold-level knowledge, with participation in appropriate educational experiences, students may develop both concepts regarding the content or substance of history (e.g., government, revolution, wealth, and trade) and concepts that regard the "doing" of history and its features (e.g., time, evidence, account, change, cause, and empathy; Lee, 2005); closely related with the development of this second set of concepts that form the core of what has been called disciplinary or second-order knowledge is the increased familiarity with the heuristics employed by historians to research and interpret the past (e.g., contextualization, sourcing, and corroboration; Bain, 2005; VanSledright, 2002). Pedagogically, the development of these concepts usually involves participation of the students in some form of historical inquiry; conversely, familiarity with the use of these concepts and heuristics enables students to gain a deeper level of understanding of any form of historical account (primary or secondary) they may encounter, an understanding that acknowledges the complexities of the factors at play and may thus help learners in recognizing and using polythetic narrative frameworks (Shemilt, 2000).

Research has shown that appropriate pedagogical practices can foster the development of second-order concepts and the use of apt heuristics, with the preponderance of data coming from studies of students between 7 and 14 years of age. Although these studies support some progression in historical thinking, they also found that students differed markedly within any given age and the development of different second-order concepts did not seem to progress in parallel (Lee & Ashby, 2000; Lee et al., 1997; VanSledright, 2002); further, the power of these concepts stands or falls with the overall conceptualization and awareness that individuals have of the *what* of the discipline and of themselves as learners, since these concepts and heuristics presuppose particular epistemological ideas regarding the nature of historical knowledge and how its knowledge claims may be justified (Lee & Shemilt, 2003; Lee, 2004). So far, such integration appears to be the mark of and be restricted to high levels of expertise, such as professional historians or graduate history students (Wineburg, 1999, 2007). In this respect, particularly worrisome are the results of research with K-12 teachers, which has reported very little evidence of such integration (Hicks, Doolittle, & Lee, 2004; Husbands, Kitson, & Pendry, 2003; Yeager & Davis, 1996), and the confusion between the critical attitude characterizing historical thinking and the generic criticism documented by Wineburg (2007) among high-school students, in what appear to be a case of "feeling of entitlement" gone awry.

As with the domains of reading and history, the novice student of science embarks on a path of development of domain-specific knowledge and process skills toward expertise. These skills and knowledge develop through repeated experience and exposure (Songer, 2006). For inquiry, in particular, investigation skills and domain knowledge are intertwined on this developmental path, bootstrapping one another along the way (Zimmerman, 2007). However, students at every level display difficulties applying higher order processes with inquiry. For example, many students tend to focus on causal factors to the exclusion of non-causal factors in experimentation, which may cause distortion of evidence (Zimmerman, 2007). As with the domain of history, the schooling context may have a direct effect on when these skills and knowledge develop. For example, research has shown some evidence that direct instruction in experimental design with elementary-school students may be more effective than pure discovery learning at teaching them inquiry skills (Klahr & Nigam, 2004). However, constructivist elementary-school classrooms, which put helping students test and revise their own ideas as paramount, may be more beneficial for students' epistemological development than traditional classrooms that emphasize learning of facts and isolated processes (C. L. Smith, Maclin, Houghton, & Hennessey, 2000).

This suggests a secondary path of development critical to higher order thinking in science: the path toward a sophisticated epistemic stance about the nature of science. Students have an evolving understanding of the nature of science, and they often focus on the outcome of an experiment as the purpose of inquiry, rather than the understanding of a phenomenon (Zimmerman, 2007). Junior-high and high-school students tend to have one of two types of epistemic beliefs about science, which Carey and Smith (1993) call commonsense epistemologies of science. Specifically, these students believe that discovering facts and inventing things is the goal of science, or that the goal of science is to engage in experimentation to see if an idea is right (Carey & Smith, 1993). Children hold naïve epistemologies that often lead to such conceptions; however, some of these naïve epistemologies (e.g., that knowledge is propagated and created) may facilitate children's epistemic development if tapped by a teacher interested in fostering such development (Hammer & Elby, 2002). Clearly, the *when* of higher order thinking in science is governed very much by the educational context (the *where*). The development of students' epistemologies, while a current area of research in science education, remains at the fringes of classroom practice despite its critical role in students' ability to engage in higher order thinking.

A summary of the domains of reading, history, and science is graphically laid out in Table 3.1 to facilitate comparisons in aspects of higher order thinking across and within these domains, as broken out in the *what, who, where,* and *when* dimensions. Table 3.1 is intended to highlight some of the very real differences across these domains in when, where, how, and for whom higher order thinking occurs, starting at the outset with differences in the *what*. At the same time, there are threads of similarities across the descriptions of the aspects for each dimension and domain, tracing back to our understanding of higher order thinking as being a particular form of engagement and reflecting a particular epistemic orientation across objects, situations, learners, and contexts. The fluid interplay between mode of engagement and epistemic orientation is evident in Table 3.1 in the pairings of perspective or view and activity or task. An important limitation of both Table 3.1 and of our discussion here is imposed by the constraints of verbal description, which require us to address or highlight in turn each of the four dimensions, which in reality form an interactive nexus.

WHAT DOES THE FUTURE HOLD?

When we first set out to reflect on the topic we were presented (i.e., the relation between higher order thinking and knowledge), we did not expect to end up posing an "unconventional" definition of higher order thinking. However, it would appear that the very topic of higher order thinking (the *what*) placed in the hands of those used to deconstructing academic constructs (the *who*) led us in this exciting direction. Of course, it was of no small consequence that our ruminations were to be set within a volume edited and populated by luminaries in our field (the *where*) and were intended not only to capture the theory and research of the past but also to provide direction for future research and practice (the *when*). Moreover, all of these dimensions of higher order thinking were amplified by our varied domain-specific experiences and orientations toward knowledge and knowing.

Table 3.1. What, Who, Where, and When of Higher Order Thinking in Reading, History, and Science

	Reading	History	Science
What	The text Relevant text characteristics: • Author presence • Controversy or ambiguity • Nesting in argumentative or otherwise participatory discourse context	The past Relevant characteristics of the past: • Accessible only partially through its remnants and its witnesses • Evoking both familiarity and estrangement with past human experiences • Invites critical, argumentative, empathetic discourse	The natural world Relevant characteristics of the phenomenon, process, or object of inquiry: • Complexity • Uncertainty, ambiguity, or controversy • Lack of clear solution path • Invites reasoning, argumentation, and justification.
Who	The learner, in relation to building knowledge of the subject-matter of text Relevant learner characteristics: • Knowledge of, interest in, and motivations toward subject-matter of text • Perception of subject-matter as ambiguous, complex, uncertain The reader, in relation to building knowledge of and about the text Relevant reader characteristics: • Knowledge of, interest in, motivations toward reading • Interest in reading as an activity • Perception of text as authored communication • Propensity to read in a participatory, conversational, or argumentative way	The learner, in relation to building knowledge about the past Relevant learner characteristics: • Awareness of author presence in historical texts • Awareness of learner positionality • Empathy • Familiarity with heuristics such as sourcing, corroboration, contextualization, and evaluation • Ability to think chronologically	The learner, in relation to building knowledge about the natural world Relevant learner characteristics: • Belief in more than one "nature" of science • Recognition that objects of scientific knowledge are in part socially-constructed • View of scientific knowledge as a coherent system of ideas; • High prior knowledge about the particular topic

(Table continues on next page)

Table 3.1. Continued

	Reading	History	Science
Where	Contexts that encourage the reader to experience texts as intelligible, questionable, and valuable Relevant context characteristics: • Attention to establishment of foundation of basic reading knowledge and skills • Provision of experience with texts as authored and as domain discourse • Use of reading to satisfy learner needs and goals • Elicitation of and respect for principled evaluative response to text	Contexts that favor encountering the past and understanding of historical method Relevant context characteristics: • Experience of and sensitivity to the characteristics of a historical text • Discussion and modeling of domain-specific heuristics • Exposure to historical inquiry • Development of a knowledge base facilitating contextualization	Contexts that allow the learner to experience complexities and uncertainties of inquiry Relevant context characteristics: • Support for belief that science is an ill-structured, but coherent system of ideas • Support for idea that science is about applying a process to transform knowledge and expand the field • Encouragement for discussion about the nature(s) of science
When	Developmental trajectory of the learner/reader Relevant developmental markers: • Greater knowledge of and interest in subject-matter/in reading • Mastery of threshold-level skills and knowledge for subject-matter/for reading • Socialization into and familiarity with conventions of domain discourse for subject-matter domain/with conventions of text as discourse • Increased propensity to approach subject-matter text/reading as invitation to discourse	Developmental trajectory of the history learner Relevant developmental markers: • Development of concepts about the substance of history, the historical method, and conventions of domain discourse • Ability to recognize and use polythetic narrative frameworks • Understanding of epistemological status of historical knowledge and of its justifications	Developmental trajectory of the student of science Relevant developmental markers: • Development of inquiry skills and processes, as applied to authentic, ill-structured problems • Development of reasoning, justification, and argumentation as habits-of-mind • Sophisticated epistemic stances about inquiry and the nature(s) of science

Collectively, we hold that this reconceptualization of higher order thinking does not set aside the decades of informative and ground-breaking theory and research, but serves to expand and improve upon that extensive literature in various ways. For one, the end to which we came—this new perspective on higher order thinking—has at its core the proposition that occasional outbreaks of reflective and transformational thought are not the site upon which to build a meaningful representation of the relation between higher order thinking and knowledge. Rather, it is the more consistent and predictable manifestations of higher order thinking that are the solid ground upon which substantive and justifiable arguments can be framed. Further, by concentrating on deep, generative, and effortful thinking that occurs with regularity we have moved beyond the more commonplace conceptualization of higher order thinking in terms of mental processes and opened that vista to beliefs about knowledge and knowing and their significant influence on both the processes and products of thought. Our forays into the domains of reading, history, and science sought to illustrate how the principles of higher order thinking we specified reveal themselves even in seemingly diverse domains, although in ways that pay homage to the knowledge and ways of knowing that distinguish those academic communities. These cross-domain exercises proved enlightening to us in our efforts to understand how the *what, who, where*, and *when* bring true dimensionality to higher order thinking.

Of course, our excitement at the understandings we have reached about higher order thinking and knowledge must be tempered with the realism that it is one thing to forward theoretical principles—even those supported by the literature—and quite another to translate those principles into research and practice. We appreciate the difficulties researchers face in devising measures and procedures that allow them to delve deeply into human thought. Here we ask even more of them. We ask them not only to develop measures with sound psychometric properties but also to attend both to the processes considered indicative of higher order mental engagement and to the beliefs about knowledge and knowing and about self as a knower that may compel effortful, generative, and transformational thought.

Much is asked of practitioners as well. As our discussion amplifies, there is no simple or easy path to higher order thinking. What transpires within schools and classrooms matters greatly and today's educational environments orchestrated toward test performance and toward normative responses to well-structured problems may be poor ecosystems for spawning such higher order thinking. There must be those *whats* of learning that invite such thinking and there must be exemplars of deep and reflective thought evident within the learning context. There must also be opportunities to build one's competence in thinking, coupled with the guidance, time, and rewards that give such occasions of unconventional thought value and argue for their regular reoccurrence.

Without such orchestrated efforts by researchers and educators, we fear that this new perspective on higher order thinking we forward will remain solely an intellectual exercise for the few and not a catalyst for transformational and unconventional empirical research or educational practice. Such a concern serves to highlight one remaining principle that must be voiced. In effect, higher order thinking should not be conceived as an end, but as means to ends. It is not merely the mental engagement with acts, ideas, objects, and situations in an analogical, elaborative, inductive, deductive or otherwise transformational manner that we prize. Nor is it just the orientation toward knowing as a complex, effortful, generative, evidence-seeking, and reflective enterprise that we hope to foster. Instead, what is ultimately to be prized or fostered is a manner of or orientation toward reflective or unconventional thinking that gives rise to intentional or deliberate human actions that are the embodiment of those deep and transformational thoughts.

We are not alone in this perception of higher order thinking as means and not as end. Indeed, Alfred North Whitehead (1929/1967), whose quote opened this chapter, shared a similar sentiment in *Aims of Education*. It is thus fitting that we close with those words.

> The ultimate motive power, alike in science, in morality, and in religion, is the sense of value, the sense of importance. It takes the various forms of wonder, of curiosity.... This sense of value imposes on life incredible labors, and apart from it life sinks back into the passivity of its lower types. (pp. 62-63)

AUTHOR NOTE

1. Author order is presented alphabetically. All authors contributed equally to the development of this chapter.

REFERENCES

Ackerman, P. L. (2003). Cognitive ability and non-ability trait determinants of expertise. *Educational Researcher, 32*(8), 15-20.

American Association for the Advancement of Science. (1989). *Project 2061: Science for All Americans Online.* Retrieved January 22, 2010, from http://www.project2061.org/

Afflerbach, P. (1990). The influence of prior knowledge on expert readers' main idea construction strategies. *Reading Research Quarterly, 25,* 31-46.

Alexander, P. A. (1997). Mapping the multidimensional nature of domain learning: The interplay of cognitive, motivational, and strategic forces. In M. L. Maehr & P. R. Pintrich (Eds.), *Advances in motivation and achievement* (Vol. 10, pp. 213-250). Greenwich, CT: JAI Press.

Alexander, P. A. (2003). The development of expertise: The journey from acclimation to proficiency. *Educational Researcher, 32*(8), 10-14.

Alexander, P. A. (2004). A model of domain learning: Reinterpreting expertise as a multidimensional, multistage process. In D. Y. Dai & R. J. Sternberg (Eds.), *Motivation, emotion, and cognition: Integrative perspectives on intellectual functioning and development* (pp. 273-298). Mahwah, NJ: Erlbaum.

Alexander, P. A. (2006). The path to competence: A lifespan developmental perspective on reading. *Journal of Literacy Research, 37*, 413-436.

Alexander, J. M., Johnson, K. E., Leibham, M. E., & Kelley, K. (2008). The development of conceptual interests in young children. *Cognitive Development, 23*, 324-334.

Alexander, P. A., Kulikowich, J. M., & Jetton, T. L. (1994). The role of subject-matter knowledge and interest in the processing of linear and nonlinear texts. *Review of Educational Research, 64*, 201-252.

Alexander, P. A., & Murphy, P. K. (1998). The research base for APA's learner-centered principles. In N. M. Lambert & B. L. McCombs (Eds.), *Issues in school reform: A sampler of psychological perspectives on learner-centered schools* (pp. 25-60). Washington, DC: The American Psychological Association.

Alexander, P. A., Murphy, P. K., Woods, B. S., & Duhon, K. E. (1997). College instruction and concomitant changes in students' knowledge, interest, and strategy use: A study of domain learning. *Contemporary Educational Psychology, 22*, 125-146.

Alexander, P. A., Schallert, D. L., & Reynolds, R. E. (2009). What is learning anyway? A topographical perspective considered. *Educational Psychologist, 44*, 176-192.

Alexander, P. A., Sperl, C. T., Buehl, M. M., Fives, H., & Chiu, S. (2004). Modeling domain learning: Profiles form the field of special education. *Journal of Educational Psychology, 96*, 545-557.

Anderson, R. C., Reynolds, R. E., Schallert, D. L., & Goetz, E. T. (1977). Frameworks for comprehending discourse. *American Educational Research Journal, 14*, 367-381.

Bain, R. (2000). Into the breach: Using research and theory to shape history instruction. In P. N. Stearns, P. Seixas, & S. Wineburg (Eds.), *Knowing, teaching and learning history: National and international perspectives* (pp. 331-352). New York, NY: New York University Press.

Bain, R. (2005). They thought the world was flat? Applying the principles of how people learn in teaching high school history. In S. Donovan & J. Bransford (Eds.), *How students learn: History in the classroom* (pp. 179-213). Washington DC: The National Academies Press.

Barak, M., & Shakhman, L. (2008). Fostering higher-order thinking in science class: Teachers' reflections. *Teachers and Teaching: Theory and Practice, 14*(3), 191-208.

Bereiter, C., & Scardamalia, M. (1986). Educational relevance of the study of expertise. *Interchange, 17,* 10-19.

Bereiter, C., & Scardamalia, M. (1993). *Surpassing ourselves: An inquiry into the nature and implications of expertise.* Chicago, IL: Open Court.

Bloom, B. S., Englehart, M. D., Furst, E. J., Hill, W. H., & Krathwohl D. R. (1956). *Taxonomy of educational objectives, Handbook 1: Cognitive domain.* Reading, MA: Addison Wesley.

Boekaerts, M., Pintrich, P. R., & Zeidner, M. (Eds.). (2001). *Handbook of self-regulation.* San Diego, CA: Academic Press.

Bransford, J. D., Brown, A. L., & Cocking, R. R. (1999). *How people learn: Brain, mind, experience, and school.* Washington, DC: National Academy Press.

Bransford, J. D., & Johnson, M. K. (1973). Consideration of some problems of comprehension. In W. G. Chase (Ed.), *Visual information processing* (pp. 383-438). New York, NY: Academic Press.

Britt, M. A., Perfetti, C. A., Van Dyke, J. A., & Gabrys, G. (2000). The Sourcer's apprentice: A tool for document-supported history instruction. In P. N. Stearns, P. Seixas, & S. Wineburg (Eds.), *Knowing, teaching and learning history: National and international perspectives* (pp. 437-470). New York, NY: New York University Press.

Bronfenbrenner, U., & Ceci, S. J. (1994). Nature-nurture reconceptualized in developmental perspective: A bioecological model. *Psychological Review, 101,* 568-586.

Brown, A. L., & Campione, J. C. (1990). Communities of learning and thinking, or a context by any other name. In D. Kuhn (Ed.), *Developmental perspectives on teaching and learning thinking skills* (pp. 108-126). Basel, Switzerland: Karger.

Brown, A. L., Campione, J. C., & Day, J. D. (1981). Learning to learn: On training students to learn from texts. *Educational Researcher, 10*(2), 14-21.

Brown, C. (2007). Learning through multimedia construction: A complex strategy. *Journal of Educational Multimedia and Hypermedia, 16,* 93-124.

Brown, R. S., & Conley, D. T. (2007). Comparing state high school assessments to standards for success in entry-level university courses. *Educational Assessment, 12,* 137-160.

Carey, S., & Smith, C. (1993). On understanding the nature of scientific knowledge, *Educational Psychologist, 28*(3), 235-251.

Chall, J. S. (1983). *Stages of reading development.* New York, NY: McGraw-Hill.

Chambliss, M. (1995). Text cues and strategies successful readers use to construct the gist of lengthy written arguments. *Reading Research Quarterly, 30,* 778-807.

Charney, D. (1993). A study in rhetorical reading: How evolutionists read "The spandrels of San Marco." In J. Selzer (Ed.), *Understanding scientific prose* (pp. 97-119). Madison, WI: University of Wisconsin Press.

Chinn, C. A., & Malhotra, B. A. (2002) Epistemologically authentic inquiry in schools: A theoretical framework for evaluating inquiry tasks. *Science Education, 86,* 175-218.

Dewey, J. (1913). *Interest and effort in education.* Boston, MA: Riverdale.

Dinsmore, D. L., Alexander, P. A., & Loughlin, S. M. (2008). Focusing the conceptual lens on metacognition, self-regulation, and self-regulated learning. *Educational Psychology Review, 20,* 391-409.

Dinsmore, D. L., Loughlin, S. M., & Parkinson, M. M. (2009, April). *The effects of persuasive and expository text on metacognitive monitoring and control.* Paper presented at the annual meeting of the American Educational Research Association, San Diego, CA.

Donovan, S., & Bransford, J. (2005). *How students learn: History in the classroom.* Washington, DC: The National Academies Press.

Dori, Y. J., Tal, R. T., & Tsaushu, M. (2003). Teaching biotechnology through case studies: Can we improve higher order thinking skills of nonscience majors? *Science Education, 87,* 767-793.

Driver, R., Asoko, H., Leach, J., Mortimer, E., & Scott, P. (1994). Constructing scientific knowledge in the classroom. *Educational Researcher, 23*(7), 5-12.

Dunbar, K., & Fugelsang, J. (2005). Scientific thinking and reasoning, In K. J. Holyoak & R. G. Morrison (Eds.). *Cambridge handbook of thinking and reasoning* (pp. 705-725). Cambridge, England: Cambridge University Press.

Elliot, A., & Harackiewicz, J. (1996). Approach and avoidance achievement goals and intrinsic motivation: A mediational analysis. *Journal of Personality and Social Psychology, 70,* 968-980.

Fisher, D., & Frey, N. (2007). A tale of two middle schools: The differences in structure and instruction. *Journal of Adolescent & Adult Literacy, 51,* 204-211.

Fox, E. (2009). The role of reader characteristics in processing and learning from informational text. *Review of Educational Research, 79,* 197-261.

Fox, E., Dinsmore, D. L., Maggioni, L., & Alexander, P. A. (2009, April). *Factors associated with undergraduates' success in reading and learning from course texts.* Paper presented at the annual meeting of the American Educational Research Associate, San Diego, CA.

Frankl, V. E. (1985). *Man's search for meaning.* New York, NY: Washington Square Press.

Gadamer, H. G. (1975). *Truth and method.* London: Continuum.

Garner, R. (1990). When children and adults do not use learning strategies: Toward a theory of setting. *Review of Educational Research, 60,* 517-529.

Geisler, C. (1994). *Academic literacy and the nature of expertise: Reading, writing, and knowing in academic philosophy.* Hillsdale, NJ: Erlbaum.

Graesser, A. C., Millis, K. K., & Zwaan, R. A. (1997). Discourse comprehension. *Annual Review of Psychology, 48,* 163-189.

Graves, B. (2001). Literary expertise and analogical reasoning: Building global themes. *Empirical Studies of the Arts, 19,* 47-63.

Gray, W. S., & Rogers, B. (1956). *Maturity in reading, its nature and appraisal.* Chicago, IL: The University of Chicago Press.

Haas, C., & Flower, L. (1988). Rhetorical reading strategies and the construction of meaning. *College Composition and Communication, 39,* 167-183.

Halpern, D. F. (1996). *Thought and knowledge: An introduction to critical thinking* (3rd ed.). Hillsdale, NJ: Erlbaum.

Hammer, D., & Elby, A. (2002). On the form of a personal epistemology. In B. K. Hofer & P. R. Pintrich (Eds.), *Personal epistemology: The psychology of beliefs about knowledge and knowing* (pp. 169-190) Mahwah, NJ: Erlbaum.

Hay, I., & Booker, G. (2006). Teachers' perceptions and classroom application of mathematical computer software. *Journal of Cognitive Education and Psychology*, *6*, 61-71.

Hicks, D., Doolittle, P., & Lee, J. (2004). Social studies teachers' use of classroom-based and web-based historical primary sources. *Theory and Research in Social Education*, *32*(2), 213-247.

Hofer, B. K., & Yu, S. L. (2003). Teaching self-regulated learning through a "learning to learn" course. *Teaching of Psychology*, *30*, 30-33.

Husbands, C., Kitson, A., & Pendry, A. (2003). *Understanding history teaching: Teaching and learning about the past in secondary schools*. Philadelphia, PA: Open University Press.

Ivey, G., & Fisher, D. (2005). Learning from what doesn't work. *Educational Leadership*, *63*(2), 8-14.

Joseph, H. S. S. L., Liversedge, S. P., Blythe, H. I., White, S. J., Gathercole, S. E., & Rayner, K. (2008). Children's and adults' processing of anomaly and implausibility during reading: Evidence from eye movements. *The Quarterly Journal of Experimental Psychology*, *61*, 708-723.

Kato, Y., Kamii, C., Ozaki, K., & Nagahiro, M. (2002). Young children's representations of groups of objects: The relationship between abstraction and representation. *Journal for Research in Mathematics Education*, *33*, 30-45.

Klahr, D., & Dunbar, K. (1988). Dual search space during scientific reasoning. *Cognitive Science*, *12*, 1-48.

Klahr, D., & Nigam, M. (2004). The equivalence of learning paths in early science instruction: Effects of direct instruction and discovery learning, *Psychological Science*, *15*(10), 661-667.

Kuhn, D. (1989). Children and adults as intuitive scientists. *Psychological Review*, *96*, 674-689.

Lee, P. (2004). Understanding history. In P. Seixas (Ed.), *Theorizing historical consciousness* (pp. 129-164). Toronto: University of Toronto Press.

Lee, P (2005). Putting principles into practice: Understanding history. In S. Donovan & J. Bransford (Eds.), *How students learn: History in the classroom* (pp. 31-77). Washington DC: The National Academies Press.

Lee, P., & Ashby, R. (2000). Progression in historical understanding among students ages 7-14. In P. N. Stearns, P. Seixas, & S. Wineburg (Eds.), *Knowing, teaching and learning history: National and international perspectives* (pp. 199-222). New York, NY: New York University Press.

Lee, P., & Shemilt, D. (2003). A scaffold, not a cage: Progression and progression models in history. *Teaching History*, *113*, 13-24.

Lee, P., Dickinson, A., & Ashby, R. (1997). "Just another emperor": Understanding action in the past. *International Journal of Educational Research*, *27*, 233-244.

Lowenthal, D. (2000). Dilemmas and delights of learning history. In P. N. Stearns, P. Seixas, & S. Wineburg (Eds.), *Knowing, teaching and learning history: National and international perspectives* (pp. 63-82). New York, NY: New York University Press.

Luna, B., Garver, K. E., Urban, T. A., Lazar, N. A., & Sweeney, J. A. (2004). Maturation of cognitive processes from late childhood to adulthood. *Child Development, 75*, 1357-1372.

Marrou H. I. (1954). *De la connaissance historique.* Paris: Editions du Seuil.

Marton, F., & Säljö, R. (1976). On qualitative differences in learning—2: Outcome as a function of the learner's conception of the task. *British Journal of Educational Psychology. 46*, 115-127.

Marton, F., & Säljö, R (1997). Approaches to learning. In F. Marton, D. Hounsell, & N. Entwisle (Eds.), *The experience of learning* (2nd ed., pp. 39-58). Edinburgh: Scottish Academic Press.

Mason, L., Gava, M., & Boldrin, A. (2008). On warm conceptual change: The interplay of text, epistemological beliefs, and topic interest. *Journal of Educational Psychology, 100*, 291-309.

Mathan, S. A., & Koedinger, K. R. (2005). Fostering the intelligent novice: Learning from errors with metacognitive tutoring. *Educational Psychologist, 40*, 257-265.

Matthews, D. B., & Burnett, D. D. (1989). Anxiety: An achievement component. *Journal of Humanistic Counseling, Education & Development, 27*, 122-131.

Mayer, R. E. (1983). *Thinking, problem solving, cognition.* New York, NY: W. H. Freeman.

Meijer, J., Veenman, M. V. J., & van Hout-Wolters, B. H. A. M. (2006). Metacognitive activities in text-studying and problem-solving: Development of a taxonomy. *Educational Research and Evaluation, 12*, 209-237.

Murphy, P. K., & Alexander, P. A. (2002). What counts? The predictive powers of subject-matter knowledge, strategic processing, and interest in domain-specific performance. *Journal of Experimental Education, 70*, 197-214.

Murphy, P. K., & Mason, L. (2006). Changing knowledge and beliefs. In P. A. Alexander & P. H. Winne (Eds.), *Handbook of educational psychology* (pp. 305-324). Mahwah, NJ: Erlbaum.

Murphy, P. K., Wilkinson, I. A. G., Soter, A. O., Hennessey, M. N., & Alexander, J. F. (2009). Examining the effects of classroom discussion on students' comprehension of text: A meta-analysis. *Journal of Educational Psychology, 101*, 740-764.

National Science Teachers Association. (2003). *Standards for science teacher preparation.* Retrieved http://www.nsta.org/main/pdfs/NSTAstandards2003.pdf

Novick, P. (1988). *That noble dream: The "objectivity question" and the American historical profession.* Cambridge, England: Cambridge University Press.

Oliver, K., & Hannafin, M. J. (2000). Student management of web-based hypermedia resources during open-ended problem solving. *Journal of Educational Research, 94*, 75-92.

Olson, G. M., Duffy, S. A., & Mack, R. L. (1984). Thinking-out-loud as a method for studying real-time comprehension processes. In D. E. Kieras & M. A. Just (Eds.), *New methods in reading comprehension research* (pp. 253-286). Hillsdale, NJ: Erlbaum.

Parkinson, M. M. (2009, April). "What did I learn?" and "How did I do?" The relation between metacognition and word learning. In P. A. Alexander (Chair), *Meta-what? Measuring monitoring and control.* Symposium presented at the annual meeting of the American Educational Research Association, San Diego.

Paxton, R. J. (1997). "Someone with a life wrote it": The effects of a visible author on high school history students. *Journal of Educational Psychology, 89,* 235-250.

Paxton, R. J. (2002). The influence of author visibility on high school students solving a historical problem. *Cognition and Instruction, 20,* 197-248.

Perry, W. G., Jr. (1959). Students' use and misuse of reading skills: A report to a faculty. *Harvard Educational Review, 29,* 193-200.

Popper, K. R. (1968). *The logic of scientific discovery.* London: Hutchinson.

Pressley, M., & Afflerbach, P. (1995). *Verbal protocols of reading.* Hillsdale, NJ: Erlbaum.

Ramsden, P. (1997). The context of learning in academic departments. In F. Marton, D. Hounsell, & N. Entwistle (Eds.), *The experience of learning* (2nd ed., p. 198-216). Edinburgh: Scottish Academic Press.

Resnick (1987). *Education and learning to think.* Washington, DC: National Academies Press.

Roth, W., & Bowen, G. M. (2003). When are graphs worth ten thousand words? An expert-expert study. *Cognition and Instruction, 2,* 429-473.

Rosenzweig, R. (2000). How Americans use and think about the past: Implications from a National survey for the teaching of history. In P. N. Stearns, P. Seixas, & S. Wineburg (Eds.), *Knowing, teaching and learning history: National and international perspectives* (pp. 262-283). New York, NY: New York University Press.

Rouet, J., Marron, M., Perfetti. C., & Favart, M. (1998). Understanding historical controversies: Students' evaluation and use of documentary evidence. In J. Voss & M. Carretero (Eds.), *International review of history education, Volume 2: Learning and reasoning in history* (pp. 95-116). London: Woburn Press.

Scardamalia, M., & Bereiter, C. (1991). Literate expertise. In K. A. Ericsson & J. Smith (Eds.), *Toward a general theory of expertise* (pp. 172-194). New York, NY: Cambridge University Press.

Schauble. L. (1996). The development of scientific reasoning in knowledge-rich contexts. *Developmental Psychology, 32*(1), 102-119.

Schraw, G. (2000). Assessing metacognition: Implications of the Buros Symposium. In G. Schraw & J. C. Impara (Eds.), *Issues in the measurement of metacognition* (pp. 297-321). Lincoln, NE: Buros Institute of Mental Measurements.

Schraw, G., & Sinatra, G. M. (2004). Epistemological development and its impact on cognition in academic domains. *Contemporary Educational Psychology, 29,* 95-102.

Schrire, S. (2004). Interaction and cognition in asynchronous computer conferencing. *Instructional Science, 32,* 475-502.

Seixas, P. (1997). Mapping the terrain of historical significance. *Social Education, 61*(1), 22-27.

Seixas, P. (2000). Schweigen! Die Kinder! Or does postmodern history have a place in the schools? In P. N. Stearns, P. Seixas, & S. Wineburg (Eds.), *Knowing, teaching and learning history: National and international perspectives* (pp. 19-37). New York, NY: New York University Press.

Seixas, P. (2004). *Theorizing historical consciousness.* Toronto, Canada: University of Toronto Press.

Shanahan, C. (2009). Disciplinary comprehension. In S. E. Israel & G. G. Duffy (Eds.), *Handbook of research on reading comprehension* (pp. 240-260). New York, NY: Routledge.

Shanahan, T. (1992). Reading comprehension as a conversation with an author. In M. Pressley, K. R. Harris, & J. T. Guthrie (Eds.), *Promoting academic competence and literacy in school* (pp. 129-148). San Diego, CA: Academic Press.

Shemilt, D. (2000). The Caliph's coin: The currency of narrative frameworks in history teaching. In P. N. Stearns, P. Seixas, & S. Wineburg (Eds.), *Knowing, teaching and learning history: National and international perspectives* (pp. 83-101). New York, NY: New York University Press.

Smith, C. L., Maclin, D., Houghton, C., & Hennessey, M. G. (2000). Sixth-grade students' epistemologies of science: The impact of school science experiences on epistemological development. *Cognition and Instruction, 18*(3), 349-422.

Smith, R. B. (1970). An empirical investigation of complexity and process in multiple-choice items. *Journal of Educational Measurement, 7,* 33-41.

Smythe, K., & Halonen, J. (2009) Using the new Bloom's Taxonomy to design meaningful learning assessments. Retrieved April 9, 2009 from the American Psychological Association Web Site: http://www.apa.org/ed/new_blooms.html

Songer, N. B. (2006). BioKIDS: An animated conversation on the development of curricular activity structures for inquiry science. In R. K Sawyer (Ed.), *The Cambridge handbook of the learning sciences* (pp. 355-370). New York, NY: Cambridge University Press.

Stearns, P., Seixas, P., & Wineburg, S. (2000). *Knowing, teaching and learning history: National and international perspectives.* New York, NY: New York University Press.

Sternberg, R. J. (1985). *Beyond IQ: A triarchic theory of human intelligence.* New York, NY: Cambridge University Press.

Stevens, R., Wineburg, S., Herrenkohl, L. R., & Bell, P. (2005). Comparative understanding of school subjects: Past, present, and future. *Review of Educational Research, 75*(2), 125-157.

Sweller, J., van Merrienboer, J. J. G, & Paas, F. G. W. C (1998). Cognitive architecture and instructional design. *Educational Psychology Review, 10,* 251-296.

Torff, B. (2003). Developmental changes in teachers' use of higher order thinking and content knowledge. *Journal of Educational Psychology, 95,* 563-569.

Tzuriel, D. (2000). Dynamic assessment of young children: Educational and intervention perspectives. *Educational Psychology Review, 12,* 385-435.

VanSledright, B. (1997). And Santayana lives on: Students' views on the purposes for studying American history. *Journal of Curriculum Studies, 29*(5), 529-558.

VanSledright, B. (2001). From empathic regard to self-understanding: Im/positionality, empathy, and historical contextualization. In O. L. Davis Jr., E. A. Yeager, & S. J. Foster (Eds.), *Historical empathy and perspective taking in the social studies* (pp. 51-68). Lanham, MD: Rowman & Littlefield.

VanSledright, B. (2002). *In search of America's past: Learning to read history in elementary school.* New York, NY: Teachers College Press.

VanSledright, B. (2004). What does it mean to read history? Fertile ground for cross-disciplinary collaborations? *Reading Research Quarterly, 39*(3), 342-346.

Vygotsky, L. S. (1978). *Mind in society: The development of higher psychological processes*. M. Cole (Ed.). Cambridge, MA: Harvard University Press.

White, H. V. (1973). *Metahistory: The historical imagination in nineteenth-century Europe*. Baltimore, MD: John Hopkins University Press.

Whitehead, A. N. (1938). *Modes of thought*. New York, NY: MacMillan.

Whitehead, A. N. (1967). *The aims of education and other essays*. New York, NY: Macmillan. (Original published in 1929)

Wimer, J. W., Ridenour, C. S., Thomas, K., & Place, A. W. (2001). Higher order teacher questioning of boys and girls in elementary mathematics classrooms. *Journal of Educational Research, 95*, 84-92.

Wineburg, S. (1998). Reading Abraham Lincoln: An expert/expert study in the interpretation of historical text. *Cognitive Science, 22*(3), 319-346.

Wineburg, S. (1999). Historical thinking and other unnatural acts. *Phi Delta Kappan, 80*(7), 488-499.

Wineburg, S. (2000). Making historical sense. In P. N. Stearns, P. Seixas, & S. Wineburg (Eds.), *Knowing, teaching and learning history: National and international perspectives* (pp. 306-325). New York, NY: New York University Press.

Wineburg, S. (2001). On the reading of historical texts: Notes on the breach between school and academy. In S. Wineburg (Ed.), *Historical thinking and other unnatural acts: Charting the future of teaching the past* (pp. 63-88). Philadelphia, PA: Temple University Press.

Wineburg, S. (2007). Unnatural and essential: The nature of historical thinking. *Teaching History, 129*, 6-11.

Wyatt, D., Pressley, M., El-Dinary, P. B., Stein, S., Evans, P., & Brown, R. (1993). Comprehension strategies, worth and credibility monitoring, and evaluations: Cold and hot cognition when experts read professional articles that are important to them. *Learning and Individual Differences, 5*, 49-72.

Yeager, E., & Davis, O. Jr. (1996). Classroom teachers' thinking about historical texts: An exploratory study. *Theory and Research in Social Education, 24*(2), 146-166.

Zimmerman, C. (2007). The development of scientific thinking skills in elementary and middle school. *Developmental Review, 27*, 172-223.

Zohar, A., & Dori, Y. J. (2003). Higher-order thinking and low-achieving students: Are they mutually exclusive? *Journal of the Learning Sciences, 12*(2), 145-181.

Zydney, J. M. (2008). Cognitive tools for scaffolding students defining an ill-structured problem. *Journal of Educational Computing Research, 38*, 353-385.

CHAPTER 4

DESIGNING ASSESSMENTS OF SELF-REGULATED LEARNING

Philip H. Winne, Mingming Zhou, and Rylan Egan

Assessment has three key features (American Educational Research Association, 1999). First, a systematic method is applied to collect information (data) that an assessor believes can provide grounds for inferences about attributes of people or objects. Usually, methods take form as an instrument, for example: a list of questions, a task with instructions for completing it or a situation in which the person being assessed behaves. Second, assessors follow a protocol to develop inferences based on the data that was gathered. Third, the inference is validated.

Issues that bear on assessing self-regulated learning (SRL) have been previously examined in major publications by Pintrich, Wolters, and Baxter (2000), Samuelstuen and Bråten (2007), Winne and Perry (2000), Winne, Jamieson-Noel, and Muis (2002) and Zimmerman (2008). Additional work that examined issues bearing on assessing SRL and its features has been contributed by Hadwin, Winne, Stockley, Nesbit, and Wosczyna (2001), Pintrich (2004), and Winne (2010). In brief and acknowledging omission of elaborations that can be found in these publications, the gist of prior analyses regarding how SRL is assessed is:

1. Assessing SRL is challenging because the target to be assessed is a dynamic *process* for which typically there are few available objective indicators or traces. As a result, think aloud protocols have often been viewed as the best method for reflecting dynamic aspects of SRL.

2. SRL processes are sensitive to changing conditions over the period of a learner's engagement in tasks. Thus, the point(s) in time at which data is gathered matters because the state of a task changes over time.

3. Two very prominent methods for gathering data about features of SRL—paper-and-pencil inventories and interviews—often suffer multiple and potentially fatal flaws, primarily because these methods depend on a respondent's memory. Memory can be less than an ideal record of information about SRL:

   - Memory is constructive and reconstructive, so it may not render an accurate account of SRL processes or products.

   - Recollections of or introspections about ongoing SRL are almost always samples from a population of relevant experiences. These samples are incomplete and often biased in unknown ways.

   - Because SRL is, by definition, sensitive to context, attributes of a current or a past context affect people's descriptions of features of SRL.

   - When people are asked to forecast how they might behave in a future context, they quite likely hold varying perceptions about attributes that constitute context.

   - Forecasts about behavior and other states (e.g., interest) are likely generated by different heuristics that are untracked and vary in degrees and kinds of inaccuracies.

   - People may report using SRL strategies because they know or believe those strategies are effective, not because they actually use them.

4. SRL is a process that generates changes in behavior over time based on preceding products of cognition. Thus, assessing SRL requires methods for gathering and articulating longitudinal data about what people do, what and how they think about what they are doing, and how these observable and covert states track along a timeline of engagement with a task. It needs to be explicitly highlighted that subsequent states inherently correlate with prior ones unless a subsequent state is a fully random event which, we believe, is exceptionally rare. Few methods have been mapped out for gath-

ering such data. Methods and tools for analyzing such data are limited.

5. Owing to (a) different theorists' accounts about fundamental elements that comprise SRL and (b) challenges in determining an appropriate grain size for states and time spans that can reflect these elements, it has proven very difficult to synthesize empirical findings and coordinate theoretical interpretations about the nature of SRL. There is no "gold standard" instrument or protocol for generating data about SRL. Nor is there a canonical approach to generating and validating inferences about SRL. In short, the field is beset by too much uniqueness in instrumentation and too much variance in findings.

6. Most skills are researched within a relatively well-defined subject matter, e.g., skills for correcting expression in an expository essay, for checking the accuracy of arithmetic computations and so forth. In contrast, skills for SRL are not situated in any particular academic subject matter or domain. People can engage in SRL while studying any academic subject, searching the Internet for information about their health, examining practices affecting their golf game, managing their finances … anything. This further complicates synthesizing understandings about assessments of SRL because it can be questioned whether the sources of variance observed in different findings lie in features of SRL or attributes of the domain.

In light of these challenges, we position this chapter as a focused review and grounded forecast about approaches to assessing SRL. We synthesize strengths of current assessment methods and approaches to analyzing data, and aim to forge a flexible and hopefully generative model for assessing SRL. Along the way, we recap specific key issues buried in the preceding general summary of work to develop a roadmap for approaching resolutions to those challenges.

ASSUMPTIONS

It is difficult to rationalize that what learners do—the tactics and strategies they enact—is utterly without purpose. Instead, we posit all tactics—basic skills that take one step in a task—and arrangements of tactics into strategies are shaped, in large part, by a learner's goals.

We construe goals as what a learner intends to accomplish by enacting a tactic or strategy. Without intentions, there are no goals; but this does not preclude that learners may act unintentionally. We do not probe here why a learner adopts a particular goal, a fundamental question about motivation. This stance allows us to avoid considerations about tailoring assessments of SRL to reflect any particular theory that was designed to explain how motivation or affect shapes behavior. (We hasten to add that shaping assessments of SRL in accord with a particular theory of motivation or affect is not to be eschewed, only that considering such methods is not our purpose.) Hence, motivation per se is addressed minimally in our analysis.

We choose the word "state" to describe qualities of a situation that a learner (a) perceives in the present or (b) forecasts about the future. Because our topic is *self*-regulated learning, states are cognitive constructions that a learner creates *in situ*. States can refer to a configuration of qualities that describe a mental context, such as a sense of confidence and an expectation about what will happen if a particular tactic is applied. States can also refer to factors in the learner's environment that create an external context, such as a time limit deemed generous for solving an algebra word problem that requires more than a usual number of algebraic manipulations. That we choose the learner as a point of reference allows that the learner's catalog of factors in a context may differ from an observer's, such as a peer's, teacher's or an experimenter's. This acknowledges that assessments of SRL have a frame of reference. What matters in our account is that SRL is a *self* phenomenon, so emphasis should be placed on how the learner perceives a state.

FACTORS IN SRL

What attributes of SRL can be assessed? What are targets for assessment? Answers are multiple owing to item 5 presented earlier in our list of challenges to developing assessments of SRL. We first introduce typologies for describing what might be assessed about SRL and facets of contexts in which SRL might be assessed. Then, we present a scenario to illustrate elements in our ontology. Following this overview and illustration, we delve into particulars of assessing SRL.

In Table 4.1, we list features of SRL that we judge can span various models found in contemporary theories and empirical research (e.g., see Zimmerman, 2008; Zimmerman & Schunk, 2001). These are topics or targets to be assessed. Our terminology is intended to be neutral yet inclusive with respect to this range of views about SRL. We suggest that, along with other data, assessments of these features of SRL can reveal whether learners self-regulate learning, distinguish kinds of SRL and, when related to other data such as achievement, contribute to assessing the effectiveness and efficiency of SRL.

Table 4.1.   Features of SRL

Feature	Description
Cue	Features of tasks, the external environment and a learner's cognitive state(s) that a learner perceives as predictive of another fundamental feature of SRL. When cues follow a learner's action, this is feedback.
Goal or Standard	Attribute a learner uses to judge whether a state is satisfactory. Goals are typically coarser-grained descriptions than standards. Standards elaborate the goal to specify more precisely, in finer grain, what constitutes accomplishment.
Tactic	Cognitive and behavioral operations a learner carries out to change a present cognitive state, a facet of context or an individual difference factor. Strategies are patterned arrangements of tactics that include decision points where the learner makes choices about which tactics are best to use given a current state.
Forecast	A learner's expectation about the product generated by a particular tactic.
Account	A learner's belief about why tactics correlate with forecasts or generate the kind or quality of product(s) that results when a tactic is applied.
Utility	A learner's judgment about the ratio of benefits to costs in applying a tactic in a context.
Likelihood	The probability a learner will enact a particular tactic.
Log	A learner's record of features of SRL: • the sequence of tactics' occurrence. • products created by tactics (or, the effect of a tactic). • correlations or conditional probabilities that relate fundamental features of SRL.

When learners engage in SRL, they are working on a task within a context; or, they are reviewing how they worked on a prior task in its context in preparation for possibly changing their approach to working on an upcoming similar task. Facets of the task's context afford or constrain a learner's work on a task per se, where the stage is set for SRL, as well as how SRL is expressed. In Table 4.2 we list facets of contexts that we posit to shape SRL in either of these two ways.

In addition to context variables that influence SRL, individual differences can affect how and how well a learner approaches focal and potential supporting tasks. This in turn can affect expressions of SRL by altering one or more factors of SRL listed in Table 4.1. Table 4.3 lists individual difference variables we posit to be critical in modeling and assessing expressions of SRL. We explicitly acknowledge this list can be extended depending on the purposes of assessment.

Table 4.2.   Facets of Contexts Where SRL is Engaged

Facet	Description
Focal Task	What kind of work is the learner undertaking? For brevity, we adopt the task language proposed in the revised Bloom taxonomy (Anderson & Krathwohl, 2001): remembering, understanding, applying, analyzing, evaluating and creating. Other typologies and ontologies could be substituted for this one.
Supporting Task(s)	As a learner works on a task (e.g., understanding a text), occasions may arise to engage in other tasks (e.g., elaborating the text in annotations) that (a) contribute to the focal task and (b) involve knowledge or skills beyond bounds of the focal task.
Access to Information	To what extent does the context afford the learner opportunity to acquire or reinstate information in working memory? The topic of information can concern: • goals set externally (e.g., by a teacher) for the focal task. • content in the domain of the focal task. Content may become available at the outset of work, during work, or upon completion. Knowledge of results feedback is common in the latter two categories but the category is open and includes elaborative information, process feedback (see Butler & Winne, 1995), and so forth. • tactics and the qualities of tactics (e.g., efficiency, risk) that are appropriate to working on the task. • features of SRL.
Information Load	What opportunity does the context provide for the learner to offload work—processes and their products—into the environment (e.g., use a calculator vs. doing mental computation, make notes, look up needed facts)?
Density	What is the ratio of demand on working memory (e.g., amount of information to read, a tactic's degree of automaticity) relative to resources available for engaging in a task?

Commonly Misrepresented Attributes of SRL

Five attributes of SRL merit explicit mention because they have been relatively underspecified or misunderstood. First, to create an opportunity to assess SRL, the learner must perceive there is a choice about: a feature of SRL, a facet of context or an individual difference that the learner can regulate. Second, to register an instance of SRL, the environment must permit the learner to make a choice in a way that can be observed.

A third key attribute of SRL is that regulation need not result in change. A learner's regulation can take form as deliberately maintaining a feature of SRL, a facet of context or the status of an individual difference. Maintaining a state is regulation when (a) the learner metacognitively

Table 4.3.   Key Individual Differences Bearing on Expressions of SRL

Individual Difference	Description
Schema Knowledge	What structural features and qualities does the learner perceive about the task and facets of its context?
Focal Task Expertise	To what extent is the learner able to carry out the focal task using current knowledge and skills versus needing to build knowledge or skill?
Supporting Task Expertise	To what extent is the learner able to carry out the supporting task(s) using current knowledge and skills versus needing to build knowledge or skill?
Focal Task Drive	To what degree does the learner want to succeed at the focal task?
Epistemic Sophistication	What attributes does the learner hold as distinguishing knowledge from other kinds of information?

monitors the state of a task then (b) exercises metacognitive control to preserve a factor that is potentially changeable.

Fourth, SRL need not correlate positively with achievement or other variables that are valued by someone other than the learner. Self-regulating learners may choose to experiment with tactics and other factors as a way of investigating what works best for them (Winne, 1997). Not every experiment results in improvements as judged by learners or observers. Another example of a more persistent approach to regulation is exemplified by self-handicapping learners who purposely avoid studying before examinations. They succeed at their goal to have an excuse for failure if they perform poorly but they will fail to achieve their teacher's goal of scoring well on the examination.

Fifth, SRL can not be assessed without multiple samples of the learner's behavior. This is because SRL can be identified only when a factor in the present is considered for change or maintenance. The following state must be observed to track regulation relative to the preceding state.

Measuring Features of SRL Within an Assessment Context— A Scenario

Italics in this scenario match corresponding elements in Tables 4.1, 4.2, and 4.3.

Cindy is a Grade 9 student studying the water cycle in her earth science course. Her teacher assigned sections 7.1-7.7 in the textbook with the *focal tasks*: understand the water cycle and factors affecting it, and prepare an analysis that addresses the question, "What effects might global warming have on the water cycle?"

Cindy has multiple *supporting tasks*, only a few of which we explicitly describe. She needs to remember previously studied terms reused in these sections and develop understanding of (learn) new ones.

Goals and Standards

Goals the teacher provided are general, so Cindy capitalizes on the latitude they afford to develop her own more specific *standards* for metacognitively monitoring her work. For example, she decides that the water cycle is understood when she can draw a complete diagram of factors involved in the cycle and their relations without having to consult the textbook. She also is free to set standards for the supporting tasks. For example, Cindy might want to experiment with a new method for using the minisummaries, as we describe shortly.

As Cindy studies, she has easy *access to information* that is potentially relevant and useful. She can reduce *information load* by looking up terms in the textbook's glossary whenever she wishes. She started studying well before her favorite TV show airs at 9 P.M., so she is not rushing metacognitive monitoring of large chunks of information (density is low). But, as she's at home, she does not have *access to her teacher* for clarification about the standards he intends for the two focal tasks.

Cindy has many options to *offload information* into her working environment. For example, she can copy information from her textbook onto sticky post-it notes or use concept mapping software to catalog, spatially organize and link information for just-in-time reference. Cindy might use the template her teacher introduced earlier in the semester about how to establish goals for learning. A scoring scheme for evaluating whether she meets her goal (drawing a diagram of factors and relations without textbook consultation) can be instantly *accessed* without having to review the entire reading assignment.

Cues and Tactics

Cindy's textbook provides a variety of *cues* that the authors intend to direct learners' studying activities. Some of these cues are: terms formatted in bold font when they are first introduced; minisummaries presented at the end of decimal-level heading (7.2, 7.3 and so forth); diagrams and tables that afford coordinating and extending information presented in the text with information presented primarily a nonverbal (graphical or symbolic) system; and, inserted questions located in the page margin near relevant material that invite elaborating the content.

Cindy has multiple opportunities to apply and experiment with various *tactics* for tasks she undertakes. For example, because there are seven instances of minisummaries, over the course of studying the assigned sections, she can carry out an informal experiment to determine whether she learns better when she reads the summary before or after studying section it summarizes.

Often-used study *tactics* in Cindy's arsenal include coding the role of information in text by colored markers (i.e., tagging), reviewing glossary terms as needed, offloading information from memory to notes, and concept mapping. Cindy started tagging information in several categories— land based factors, meteorological factors, and so on—but decided this was unproductive, so simplified her scheme to use just one color for "important" information.

Forecast and Account

Cindy makes a *forecast* that reading minisummaries, which the textbook authors positioned to follow the section each one summarizes, might help her "zero in" on key information in a section. Being quite an adept learner, her *account* is that the authors are experts and a summary is supposed to provide key information about a topic. However, rather than relying on the textbook summaries, Cindy also supplements them with the entries in her concept map. Cindy expects that, if her tactic works, she'll have fewer highlights, since she will highlight only the key information; and there will be a better match of information highlighted to entries in her concept map.

Log

Cindy decided to *log* results of her experiment by putting marking a + or a – next to the minisummary to record whether pre-reading it was helpful or not. Depending on how these results accumulate, Cindy might revise her account. As well, Cindy inherently builds up an internal log of her experiences. If we asked her, she might report that she spent too much time reading summaries before studying the main material, and that led her to further revise her account to incorporate the cost of increased *density*.

Utility

Cindy judged that reading a minisummary before the section it summarized was better (had greater *utility*) than reading it after studying that section. Both methods offered roughly the same benefit to learning. But, when she read minisummaries after reading the corresponding section, she had to work harder (experienced greater *information load*) to identify key information to highlight and she needed to re-examine the section to make sure she highlighted all the key information (increased *density*). Those costs weren't matched by greater benefits.

Likelihood

Cindy decides her experiment for this assignment was sufficiently convincing that, next time, she'll read minisummaries before reading the sections they summarize. Being an eager, self-regulating learner, she invents two new experiments. What would happen if she read all the minisummaries at the outset of her study session? Would it be beneficial to write summaries of sections in her other courses where the textbook authors do not provide them?

METHODS FOR GATHERING ASSESSMENT DATA

There are two fundamental methods for gathering assessment data about SRL from learners. The first and most prevalent method is asking learners to describe features of SRL, facets of tasks or individual differences they perceive to influence states and processes. The second method is a performance-based measure called traces.

Ask Learners About SRL

Learners can be asked questions about features of SRL, facets of contexts in which SRL is engaged and individual differences that assessors or learners themselves believe to influence SRL. While this technique rarely generates error-free data about actual events, as noted earlier, it has the strong advantage of revealing how learners interpret features of SRL, contextual factors and individual differences they consider relevant. Because SRL is a self phenomenon, learners' accounts contribute to a fuller assessment of SRL. Also, changes in learners' perceptions or the accuracy of those perceptions are themselves indicators of SRL. Thus, while research does not clearly validate direct links between observable behavior and what a learner has "in mind," self reports provide important information in assessing SRL.

Questions can be posed at varying grain sizes with respect to what the learner should consider in answering a probe about learning, motivation or affect. Here, grain size refers to the scope of information the learner needs to consider in responding. A fine grain size focuses on a single kind of event usually in one, clearly demarcated context for which data is intended to reflect a specific quality of thought or behavior. An example is: "In this article, did you highlight the definition of bold phrases in the section titled Introduction?" A coarse grain size falls at the other end of one or more of the continua that define the event, its context, individual differences or temporal qualities. Examples are: "Do you usually highlight?" "Do you prefer to highlight or to make notes?" Most prevalent by far among methods for asking students about features of SRL are paper-and-pencil or online Likert response surveys. This format affords gathering a great deal of data in a short time at relatively little cost to learners or researchers. Prominent examples of surveys used in research and practice are the *Learning and Study Strategies Inventory* (Weinstein, Schulte, & Palmer, 1987) and the *Motivated Strategies for Learning Questionnaire* (Pintrich, Smith, Garcia, & McKeachie, 1991).

In a single survey, features of SRL often vary across items from fine-grained (e.g., using images to encode word meanings) to coarse-grained (e.g., planning for studying). The context is usually coarse grained (e.g., what is typical of a learner or what is typical for a particular undergraduate course). Individual differences sometimes explicitly name the construct asked about (e.g., procrastinate) or use a synonym or euphemism for it (e.g., put off work, find other things to do). Response scales may be dichotomous (e.g., true/false) or ordinal (e.g., 1 to 5 and 1 to 7 are popular). A challenge about both dichotomous and ordinal response scales is the precision with which learners can discern their response. It is not common that a question refers to something a learner never does or always does—few experiences are entirely plus or minus. Regarding ordinal Likert scales, the divisions between response options are elastic. Thus, intervals may differ across respondents and items, and are not necessarily linear. When scales are long (e.g., 0 to 100 points), questions can be raised about the reliability of learners' abilities to differentiate adjacent points on the scale. When scales are short (e.g., 1 to 3 or 4 or 5), questions can be raised about how precisely a learner can represent qualities of SRL.

Interview schedules are another format for gathering data about SRL in which learners are asked about their experiences and reply in "free" form. The most cited interview protocol is Zimmerman and Pons' (1986) interview schedule in which learners are posed open-ended questions from which were generated 14 SRL tactics. Questions in this interview took the form of a brief context plus a focal task. For example: "Most teachers give tests at the end of marking periods, and these test greatly determine report card grades. Do you have any particular method for preparing or this type of test in English or history?" (p. 617). Interview responses are qualitatively analyzed to discern categories, relations among categories and other qualities of learners' responses.

When gathering assessment data using surveys and interviews, it is important to investigate whether items satisfy the psychometric requirement of local independence. Essentially, this requires that experience answering preceding items does not affect responses to following items. When local independence is not achieved, data are unreliable due to confounds introduced by order effects. This is another manifestation of the influence of context data in assessing SRL.

Diaries are instruments where a learner writes relatively free-form descriptions of their perceptions about occurrences and qualities of events. Entries may be scheduled (e.g., every evening) or when the learner "feels like" adding an entry. For example, Schmitz and Wiese (2006) invited participants to answer both Likert scale items and open ended questions every day during a program that provided training in features SRL. Diary responses are qualitatively analyzed to identify learners' interpretive accounts about features of SRL, factors of context and individual differences.

Think Aloud Protocols

Having learners report about their thinking in the midst of working on a task gained prominence following the publication Ericsson and Simon's (1980) seminal paper on verbal reports as data (see also Ericsson & Simon, 1993). In this approach to gathering data, learners are invited before starting work on a task to describe what they think about by talking aloud as the task unfolds. Throughout the work period, when the learner is not vocalizing as much as the researcher intends, a prompt may be provided such as, "Please keep speaking." Formally, think aloud protocols are designed as a situation where learners "verbalize their thoughts without any, or at worst with minimal, reactive influences on their thinking" (Ericsson & Simon, 1993, p. 181). These data are intended as indicators of the awareness learners have about what they are doing. Think aloud data can be contrasted with self-report or interview data, where the learner remembers about what was done; and study traces that record what the learner did. Because think aloud methods are quite frequently used and have not been as thoroughly analyzed as other methods, we examine them here.

At first blush, it might seem appropriate to investigate the accuracy of think aloud reports about SRL by correlating think aloud data with self-report inventory data playing the role of a criterion. This would be controversial for two main reasons. First, the response scale of self-report inventories is a Likert scale of options describing an ordinal property (e.g., very true of me) of an SRL event which the learner recalls as being typical of performance across various tasks usually nested in a broad context (e.g., this course). Think aloud data, on the other hand, are discrete and event specific. Correlations, therefore, would gauge the extent to which a sum of tallies recording distinct events reported in a think aloud session covary with aggregate recollections about the relative occurrence of events in many contexts. This approach does not indicate whether think aloud data accurately depict the learner's account of cognitive processes or content when think aloud data were gathered. If trace data are unavailable, validating think aloud data with specific interview responses may be useful.

Second, several studies suggest that think aloud data violate Ericsson and Simon's requirement that thinking aloud does not modify or interfere with the learner's cognitive engagement. Leow (2002) argued that by thinking aloud, participants' cognition may differ from what would have been the case had they not verbalized. Karahasonovic, Hinkel, Sjoberg and Thomas (2009) reported in a study of computer programming that "performance of participants who used the [concurrent think aloud] method declined, with respect to both time and correctness" (p. 159). Similarly, in their study of the usability of a software system, Van Den Hakk, De Jong, and Schellens (2003) found thinking aloud caused "participants to make more errors in the process of task performing and to be less successful in completing the [tasks]" (p. 349). Although Crisp (2008) reported there was no statistically detectable impact of thinking aloud on essay performance, approximately one-third of participants reported difficulty reading and synchronously reporting their thoughts. In these instances and other settings where information load and density are high, we hypothesize thinking aloud interferes with work on the task per se. In turn, this increases the likelihood that learners may self regulate, to recover from this disruption, thereby probably changing the flow of work on the task and the frequency and forms of SRL.

Trace Learners' SRL Performance

In performance assessment, a learner carries out an activity. Products constructed as the activity unfolds, as well as final products, are observed by an assessor. These data provide grounds for drawing inferences about qualities of knowledge and processes the learner used to generate those products. The number and variety of products and processes can be large. Assessors often use checklists to denote the discrete presence or absence of a factor or, where appropriate, rating scales to record their ordinal judgments about the degree or extent to which a product or process corresponds to a standard. The collected set of checklist and rating data, sometimes supplemented with an assessor's qualitative account regarding the learner's performance, is called a scoring rubric. Performance assessments of SRL (and learning in general) are rare. We describe one method that, in our judgment, offers significant potential for assessing SRL.

Winne (1982) introduced the operational definition of "trace" to describe data that reflect learners' cognitive engagements in learning tasks. Traces are accretion data gathered relatively unobtrusively (Webb, Campbell, Schwartz, & Sechrest, 1966) as learners work on tasks. The medium in which the learner enacts the tactic affords a record of some or all of: a metacognitive monitoring event, standards used in metacognitive monitoring, and cognitive processes embodied in the physical expression of a tactic. In general, traces can be modeled as condition-action rules: IF metacognitive monitoring of information or a state indicates the information or state meets standards, THEN enact a tactic.

For example, when Cindy highlights a phrase in her textbook, that highlight traces several cognitive events: (a) Cindy engaged metacognitive monitoring to identify particular phrases in the textbook. (b) The phrase she highlighted met standards she used for metacognitively monitoring. (c) Cindy forecasts a useful product was created—the visually distinguished text and perhaps a memorial representation of it generated as she rehearsed the text while highlighting it—because she spent effort to highlight the phrase. (d) She exercised metacognitive control by choosing to use a highlight tactic versus some other tactic, such as copying the sentence into her notebook or interpreting it in an annotation recorded in the margin of the page.

Simple traces, such as a highlight, may not reveal details about some of SRL's features in which assessors are interested or may not generate data for drawing inferences about other features of SRL. Some artifice often needs to be introduced, a designed *tool*, that learners use such that using the tool traces features of SRL the assessor wants to observe. For example, Cindy a peer or researcher may suggest to Cindy that she use several color markers as a way to catalog information in her textbook using highlights: green signifies a "glossary term to learn," pink marks a "major principle" and yellow marks anything else that Cindy judges to be "important" to learn for exams or with respect to her interests. If Cindy discloses her mapping of colors to categories or she was trained to use a particular mapping, when she highlights text using these colors, those highlights trace cognition in more detail. Specifically, an assessor can infer that Cindy has a goal to differentiate information into four categories (the three represented by each highlight color plus at least one other category for information she does not highlight). Also, in choosing among highlight colors, Cindy traces which standards she used to metacognitively monitor information in the text: Was the information a glossary term to learn, a major principle or important for other reasons?

Designing a Data Gathering System

Each method for gathering data for assessing SRL exhibits relative strengths and weaknesses. For example, an advantage of traces is that they avoid (a) memory buffering that can distort self-reports and interviews and (b) interrupting cognitive processes, as in a think aloud protocol. However, traces are not inherently best for gathering data about SRL. First, as noted earlier, because SRL is a self phenomenon, learners' views of what they are doing and how they SRL are important. Second, assessors who interpret traces are not immune from the same biases that confound learners' self reports. They and other experts also fall victim to biases such as assumptions of control, baseline neglect, and availability (for a reviews see Kahneman, Slovic, & Tversky, 1982; Koehler & Harvey, 2004). Assessing complex phenomena like SRL typically requires triangulation across multiple methods for gathering data so that omissions and biases can be identified, and useful trade offs in practicality and be realized.

DESIGNING ASSESSMENTS OF SRL

Each factor listed in Tables 4.1, 4.2 and 4.3 is a potential element in designing methods for gathering assessment data that can support inferences about features of SRL. While we segregated factors within each table (each row) and across separate tables, we do not imply that factors can be treated independently of one another. Such a view is simplistic. SRL is a complex, multidimensional, temporally extended orchestration of successively conditionally dependent events. As a result, capturing the fullness of SRL in any single assessment may not be achievable. Advanced psychometrics and sophisticated guidelines for designing assessments of states of knowledge, such as might be manifested as a multiple-choice test or a brief essay scored against a rubric, are not well groomed for assessing a dynamic process like SRL. Given the newness of thinking about assessing SRL as performance, we acknowledge that descriptions we present here are first steps.

In this section, we first briefly recap common information about scales for data, Then, keeping in mind our caveat about challenges in assessing the full spectrum of features of SRL, we consider how data might be gathered to assess features of SRL listed in Table 4.1. A summary of issues is provided in Table 4.4.

Scales for Assessment Data

Data, including data about factors related to SRL, are scaled in one of three classes: discrete, ordinal, and continuous. Data on a discrete scale identify whether a feature of SRL is present or absent or whether an event falls in one of several mutually exclusive categories. For example, did Cindy recognize that information in diagrams and figures was identical to the textual presentation? Did she forecast possible consequences of not reading summaries or alternative tactics that might be substituted for using the textbook's summaries?

Ordinal data describe differences in a factor along a dimension of relative magnitudes but these data do not have a unit. Comparisons of ranks can not say how much more or less one rank is relative to another rank. For example, ordinal data about the likelihood to highlight may indicate

Table 4.4.   Inferences About Features of SRL

Feature	Inferences
Cue	What cues does a learner identify?
	How reliably does a learner identify a cue?
	What feature of regulation does a learner correlate to a cue's value?
Goal or Standard	What explicit goal does a learner set?
Tactic	What tactics are in a learner's repertoire?
	What is a learner's expertise with a tactic?
Forecast	Is a forecast made?
	What product is forecast?
	What is the conditional probability of a product given a tactic?
Account	Does the learner explain why tactics generate products?
	What reasons appear in a learner's accounts?
Utility	What costs and benefits does a learner associate with a tactic?
Likelihood	What is the probability that a particular tactic will be enacted in a given context?
Log	Is a log kept?
	How specifically are factors described in log entries?
	To what degree do log entries correspond to other assessment data?

it is greater than the likelihood to create notes but it is not possible to specify by how much it is greater.

Continuous data are represented using a scale that has equal units of measurement. With continuous data, one can answer how much greater the likelihood is to highlight than to create notes. If there is a genuine zero point to the data—that is, a learner can be considered to have zero amount of a feature of SRL—indexes (ratios) and other nonlinear descriptions can be created. For example, Cindy could be described as having created 0 notes or 4 notes per hour.

Data About Cues That Trigger SRL Activities

Cues afford the learner an opportunity to metacognitively monitor work on a task in parallel with metacognitively monitoring factors that relate to self-regulating work on that task. Metacognitive monitoring generates a profile that characterizes differences between attributes of an event and standards for that event. This sets the stage for the learner to exercise metacognitive control by making and implementing choices about features of SRL (Table 4.1), by changing a facet of context (Table 4.2), or by managing (to the extent possible) an individual difference factor that interacts with work on the task.

We propose that assessments regarding the learner's engagement with cues can involve three main inferences.

What cues does a learner identify? The inference to be drawn in this case is whether a learner detects cues that are embedded in the flow of work on a task. Cues can be defined relative to a frame of reference—that of the task designer (e.g., a teacher or assessor) and that of the learner. Some cues that a learner observes (e.g., a multiple-choice test author's inadvertent high probability of making option c the correct answer) are not cues designed or intended by a task designer.

To assess cues (e.g., bolded words, inconsistent text, headings, etc.) that learners identify, there are two basic approaches. First, a trace needs to be designed that can reveal whether a learner detects a cue. For example, the learner might be asked to highlight content that is judged essential to meet a particular learning objective, say, explaining the difference between mitosis and meiosis. In this case, learning content critical to meeting the objective would be the focal task and tracing (highlighting) would constitute the secondary task. In contrast, if the task was to highlight all cues then highlighting becomes the focal task.

If the assessor defines the cues in material the learner studies, this performance assessment is scored as a tally of hits and a tally of misses. If the assessor is interested to learn what standards the learner uses to metacognitively monitor what is a cue, data generated can be analyzed qualitatively to create clusters of cues the assessor hypothesizes to be (a) homogeneous and (b) associated with distinct features of SRL. Over time, changes to clusters the learner uses as SRL cues provide evidence of SRL.

By gathering other data using other instruments—think aloud protocols, interviews or self-reports—these hypotheses about SRL in action can be tested relative to the learner's perceptions of these features of SRL. Another approach is to design a trace of the feature of SRL that a cluster predicts. Occurrences of the trace indicate the learner perceives cues that trigger that trace.

How reliably does a learner detect a cue? If it has been determined that a learner can detect a cue within a particular context, it is then possible to ask how reliably that cue is detected. Assessments of this kind share a common design. Multiple instances of a cue are embedded in a task and the learners is taught a trace designed to signal when the learner detects that cue. Traces can be simple—a highlight, a √ in the margin of a textbook's pages, or hyperlinks clicked in multimedia software. A tally of traces applied divided by the total number of cues represents a hit rate, the conditional probability of a trace of cognitive processing given a cue. The assessor might use signal detection analysis when there is interest in false alarms (a trace is applied to a noncue), misses (a trace is not applied to a cue) and correct rejections (foils are not traced). To verify these interpretations think aloud protocols and posttask self-report methods can assess learners' online cognitions for false alarms and misses.

What feature of regulation does a learner correlate to a cue's value? Cues are inherently relational—they predict something. The author predicts a learner will engage in other-than-usual or an additional tactic because a term or phrase is bolded. A learner may correlate words in bold with a particular 2-tactic strategy: create a flash card with the term on one side and the definition on the other, then plan to use the flash card to rehearse the term and its definition in a self-test mode on the night before an exam. Assessors need to be sensitive to learners' capacity for adaptation. After internalizing a particular cue-tactic (IF-THEN) link, the learner may apply a different tactic when reviewing material, e.g., a simple rehearsal strategy that involves restudying the flash card. Links between cues and tactics can change as studying unfolds.

In terms of IF-THEN structures, we are interested to assess which THENs a learner correlates to a cue under a particular context supplemented by an array of individual differences. This is another way of describing what the learner understands about the cue—what is the cue "good" for?

Making assessments of THENs that a learner correlates to a cue requires that the learner can reliably detect a cue. More about assessing THENs is presented in following sections.

Data About Goals and Standards

A goal is an organized set of standards that describes a desired state. Standards can function proactively, as cues that activate potential actions on factors in the task, and retrospectively, as gauges for judging the adequacy of a quality of work on a task. We propose two methods for assessing goals learners hold and the standards that comprise goals.

What Explicit Goals Does a Learner Set? In this approach, well before assessment data are gathered, learners are trained to develop goal statements (e.g., Morgan, 1985). The quality of goals they are able to develop can be assessed after training as a measure of maximum achievement using conventional methods, such as this task: "Develop a goal for studying [subject matter] and justify why your goal fully meets the requirements for goals as you were taught in training."

To assess explicit goal setting at the start of a task or during engagement with a task, provide a tool—for example, a paper-and-pencil log, an online annotation tool, an audio recording —for learners to record goals explicitly when they deem it appropriate. This yields several kinds of information. Are goals set? Under what conditions (IFs) are goals set? Do goals exhibit the attributes of goals in which learners were trained?

Does recording goals in this way differ from inviting think aloud reports about goals? Research cited earlier lends support to our conjecture that it does. In a think aloud protocol, the learner is urged to report thoughts as they occur. This is a demand an assessor makes to create an assessment task. We posit it taxes working memory resources because the learner must metacognitively monitor for conditions (IFs) that trigger if it is appropriate to report. In contrast, by allowing learners to judge when it is appropriate to form and record goals as *they* deem appropriate, the learner sets a task that generates assessment data without imposing an additional assessment task.

Second, when learners trace goals, they create a permanent record that they can review without having to retrieve goals from memory. This increases accuracy and reduces information load. Thus, more of the learner's cognitive resources can be dedicated to the task versus allocating resources to trying to recall goals and re-express them.

An advantage arises when goals are available as a permanent record. When learners access these records, a time-stamped trace can be created showing that and when goals were considered in the work flow of the task. Goals reviewed but not edited indicate the learner reinstated a goal in working memory. If the learner edits or replaces a goal, changes identify elements of the prior version of the goal that were monitored and judged inappropriate. Qualitative analysis by an assessor can lead to inferences about what differentiates the new goal from the prior version. Posttask interviews, self-reports or online think aloud protocols can be used in triangulation and to provide indicators for cases where learners don't edit goals because they judged the goals were still appropriate.

Under our assumption that behavior is goal directed, inferences that the learner operated under the direction of a goal can be associated with *any* trace the learner generates. For example, when a learner highlights, the trace supports an inference about a goal to locate and permanently mark particular kinds of information. A learner who applies several colors in highlighting or multiple tags in an online environment (e.g., "Review this" or "Search for more") traces a goal to search for and permanently mark different kinds of information. Where tags are titled, the title of the tag reveals the standard.

Data About Tactics and Expertise

The learner's workhorses for accomplishing tasks are tactics and strategies that arrange tactics into patterns. Very basic tactics, such as creating categories and maintenance rehearsing, develop early in life and play important roles in learning throughout a learner's lifespan. More complex tactics, such as building first-letter mnemonics or surveying an assignment to catalog its qualities as a basis for forecasting what a teacher will test, are developed by direct instruction, observation and a learner's self-directed experimentation with them (see Winne, 1997). There are two major inferences to be considered in assessing tactics.

What Tactics Are in the Learner's Repertoire? A direct assessment of whether a tactic is available to a learner involves presenting a task for which the target tactic is appropriate and inviting the learner to apply it. These are basic performance tests. They have two main steps. First, create a situation in which a particular tactic can be applied—that is, design IFs that a learner can be expected to pair with the assessor's target THENs. Second, present the task to the learner with clear instructions that THENs are to be displayed. We suggest providing an example other than the tactic(s) being assessed to maximize the correspondence between the assessor's intent and the learner's interpretation of the focal task, cues and the tactics correlated to those cues.

Care must be taken so these assessments are not invalidated because there is a less then perfect conditional probability (< 1.0) relating the tactic's THEN to its IF. This can happen in two ways. The first is a production deficiency. This is a case where the learner fails to recognize a cue that signals the tactic can be applied *and*, had that cue been recognized, the tactic could have been applied. This is like a missed opportunity. Another factor that can invalidate these assessments is self-regulation. In this case, the that avoids using the tactic due to a utilization deficiency. A utilization deficiency is a case where a learner's inexpert use of a tactic degrades performance on the task. While degraded performance on the task is not the focus in a performance assessment of a tactic the learner can nonetheless self-regulate during the performance assessment. Thus, depending on features of SRL, such as the learner's forecast about the tactic and the utility the learner ascribes to the tactic, the learner may self regulate and thereby not follow instructions to apply the tactic despite the assessor's intent.

What is the Learner's Expertise with a Tactic? For each tactic in the learner's repertoire, a question can be posed about how expertly the learner can apply that tactic. What does it mean to apply a tactic "expertly?" At least three answers are available.

First, with what reliability does the tactic generate its intended product? Because of other facets of context and individual differences, the probability that a tactic produces an ideal or flawless product is likely less than 1.0. In this case, assessments can vary facets of context to qualitatively and quantitatively profile the reliability that a tactic generates its intended product.

Second, how efficiently does the learner execute the tactic? The inference here is the degree to which a tactic is automated. Automated tactical skills can be carried out relatively quickly and demand less of working memory's limited resource than non-automated skills. Ideally, tactics are applied in appropriate contexts. These qualities suggest kinds of data to gather in gauging efficiency of a tactic. Regarding speed of execution, what is the latency between start up and completion of a tactic relative to other tactics that involve similar cognitive work and span a similar number of "steps"? Answering this question requires detailed qualitative descriptions of tactics in terms we have rarely observed in research. Progress on this issue requires generating clearer and more complete descriptions of what tactics are, an accomplishment that would benefit theories, empirical research and assessments of SRL.

Third, how much working memory is required? Regarding lesser demand on working memory, a possible method borrows the secondary task protocol from experimental research where the latency to respond to a secondary stimulus—often a tone meant to signal pressing a key—is inversely proportional to the demand a tactic makes on working memory.

Data About Forecasts

In IF–THEN representation, a tactic equates to a THEN. Tactics are applied when conditions the learner perceives about a task fit IFs, *and* when the learner judges that tactic will generate a product that meets the learner's standards (goals). However, the real world is probably more complex than represented by a theoretical IF-THEN structure. Two tasks, even ones designed to be psychometrically parallel and closely sequenced, are rarely identical in every sense. For example, if memory for work on a previous successfully completed task is still accessible at the outset of work on a subsequent task—such as a problem just solved or an internet search expression and its results just retrieved—this adds a worked example to the learner's context. Individual differences also may vary across apparently "identical" tasks as the learner metacognitively monitors experience with a prior task. A facet of context not previously perceived may come into the learner's field of awareness.

Forecasts about products generated by tactics that are candidates for execution are valuable complements to IF-THEN tactics because subsequent tasks are rarely identical to prior ones and because individual differences that evolve as learners gain through experience modulate the learner's mental state. We posit three main inferences pertain to assessments about forecasts about products that tactics generate.

Is a Forecast Made? Learners may not fully or automatically forecast attributes of product(s) that a tactic generates. Obvious examples are unintended side effects.

Data to assess whether a forecast is made are discrete. As was the case with goals, these data can be gathered by providing the learner with a tool to record their forecasts. Using the tool traces making a forecast. As before, if the learner can access records about forecasts during a task, reviews of those records trace that the learner reinstated product-related information in working memory. Interview, self-report, and think aloud data can be useful in verifying the learner's intent to revisit forecasts and intentions to feed-forward that affects how the learner approaches future tasks.

What Product is Forecast? The product a learner forecasts is inherently available to an assessor if the learner records forecasts. We suggest attributes of learners; forecasts will typically be assessed as discrete data (e.g., Does the forecast include content about a specific topic?) and ordinal data (e.g., How complex is the product?). Continuous data are possible but fit only some kinds of tasks where products can be described on genuine continua such as number of words.

What is the Conditional Probability of a Product Given a Tactic? Because a tactic is not guaranteed to render a particular product that has particular qualities, the accuracy of a learner's forecast is a probability rather than a certainty. Learners could be trained to record their forecasts in a way that makes data about the learner's judgment of probability available to an assessor. Research on judgments of learning provide an example (see

Dunlosky & Lipko, 2007). At first blush, data about forecasts may appear continuous but, to our knowledge, this property has not been demonstrated empirically. Pending research, conditional probabilities that learners estimate or report probably should be treated as ordinal data.

Data About Accounts

As learners seek to understand what happens in their world, they generate explanations for correlations they perceive among features of SRL, facets of context and individual differences. When these play a role in subsequent SRL, tactics are selected or rejected in relation to these explanations. When these accounts become explicit grounds for action, learners have created standards for monitoring (a) how work should unfold and (b) thresholds for satisfactory progress that may set the stage for adapting studying tactics (but see Kornell & Bjork, 2007). For learners who work within bounded rationality (Simon, 1957), beliefs about why tactics correlate with forecasts or why tactics generate product(s) with particular qualities will influence whether a tactic is adopted, maintained, adapted or replaced. This decision can be affected by all the factors listed in Tables 4.1, 4.2, and 4.3.

Does the Learner Explain Why Tactics Generate Products? Assessors can gather information about learners' accounts only if learners record their reasons for using a tactic. As noted earlier, this can be accomplished by inviting or training learners to record diary entries that reflect their accounts as they wish; or by obtrusively soliciting data using a survey, interview or think aloud protocol. As described before, each method's strengths play off against another's weaknesses. Triangulation is important in considering these data.

What Reasons Appear in a Learner's Accounts? The IF-THEN representation of tactics provides a format for correlating a reason (THEN) to a state (IF): "IF my product has such-and-such a quality, THEN the reason is ...." For example, a learner who shares our vocabulary might record in a diary of study activities: "If my summary omits key information, I must have not monitored the materials using the right standards." Both states and reasons can be represented as discrete data (the summary is incomplete, a standard is not appropriate), ordinal data (the summary today was better than yesterday's, I applied more effort today than yesterday) or continuous data (the summary included 10 of 14 key points, I checked my summary for key points 3 times).

When there are multiple instances of a state and a reason, and states and reasons form separate lists of mutually exclusive items, another representation for these data is a conditional probability. Given a particular state, what is the conditional probability that a particular account was the learner's explanation for that state? Post-task interviews, self-reports or online think aloud protocols interviews can be used to address this issue.

Data About Utility

Because people have bounded capacity for processing information (Simon, 1957; see also Gigerenzer & Goldstein, 1996) they do not frequently find optimal solutions to problems. Moreover, there often is more than one tactic that can generate a product with high probability (as discussed previously in the section on forecasts) and more than one strategy for approaching goals of a task. In this context, learners have options about how they work as a function of effort and other costs balanced against rewards and other benefits. Indeed, we hypothesize that a significant influence on qualities of SRL is the relative utility a learner assigns on the basis of alternative cost-benefit ratio for available tactics.

Very little is known about this topic in the context of learners' choices in SRL. Assessors can gather information about utility in several ways but, as before, these divide into two main paradigms: tracing and asking learners. The latter is relatively straightforward and requires an assumption that the learner's reports are veridical. The former has been infrequently addressed and thus merits brief discussion.

What Costs and Benefits Does a Learner Associate with a Tactic? Possible indicators of costs in applying a tactic are: duration relative to time available or time preferred, rate of progress, loss of opportunity (e.g., to experiment with whether an untested tactic is productive, to access potentially useful information), increased information load and unwanted density (see Table 4.2). Assessing these as costs in the form of discrete, ordinal or continuous data cannot be accomplished in tasks where learners are graded or rewarded for products because that would confound a determination of what is a cost with the utility of more or less costly alternatives. Instead, to assess what the learner considers costly requires designing a task in which the learner can freely choose among options under the unusual constraint success or failure has value but neither is extraordinary. Similarly, determining what are perceived as relative benefits requires a context in which the learner can freely gain those benefits without suffering significant costs.

Once costs and benefits have been independently established, utility can be traced in a task design that includes two features. First, learners should be instructed to carry out each in a set of alternative tactics to gain experience with their costs and benefits. Then, with this experience as backdrop, the learner should be afforded free choice. Choices indicate relative (ordinal) utility values among tactics.

Under an assumption that the likelihood of applying a tactic is proportional to its utility, checks on tactics' utility rankings within a given context can be made by manipulating costs associated with learning tactics and tracing choices.

Data About Likelihood

No useful model, be it the learner's or an assessor's, is fully specified—were it so, the model would not afford the benefit of parsimony. As well, data are not perfectly reliable due to instrument insensitivity and random influences on measurements. In this light, whatever the profile of data about features of SRL, there is only a probability that a particular tactic will be enacted in a given context.

What is the probability a particular tactic will be enacted? Assessing the likelihood of a tactic's implementation requires longitudinal data that describes the conditional probability of a tactic's use (THEN) in situations (IFS) that are "sufficiently the same." Of course, situations are not absolutely identical. There is no perfectly reliable method for tracing likelihood.

Perhaps the only method for assessing likelihoods that tactics are applied is one of the methods for asking learners to estimate likelihoods. When self-report data are considered in light of issues we raised earlier and when inferences about learner performance are qualified in proportion to the influence of factors that lower precision, cautious assessments can be useful.

Data About Logs

A log of SRL is a learner's self-reported archival, selective catalog of features of SRL possibly supplemented with introspective descriptions of facets of context and qualities of individual differences. Learners who carry out a personal program of research to discover "what works," as Winne (1997) hypothesized, may profit from logs because log entries reduce dependence on fallible memory.

Is a Log Kept? Data describing logs are straightforward. Whether a log is kept may be most easily determined by providing learners with a tool for diarizing their SRL. Training learners in a vocabulary for expressing factors relating to SRL will increase the validity of inferences assessors make about learners' log entries.

How Specifically Are Factors Described in Log Entries? We conjecture that, in general, it is more difficult for learners to track or modulate a vaguely described factor than a factor that is described explicitly and precisely. Consequently, it may prove useful to assess log entries for their specificity.

One way to conceptualize this for tactics and facets of context is in terms of operational definitions. Learners' descriptions of individual differences are not likely to be operationally defined, however.

The specificity of an operational definition can be gauged by judging whether the log entry can be replicated or reinstated accurately. These judgments likely will be expressed in terms of an ordinal scale.

Do Log Entries Correspond to Other Assessment Data? Data in logs must be veridical to provide solid grounds for productive SRL. Learners may struggle to achieve this (Winne & Jamieson-Noel, 2002). Discrepancies can be gauged using statistical techniques described in research on the accuracy of learners' metacognitive judgments (see Schraw, 2009). There are two "families" of approaches. One gauges the match at a fine-grained level where a report about a factor is compared to a trace (or other forms of self-report) of that factor, pair by pair. Data are then aggregated over instances to compute an index of correspondence between log entries and traces. The other approach provides a coarser-grained index of correspondence. A log entry refers to a collection of instances, such a learner's estimate of how many times metacognitive monitoring was applied in a study session. This is compared to the sum of traces of metacognitive monitoring tallied over the study session.

A GRAPH THEORETIC METHOD FOR
ANALYZING ASSESSMENT DATA

As already illustrated in the preceding section, one method for analyzing assessment data is to tally instances. Provided that instances are homogenous, tallies of traces describing SRL-in-action can be summed to gauge a factor's frequency of occurrence in a specified time span. Indexes of correspondence or correlation can be generated using techniques for mixtures of discrete, ordinal and continuous data.

What has not yet been deeply explored are methods for describing temporal qualities of events in SRL or their patterns. Winne, Gupta, and Nesbit (1994) proposed graph theoretic indexes to quantify patterns. In their method, traces are ordered in sequence of occurrence along a timeline. A list is formed of the kinds of traces and used to define rows and columns of a matrix such that the order of traces across rows must be the same as the sequential order of columns. An example of this method is shown in Figure 4.1.

The first trace in the timeline, A, is used to identify a row of the matrix. The next trace in the timeline, B, identifies the column of the matrix. A tally is entered in the intersecting cell to represent a transition from the first trace to the second trace. Next, the trace that had identified a col-

Event Sequence: A B D B C E D B C E D A C E D A B C F ...

Transition Matrix

	A	B	C	D	E	F
A		//	/			
B			///	/		
C					///	/
D	//	//				
E				///		
F						

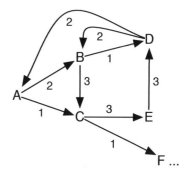

Figure 4.1.   A sequence of events, the transition matrix and a graphical display of the pattern represented by the sequence.

umn is used to identify a row in the matrix, B. The trace observed third in the timeline, D, now identifies a column of the matrix. A tally is entered to represent a transition from the second trace to the third trace is entered in the intersecting cell, and so on until the last trace in the time-line has been recorded as having a trace preceding it.

While real data rarely will be as "clean" as this hypothetical illustration, graphs of patterns can help to visually identify features of SRL. For example, suppose (a) E represents looking up a term in a glossary, (b) D and B represent various ways of cognitively processing that information (e.g., making a note, adding the term to a concept map, etc.) and (c) the pattern depicted in Figure 1 describes studying early in a learning session. Later in this same study session, segments B C E D A and B C E D B are not observed. At this later time, the learner proceeds from "straight" A to C to F. Differences in the graph of studying activities early vs. late invite an inference that the learner judges terms are learned in the latter part of the study session and need not be reviewed, as was the case in the early part of the study session.

From a transition matrix, a variety of quantitative indexes can be generated to describe features of SRL. For example, the sum of tallies in a cell divided by the sum of tallies for the cell's row describes the conditional probability that the column event follows the row event. Other graph theoretic indexes can describe: the degree to which transitions across traced events are patterned versus random; (b) the degree to which one set of traces has a pattern that is congruent to a different set of traces, thus inviting inferences about whether superficially different traces initially hypothesized to represent different approaches to working on tasks may be used by a learner in similar ways for similar goals; and, (c) whether two superficially different traces play equivalent roles in relation to a common pattern of other traces. To our knowledge, graph theoretic indexes like these offer unique quantitative value for describing patterns of factors in SRL. See Winne et al. (2002) for elaboration.

CONCLUSION

Winne and Perry (2000) distinguished two classes of SRL measures. Modeling SRL as an aptitude "describes a relatively enduring attribute of a person that predicts future behavior [where] a single measurement aggregates over or abstracts some quality of SRL based on multiple SRL events." SRL also can be modeled as an event, "a transient state embedded in a larger, longer series of states unfolding over time" (p. 534). Following Winne, Jamieson-Noel, and Muis (2002), we agree with Zimmerman (2008) that "aptitude measures of SRL will continue to provide useful information regarding students' methods of learning [but] online event measures of SRL offer detailed information concerning the interaction of processes in real time (p. 181). Thus, here we emphasized traces as data for assessing features of SRL with an explicit acknowledgment that other forms of data are both useful and necessary in many instances.

We offered a typology keyed to the complex landscape of SRL within which features can be selected as targets for assessment. As noted earlier, creating a full-spectrum assessment of SRL that taps all features simultaneously may not be possible. Like other assessments of multifaceted human phenomena, assessments of SRL will need to focus on select features, facets and individual differences. As a result, assessments afford triangulation rather than equivalency.

Assessing SRL is further complicated by the fact that it can be reflected not only in a steady state (maintenance) but as changes in states across a time period of the assessment. Validating alternative assessments of SRL relative to one another or successive assessments of a single learner therefore will be challenging because rarely will different assessments satisfy the condition that "all other things be equal." Thus, it is critical to carefully operationalize and fully report assessment methods. We look forward to new instruments and methodologies for assessing complex, dynamically changeable, contextually sensitive skills such as SRL.

REFERENCES

American Educational Research Association, American Psychological Association and National Council on Measurement in Education. (1999). *Standards for educational and psychological testing.* Washington, DC: Author

Anderson, L. W., & Krathwohl, D. R. (Eds.). (2001). *A taxonomy for learning, teaching and assessing: A revision of Bloom's Taxonomy of Educational Objectives.* New York, NY: Longman.

Crisp, V. (2008). The validity of using verbal protocol analysis to investigate the processes involved in examination marking. *Research in Education, 79,* 1-12.

Butler, D. L., & Winne, P. H. (1995). Feedback and selfregulated learning: A theoretical synthesis. *Review of Educational Research, 65,* 245-281.

Dunlosky, J., & Lipko, A. R. (2007). Metacomprehension: A brief history and how to improve its accuracy. *Current Directions in Psychological Science, 16,* 228-232.

Hadwin, A. F., Winne, P. H., Stockley, D. B., Nesbit, J. C., & Woszczyna, C. (2001). Context moderates students' self-reports about how they study. *Journal of Educational Psychology, 93,* 477-487.

Ericsson, K. A., & Simon, H. A. (1980). Verbal reports as data. *Psychological Review, 87,* 215-251.

Ericsson, K. A., & Simon, H. A. (1993). *Protocol analysis: Verbal reports as data* (2nd ed.). Cambridge, MA: MIT Press.

Gigerenzer, G., & Goldstein, D. G. (1996). Reasoning the fast and frugal way: Models of bounded rationality. *Psychological Review, 103,* 650–669.

Kahneman, D., Slovic, P., & Tversky, A. (Ed.). (1982). *Judgment under uncertainty: Heuristics and biases.* New York, NY: Cambridge University Press.

Karahasonovic, Hinkel, U. N., Sjoberg, D. I. K., & Thomas, R. (2009). Comparing of feedback-collection and think-aloud methods in program comprehension studies. *Behaviour & Information Technology, 28,* 139-164.

Koehler, D. J., & Harvey, N. (2004). *Blackwell handbook of judgment and decision making.* Oxford, England: Blackwell.

Kornell, N., & Bjork, R. A. (2007). The promise and perils of self-regulated study. *Psychonomic Bulletin & Review, 14,* 219-224.

Leow, R. P. (2002). Models, attention, and awareness in SLA: A response to Simard and Wong's (2001) "Alertness, orientation, and detection: The conceptualization of attentional functions." *Studies in Second Language Acquisition, 24,* 113–119.

Morgan, M. (1985). Self-monitoring of attained subgoals in private study. *Journal of Educational Psychology, 77,* 623-630.

Pintrich, P. (2004). A conceptual framework for assessing motivation and self-regulated learning in college students. *Educational Psychology Review, 16,* 385-407.

Pintrich, P. R., Smith, D.A., Garcia, T., & McKeachie, W. J. (1991). *A manual for the use of the motivated strategies for learning questionnaire (MSLQ)* (Technical Report No. 91-B-004). Ann Arbor, MI: University of Michigan, School of Education.

Pintrich, P. R., Wolters, C. A., & Baxter, G. P. (2000). Assessing metacognition and self-regulated learning. In G. Schraw & J. C. Impara (Ed.), *Issues in the measurement of metacognition* (pp. 43-97). Lincoln, NB: Buros Institute of Mental Measurement.

Samuelstuen, M. S. & Bråten, I. (2007). Examining the validity of self-reports on scales measuring students' strategic processing. *British Journal of Educational Psychology, 77*, 351-378.

Schmitz, B., & Wiese, B. S. (2006). New perspectives for the evaluation of training sessions in self-regulated learning: Time-series analyses of diary data. *Contemporary Educational Psychology, 31*, 64-96.

Schraw, G. (2009). Measuring metacognitive judgments. In D. J. Hacker, J. Dunlosky & A. C. Graesser (Eds.), *Handbook of metacognition in education* (pp. 415-429). New York, NY: Routledge.

Simon, H. (1957). *Models of man, social and rational: Mathematical essays on rational human behavior in a social setting.* New York, NY: Wiley.

Van Den Haak, M. J., De Jong, M. D. T., & Schellens, P. J. (2003). Retrospective vs. concurrent think-aloud protocols: Testing the usability of an online library catalogue. *Behaviour & Information Technology, 22*, 339-351.

Webb, E. J., Campbell, D. T., Schwartz, R. D., & Sechrest, L. (1966). *Unobtrusive measures.* Skokie, IL: Rand-McNally

Weinstein, C. E., Schulte, A. & Palmer, D. (1987). *LASSI: Learning and Study Strategies Inventory.* Clearwater, FL: H & H.

Winne, P. H. (1982). Minimizing the black box problem to enhance the validity of theories about instructional effects. *Instructional Science, 11*, 13-28.

Winne, P. H. (1997). Experimenting to bootstrap self-regulated learning. *Journal of Educational Psychology, 89*, 397-410.

Winne, P. H., & Jamieson-Noel, D. L. (2002). Exploring students' calibration of self-reports about study tactics and achievement. *Contemporary Educational Psychology, 27*, 551-572.

Winne, P. H. (2010). Improving measurements of self-regulated learning. *Educational Psychologist, 45*, 267-276.

Winne, P. H., Gupta, L., & Nesbit, J. C. (1994). Exploring individual differences in studying strategies using graph theoretic statistics. *Alberta Journal of Educational Research, 40*, 177-193.

Winne, P. H., Jamieson-Noel, D. L., & Muis, K. (2002). Methodological issues and advances in researching tactics, strategies, and self-regulated learning. In P. R. Pintrich & M. L. Maehr (Eds.), *Advances in motivation and achievement: New directions in measures and methods* (Vol. 12, pp. 121-155). Greenwich, CT: JAI Press.

Winne, P. H., & Perry, N. E. (2000). Measuring self-regulated learning. In M. Boekaerts, P. Pintrich, & M. Zeidner (Eds.), *Handbook of self-regulation* (pp. 531-566). Orlando, FL: Academic Press.

Zimmerman, B. J. (2008). Investigating self-regulation and motivation: Historical background, methodological developments, and future prospects. *American Educational Research Journal, 45*, 166-183.

Zimmerman, B. J., & MartinezPons, M. (1986). Development of a structured interview for assessing students use of self-regulated learning strategies. *American Educational Research Journal, 23*, 614628.

Zimmerman, B. J., & Schunk, D. H. (2001). *Self-regulated learning and academic achievement: Theoretical perspectives* (2nd ed.). Mahwah, NJ: Erlbaum.

PART II

COGNITIVE ASSESSMENT MODELS

TEST DESIGN WITH HIGHER ORDER COGNITION IN MIND

Joanna S. Gorin and Dubravka Svetina

Test design has often been characterized as an art more than a science. Recent efforts on the part of test developers, educators, and psychometricians, however, have encouraged an increase in the "science" of test development. This shift is no more evident than in the 2001 National Research Council's report *Knowing What Students Know: The Science and Design of Educational Assessment* (KWSN; NRC, 2001). In its introductory chapter and throughout the report, the authors lay out a contemporary approach to assessment design that is more complex and multidisciplinary than traditional methods described in the majority of measurement and psychometric textbooks. The most significant change is the centralized role of cognition—including theories and methods of cognitive psychology—as the foundation and guiding ruler for the test development process.

Though the role of cognition in educational and psychological assessment has previously been heralded by a small number of researchers for decades (e.g., Carroll & Maxwell, 1979; Pellegrino, 1988; Snow & Lohman, 1989), the implementation of methods incorporating cognition into the test design and development process has only recently taken hold. Rather, the main impact of cognitive theory continues to play only a

Assessment of Higher Order Thinking Skills, pp. 121–149

role in guiding test interpretations, rather than test construction. The most significant and innovative recommendations of the NRC's 2001 report for purposes of test design could be separated into three key points, each targeting distinct, yet interconnected, steps in the test design process: (1) a focus on cognitive definitions of the construct of interest, (2) a direct and testable link between test items and tasks and a cognitive model of the construct, and (3) the use of complex psychometric models to estimate student proficiency in terms of cognitive skills and processes.

Although the recommendations described above are somewhat universal and can be applied to designing tests for all purposes, test design for higher order thinking skills offers a unique opportunity to leverage the advantages associated with a cognitively-based approach. Specifically, whereas many traditional educational and psychological assessments of basic (versus higher order) cognitive skills are typically unidimensional in nature, higher order thinking (HOT) skills are more likely to be multidimensional in nature. Unlike basic cognitive skills, which may become automated over time, we define HOTs as skills that require effortful coordination of multiple cognitive (and sometimes metacognitive) processes in order to solve a problem or resolve an issue. Further, the types of inferences one would like to make about individuals' ability to perform HOT skills may be more complex, with target inferences including situated cognition and metacognition, in addition to declarative and procedural knowledge. The current chapter presents an overview of the contemporary view of test design described in the NRC's KWSN report, including specific details about two test design frameworks that incorporate the reports' key recommendations. We then examine how contemporary views of test design can enhance the development and usefulness of tests to measure higher order skills. Incorporating two illustrative examples of HOT assessments, we turn to three critical steps in test design and consider how test developers might reconsider their traditional methods. First, construct definitions are reconsidered in terms of cognitive theories and cognitive models. Next, implications for item and task design are considered. Finally, new advances in psychometric modeling of assessment data are presented, with specific attention paid to models appropriate for multidimensional data.

Contemporary Test Design Frameworks

Traditional descriptions of test development often present the process as a series of discrete steps that must be completed in order to support the quality of score interpretations. Conversely, several contemporary test design frameworks gaining popularity in the tests and measurement literature present the test development process as a coherent system, with each step directly connected to one another. The cohesive link to the process is the centralized role of cognitive theory at all stages of test development. The end result is a test that yields scores based strongly in cognitive theories that provide rich descriptions of individuals and groups' abilities, skills, proficiencies, and knowledge. Two frameworks that have been most widely applied are Embretson's cognitive design system (CDS; Embretson, 1993, 1998) and Mislevy's evidence-centered design (ECD; Mislevy, 1994; Mislevy, Steinberg, & Almond, 2003). Both approaches, improve upon previous test development procedures at specific points in the test development process—(1) construct definition, (2) item writing and revision, and (3) parameter estimation and validation procedures. Though developed and reviewed here separately, many similarities between ECD and CDS can be observed, chiefly, the central role of cognitive theory and evidence gathering through empirical model testing as a basis for item development.

Embretson's (1998) Cognitive Design System. The cognitive design system (CDS; Embretson, 1998) was developed as an approach to generate ability and achievement test items as complex tasks that involve multiple processes and often more than one strategy. This makes the system particularly well suited for assessments designed to measure higher order thinking skills. The goal of the CDS approach is to develop items explicitly based on hypotheses regarding the way in which different characteristics of the item impacts students' cognitive processes. For example, in reading comprehension assessment, the CDS approach to item development would pay particular attention to how vocabulary level of the text, linguistic complexity of the sentences, and propositional density impact students' encoding and coherence processes when building a text representation. To achieve this goal, the test developer must begin with a detailed description of the cognitive processes of interest. This "model" must then be linked both theoretically and mathematically to characteristics of the test questions and ultimately to differences in patterns of examinee responses. That is, differential responses to test items should be interpretable as differences in cognitive ability—specifically differences in the cognitive abilities of interest to the test developers.

To facilitate the implementation of the CDS system, a procedural framework is explicated that not only elaborates the stages involved in developing processing models of item performance, but also relates item processes to issues of score interpretation. The seven CDS stages are presented in Figure 5.1, beginning at the top (Specify Goals of Measurement) and proceeding in a clockwise manner. The most unique stages in comparison to traditional test development are the early stages (i.e., Stages 1-3) and model evaluation (i.e., stage 5). Researchers must develop a model

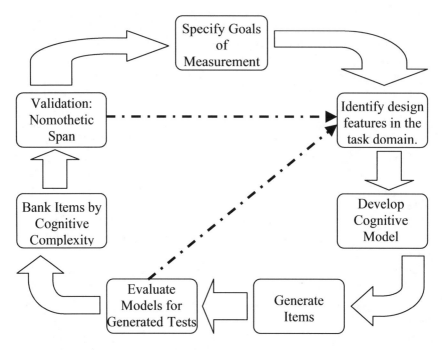

Figure 5.1.   Cognitive design system framework procedural framework.

of the construct (or content domain) by identifying its most basic units (e.g., subskills, processes, abilities). This model is then incorporated into and compared with a similar cognitive processing model of the developed items. In model evaluation, advanced psychometric models (e.g., componential IRT models, diagnostic classification models) that incorporate cognitive parameters are applied to evaluate the fit of item responses to the cognitive model of the construct. Thus, researchers can mathematically validate the interpretation of the test scores through a formal test of the item features. Items that fit the cognitive model can be interpreted as providing strong evidence of the construct. More specific discussion of cognitive model development, item design, psychometric parameterization, and validity evidence is reserved for separate sections later in the chapter. Finally, although the CDS stages are presented in a suggested order, one should note that the entire process is iterative, and the continued improvement of items may require returning to earlier stages of the framework. The sequence of the framework is intended to emphasize the importance of early stages of assessment development, which should be given equal attention and methodological rigor as the later statistical analysis that is so heavily emphasized in traditional test design.

Evidence-Centered Design. Evidence-centered design (ECD; Mislevy, Steinberg, & Almond, 2003) is a framework that provides a conceptual approach to a coherent test design characterized by gathering evidence to support inferences about individuals. Its conceptual approach to assessment is one for which the evidence gathered describes evidentiary reasoning. In addition to evidentiary reasoning, ECD also provides guides for gathering such evidence in terms of production and delivery of the assessment (Almond, Steinberg, & Mislevy, 2002). ECD breaks down a complex system of design, implementation, and delivery of an educational assessment into several subsystems (i.e., layers), with an idea that each subsystem can be better handled at a subsystemic, individual, level. For each layer, key entities and knowledge representation are well specified (for details, see Mislevy & Riconscente, 2006).

The comprehensive ECD framework has five layers, which include domain analysis, domain modeling, conceptual assessment framework, assessment implementation, and assessment delivery. In this chapter, the focus is on the formal design portion for the assessment—the conceptual assessment framework (CAF; see Figure 5.2). In the CAF, a blueprint for the operational elements of an assessment is provided. There are three submodels which essentially connect the assessment argument and operational activities of the assessment: student, evidence, and task models. The *student model* contains variables that represent some aspect of knowledge, skills, and abilities (KSA) of an examinee about which inferences are to be made (Mislevy, Almond, & Lukas, 2003). Variables in the student model define the target of inference and ought to be in line with the purpose of the assessment. The student model represents our beliefs about what knowledge a student has based on evidence we collected so far.

The *evidence model* of ECD is partitioned into the evidence rules and statistical models. The evidence rules model is concerned with extracting salient features of what the student does or says in a task situation. This

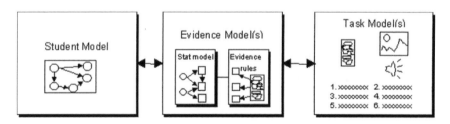

Note: Diagram adopted from Mislevy et al. (1999).

Figure 5.2.   Conceptual assessment framework of Evidence Centered Design.

information is then used to update the beliefs about student model variables via the statistical part of the model. In other words, the statistical component of the evidence model quantifies the relationship between the evaluative component and the student model (Mislevy et al., 2003). The statistical component of the model specifies the numeric parameters connecting student behaviors (i.e., responses) to their estimated proficiency or ability level. Within this model are parameters that specify the relationship between a student response and how it is related to a particular measured dimension (e.g., a factor loading, as well as the relationship between that dimension and the overarching construct to be measured). At the beginning of the each assessment, we know very little about the ability of a student (examinee). As we observe the student's performance, evidence for inferencing about the student proficiency is gathered and the update of our beliefs about the student's ability is modeled; that is, we move from a state of greater uncertainty to a state of less uncertainty as the assessment progresses.[1] Generally, the evidence model can be represented by psychometric models, including models of classical test theory and item response theory, cognitive diagnosis models, and latent trait models (Mislevy et al., 2003).

The last submodel, the task model, serves to create and define an environment in which a test ought to be performed. This environment creates possibilities to gather evidence for the evaluation part of the evidence model. Additionally, the task model describes relevant task features and relates these task features to work products. Generally speaking, the primary goal of the task model is to create an environment in which a student will exhibit observable behaviors that correspond closely to the evidence models. Once a task model is generated and a connection between the student and the evidence models is established, generation of an infinite number of items is possible. The task model is useful because it provides tools to assess the cognitive processes as evidenced by performance on a task and make inferences regarding individuals' mastery or ability levels on an assessment possible.

Advantages of ECD and CDS. More so than the traditional disjointed approaches to test design, frameworks such as ECD and CDS integrate the way we gather evidence and make interpretations about individual's underlying knowledge. Because the frameworks have a common design structure, coordination among the work of statisticians, item writers, and delivery-process developers is ensured. Several other advantages result as well. First, construct validity is more completely understood. Mislevy (2007) and Embretson and Gorin (2001) explicate these advantages, highlighting specifically the explicit approaches to elaboration of construct representation throughout the test development process. Second, construct validity may be understood at the item level, which can facilitate development of new items with more fully understood properties. The mathematical models incorporated into ECD and CDS can indicate the sources of cognitive complexity in each item which permits good predictions of psychometric properties for any new item from its stimulus features. Thus, items may be developed for specified sources of cognitive complexity, which can make testing more efficient for specific purposes or populations. Finally, as a consequence of the previously cited advantages, enhanced score interpretations are feasible such that persons may be described by the kinds of items that they are likely or unlikely to solve.

Illustrative Examples

To support the discussion of test design principles for HOT assessment, we draw upon two examples of tests developed upon these principles. The first example is a test of abstract reasoning skills, a long-researched higher order cognitive skill. The second test is a recently developed, operational certification test that measures electrical circuit construction and troubleshooting. A brief description of the two tests is provided here and more detail is given throughout the chapter where relevant.

Abstract Reasoning Test (ART). Among the many cognitive abilities of interest to individual differences researchers, abstract reasoning is one of the most commonly researched higher order processes. A traditional item type used to measure the ability is the progressive matrix. These items were first introduced on the classic Raven's Progressive Matrix test (Raven, 1940) and then have been reintroduced as an online assessment called the Abstract Reasoning Test (ART; Embretson, 1998). For these problems, students are provided a 3 x 3 matrix of shapes, with one blank cell with a missing shape that would complete the sequence in the matrix (see Figure 5.3). The examinee's task is to identify the appropriate shape for the missing cell based on patterns (i.e., rules) governing the completed portions of the matrix. A multiple-choice item type is used, wherein six response options combining different shapes, colors, and patterns are presented, only one of which correctly completes the matrix. The shapes in each of the matrix cells are organized according to rules of association between aspects of the figures. The rules can vary in number and complexity. If the examinee is able to infer the rules of association, then the correct response option for the missing cell is selected to complete the pattern.

Networking Performance Skill System (NetPASS). The second assessment example used throughout the chapter is a less traditional higher order cognitive skills assessment system, Cisco System's *Networking Performance Skill System (NetPASS)* (Behrens, Mislevy, Bauer, Williamson, & Levy,

Item Stem   Response Options

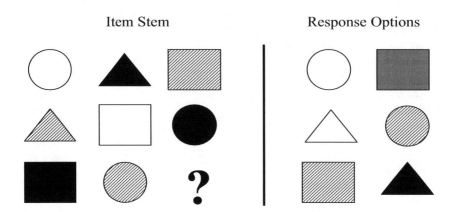

Figure 5.3.   Abstract Reasoning Test (ART) progressive matrix item.

2004). The goal of NetPASS is to develop an online performance assessment of networking proficiency that provides feedback to e-learning students and instructors as well as use for certification decisions. It is a simulation-based assessment mimicking actual Cisco networking equipment with specific design constraints similar to real world "scenarios" of network troubleshooting, design, and implementation (Williamson, Bauer, Steinberg, Mislevy, Behrens, & DeMark, 2004). Figure 5.4 shows a sample screenshot of the examinee workspace for one of the simulations. Three task types with varying degree of difficulty (low, moderate, high) are included in the assessment, each targeting different skills of interest: a design task, a troubleshooting task, and an implementation task. Examinees are required to design, implement, and/or troubleshoot networks based on typical network failures, configuration requirements, and design constraints, including elements of a network, and relations and connections between elements. Logs of all computer workstation commands are collected and evaluated for completeness and the correctness of procedures while solving the problem, as well as the final outcome. In addition to certification decisions and overall scores, diagnoses of specific problems are made by comparing process and outcome of student logs to previously identified processing patterns associated with known weaknesses or misconceptions.

Cognitively Based Construct Definitions

It is universally recommended to begin test development by initially defining that which one would like to measure (DeVellis, 1991; Nete-

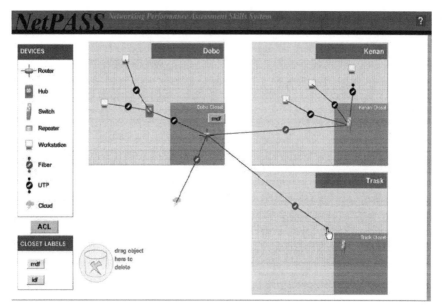

Figure 5.4.   NetPASS simulation item.

meyer, Bearden, & Sharma, 2003; Wilson, 2005). For higher order think-ing measurement, this would entail a definition of the construct (i.e., the cognitive ability/abilities) of interest. The ECD and CDS frameworks also begin with construct definitions, but from a slightly different vantage, one that relies more heavily on detailed cognitive descriptions of the con-struct. Whereas traditional construct definitions are often provided in a two or three sentence description of the cognitive ability, greater empha-sis on the specific aspects of cognition that are and are not targeted by the test developers is made. Detailed construct definitions, including descrip-tions of individual cognitive processing and theoretical relationships among trait dimensions, have been advocated (Embretson & Gorin, 2001; Mislevy, 2007; Messick, 1989, 1995). This finer grained construct defini-tion is the foundation for the remainder of the test development process by maintaining the focus of item and test development on the trait of interest.

Within the CDS framework, the construct definition process is incor-porated into Step 1: *Specify the Goals of Measurement*. The CDS approach includes defining at least two entities: (1) the construct representation of the test, and (2) the nomothetic span of the test. The first of these entities should rely heavily on a cognitive understanding of the con-struct of interest. The construct representation should address questions such as "What are the targeted cognitive processes to be measured?", "What discrete (declarative) knowledge is assessed?", "What differentiates different cognitive levels of performance?" The nomothetic span specifies the expected relationships among scores on the developed tests and other measures. Clearly, the nomothetic span is defined largely by the construct representation and theories associating its cognitive components to other measures of cognitive abilities. It is at this early stage in the CDS that we begin to see a more concerted effort to engage test developers with cognitive theories and models as part of the entire test development process.

Table 5.1 provides an example of a cognitively based construct definition for the progressive matrix items from Embretson's Abstract Reasoning Test (ART) based on the principles of the classic Raven's Progressive Matrix test (Raven, 1940). Notice that elements of both construct representation and nomothetic span are incorporated. When the intended use and interpretation of test scores are defined with great clarity and specificity, the likelihood that appropriate items will be written to achieve those goals increases. Further, when validation analyses are implemented, the criterion for determining the success with which the test measures the appropriate construct is made explicit at the outset.

Within the ECD framework, the construct definition is instantiated as the student model of the conceptual framework. The purpose of the student model in ECD is the same as CDS's Stage 1: Specify the Goals of Measurement though the structure and phrasing of the construct definition differ slightly. The ECD's student model is typically phrased in terms of the inferences or claims that a test developer wants to make about individuals based on the test scores. These claims are often formulated in terms of individual students' behaviors and skills. A student model for the NetPASS Troubleshooting Task is presented in the top portion of Figure

Table 5.1.   Cognitive Model of Abstract Reasoning Construct

Construct Representation	*Nomological Network*
• Involves inference independent of specific knowledge	• Correlates with other measures of fluid ability

o   Specific skills
  (a) Find correspondences
  (b) Induce relationships
	• Correlations with reasoning and judgment should be higher than correlations with verbal comprehension or knowledge

• Akin to fluid intelligence	
• Does not depend on prior knowledge	

Source: Based on Carroll's (1993) definition.

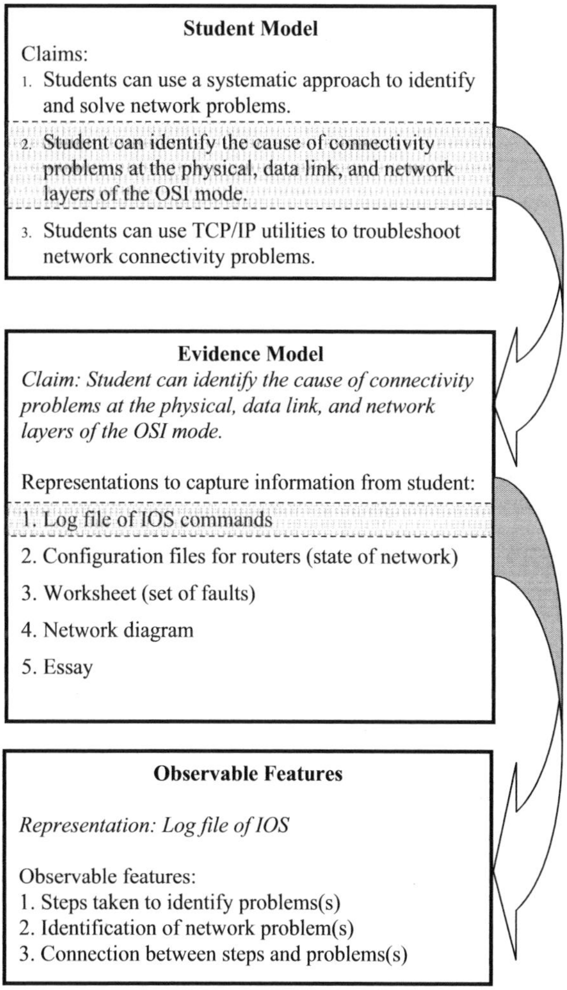

Student Model

Claims:

1. Students can use a systematic approach to identify and solve network problems.

2. Student can identify the cause of connectivity problems at the physical, data link, and network layers of the OSI mode.

3. Students can use TCP/IP utilities to troubleshoot network connectivity problems.

Evidence Model

Claim: Student can identify the cause of connectivity problems at the physical, data link, and network layers of the OSI mode.

Representations to capture information from student:

1. Log file of IOS commands

2. Configuration files for routers (state of network)

3. Worksheet (set of faults)

4. Network diagram

5. Essay

Observable Features

Representation: Log file of IOS

Observable features:
1. Steps taken to identify problems(s)
2. Identification of network problem(s)
3. Connection between steps and problems(s)

Figure 5.5.   ECD student, evidence, and task models for NetPASS Troubleshooting task.

5.5. The student model cognitive variables for this task include networking disciplinary knowledge, and network modeling.

Item Writing With Cognitive Models

By this point in the test development process, a model of the cognitive processes to be measured should have already been well defined as part of the construct definition. We can refer to this as the *cognitive model of the intended construct* (Ferrara et al., 2004; Gorin, 2007). However, unless the test items represent the exact cognitive processes of interest, that is they are completely authentic assessments, then the items will likely require some cognitive processes that are not of interest. Messick (1995) refers to the variance attributable to these processes as *construct irrelevant variance*. Additionally, it is likely that the items do not require all of the cognitive processes of interest, a problem referred to as *construct underrepresentation*. The goal in selecting item types and developing items is to design tasks[2] that simultaneously reduce sources of construct irrelevant variance and maximize construct representativeness. One effective approach is to develop a second cognitive model, one that specifies the expected cognitive processes that an individual must enact in order to correctly solve the test item—a *cognitive model of the enacted construct* (Gorin, 2006).

Models of enacted constructs should be capable of describing the observable data generated from item responses, including accounting for the difficulty of items. For this reason, the model of the enacted construct can be thought of as an *item difficulty model* (IDM), so named because the difficulty of an item should depend on the complexity of the cognitive processes specified in the model. For example, as the cognitive processes required to solve an item become more complex (i.e., higher working memory loads, more cognitive complexity) we would expect that (a) fewer examinees answer the items correctly and (b) item responses are generated more slowly. Similarly, items for which the cognitive processes are relatively simple (i.e., low level cognitive processes) the majority of respondents should answer correctly and relatively quickly. Both the number of respondents answering an item correctly (i.e., the item's difficulty) and the amount of time needed to answer an item (i.e., response time) are observable entities that can be statistically evaluated. The quality the IDM can be judged by its ability to account for variations in item characteristics. A formal statistical test of the fit of IDM to the test data will be conducted later in the test development process, once data has been collected. However, at least initially, test developers can compare informally the cognitive components of the intended construct with those of the IDM to determine the likelihood that an appropriate item type has been selected.

Returning to the CDS approach, the IDM is developed at Stages 2 and 3. An item difficulty model typically includes a list of cognitive processes or skills organized in terms of the sequence of item processing. To test these models, each process is defined by observable features of an item that can be systematically coded and entered into statistical analyses to test the impact of the process on item difficulty. A model that includes processes and features describing the majority of variability in item difficulty are thought to accurately describe the true processes and skills measured by an item. Studies that examine the connections between item features and processing models, such as the correlational studies, analysis of verbal protocols and eye-tracking data, and experimental manipulations can play a critical role in the item writing process (Embretson, 1998; Embretson & Gorin, 2001; Gorin, 2006, 2007). To illustrate the structure of an IDM, let us return to the progressive matrix items of the Abstract Reasoning Test (ART; Embretson, 1998). Recall the construct definition of the intended cognitive processes described earlier in the chapter. The targeted construct to be measured by these items is abstract reasoning, which includes the ability to infer associations between concepts and to apply them in new situations. Figure 5.6 provides an IDM of the multiple-choice items appearing on the test. In terms of construct relevant cognitive processes, studies of these problems showed that item difficulty could be deconstructed into two general processes—inferring rules and applying them—which is controlled by working memory and abstraction processes (Carpenter, Just, & Shell, 1990; Embretson, 1998). The cognitive complexity of these processes for any individual item comes primarily from two features/characteristics of the item: (1) the number of rules, and (2) the complexity of the rules. The working memory load for an item is determined by these two characteristics. Items written with multiple rules rather than a single rule, and those with more complex versus simpler rules, should be more difficult to solve than other items. Further, the level of abstraction needed is controlled by several other perceptual features, including overlay (i.e., one shape is placed over another), distortion (i.e., one aspect of a shape is expanded or modified to alter its appearance slightly), and fusion (i.e., two shapes are joined to form a single new shape that contains aspects of each original shape). Looking solely at the schematic representation of the cognitive model for the items in comparison to the cognitive model of the intended construct, there appears to be considerable correspondence, an assumption that will be tested later during psychometric parameterization.

Within an ECD context, items and tasks are developed based on a similar though slightly different logic. Since the student model used as a construct definition is phrased in terms of claims that one would like to make about student abilities, then the task should be designed to provide observable behaviors that provide evidence relevant to these claims. For every claim to be made, at least one, if not more, sources of evidence should be provided by the task—the second and third models in the ECD conceptual assessment framework (see Figure 5.4). Let us return to the NetPASS Troubleshooting task developed within the ECD framework focusing on one particular student model variable—*Claim: Student can identify the cause of connectivity problems at the physical, data link, and network layers of the OSI mode* (see Figure 5.5). In this task, students are introduced

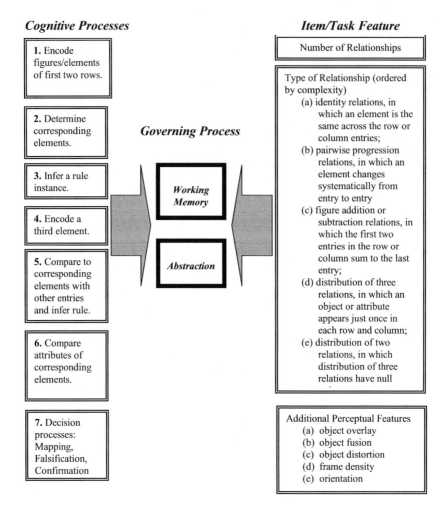

Figure 5.6.   Cognitive processing model for ART items.

to a simulated network for which certain failures exist and corresponding "fixes" are needed. Students are provided with user reports, based on which they must identify faults and fix them. The design of the simulated network is specified by the test developers according to the types of faults that elicit the troubleshooting processes of interest. In NetPASS, task models were generated for each area of emphasis (i.e. design, implement, troubleshoot). Each task model targeted different degrees of knowledge and skills (low, moderate, high), which resulted in a total of nine tasks students needed to complete. A student is introduced to an existing network with specified properties for which he/she must determine the fault or faults of the network and to fix them. These specified properties (e.g., type and number of faults, structure of the network, resources available) constitute the task model. The evidence model is comprised of the observable student behaviors that are collected. In the case of the network troubleshooting task, these include students' commands and sequences of commands which are placed into categories that describe the actions— *information gathering about router, changes to router, testing network after fixes*, and *gathering information about commands*. Later stages in test development, specifically psychometric modeling, will complete the evidence model with the statistical parameters connecting behavioral evidence, task features, and student model claims.

Psychometric Scaling and Analysis

We now turn to the least favorite part of test and scale development for all non-statistician/psychometricians—item and scale analysis. Typical analyses include calculation of classical true score (CTS) item statistics (e.g., *p*-values, item-total correlations, scale means and standard deviations), some form of reliability estimate (e.g., coefficient alpha, test-retest, parallel forms), and often dimensionality analysis incorporating some form of factor analysis or multidimensional scaling. Alternatively, modern psychometric testing models based on item response theory (IRT) can be used to estimate similar item statistics. The typical IRT model provides estimates of item difficulty, discrimination, and potentially guessing, though the meaning of these parameters is slightly distinct from the CTS item statistics. IRT models for both dichotomous and polytomously scored item types have become commonplace for high stakes tests in education and are growing in popularity in psychological assessment (Hambleton & van der Linden, 1982). These methods are often preferred over the classical test models due to the increased substantive interpretability of test scores and the independence of the item and person parameters that are estimated by the models.[3]

While we do not suggest that CTS or IRT statistics should not be calculated for completeness, they are limited in their utility within the cognitively-based framework we advocate. With all of the effort up to this point that has been recommended to incorporate cognitive psychology principles and theory into test development, it is logical that the psychometric analysis provide an opportunity to examine item responses with a cognitive lens. For that reason, our focus in this section on psychometric models that can assess the full cognitive model of the IDM, as well as provide individual item parameters. Using the ECD language, the connection between student model variables and observable variables can be provided via psychometric models. We provide a brief summary of the most frequently cited models in the recent psychometric literature, primarily to expose the reader to what is available. Table 5.2 provides a list of the selected psychometric models and the source citations for each. Interested readers are encouraged to reference these sources for more detailed information about the mathematical structure of the models, issues and assumptions of the model, and estimation procedures and computer applications available for each.

Cognitively-based latent trait models. The simplest extension of the traditional IRT models that are useful for examining the cognitive components of test items and scores are linear latent trait models with additional cognitive parameters. In such models, rather than estimating directly the difficulty or discrimination of an item, the impact of individual cognitive processes *on* item difficulty or discrimination is estimated. One such model that has shown promise for cognitively-based test development is the linear logistic latent trait model (LLTM; Fischer, 1973). Without delving into the mathematical complexities of the nonlinear form of the model and its assumptions, let us focus on the advantage of the model from a cognitive test development perspective. The LLTM incorporates content information into the calculation of probabilities of a correct response to an item. The model includes this information in the form of weights, representing the impact that any cognitive component of a trait may have on the difficulty[4] of an item. The user begins by specifying the

Table 5.2.   Selected List of Potential Models for Psychometric Analysis of HOT

Model	Name	Reference
LLTM	Linear logistic latent trait model	Fischer, 1973
GDM	General diagnostic model	von Davier, 2005
MIRT	Multidimensional IRT	Reckase, 1997
MLTM	Multicomponent Latent Trait Model	Embretson, 1997
DINA	deterministic inputs, noise, "and"	Doignon & Famagne, 1999 Tatsuoka, 1995
NIDA	noise inputs, deterministic, "and"	Marris, 1999 DiBello, Stout, & Roussos, 1995
RSM	Rule-space method	Tatsuoka, 1983, 1985
Fusion	Fusion model	Hartz, Roussos, & Stout

presence or absence of a particular cognitive skill for solving a particular item, which is represented often in the form of an incidence, or Q-, matrix. The incidence matrix simply indicates whether an item requires a skill (coded mathematically as a "1") or does not require the skill (coded mathematically as a "0"). Formulating this incidence matrix is a matter of examining the cognitive processes required to solve a question. If one has followed the CDS or ECD steps, this is an easy task. After all, the item writing process was driven by an IDM that included specification of each cognitive skill or component and how it is represented in each item. The presence or absence of a particular cognitive attribute in an item's solution path is represented by a design matrix relating items to processing components. Essentially, a regression equation, regressing item difficulty on the cognitively-based item features, replaces the typical value of item difficulty. When we fit the LLTM model to the data and estimate the cognitive parameters, the result is a formal test of the quality of our cognitive model. Any cognitive parameters that are significant suggest that the associated cognitive process was invoked in problem solving and affects the difficulty of an item. Further, the extent to which the overall model fits the data, one can infer that a complete description of the construct measured by the item has been represented. This is a critical result for examining the quality of the items and the validity of score meaning, a topic we will return to later in the chapter.

Multidimensional models. A different approach to psychometric modeling that provides cognitively-rich information about people and items are multidimensional models, specifically IRT-based multidimensional models. These models have been most popular in testing program for which diagnostic score reports are desired and/or complex item types are used (e.g., Tatsuoka's (1995) Rule Space; Hartz, Roussos, & Stout's (2002) Fusion model; von Davier's (2005) general diagnostic model). These models have several advantages over traditional psychometric models. Most significantly, they provide test designers with greater reliability when estimating ability (proficiency) scores at the subscale level. The increased reliability comes from estimating subskill scores based on information from a larger number of items than go into a simple summed subscale score. Further, test banks may be reorganized with items classified (grouped) based on their skill structure rather than simply according to difficulty. Taking advantage of this latter point allows for item selection that is skill oriented which in turn may yield more informative test score for any one individual test taker.

One type of model in this category is multidimensional compensatory IRT model (MIRT; Reckase, 1997). Unlike unidimensional IRT models, MIRT allows for the contribution of two or more constructs to the solution for an item or set of items. MIRT decomposes the unidimensional person parameter into an item-dependent linear combination of latent traits (Junker & Sijtsma, 2001, p. 259). Compensatory here suggests (assumes) that an examinee need not master all of the attributes associated with any one item in order to answer it correctly. Rather, a high level of ability on one attribute may compensate for lower level ability on a different attribute, both of which are associated with that same item. However, according to Junker and Sijtsma, while these models made advances in blending IRT and cognitive assessment, however, are not sensitive to all aspects of cognition. Thus, noncompensatory approaches, such as the multicomponent latent trait model (MLTM, Embretson, 1997) might be more appropriate. MLTM is suggested to be more sensitive to "finer variations among examinees in situations in which several cognitive components are required simultaneously for successful task performance" (Junker & Sijtsma, 2001, p. 259). In other words, performance on tasks involved the conjunction of successful performances on multiple subtasks, where each subtask may be thought of as unidimensional IRT model. Such conjunctive (noncompensatory) approach might be preferred in cognitive assessment models, especially if the focus is on a single strategy for performing tasks (Corbett, Anderson, & O'Brien, 1995; Tatsuoka, 1995).

An alternative to the linear models, MIRT and MLTM, is an approach based on classification into latent classes which has shown some promise. These models are analogous to the MLTM model but with fewer assumptions about the relationship between the cognitive attributes of the items and task performance. Two of the more frequently cited models include DINA (deterministic inputs, noise, "and," Doignon & Famagne, 1999; Tatsuoka, 1995) and NIDA (noise inputs, deterministic, "and," Maris, 1999; DiBello, Stout, & Roussos, 1995) gate models. Similar to the MLTM and LLTM models, the user specifies the cognitive skills required by each item, typically specified within the IDM. The mathematical model then estimates the effect of each of these skills on item responses. However, for the classification models, examinee proficiency is reported in terms of the current "knowledge state" of the student as either a "master" or "nonmaster" of each of the cognitive skills. In general, no continuous ability estimate, such as a z-score, total test score, or theta estimate, are generated. For this reason, These models have been used as tools to make several types of inferences, including inferences about mastery and nonmastery of hypothesized cognitive attributes, or inference about the relationship between these attributes and observed task performance (Junker & Sijtsma, 2001).

Bayes Inference Networks. A third contemporary modeling approach that has increased in popularity as the computing power for mathematical calculations has improved is a complex probabilistic modeling system. As the number of observable variables (scores) for an item increases the use of the aforementioned models that typically handle one variable per item are insufficient. It is preferable to construct a model consisting of a complex system of variables. One approach that has had some success is the use of Bayesian inference networks (BINs; Jensen, 1996, 2001; Pearl, 1988; for examples in educational assessment, see e.g., Almond, DiBello, Moulder, & Zapata-Rivera, 2007; Levy & Mislevy, 2004; Martin & Van-Lehn, 1995, Mislevy, 1994). BINs are graphical models in which we transmit complex observational evidence within a network of interrelated variables. In ECD language, student model variables characterize the skills, knowledge, and strategies to make claims about. Given their unobservable nature, we use observable measures that characterize salient aspects of performance. Conditional relationships between the observables variables, the underlying proficiency variables (i.e., student level variables), and characteristics of the task are graphically diagramed as a network. Then, using Bayes theorem of conditional probabilities, the strength of the relationships and the fit of the overall model to the data can be tested. The key, of course, is to construct a BIN based on a nonarbitrary model of cognition and the tasks. The model ought to be "consistent with knowledge about the underlying scientific problem and the data collection process" (Gelman, Carlin, Stern, & Rubin, 1995, p. 3). All of the work up to this point on the student model and item/task development pays off here.

Building the Validity Argument

The culminating analyses for any newly developed or revised assessment typically include examination of the validity of score interpretations. Recent conceptualizations of validity (which will not be discussed in detail here) advocate an evidence-based approach to the construction of a validity argument through a variety of analyses, each addressing different aspects of validity (Kane, 1992, 2006; Messick, 1989, 1995). It is here that the cognitive components previously included in the construct definition, item design, and psychometric analysis will be compared and contrasted to draw conclusions regarding the skills represented by the resultant test scores. Evidence of the content aspect of validity is provided in the initial cognitive model of the intended construct as well as the cognitive model of the enacted construct. Evidence of the external aspect of validity can be generated using traditional correlational approaches. Within the CDS framework, the external variables to be included have likely been specified in the early stages of test development as part of the nomothetic span component of the goals of measurement. Further, application of the psychometric models can provide evidence of the structural aspect of validity by indicating the number of latent dimensions that best fit the data. In particular, evidence of the substantive aspect of validity is enhanced by the CDS and ECD approaches to test design.

Central to the substantive aspect of construct validity is the question of whether the processes measured by items and tests are those that were intended by the researcher. The alignment between the *intended* cognitive processes specified by test developers, and the *observed/enacted* processes applied by the examinees when solving an item is of critical interest (Ferrara et al., 2004; Gorin, 2007). Unfortunately, comparison of the intended and enacted cognitive processes is challenging, particularly for HOT items that often use complex cognitive tasks to measure multiple complex cognitive processes. By this point in the test development process, the intended cognitive processes should have already been well defined as part of the construct definition. We can refer to this as the *cognitive model of the intended construct*. What remains to be developed is the description of the cognitive processes elicited by the items—a *cognitive model of the enacted construct*. Once both models are formulated, they can be compared for alignment and the validity argument is made (see Figure 5.7). Close alignment between these cognitive processes supports strong and valid score interpretations. The final section of this chapter reviews the previously discussed IDM as an approach to developing cognitive models of the enacted construct.

As one may have inferred from the previous discussion of psychometric modeling, parameter estimation from multidimensional or cognitively-based psychometric models can provide test developers with evidence regarding the alignment of the intended and enacted cognitive models via that item difficulty model. Two characteristics of item difficulty models should be evaluated. First, to what extent do model-related item features account for variations in item properties? The parameter estimates from the psychometric modeling exist to answer this question. Alternatively, methods such as regression can be used to estimate the strength of the relationship between item features and the statistical properties of the item (e.g., item difficulty, item discrimination, response time).

Returning to our illustrative examples, psychometric modeling of data from both the ART and NetPASS tests have been used to support validity arguments regarding the meaning of test scores from these tests. For the ART progressive matrix items, IDM studies implementing the IRT-based LLTM model have been used to argue for the validity of the score interpretation of the items. When the impact of individual cognitive processes on item difficulty were examined, 80% of the variance in item difficulties for matrix questions could be explained by the IDM features (Embretson, 1998). These item features included (a) working memory load as represented by number and complexity of the rules in the item, (b) overlay, (c) fusion, and (d) distortion (see Table 5.3). This high proportion of explained

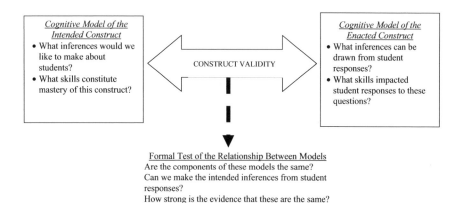

Figure 5.7.   Representation of the validity argument as the alignment between cognitive models of the intended and enacted constructs.

variance in item difficulty suggests strong evidence that scores from these items can be interpreted in terms of the typical skills associated with the ability to think abstractly. An alternative approach, BINs modeling was incorporated into the NetPASS development. Unlike the LLTM, BINs can model multiple latent variables (i.e., multidimensional data) with multiple observable variables. Given the nature of the simulation tasks and the number of observables in the evidence model, this is required for the NetPASS Networking Assessment. Figure 5.8 shows a fragment of a conditional probability model specifying the expected relationships between the student model and task model variables with the observables. Using BINs, test developers were able to verify the relationship between the student model, task model, and evidence model variables. The strength of the conditional relationships between observable variables from the tasks and the student proficiency variables and the fit of the overall model provides evidence in support of the hypothesized underlying cognitive processes.

A second, perhaps more important, issue relevant for validity argumentation for test developers is whether the skills and knowledge validated in the IDM are the same as those of the cognitive model of the intended construct? Compared to the first question, the alignment of the cognitive processes is a more subjective issue, one that is central to the validity of score interpretations. Whether the processes described in that model are the same as the processes and skills of the intended construct is not assessed in the psychometric analysis. Further consideration of methods for making these evaluations should be explored as more item difficulty models are developed for existing and newly developed tests.

**Table 5.3. LLTM Parameter Estimates for
IDM Cognitive Features of ART Progressive Matrix Items**

	Item Difficulty		Response Time	
Variable	Weight	Error	Weight	Error
Memory Load	.25	.02	.06	.01
Perceptual Features				
Overlay	.62	.18	.18	.06
Distortion	.55	.26	.07	.08
Fusion	−.42	.22	−.15	.07

Source: Embretson (1998).

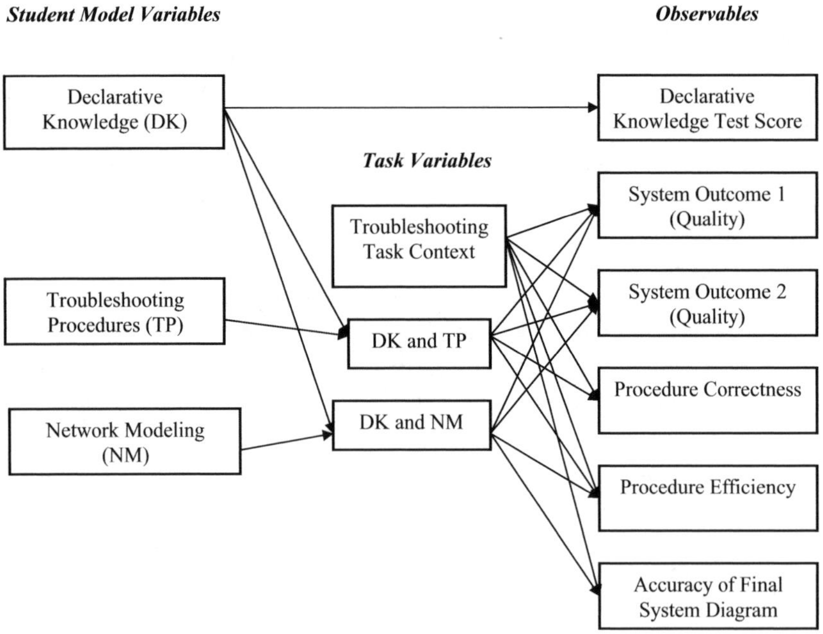

Source: Adapted from Levy and Mislevy (2004).

Figure 5.8.   Fragment of conditional probability model for estimation with BINs for NetPASS.

The Iterative Test Development Process

As was alluded to previously, test development via CDS or ECD are iterative processes. The validity analysis provides not only summative information for test developers regarding their success or failure in test development, it provides formative information that can be used to either revise items or increase the size of the available item pool for future testing. Linking HOT item writing to cognitive models can have substantial benefits for further item revision or development. It is typical for a small number of items to be written initially, though for test development purposes, a large number of items are often desired, particularly if test security is an issue. Thus, a mechanism that can quickly generate pools of items based on an initial subset, about which much is known, is advantageous. One such approach is called *item generation* (Bejar, 1993; Irvine, 2002).

Item generation is the process of streamlining item development by specifying a priori the structure of an item, including all of the ways in which items can vary and how those variations affect student processing. Based on the characteristics of a validated and statistically parameterized item difficulty model, an implied *item structure* can be generated (Bejar, 1993; Hornke, 2002). An item structure specifies the physical characteristics of the test questions and the ways in which it can be manipulated to vary the processing requirements. Essentially it is a structural blue-print for writing an item with a priori known statistical and cognitive component. Once an item structure is in place, test developers can produce virtually limitless numbers of items with known cognitive and statistical properties to improve the efficiency and security of a test, while reducing the development costs.

Item generation in its most sophisticated form entails computers generating test items *on-the-fly* as a test is in progress (Bejar, 1993; Bennett, 1999; Bennett & Bejar, 1999). The entire item writing process is incorporated into a computer algorithm that is invoked after each item response, much like an item selection algorithm applied in computerized adaptive tests with item banks. In most content areas, technological requirements for programming automated item generation are well within our capabilities. Computerized item generators have already been developed that automatically generate spatial and abstract reasoning tasks. Embretson (1998) successfully developed a fully automated item generator for the progressive matrix items on the ART that can assemble sets of items with predictable item difficulty based on the IDM structure. The test scores generated from the automatically generated tests are comparable in reliability and validity of meaning as those from a humanly constructed test, though the efficiency of the test generation and the security of the test itself is vastly improved in the automated situation. Applications of automated item generators for complex item types measuring more complex IDMs are currently underway. The implications for more efficient and effective item development as compared to current human-generated tests are promising.

Benefits of Cognitive Models for HOTs Assessment Design

Our discussion of cognitively-based assessment design versus more traditional intuitive or statistically-driven approaches imply a significant increase in effort needed to develop and validate tests, items, and score interpretations. However, we would argue that rather than an increase in the work to develop HOT assessments based on strong cognitive models of the construct, there is a shift in the effort onto the front end of the assessment design, one that ought to pay off in the end by yielded more useful and reliable test scores. Embretson and Gorin (2001) include the following among the benefits of cognitively-based approaches to assessment design: (1) improved construct definition as a foundation of validity investigations, (2) an empirical basis for selecting items based on the relationship between characteristics of items and cognitive components to be measured, (3) increased accuracy of item parameter estimation based on auxiliary information about item features, (4) a basis for diagnostic score interpretations regarding skill strengths and weaknesses, (5) defining principles for automated scoring of complex item types that are useful for HOTs measurement, and (6) providing a structure for algorithmic item generation.

For psychometricians, the primary advantage relates to the contribution of cognitive models to parameter estimation. Well specified cognitive models that predict the difficulty of items (or even the guessing level or discrimination of items) can greatly reduce the computational burden of item parameter estimation that often requires large pretest/calibration samples. Several researchers have show that item parameters can either be (a) predicted (Embretson & Gorin, 2001) or (b) estimated with increased precision by incorporating auxiliary information about item features and cognitive properties in the estimation algorithm (Mislevy, 1988). Mislevy, Sheehan, and Wingersky (1993) went so far as to illustrate how cognitive models of item processing could be used to facilitate test equating when little or no data exists. The mathematical modeling of item difficulty based on cognitive models of processing permits good predictions of psychometric properties for new item constructed with similar item features. from its stimulus features.

For the item writer, the primary advantage is the utility of cognitive models for efficient item development. Fulkerson, Nichols, and Mittelholtz (2009) contrast an "item-construction-as-science" approach, based on knowledge of the cognitive requirements of item solutions to the traditional "item-construction-as-art" approach, recommending the former as a more promising approach to targeted item development. The "science" approach uses a predefined cognitive model of items to help item writers to systematically manipulate item and task features that result in items of different difficulty levels. This capability can increase the efficiency of targeted test design such that items with maximum discriminatory power (i.e., maximized information) for the targeted testing population can be generated explicitly because the varying and constant features across items are clearly defined. When given a targeted test information curve and cognitive models describing the characteristics of items at different locations on the latent trait continuum, item writers can develop multiple variants of items that increase information at the desired ability levels without wasting energy developing items targeting unintended examinees.

Conclusion

As we progress into the twenty-first century of ability testing, remarkable changes and advances are evident. Perhaps more than in any other arena, higher order thinking skill assessment will likely be impacted by these changes. Technological advances have made innovative item types capable of capturing higher ordering thinking skills, including complex item types such as computer simulations, a reality for large scale testing. Simultaneously, the increased computational capability of computers has made parameter estimation for the complex psychometric models needed to model complex items a nonissue. When we combine these advances with the rich cognitive theory that exists for many higher order cognitive skills, a unique opportunity is presented. In order to take advantage of this opportunity, researchers in cognitive psychology, educational learning theory, psychometrics and statistics, and computer science must join forces to develop assessments that leverage the cutting-edge knowledge from each discipline. We have tried, in this chapter, to provide some guidance as to how teams of researchers from these disparate fields might approach the test development process. Our hope is that with increased dissemination of contemporary test design frameworks ideal for higher order thinking assessment we will see an increase in the operational use of tests that provide the richest possible information about individuals' abilities and skills.

NOTES

1. Bayesian approach is often used in updating of the beliefs via modeling (see chapter section on Psychometric Scaling and Analysis).
2. The terms *item tasks, item types,* and *items* are used somewhat interchangeably. Test items refer typically to individual test questions found on traditional tests. However, many modern assessments include more complex and open ended questions that are often referred to as tasks.
3. Readers interested in the advantages of IRT over CTS are referred to Embretson & Reise (2001).
4. IRT item difficulty is typically defined as the latent trait level associated with having a 50% chance of correctly answer an item.

REFERENCES

Almond, R. G., DiBello, L. V., Moulder, B., & Zapata-Rivera, J. D. (2007). Modeling diagnostic assessments with Bayesian networks. *Journal of Educational Measurement, 44*, 341-359.

Almond, R. G., Steinberg, L. S., & Mislevy, R. J. (2002). Enhancing the design and delivery of assessment systems: A four-process architecture. *Journal of Technology, Learning, and Assessment, 1*(5). Retrieved from http://www.bc.edu/research/intasc/jtla/journal/v1n5.shtml

Behrens, J. T., Mislevy, R. J., Bauer, M., Williamson, D. M., & Levy, R. (2004). Introduction to evidence-centered design and lessons learned from its application in a global e-learning program. *International Journal of Testing, 4*, 295-302.

Bejar, I. I. (1993). A generative approach to psychological and educational measurement In N. Frederiksen, R. J. Mislevy, & I. I. Bejar (Eds.), *Test theory for a new generation of tests* (pp. 323-359). Hillsdale, NJ: Erlbaum.

Bennett, R. E. (1999). Using new technology to improve assessment. *Educational Measurement: Issues and Practice., 18*, 5-12.

Bennett, R. E., & Bejar, I. I (1999). Validity and automated scoring: It's not only the scoring. *Educational Measurement: Issues and Practice, 17*(4), 9-16.

Carpenter, P. A, Just, M. A., & Shell, P. (1990). What one intelligence test measures: A theoretical account of processing in the Raven's Progressive Matrices Test. *Psychological Review, 97*, 404-431.

Carroll, J. B. (1993). *Human cognitive abilities: A survey of factor analytic studies.* New York, NY: Cambridge University Press.

Carroll, J. B., & Maxwell, S. E. (1979). Individual difference in cognitive abilities. *Annual Review of Psychology, 30*, 603-640.

Corbett, A. T., Anderson, J. R., & O'Brien, A. T. (1995). Student modeling in the ACT programming tutor. In P. D. Nichols, S. F. Chipman, & R. L. Brennan (Eds), *Cognitively diagnostic assessment* (pp. 19-41). Hillsdale, NJ: Erlbaum.

DeVellis, R. F. (1991). *Scale development: Theory and applications.* Thousand Oaks, CA: SAGE.

DiBello, L., Stout, W., & Roussos, L. (1995). Unified cognitive/psychometric diagnostic assessment likelihood-based classification techniques. In P. D. Nichols, S. F. Chipman, & R. L. Brennan (Eds.), *Cognitively diagnostic assessment* (pp. 361-389). Hillsdale, NJ: Erlbaum.

Doignon, J. -P. & Falmagne, J. -C. (1999). *Knowledge spaces.* New York, NY: Springer-Verlag.

Embretson, S. E. (1993). Construct validity: Construct representation versus nomothetic span. *Psychological Bulletin, 93,* 179-197.

Embretson, S. E. (1998). A cognitive design system approach to generating valid tests: Application to abstract reasoning. *Psychological Methods, 3,* 380-396.

Embretson, S. E. (1997). Multicomponent response models. In W. J. van der Linden & R. K. Hambleton (Eds.), *Handbook on modern item response theory* (pp. 305-322). New York, NY: Springer-Verlag.

Embretson, S. E., & Gorin, J. S. (2001). Improving construct validity with cognitive psychology principles. *Journal of Educational Measurement, 38*(4), 343-368.

Ferrara, S. Duncan, T. G., Freed, R., Vélez-Paschke, A., McGivern, J., Mushlin, S., Mattessich, et al. (2004, April). *Examining test score validity by examining item construct validity: Preliminary analysis of evidence of the alignment of targeted and observed content, skills, and cognitive processes in a middle school science assessment.* Paper presented at the 2004 annual meeting of the American Educational Research Association.

Fischer, G. H. (1973). Linear logistic test model as an instrument in educational research. *Acta Psychologica, 48,* 315-342.

Fulkerson, D., Nichols, P. D., & Mittelholtz, D. J. (2009, April). *The psychology of writing items: Improving figural response item writing.* Paper presented at the 2009 annual meeting of the American Educational Research Association, San Diego, CA.

Gelman, A., Carlin, J. B., Stern, H. S., & Rubin, D. B. (1995). *Bayesian data analysis.* London: Chapman & Hall.

Gorin, J. S. (2006). Item design with cognition in mind. *Educational Measurement: Issues and Practice, 25*(4), 21-35.

Gorin, J. S. (2007). Test construction and diagnostic testing. In J. P. Leighton & M. J. Gierl (Eds.), *Cognitive diagnostic assessment in education: Theory and practice.* Cambridge, England: Cambridge University Press.

Hambleton, R. K., & van der Linden, W. J. (1982). Advances in item response theory and applications: An introduction. *Applied Psychological Measurement, 6,* 373-378.

Hartz, S., Roussos, L., & Stout, W. (2002). *Skills diagnosis: Theory and practice.* (User manual for Arpeggio software) Princeton, NJ: ETS.

Hornke, L. F. (2002). Item-generation models for higher order cognitive functions. In S. H. Irvine & P. C. Kyllonen (Eds.), *Item generation for test development* (pp. 159-178). Mahwah, NJ: Lawrence Erlbaum.

Irvine, S. H. (2002). The foundations of item generation for mass testing. In S. H. Irvine & P. C. Kyllonen (Eds.), *Item generation for test development* (pp. 3-34). Mahwah, NJ: Lawrence Erlbaum

Jensen, F. V. (1996). *An introduction to Bayesian Networks.* London: UCL Press.

Jensen, F. V. (2001). *Bayesian Networks and Decision Graphs*. New York, NY: IEEE Computer Society. London: Chapman & Hall.

Junker, B. W., & Sijtsma, K. (2001). Cognitive assessment models with few assumptions, and connections with nonparametric item response theory. *Applied Psychological Measurement, 25*, 258-272.

Kane, M. T. (1992). An argument-based approach to validation. *Psychological Bulletin, 112*, 527-535.

Kane, M. T. (2006). Validation. In R. L. Brennan (Ed.), *Educational measurement* (4th ed.). Washington, DC: American Council on Education/Praeger.

Levy, R., & Mislevy, R. J. (2004). Specifying and refining a measurement model for a computer-based interactive assessment. *International Journal of Testing, 4*, 333-369.

Maris, E. (1999). Estimating multiple classification latent class models. *Psychometrika, 64*, 187- 212.

Martin, J., & VanLehn, K. (1995). A Bayesian approach to cognitive assessment. In P. Nichols, S. Chipman, & R. L. Brennan (Eds.), *Cognitively diagnostic assessment* (pp. 141-165). Hillsdale, NJ: Erlbaum.

Messick, S. (1989). Meaning and values in test validation: The science and ethics of assessment. *Educational Researcher, 18*(2), 5-11.

Messick, S. (1995). Validity of psychological Assessment: Validation of inferences from persons' responses and performances as scientific inquiry into score meaning. *American Psychologist, 50*, 741-749.

Mislevy, R. J. (1994). Evidence and inference in educational assessment. *Psychometrika, 59*, 439-483.

Mislevy, R. J. (1988). Exploiting auxiliary information about items in the estimation of Rasch item difficulty parameters. *Applied Psychological Measurement, 12*(3), 281-296.

Mislevy, R. J. (2007). Validity by design. *Educational Researcher, 36*(8), 463-469.

Mislevy, R. J., Almond, R. G., & Lukas, J. F. (2003). *A brief introduction to Evidence Centered Design* (Technical Report RR-03-16). Princeton, NJ: Educational Testing Service.

Mislevy, R. J., & Riconscente, M. M. (2006). Evidence-centered assessment design: Layers, concepts, and terminology. In S. Downing & T. Haladyna (Eds.), *Handbook of test development* (pp. 61-90). Mahwah, NJ: Erlbaum.

Mislevy, R. J., Sheehan, K. M., & Wingersky, M. (1993). How to equate tests with little or no data. *Journal of Educational Measurement, 30*(1), 55-78.

Mislevy, R. J., Steinberg, L. S., & Almond, R. G. (2003). On the structure of educational assessments. *Measurement: Interdisciplinary Research and Perspectives, 1*(1), 3-67.

National Research Council. (2001). *Knowing what students know: The science and design of educational assessment*. Washington, DC: National Academy Press.

Netemeyer, R. G., Bearden, W. O., & Sharma, S. (2003). *Scaling procedures: Issues and applications*. Thousand Oaks, CA: SAGE.

Pellegrino, J, W. (1988). Mental models and mental tests. In H. Wainer & H. Braun (Eds.), *Test validity* (pp. 49-59), Hillsdale, NJ: Erlbaum.

Pearl, J. (1988). *Probabilistic reasoning in intelligent systems: Networks of plausible inference*. San Mateo, CA: Kaufmann.

Raven, J. C. (1940). Matrix tests. *Mental Health, 1,* 10-18.

Reckase, M. D. (1997). A linear logistic multidimensional model for dichotomous item response data In W. J. van der Linden & R. K. Hambleton (Eds.), *Handbook on modern item response theory* (pp. 271-286). New York, NY: Springer-Verlag.

Snow, R. E., & Lohman, D. F. (1989). Implication of cognitive psychology for education measurement. In R. L. Linn (Ed.), *Educational Measurement* (3rd ed., pp. 263-331). New York, NY: Macmillan

Tatsuoka, K. K. (1983). Rule space: An approach for dealing with misconceptions based on item response theory. *Journal of Educational Measurement, 20,* 345-354.

Tatsuoka, K. K. (1985). A probabilistic model for diagnostic misconceptions in the pattern classification approach. *Journal of Educational Statistics, 10,* 55-73.

Tatsuoka, K. K. (1995). Architecture of knowledge structures and cognitive diagnosis: A statistical pattern recognition and classification approach. In P. D. Nichols, S. F. Chipman, & R. L. Brennan (Eds.), *Cognitively diagnostic assessment* (pp. 32-359). Hillsdale, NJ: Erlbaum.

von Davier, M. (2005). *A general diagnostic model applied to language testing data* (ETS Research Report: RR-05-16). Princeton, NJ: Educational Testing Service.

Williamson, D. M., Bauer, M., Steinberg, L. S., Mislevy, R. J., Behrens, J. T., & DeMark, S. F. (2004). Design rationale for a complex performance assessment. *International Journal of Testing, 4,* 303-332.

Wilson, M. (2005). *Constructing measures: An item response modeling approach.* Mahwah, NJ: Erlbaum.

CHAPTER 6

A COGNITIVE MODEL FOR THE ASSESSMENT OF HIGHER ORDER THINKING IN STUDENTS

Jacqueline P. Leighton

The assessment of student learning has become an increasingly specialized activity. In response to many external pressures, including federal legislation in the form of No Child Left Behind (NCLB, 2002) and international testing competitions such as the Programme for International Student Assessment (Organization for Economic Cooperation and Development, 2007), professional test developers and psychometricians are searching for innovative methods to develop standardized large-scale assessments, which measure the kinds of knowledge and skills that place students at the forefront of human intellectual mastery and economic growth (Hanushek, 2003). Teachers are also searching for better ways to instruct students in the classroom, assess their knowledge and skills, and prepare their path to newfound proficiency on state-wide and other large-scale assessments.

Knowledge and skills are often described as representing a range of complexity. Over 50 years ago, Bloom, Englehart, Furst, Hill, and Krath-

Assessment of Higher Order Thinking Skills, pp. 151–181

wohl (1956) outlined this range of complexity in the book, *Taxonomy of Educational Objectives, Handbook 1: The Cognitive Domain*. According to Bloom et al., *knowledge* represented the most basic type of cognition or level of thinking as it simply meant the student could recall or remember facts. Following this most basic level of thinking and in ascending order of complexity, more advanced levels included *comprehension, application, analysis, synthesis*, and *evaluation* (see Figure 6.1). The most sophisticated level of thinking, *evaluation*, meant that the student could make judgments about the value of ideas, solutions, or material. Inherent to this ordering is the expectation that the quality of human thinking is hierarchical such that a student cannot attain higher levels without first mastering previous levels,[1] and that assessment tasks can be designed to measure increasingly higher levels of thinking. For example, at the end of an elementary course in statistics, a student who only responds correctly to comprehension measures of central tendency can be said to have a lower level of proficiency than a student who can apply different concepts of central tendency to solve problems in novel situations.

Bloom's taxonomy has played a major role in the design of student assessment (both large-scale and classroom-based). In fact, Bloom's taxonomy is often used in tables of test specifications to identify the thinking levels students are expected to employ as they respond to test items (Downing & Haladyna, 2006; Gierl, 1997; Haladyna, 2004; Schmeiser & Welch, 2006; Sheppard, 2006). However, the use of this taxonomy does not assure that students will actually employ those thinking levels as they respond to test items. For example, Gierl found that there was, approximately, a 50% match between the thinking levels expected by item writers and the thinking levels used by Grade 7 students to solve large-scale math test items designed to reflect Bloom's taxonomy. Gierl concluded from the results of his study that Bloom's taxonomy did not provide an accurate framework to guide the development of test items intended to measure increasingly sophisticated levels of thinking in students. Likewise, Schmeiser and Welch (2006) state that "unfortunately, no current cognitive taxonomy seems to be supported by documented validation evidence" (p. 316).

Recent developments in the learning sciences indicate that measuring higher order thinking in students may be more challenging than anticipated (National Research Council, 2001). The challenge is threefold: first, educators and test developers (assessment specialists) must agree on what is meant by higher order thinking; second, once there is agreement about what levels of thinking can be rightly designated as higher order, these levels must be coordinated into a model or framework that can guide test item and assessment design; and third, items and assessments designed to measure higher order thinking in students must be evaluated for whether they in fact elicit expected levels of thinking. The purpose of

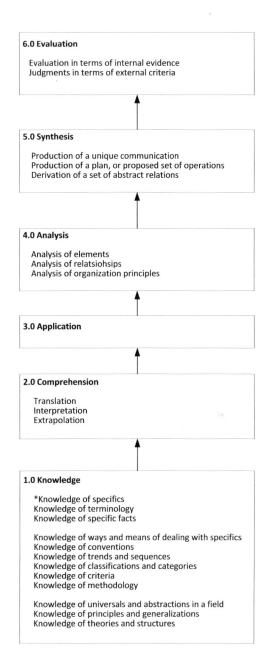

Figure 6.1.   A representation of Bloom's original taxonomy of educational objectives. *Wording of levels and skills as found in Krathwohl (2002, p. 213).

the present chapter, then, is threefold: to provide a working definition of higher order thinking based on the research literature; to identify a cognitive model of higher order thinking, which maps onto our working definition, and can serve as a framework for the design of student assessments; and to identify the types of assessments that can be expected to be appropriate measures of the knowledge and skills identified in both our definition and model of higher order thinking. Finally, the chapter concludes with a summary of the working definition and model presented to design assessments of higher order thinking.

SECTION 1—WHAT IS HIGHER ORDER THINKING?

In the first chapter of the *Cambridge Handbook of Thinking and Reasoning*, the cognitive scientists Holyoak and Morrison (2005) define thinking as "the systematic transformation of mental representations of knowledge to characterize actual or possible states of the world, often in the service of goals" (p. 2). This first chapter, "Thinking and Reasoning: A Reader's Guide," goes on to describe thinking in relation to more specific cognitive activities such as conceptualizing, remembering, reasoning, reading, deciding, and planning. According to Holyoak and Morrison, thinking is viewed as the superordinate term in relation to these other subordinate cognitive activities. The task of defining higher order thinking is extensive as the authors of this 858-page volume begin to describe the contents of the 33 chapters and 7 subparts of the volume; each subpart of the volume focusing on a specific aspect of thinking, and many of these describing higher order forms—the nature of human concepts, reasoning, judgement and decision making, problem solving, and complex learning. Clearly the study of thinking is broad and rich, and a comprehensive review of all the possible manifestations of higher order thinking extends far beyond what can be covered in a single chapter. However, in the balance of this section, *higher order thinking* is described from both an educational and psychological perspective, and then defined for the purpose of assessment design. The emphasis given to this section is deliberate; the single most important challenge in the assessment of higher order thinking has been failure in its description and definition (Haladyna, 1997, p. 97; see also Haladyna, 2004).

Higher Order Thinking: Performance or Underlying Process?

An educational perspective. Higher order thinking is a term often used in educational parlance. The term is associated with educational reform, standards-based assessment, and the measurement of complex thinking with alternative item formats (Koretz & Hamilton, 2006; Krathwohl, 2002; Lane & Stone, 2006; see also Sobocan, Groarke, Johnson, & Ellet, 2009). It is also a term that has been used in critiques of what standardized tests do not measure, and should be measuring. If one were to do an internet search of the term, many of the results would point to educational websites focusing on instruction and assessment. For example, an internet search of *higher order thinking* on Google leads to the Wikipedia entry that ties the origins of the term to the publication of Bloom et al.'s (1956) *Taxonomy of Educational Objectives*. Shown in Figure 6.1 is the original Bloom's taxonomy. As mentioned previously, an important observation to make about this taxonomy is that it is frequently used among teachers and assessment specialists to design test items measuring a range of thinking skills (Haladyna, 2004; Schmeiser & Welch, 2006). This is not surprising as the taxonomy was originally designed for the assessment of educational objectives; in particular, it was "conceived as a means of facilitating the exchange of test items among faculty at various universities in order to create banks of test items, each measuring the same educational objective" (Krathwohl, 2002, p. 212).

Normally the way Bloom's taxonomy is incorporated in assessment design is with a table of test specifications or blueprint. As an example, Figure 6.2 illustrates the 2008 test blueprint for the Grade 9 Mathematics Achievement Test for the province of Alberta in Canada (Alberta Education, 2008). A table of test specifications is a 2 by 2 matrix that shows the curricular content to be assessed crossed with the reporting category or level of thinking skills. The cells within the table of test specifications catalogue the items that measure the content by skill interaction. For example, as shown in Figure 6.2, there are four curricular content areas (e.g., number, patterns and relations, shape and space, and statistics and probability) and two levels of reporting category (e.g., knowledge and skills). Notice that the reporting category of knowledge is positioned as lower-order relative to the category of skills. The knowledge category includes the measurement of *recall* of facts, concepts, procedures, and terminology, all essentially measures of lower order thinking according to Bloom's taxonomy. In contrast, the skill category includes the measurement of *application* of facts, concepts, procedures, terminology, and relationships, all measures of higher order thinking according to Bloom's taxonomy.

Another observation to make about Bloom's taxonomy, at least in the way it is typically used by teachers and assessment specialists, is that it stresses the *performance* of higher order thinking. In other words, Bloom's taxonomy identifies the kinds of *behaviors* (i.e., application, analysis, synthesis, or evaluation) that should be observed in students if higher order

| Test Sections (Curricular Content Areas) | Reporting Category | | Number of items and Percentage of Released Test |
| | Knowledge | Skills | |
	Recall facts, concepts, procedures, and terminology	Apply facts, concepts, procedures, terminology, and relationships to solve problems in a variety of situations	
Number • Number Concepts • Number Operations	5, 36	4, 10, 13, 24, 34, NR1	**8** **(16%)**
Patterns and Relations • Patterns • Variables and Equations • Relations and Functions	21	6, 12, 15, 19, 20, 22, NR3	**8** **(16%)**
Shape and Space • Measurement • 3-D Objects and 2-D Shapes • Transformations	35, 43, 44	8, 14, 27, 33, NR6	**8** **(16%)**
Statistics and Probability • Data Analysis • Chance and Uncertainty	7, 37	30, 31, 32, NR5	**6** **(12%)**
Number of items and Percentage of Released Test	**8** **(16%)**	**22** **(44%)**	**30** **(60%)**

Figure 6. 2.   An exemplar of a test blueprint for 30 released items from the 2008 Grade 9 Mathematics Achievement Test in the Province of Alberta, Canada. Reprinted from Released 2008 achievement test: Mathematics Grade 9, Alberta Education, p. 20, 2008, with permission from Alberta Government.

thinking is being engaged. The emphasis placed on behavior or performance represents a difference from the way in which higher order thinking is conceptualized by other professionals, such as cognitive and developmental psychologists. In particular, cognitive and developmental psychologists do not often refer to 'higher order thinking' unless they are writing for educators about education. For example, in the 2005 *Cambridge Handbook of Thinking and Reasoning*, described in the preceding section, there is not a single chapter with the term higher order thinking in the title. This is not an omission but simply a difference in the way that cognitive and developmental psychologists order and classify thinking compared to teachers and assessment specialists.

A cognitive psychological perspective. While psychologists identify many types of thinking such as conceptualizing, remembering, reasoning, deciding, judging, and planning among others, many of them would argue that any form of thinking has the potential to be of higher order depending on its underlying process or structure. For example, consider the act of recall. According to Bloom's taxonomy, recall of knowledge is the lowest in the hierarchy of thinking skills. In contrast, for psychologists who study the development of expertise, recall often reflects the automation of knowledge and skill in response to a task, a desirable goal state achieved after many years of deliberate practice and indicative of well-organized and efficient underlying structures of understanding (e.g., J. Anderson & Schunn, 2000; Chi, Glaser, & Farr, 1988; Ericsson, 2006; Gobet, 2005; Holyoak & Morrison, 2005; Johnson-Laird, 2004; Kilpatrick, Swafford, & Findell, 2001; Kintsch & Kinstch, 2005; Shrager & Siegler, 1998). Likewise, Kintsch and Kintsch (2005) explain that a multiple choice item may elicit simple recall in a student who studied the material the night before and therefore can remember the correct answer, and probabilistic reasoning (and evaluation) in another student who is trying to eliminate incorrect response options based on the likelihood of their inaccuracy given the question. While the latter student may be evaluating, few would agree that the underlying structure of this manifestation of probabilistic reasoning is indicative of knowledge and skill mastery in the subject domain. It is therefore problematical for psychologists to say whether recall or evaluation always reflects lower order or higher order thinking, respectively, in the absence of more information about the task in which recall or reasoning is being applied and a student's learning history (Lewis & Smith, 1993).

In his 25 years of research on human cognition, J. Anderson (1996; see also, e.g., J. Anderson, 2007; Anderson, Bothell, Byrne, Douglass, Lebiere, & Qin, 2004) has consistently found evidence for the claim that all of human cognition, from simple recall to evaluation, and adaptive problem solving, is based on two types of underlying knowledge structures—knowledge of concepts (declarative) and knowledge of skills (procedural). What characterizes a form of thinking as lower order or higher order depends on the organization and cohesion (cross-referencing) of networks of declarative and procedural knowledge structures. In particular, skilled performers after years of extensive study develop highly organized, cohesive, and interconnected declarative and procedural knowledge networks that shape the interpretations they generate (i.e., mental representations) when presented with task information by influencing the task features they view as relevant to understanding a problem (see Chase & Simon,

1973; Chi, Feltovich, & Glaser, 1981; Ericsson, 2006, 2009; Gobet, 2005; Holyoak & Morrison, 2005; Johnson-Laird, 2004; Klahr, 2000; Newell & Simon, 1972; see also Lewis & Smith, 1993). For example, in a now classic study, Chi et al. (1981) found that when asked to classify physics problems, experts based their classifications on structural characteristics such as the rules or principles needed to solve the problems (e.g., conservation of energy), thereby showing their recognition of the key conceptual features; in contrast, novices classified the problems based on surface characteristics such as elements in background stories shared by some of the problems. Similar results have been found in other domains such as medicine, surgery, software design, history, arts, sports, and music (see Ericsson, 2009; and Ericsson, Charness, Feltovich, & Hoffman, 2006, for a review; Holyoak & Morrison, 2005). In addition to their highly organized and cohesive knowledge networks, skilled performers are uniquely characterized by vastly efficient search processes through long term working memory (Ericsson & Kintsch, 1995; Klahr, 2000). Rapid, directed search processes through long term working memory facilitate the efficient and effective consideration, selection, and implementation of strategies to solve problems. In light of such psychological advances in the underlying structure of thinking, revisions were made to the original Bloom's taxonomy (see L. Anderson et al., 2001).

Bloom's revised taxonomy and contemporary educational perspectives on higher order thinking. Shown in Figure 6.3 is the revised taxonomy proposed by L. Anderson et al. (2001). In the revised taxonomy, knowledge is distinguished from the other skill categories and identified as a separate dimension to underscore the role that knowledge plays in all levels of thinking. Consequently, in the revised taxonomy, knowledge includes four levels: factual knowledge, conceptual knowledge, procedural knowledge, and metacognitive knowledge. In addition to the knowledge dimension, there is a skill[2] dimension that includes six levels: remembering, understanding, applying, analyzing, evaluating, and creating. Some of these levels are new. For example, the lowest level of skill in Bloom's revised taxonomy is now labelled remembering, understanding is next and replaces the skill of comprehension used in the original taxonomy; applying and analyzing are kept as in the original, but now synthesis is replaced with evaluating, and a new skill, creating, is added to the top of the hierarchy. What the revised taxonomy allows for, then, is the ability to cross higher order forms of knowledge (e.g., conceptual knowledge) with higher order forms of skill (e.g., create). Overall, compared to the original, the revised taxonomy presents thinking as involving two dimensions instead of one, which brings it in more in line with the psychological research literature on the underlying structure of thinking.

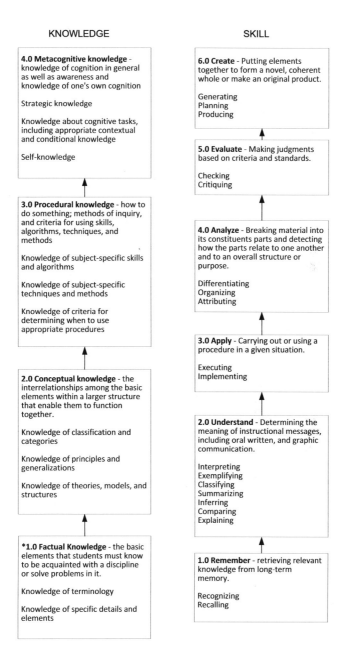

Figure 6.3.   A representation of Bloom's revised taxonomy of educational objectives. *Wording of levels and skills as found in Krathwohl (2002, pp. 214-215).

Although the revised taxonomy reflects advances in the underlying structure of thinking by distinguishing knowledge from skill, the hierarchy of skills continues to place remembering or recall at the lowest level. It is therefore of little wonder that teachers and assessment specialists schooled in either the original or revised version of Bloom's taxonomy continue to perceive *recall* of knowledge or *remembering* as a lower order thinking skill. Based on both taxonomies, it would seem that recall does not require the cognitive effort assumed of alternative forms of thinking such as understanding, applying, analyzing, evaluating, and creating. This is an aspect of both taxonomies that is not in line with psychological research on thinking.

Additional educational perspectives on higher order thinking can be found in the writings of Resnick (1987), Facione (1990), and more recently Zohar (2006; see also Williams, 2003). Empirical support for manifestations of higher order thinking can be found in Kuhn (2005), Quilici and Mayer (2002), and Pintrich and Schrauben (1992) among others. For example, Resnick (1987) indicates that higher order thinking has the following characteristics: it is nonalgorithmic, complex, effortful, and yields multiple solutions. Furthermore, she states that higher order thinking involves uncertainty, nuanced judgment, imposing meaning, application of multiple criteria, and self-regulation. According to the American Philosophical Association's *Delphi Report* (Facione, 1990), a term that is often used interchangeably with higher order thinking (Giancarlo-Gittens, 2009; Williams, 2003), critical thinking, is defined as consisting of six core components: interpretation, analysis, evaluation, inference, explanation, and self-regulation. Each of these six components is made up of additional components. For example, interpretation is made up of the sub-skills, categorization, decoding significance, and clarifying meaning. Found within the report is also a definition of critical thinking: "[It is] purposeful, self-regulatory judgement which results in interpretation, analysis, evaluation, and inference, as well as explanation of the evidential, conceptual, methodological, criteriological, or contextual considerations upon which judgement is based" (Facione, 1990, p. 2).

In a similar vein, Zohar (2006, p. 336; see also Zohar, 2004) describes higher order thinking as involving the traditional components of analysis, synthesis, and evaluation, but also newer components such as the construction of arguments, posing research questions, drawing comparisons, resolving nonalgorithmic complex problems, handling controversies, identifying implicit or hidden assumptions, categorizing, classifying, determining causal relationships, and the activities often associated with scientific inquiry, such as generating hypotheses, organizing experiments, planning for the control of variables, and drawing conclusions. In support of these latter inquiry skills especially, Kuhn (2005, p. 40; see also Kuhn,

2001; Kuhn & Dean, 2004; Zimmerman, 2007) identifies the following as important indicators of sound thinking across academic domains:

- identifying questions that can be answered by means of empirical investigations;
- designing and conducting empirical and/or scientific investigations;
- using appropriate tools and techniques to systematically gather, analyze, and interpret data (evidence);
- developing descriptions, explanations, predictions, and models using evidence; and
- thinking critically and logically to coordinate the relationships between evidence and explanations.

Defining Higher Order Thinking as Skilled Performance

That the term "higher order thinking" is not often used among cognitive and developmental psychologists does not mean that differences in thinking are not recognized. It is evident that such differences are recognized, otherwise research on expertise (e.g., Chi, Glaser, & Farr, 1988 Ericsson, 2006, 2009) or individual differences (e.g., Stanovich, 2009; Sternberg, 1999) would probably not exist. However, the level of analysis at which cognitive and developmental psychologists choose to order and categorize thinking is different from the level of analysis at which teachers and assessment specialists choose to order and categorize thinking. Although the revised form of Bloom's taxonomy reflects an attempt to bring the taxonomy more in line with the psychological literature on the structure of thinking, it continues to classify thinking skills as behaviors that can be unequivocally rated as either low or high. As already mentioned, cognitive and development psychologists prefer to focus on the underlying structures and processes of thinking (e.g., types of knowledge representations, strategies used to operate on representations, and combinatorial processes for transforming representations) to rate thinking as low or high. One focus is not better than the other, but each has implications for how higher order thinking is defined, modeled, and ultimately assessed.

While there are differences in how higher order thinking is conceptualized by educators and psychologists, in the present chapter, a definition is proposed that focuses on higher order thinking solely as the manifestation of *skilled performance*, and not as a category of thought based on its underlying structure or process (e.g., see Anderson et al., 2004; Ericsson,

2006; Johnson-Laird, 2004). Focusing on higher order thinking as skilled performance is chosen as it is the level of description typically considered and used in educational domains. Based on a synthesis of the multiple and complimentary perspectives discussed in the preceding section, common components emerge in the characterization of higher order thinking. According to these common components, our working definition of higher order thinking for the purpose of assessment design involves the following four core components of knowledge and skills:

1. inquiring or identifying questions, assumptions, or issues to investigate (e.g., student should be able to answer the question *what is to be verified, known, or investigated?*);

2. applying multiple and appropriate criteria and tools to systematically collect, analyze, and interpret evidence and/or data from a variety of perspectives (e.g., student should be able to answer the question *what/which are the best strategies for investigating claims to knowledge?*);

3. developing and/or generating coherent descriptions, inferences, predictions, explanations, evaluations, and/or arguments that are aligned with evidence and sensitive to logical and contextual considerations (e.g., student should be able to answer the question *what/which claims to knowledge does the evidence and/or data support?*); and

4. regulating and appreciating the cognitive effort required to substantiate claims to knowledge by being willing to use novel, non-algorithmic approaches to problem solving (see Facione, 1990; Kilpatrick et al., 2001; Kuhn, 2001, 2005; Resnick, 1987), recognizing the limitations of human information processing activities, and engaging in inquiry activities designed to evaluate claims to knowledge (e.g., student should be able to answer the question *is there value in seeking knowledge? What/how do strategies for investigating claims to knowledge enrich my process of knowing?*).

This latter, *self-regulatory* component has acquired increasing support in the literature as being instrumental in the application of higher order thinking (Baron, 2000; Kuhn & Dean, 2004; Murphy & Alexander, 2002; Resnick, 1987; Schommer & Walker, 1995; Schraw, 1998; Stanovich, 2009; Stanovich, Sá, & West, 2004; Winne, 1996). Resnick (1987) claims "we have good reason to believe that shaping [a] disposition to critical thought is central to developing higher order cognitive abilities in students" (p. 41).

According to Schraw (1998) regulation of cognition refers "to a set of activities that help students control their learning" (p. 114). Moreover, Baron (2000; see also Murphy & Alexander, 2002) explains that personal dispositions or self-regulatory habits toward open-minded thinking may represent an important variable in understanding higher order thinking, especially as required on formal reasoning tasks. For example, open-minded thinking that includes engaging in epistemological evaluativism (i.e., seeing knowledge as fluid and subject to empirical challenge), willingness to change perspectives, willingness to separate a problem or issue from its context, and the tendency to weigh alternative opinions and sources of evidence (see also Schommer & Walker, 1995; Stanovich, 2009) may spur individuals to seek additional sources of information as they reason on academic and nonacademic tasks. These personal dispositions are understood as signalling a person's values and goals in relation to information, tendency to self-regulate in the face of epistemic understanding, and need for cognition. In a test of the effect of personal dispositions for predicting performance on formal reasoning tasks, Stanovich et al. (2004) used an additive, multiscale instrument to measure students' dispositions to self-regulate, weigh new evidence in light of a highly favoured belief, spend the necessary time on a problem before giving up, and consider the opinion and thoughts of others to inform one's own opinion. Stanovich et al. found that students' personal disposition scores correlated significantly with their performance on seven reasoning tasks comprising a composite test score even after cognitive ability was controlled in the analysis.

Higher order thinking, then, comprises cognitive and dispositional, self-regulatory aspects. Not only is higher order thinking about the methods used to question and manipulate information but also about the effort expended and value attached to the possession of well-reasoned and coherent sets of knowledge and beliefs. Interestingly, while the self-regulatory component may be the linchpin in facilitating higher order thinking, it is a component that is not often measured in educational assessments (however, see Kuhn, Iordanou, & Wirkala, 2008, for a psychological measure of the disposition to evaluate multiple sources of information or perspectives). In fact, it is the one component of higher order thinking whose presence is less overtly observed and more often inferred from the observation of other components such as identifying questions, assumptions, or issues, applying multiple and appropriate criteria and tools for the systematic collection of evidence, and developing coherent descriptions, inferences, predictions, explanations, and/or evaluations about the evidence gathered. In the next section, a model for the assessment of higher order thinking is presented that reflects the working definition proposed in this section.

SECTION 2—A MODEL FOR THE ASSESSMENT OF
HIGHER ORDER THINKING

While components of higher order thinking were discussed in the previous section, leading to our working definition, there are surprisingly few formal models or illustrations of how these components relate or interact with each other. Exceptions are Bloom's original and revised taxonomies shown in Figures 6.1 and 6.3. Although both of Bloom's taxonomies show a relatively simple, linear hierarchy of skills, they are nonetheless useful in visually illustrating the relationships among skills. Another exception is Kuhn's (2001) model of knowing. In fact, Kuhn's model overlaps substantially with our working definition of higher order thinking, exemplifying many of its components as illustrated in Figure 6.4. For example, the first component in our working definition (i.e., inquiring or identifying questions, assumptions, or issues) is exemplified by what Kuhn labels *metalevel declarative knowing*, shown in the right-hand side of Figure 6.4. *Metalevel declarative knowing* requires isolating the objective of an investigation; that is, asking the appropriate questions and therefore distinguishing what is known from what is unknown. Toward this end, it is useful to recognize differences between facts, opinions, and claims; for example, a fact (e.g., the rate of diabetes is increasing among Americans) may lead to an opinion about how the fact originated (e.g., lack of exercise and overeating) but in order to substantiate the opinion as a claim, it must be supported with evidence. The second component (i.e., applying multiple and appropriate criteria and tools to systematically gather evidence), and the third component (i.e., developing and/or generating coherent descriptions, inferences about the evidence gathered) in our working definition are exemplified by Kuhn's *knowledge seeking strategies* and *metalevel procedural knowing*, shown in the middle and left-hand side of Figure 6.4, respectively. The *knowledge seeking strategies*, including inquiry, analysis, inference, and argument, reflect the skills needed not only to gather evidence but also to generate conclusions about the evidence gathered. *Metalevel procedural knowing* reflects an understanding of when, where, and why to use multiple and appropriate criteria for gathering evidence and how these skills relate to interpreting the evidence for the development of sound inferences. The fourth component in our working definition is reflected prominently in Kuhn's model. The self-regulatory component is exemplified by values of thinking, dispositions to apply these values, and even by the metalevel procedural knowledge required to answer the question: *what do knowing strategies accomplish?*

An advantage to mapping our working definition of higher order thinking to Kuhn's model of knowing is two-fold: first, Kuhn and others have collected substantial evidence in support of specific parts of the

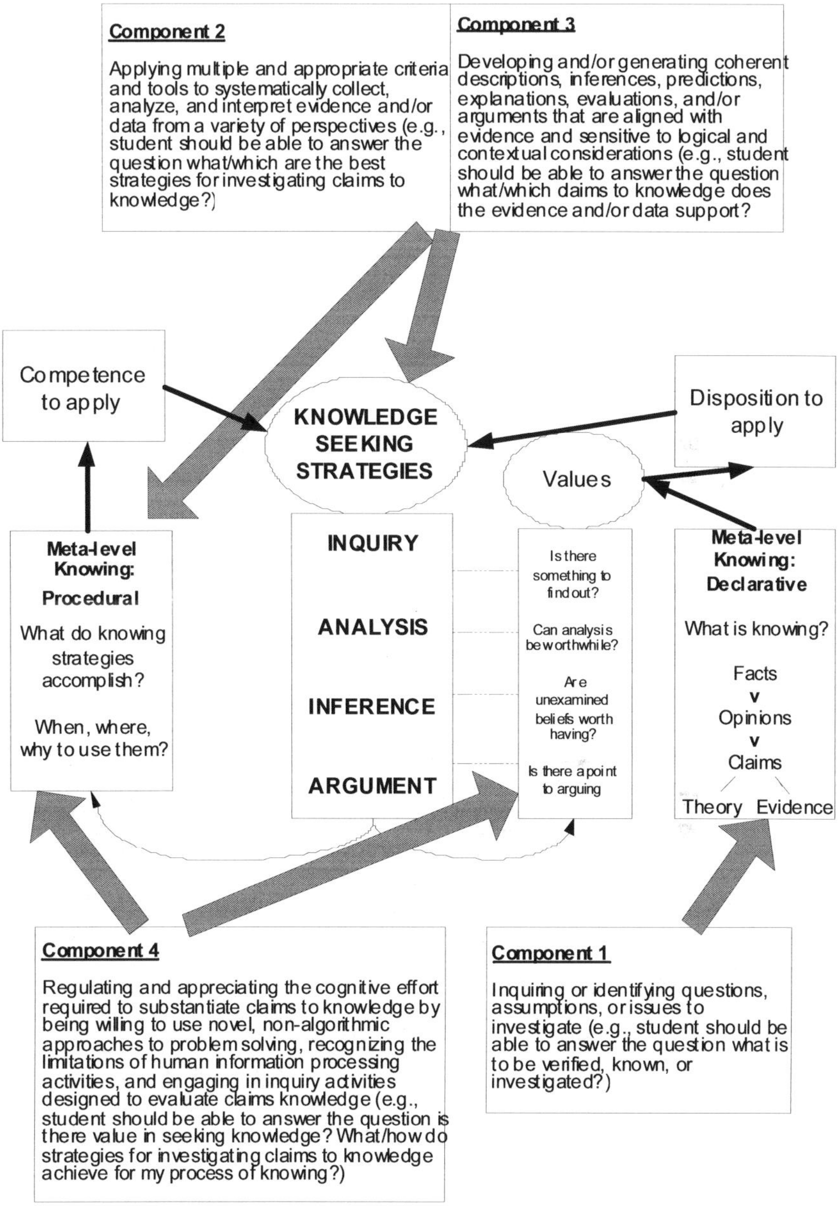

Component 2

Applying multiple and appropriate criteria and tools to systematically collect, analyze, and interpret evidence and/or data from a variety of perspectives (e.g., student should be able to answer the question what/which are the best strategies for investigating claims to knowledge?)

Component 3

Developing and/or generating coherent descriptions, inferences, predictions, explanations, evaluations, and/or arguments that are aligned with evidence and sensitive to logical and contextual considerations (e.g., student should be able to answer the question what/which claims to knowledge does the evidence and/or data support?

Competence to apply

Disposition to apply

KNOWLEDGE SEEKING STRATEGIES

Values

Meta-level Knowing: Procedural

What do knowing strategies accomplish?

When, where, why to use them?

INQUIRY

ANALYSIS

INFERENCE

ARGUMENT

Is there something to find out?

Can analysis be worthwhile?

Are unexamined beliefs worth having?

Is there a point to arguing

Meta-level Knowing: Declarative

What is knowing?

Facts
∨
Opinions
∨
Claims

Theory   Evidence

Component 4

Regulating and appreciating the cognitive effort required to substantiate claims to knowledge by being willing to use novel, non-algorithmic approaches to problem solving, recognizing the limitations of human information processing activities, and engaging in inquiry activities designed to evaluate claims knowledge (e.g., student should be able to answer the question is there value in seeking knowledge? What/how do strategies for investigating claims to knowledge achieve for my process of knowing?)

Component 1

Inquiring or identifying questions, assumptions, or issues to investigate (e.g., student should be able to answer the question what is to be verified, known, or investigated?)

Figure 6.4.   Working definition of higher order thinking mapped onto representation of Kuhn's (2001) model of knowing. Boxes show the four components proposed in our working definition and their links to the model.

model (e.g., see Zimmerman, 2007, for a review); second, the model helps to illustrate the relationships among higher order thinking components and, therefore clarifies and even provides ideas for ways in which to design assessments to measure higher order thinking. Although the model may not include all aspects of our working definition, for example, it does not include the role of complexity or nonalgorithmic thinking, it nevertheless provides a framework from which to begin envisaging the connections among higher order thinking components. One of the desirable features of Bloom's original and revised taxonomies is that it scaffolds for test developers, in the form of a visual illustration, the specific knowledge and skills that can be assessed and, perhaps most importantly, their interrelationships. A similar function is provided by Kuhn's model, except that it offers a more complex set of interrelationships among higher order components than the linear hierarchies illustrated by Bloom's taxonomies. In the next section, assessment formats designed to measure components of our working definition are discussed.

SECTION 3—ASSESSMENTS OF HIGHER ORDER THINKING

In the late 1980s, the question of how to assess higher order thinking began with earnest as the reform-minded, standards-based movement in the U.S. permeated the literature on educational assessment (Koretz & Hamilton, 2006; Lane & Stone, 2006). The focus of this reform-minded movement, which quickly spread to neighboring countries such as Canada, was on promoting all students to perform at high levels on state-wide large-scale assessments, improving education through measurement-driven instruction, and ensuring that item types elicited meaningful responses from students. In other words, the focus was on "high literacy" for all (Resnick, 1987). However, the measurement of higher order thinking has eluded teachers and test developers for years (Stiggins, Griswold, & Wikelund, 1989; Wiggins, 1989), and the challenge as expressed by Haladyna (1997) is substantial:

> the heart of this problem is our failure to define such terms as *critical thinking*, *problem solving*, *metacognition*, *reasoning*, and *abstract thinking*. Without adequate definitions and training, teachers lack the knowledge and skills to teach and test for these desirable but elusive human qualities. (p. 97, emphasis in original)

While definitions and models of higher order thinking have been generated over the years (e.g., Bloom's taxonomy), the real test may ultimately be whether such definitions and/or models can be used by teachers and assessment specialists to operationalize the design of psychometrically-sound assessments that do, in fact, measure the quality of thinking expected (see Lane & Stone, 2006; Leighton & Gierl, 2007). This is therefore an empirical issue that, so far, has garnered relatively little data (Ferrara & DeMauro, 2006; Haladyna, 2004; Leighton & Gierl, 2011; Schmeiser & Welch, 2006; Stiggins, 2004; see also Gierl, 1997).

Despite an absence of empirical evidence to show that models of higher order thinking can be used to generate assessments that elicit these knowledge and skills, there has been general agreement that *performance items* or tests may be the better format to use for assessing higher order thinking (Lane & Stone, 2006). A performance item or test (if based on many items) involves a "constructed-response format where either a high-inference rating scale or a low-inference observation method is used to score the response" (Haladyna, 1997, p. 94). Examples of performance item formats include portfolios, projects, research papers, reviews or critiques, peer or self-assessments, short-answer completion questions, visual observation, and writing samples. One of the attractive features of performance tests, according to Fitzpatrick and Morrison (1971), is that they simulate to a relatively high degree the criterion for the test. For example, an essay is normally considered a performance item because the substantive and technical skills required to write a good essay for a school assignment are similar as those required by a professional writer to compose a good story. Performance tests are therefore believed to be better candidates for eliciting and measuring higher order thinking skills than traditional multiple choice items because they require the complexity of skills of real-life problem solving.

Although performance items are designed to elicit nonalgorithmic and complex forms of thinking as they often provide students with choices in the structure, content, and presentation of their responses, the empirical evidence suggests that these items may not be functioning as expected (Koretz & Hamilton, 2006; Lane & Stone, 2006). For example, Koretz and Hamilton state that "several studies have demonstrated that performance tests frequently fail to tap the processes and skills their developers intended ... and that they are not immune to score inflation" (pp. 535-536). A possible reason for the inconsistency in how well performance items elicit desired higher order thinking skills may have to do with confusion about the nature of these knowledge and skills. For example, in a study to determine whether performance items in science elicited either basic knowledge and reasoning, spatial-mechanical reasoning, or quantitative reasoning skills in students, Ayala, Yin, Schultz, and Shavelson (2002) found that performance items did not consistently elicit the thinking skills expected in students. For example, a task, called *Daytime Astronomy*, was designed to elicit spatial-mechanical reasoning but students were found to be primarily using quantitative reasoning to solve it. Findings such as these raise questions about whether assessment specialists need more background information or training about the types of tasks, including their content and their development, that elicit higher order thinking skills. Lane and Stone (2006) indicate that these findings underscore the need to validate the thinking skills measured by performance items, using think-aloud and/or cognitive labs, just as one would validate traditional multiple choice items.

Item Formats Expected to Measure Higher Order Thinking Skills

Although any measure of higher order thinking requires a rigorous process of validation, there are certain item features that can be *expected* to elicit components of higher order knowledge and skills. Toward this end, both multiple choice and performance items can be designed to measure components of higher order thinking (Haladyna, 1997, 2004). These item development procedures can be used by classroom teachers in their design of unit exams or by test developers in their design of standardized items for large-scale assessments. In the next section, specific item features for measuring higher order knowledge and skills, such as the components in our working definition, are presented.

Multiple choice items. Developing multiple choice items involves not only clearly worded stems or questions, but also clearly appropriate correct or best answers, and distracters that are sufficiently plausible to attract those examinees who have not mastered the knowledge and skills being measured. Haladyna (1997) suggests using *item shells* or specific stem wording to elicit certain forms of higher order thinking skills in relation to the content being measured. For example, to measure understanding, Haladyna recommends using specific stem wording such as *Which best defines_____?* or *Which is characteristic (or uncharacteristic) of _____?* or *Which of the following is an example of _____?* After this specific wording is used to elicit understanding, the relevant content of interest is inserted such as "Which of the following is an example of *a parameter*?" While these specific item stems map more closely to Bloom's taxonomy than to Kuhn's model described in the previous section, the stems can be modified to elicit the components in our working definition. For example, to probe the first component, that is, identifying questions, assumptions or issues, an item could be worded as follows: *Which question best identifies _____?* or *Which is characteristic of the assumption made in _____?* or *Which of the following issues is an example of _____?* The relevant content of interest would then be inserted in the blank.

Haladyna (1997, p. 68) recommends the following stem wording to elicit critical thinking (evaluating), critical thinking (predicting), and problem solving:

1. *Critical thinking (evaluating)*: What is most effective (appropriate) for___? Which is better (worse) ___? What is the most effective method for ___? What is the most critical step in this procedure___? Which is unnecessary in this procedure___?
2. *Critical thinking (predicting)*: What would happen if ___? If this happens, what should you do ___? On the basis of ___what should you do? Given___, what is the primary cause of ___?
3. *Problem solving (given a scenario)*: What is the nature of the problem? What do you need to solve this problem? What is a possible solution? Which is a solution? Which is the most effective (efficient) solution? Why is ___ the most effective (efficient) solution?

These stem wordings could be modified to measure components two and three of our working definition. For example, to measure component two of our definition, that is, applying multiple and appropriate criteria and tools to gather evidence, an examinee could be presented with a research scenario or problem and asked to answer questions such as *What is the most effective criteria (or method) for evaluating this claim (or answering this research question)? Which technique is better for collecting (or inquiring or analyzing or interpreting) ____?* Questions designed to measure component three might include *Given the information ___, which of the following inferences (or explanations or evaluations) would you make?* or *Why is ____ the most effective argument given the data?* "Why" questions in particular have been found to elicit higher levels of thought (see Kilpatrick et al., 2001; Kintsch & Kintsch, 2005).

The next task is to design distracters that are attractive to students who have not mastered the high level of knowledge or skill being measured by the item. Generating such distracters is challenging. One method for accomplishing this task, which also can provide useful information about the learning difficulties students are experiencing, is to generate distracters that reflect student misconceptions or faulty ways of conceptualizing the material (see Briggs, Alonzo, Schwab, & Wilson, 2006). For example, in scientific inquiry, the control of variables is a critical skill for generating useful data about the relationship between two variables. In a question designed to probe for knowledge of this skill, examinees could be asked *Which procedure is better for inquiring about the nature of the relationship between the following variables ___?* The distracters could include procedures that fail to control for the confounding variables mentioned in the background story of the item. In addition to the use of key wording in the stem and the inclusion of relevant, and appropriate distracters, well-established guidelines for developing multiple choice items should also be followed (e.g., varying the position of the keyed response, keeping alternatives independent, keeping length of alternatives approximately the same, see Haladyna, 2004, for a comprehensive review). Once these items are developed, a major benefit is that scoring is objective and complaints about the consistency of grading procedures are rare. In the next section, specific features of performance items are discussed for measuring higher order thinking and scoring responses.

Performance items. Haladyna (1997) lists 11 decisions that need to be made when performance items are being designed; for example, developers need to ask: Should the task require responses that integrate multiple subject-matters? Is process or product or both being evaluated? What is the meaningful context for the task? Are the instructions clear? If materials are to be provided, what type and how many should be provided? Are there time limits? What is the appropriate scope or length for the response? Are students able to consult with each other? Or collaborate? Is the response considered a final draft or is feedback allowed? Can students use computers to work on their task?

An example of a performance task developed by Kuhn et al. (2008) to measure students' skills at *using data* about risk factors to *make predictions* about avalanches (i.e., component three of our working definition) included: (a) a chart containing both visual and textual data about a set of five factors (three causal variables and two noncausal) associated with the risk of avalanche; (b) the context of the task, as shown in Figure 6.5, which included instructions prompting students to use the given data to make predictions about the risk of an avalanche; and (c) a reflection sheet for recording the variables believed to be causal and justifying predictions. Kuhn et al.'s performance task offers an opportunity to illustrate Haladyna's list of 11 decisions that need to be made in relation to the design of performance items. For example, Kuhn's performance task measured non-integrated higher order thinking skills as students worked primarily in the science domain to evaluate data, and generate defensible predictions about the risk of an avalanche; although both process and product were requested, students' justifications were used for informational purposes and only students' predictions were graded; a meaningful context in science (e.g., risk of avalanches) was selected and it was expected that students would complete the assignment during the time limits of the study; students were provided with verbal and written instructions, which were included in the visual and textual data they were given about the set of five variables to consider in relation to predicting outcomes; students were guided in the scope of their responses by the questions and spaces included in the reflection sheet provided; consultation with teachers and/

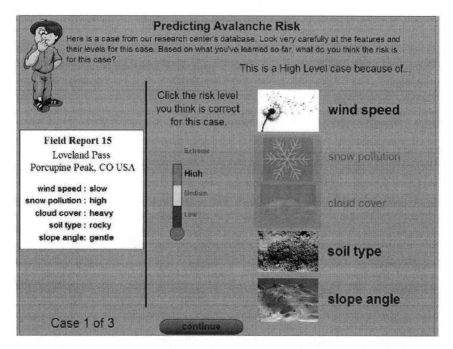

Figure 6.5. The performance item (case 1 of 3) used by Kuhn, Iordanou, Pease, & Wirkala (2008). Reprinted from *Cognitive Development*, 23, Kuhn, D., Iordanou, K., Pease, M., & Wirkala, C., Beyond control of variables: What needs to develop to achieve skilled scientific thinking? p. 438, 2008, with permission from Elsevier.

or the experimenter was not allowed but some students were allowed to work collaboratively in pairs; and, finally, the task was presented via computer (see Figure 6.5 for the first of three tasks presented).

A major hurdle in the development of performance items is the creation of adequate scoring criteria to evaluate responses. Therefore, the next step to consider in the development and use of performance items is the point values and the criteria or scoring rubric for grading responses. Rating scales are the tools of choice for recording observations about student performance and classifying responses into levels or categories; especially for performance items that involve extended work samples such as portfolios, projects, research papers, reviews or critiques, visual observation, and writing samples (Haladyna, 1997). While there are a variety of scales as shown in Figures 6.6 and Table 6.1, such as the numerical, graded-category, and descriptive rating scales, the latter is frequently prescribed because it involves richer-level descriptions of the perfor-

(a)

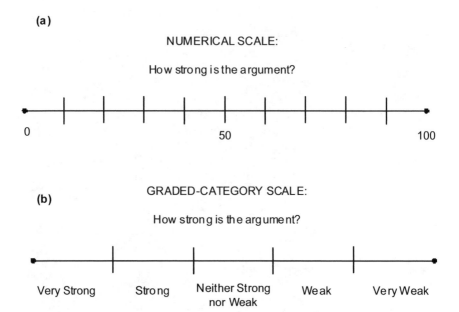

Figure 6.6.   Examples of numerical (a) and graded-category (b) scales to rate strength of an argument.

mance being evaluated compared to the other scales, and therefore promotes consistency in its use.

The benefits of the descriptive scale are reaped when considerable effort is expended to generate clear and accurate descriptions of performance. Decisions need to be made about (a) whether to generate a holistic versus an analytic descriptive rating scale, (b) whether it will be generic or task-specific in its relation to the performance being evaluated, and (c) how many point values to include. Holistic scales frequently involve singular, global judgements about, for example, the writing ability reflected in an essay. Analytic scales frequently involve localized judgements about specific categories of writing ability (e.g., strength of arguments, cohesion or logic, grammar, and style or format); each of the analytical categories would comprise a separate rating scale. Furthermore, generic descriptive scales can be applied to a variety of tasks within a subject domain, whereas task-specific scales are developed for single tasks. The number of point values to include in graded-category and descriptive scales should allow raters to adequately differentiate among different levels of performance. Therefore, four to seven point values (as shown in Figures 6.6b and Table 6.1) are often recommended because fewer values have been found to

**Table 6.1. Sample Descriptive Rating Scale
(Holistic and Generic) to Rate Strength of an Argument**

	Scoring Category
U	***Cannot be scored*** because the paper is totally illegible or obviously not written on the assigned topic.
1	***No real argument or extremely disjointed and weak.*** Fails to identify or analyze most of the important features of the argument. Although some analysis is present, it is largely disjointed and suffers from development of ideas. There is little, if any support provided for choice of premises and connection to conclusion.
2	***A reasonably well articulated argument.*** Is able to identify and capably analyze some important features of the argument. Although some analysis is present, only some of it is organized and developed. Parts are inconsistent. There is brief support provided for choice of premises and connection to conclusion.
3	***A good argument.*** Clearly identifies some to most important features of the argument and analyzes these features. Analysis presented is organized and most of the analysis is developed for the reader to show consistency. There is systematic support for most of the premises presented and the connection to conclusion is articulated clearly.
4	***An excellent argument.*** Clearly identifies and analyzes all features of the argument. Analysis is presented smoothly, insightfully, and development shows depth, consistency, cogency and originality of ideas and evidentiary support. There is systematic logical, support and elaboration for all premises and connections to conclusions. There is not second-guessing on what intent or ideas are being conveyed.

restrict the number of possible distinctions that can be made about the performance (DeVellis, 2003) and more than seven tends to be too many for practical use. Analytic and task-specific descriptive rating scales, with four to seven points, are the types of scales most often recommended for consistency, accuracy of use, and quality of diagnostic feedback provided to students about their performance. However, they are also most time-consuming and expensive to develop.

In the performance task shown in Figure 6.5, Kuhn et al. (2008) did not use a rating scale to grade responses as the task required short-answer responses (i.e., the identification of the variables believed to be causal in the risk of an avalanche) that were relatively simple to grade. Students were therefore evaluated according to (a) the number of variables they listed as causal, and (b) their consistency in listing specific variables as causal (or not causal) across three cases or versions of the task. The justifications provided by students for their selections were not graded in the study as the investigators requested this information only as background material for the predictions made. However, if the justifications had been graded, a rating scale would have been required. If a scale had been used to grade the student justifications, Kuhn et al. would have needed a minimum of two raters, working independently, to evaluate the justifications. The *reliability* of ratings made by each rater would have been examined for intrarater consistency; that is, the consistency of each rater for evaluating justifications (performances) across students (e.g., rater A graded Sally's justification, which was similar to Bob's justification, equivalently) and across time (e.g., rater A was consistent in his or her rating of a certain quality or level of justification across multiple occasions).

The *inter-rater consistency* of rater A and B's ratings would also have been examined to determine the proportion of agreement between the raters in their evaluation (grading) of justifications (see McIntire & Miller, 2007). Haladyna (1997) outlines four ways to improve inter-rater consistency and reliability (intrarater consistency) of ratings: (1) develop clear and specific descriptive rating scales, (2) train raters on the proper meaning and interpretation of point values and performance category-level descriptions, (3) use as many performance categories as is appropriate for the performance being evaluated, and (4) use between four to seven point values for each category level. Training raters on the proper interpretation and use of ratings scales is critical. Biases such as the tendency to give high ratings or low ratings without discriminating differences in performance or to be influenced by boredom or first impressions can often skew the interpretation and evaluation of performances. Ultimately, both multiple choice and performance items can be designed to measure higher order thinking in students. However, whether or not an item is successful at eliciting a specific form of thinking in students is an empirical matter, which needs to be investigated with proper validation techniques (see Kane, 2006; Lane & Stone, 2006).

SECTION 3—SUMMARY

Although the assessment of higher order thinking has proven to be elusive (Haladyna, 1997; Lane & Stone, 2006), there is value in continuing our attempts to define and measure this construct. Higher order thinking is the "high literacy" of educational outcomes (Resnick, 1987) and it will require extensive and repeated formulations to define it and measure it appropriately. It is no secret that the push for the teaching and assessment of higher order thinking is partly driven by its association to economic growth (Hanushek, 2003). If this were not the case, countries would not be competing and mobilizing their resources to revamp and upgrade school systems that underperform on international assessments that purport to measure these sophisticated skills. Kuhn (1992, p. 202) comments on the sophistication of these skills by reminding us of a continuum of knowing: "At one pole, knowing prevails in the comfortable ignorance of the knower never having considered that things could be otherwise. At the other pole, knowing is an ongoing, effortful *process* of evaluation, one that the ever-present possibility of new evidence and new arguments leaves never completed." However, while many assessments might include test items designed to measure higher order thinking, there is often little, if any, empirical evidence offered to show that students actually engage in higher order thinking when they respond to the items (Schmeiser & Welch, 2006). Validating measures, both classroom or large-scale, of higher order thinking is as important as their development since there is no guarantee that specific item features or item formats (e.g., performance items) will necessarily elicit the desired skills and responses of interest (Koretz & Hamilton, 2006; Lane & Stone, 2006).

Decades of empirical research on the topic of higher order thinking have made it evident that some components are central to its definition. In this chapter, a working definition of higher order thinking based on *skilled performance* was presented. This definition focused on the overt activities educators can observe and measure such as the tendency for students to ask questions, apply multiple and appropriate criteria and tools to systematically collect, analyze, and interpret evidence from a variety of perspectives, and develop coherent descriptions, inferences, predictions, explanations, evaluations, and arguments that are aligned with the evidence gathered. An additional component to our definition is students' ability to regulate and appreciate the cognitive effort required to substantiate claims to knowledge by being willing to use novel, nonalgorithmic approaches to problem solving. Although this latter component is covert and not often directly evaluated, it is considered to be instrumental in facilitating students' tendencies to exercise the other three components (i.e., asking questions, gathering evidence, and interpreting evidence to generate sound inferences).

In addition to the definition of higher order thinking, a model of how these components inter-related was offered. It was considered important to map the components of the definition to a model so as to provide a visual illustration of the links among components that then might facilitate the design and development of items to measure higher order thinking. Bloom's taxonomy has been used by assessment specialists for decades as a tool with which to organize the measurement of cognitive skills. One of the desirable qualities of Bloom's taxonomy is that it provides a straightforward representation of the hierarchy of skills. By mapping the components of our definition to Kuhn's model of knowing, the intention was to offer the support or scaffolding needed by teachers and assessment specialists to see the interaction among components for ease of use in the design and development of test items. Finally, a discussion of the item features, for both multiple choice and performance items, that are recommended to measure higher order thinking was provided. The recommendations are well-established and have been used by assessment specialists to develop standardized items and can also be used by class-room teachers to design assessments or unit tests. A word of caution, how-ever, is in order. Future research needs to focus on investigating and validating how well definitions and models of higher order thinking translate into the design and development of well-functioning test items. Although there is empirical evidence in support of the components included in the definition presented in this chapter and for Kuhn's model of knowing (e.g., see Zimmerman, 2007, for a review), there needs to be a concomitant focus on gathering evidence to help determine whether the model-based measurement of higher order thinking is indeed feasible, accurate, and most importantly useful.

ACKNOWLEDGMENTS

Preparation of this chapter was supported by a grant to the author from the Social Sciences and Humanities Research Council of Canada (SSHRC Grant No. 410-2007-1142). Grantees undertaking such projects are encouraged to express freely their professional judgment. This paper, therefore, does not necessarily represent the positions or the policies of the Canadian government, and no official endorsement should be inferred. Correspondence pertaining to this chapter should be directed to Jacque-line P. Leighton by airmail at 6-110 Education North, Centre for Research in Applied Measurement and Evaluation (CRAME), Dept. of Educational Psychology, Faculty of Education, University of Alberta, Edmonton, Alberta, CANADA T6G 2G5 or e-mail at jacqueline.leighton@ualberta.ca

NOTES

1. Some educational scholars disagree with the proposal that thinking skills are ordered or hierarchical (see Nitko & Brookhart, 2007; see also Zohar, Degani, & Vaaknin, 2001). Although it is beyond the scope of the present chapter to review the evidence in relation to this claim, it is a topic that is not settled and is in need of additional research. Even cognitive scientists have differing perspectives, for example, Gobet (2005; see also Gobet & Lane, 2007) contends that based on his simulation work with CHREST knowledge is ordered and, therefore, teaching of knowledge and skills should follow a simple to complex sequence. However, J. Anderson (1987)

suggests, based on his ACT-R model, that sequencing problems during instruction based on complexity should not influence performance.

2. In Airasian et al. (2001), the skill dimension is called "cognitive process" but I will not use this term in the present chapter so as to not confuse the Airasian et al. use of the term 'process' with the way in which many psychologists use the term, which often connotes underlying cognitive structures.

REFERENCES

Alberta Education. (2008). *Released 2008 achievement test: Mathematics Grade 9.* Author.

Anderson, L. W., Krathwohl, D. R., Airasian, P. W., Cruikshank, K. A., Mayer, R. E., Pintrich, et al. (2001). *A taxonomy for learning, teaching, and assessing: A revision of Bloom's taxonomy of educational objectives.* New York, NY: Longman.

Anderson, J. R. (1987). Production systems, learning, and tutoring. In R. Neeches (Ed.), *Production systems models of learning and development* (pp. 437-458). Cambridge, MA: MIT Press.

Anderson, J. R. (1996). ACT: A simple theory of complex cognition. *American Psychologist, 51,* 355-365.

Anderson, J. R. (2007). *How Can the Human Mind Occur in the Physical Universe?* New York, NY: Oxford University Press.

Anderson, J. R., Bothell, D., Byrne, M. D., Douglass, S., Lebière, C., & Qin, Y. (2004). An integrated theory of the mind. *Psychological Review, 111,* 1036-1060.

Anderson, J. R., & Schunn, C. D. (2000). Implications of the ACT-R learning theory: No magic bullets. In R. Glaser (Ed.), *Advances in instructional psychology: Educational design and cognitive science* (Vol. 5, pp. 1-33). Mahwah, NJ: Erlbaum.

Ayala, C. C., Yin, Y., Schultz, S., & Shavelson, R. (2002). *On science achievement from the perspective of different types of tests: A multidimensional approach to achievement validation* (CSE Technical Report 572). Los Angeles, CA: UCLA, Center for Research on Evaluation, Standards, and Student Testing.

Baron, J. (2000). *Thinking and deciding* (3rd ed.). New York, NY: Cambridge University Press.

Bloom, B., Englehart, M., Furst, E., Hill, W., & Krathwohl, D. (1956). *Taxonomy of educational objectives: The classification of educational goals. Handbook I: Cognitive domain.* New York, NY: Longmans, Green.

Briggs, D. C., Alonzo, A. C., Schwab, C., & Wilson, M. (2006). Diagnostic assessment with ordered multiple-choice items. *Educational Assessment, 11*(1), 33–63.

Chase, W. G., & Simon, H. A. (1973). Perception in chess. *Cognitive Psychology, 4,* 55-81.

Chi, M., Feltovich, P., & Glaser, R. (1981). Categorization and representation of physics problems by experts and novices. *Cognitive Science, 5,* 121-152.

Chi, M. T. H., Glaser, R., & Farr, M. J. (Eds.). (1988). *The nature of expertise.* Hillsdale, NJ: Erlbaum.

DeVellis, R. F. (2003). *Scale development: Theory and applications* (2nd ed.). Thousand Oakes, CA: SAGE.

Downing, S. M., & Haladyna, T. M. (Eds.). (2006). *Handbook of test development.* Mahwah, NJ: Erlbaum.

Ericsson, K. A. (2006). Protocol analysis and expert thought: Concurrent verbalizations of thinking during experts' performance on representative tasks. In K. A. Ericsson, N. Charness, P. J. Feltovich, & R. R. Hoffman (Eds.), *The Cambridge handbook of expertise and expert performance* (pp. 223-241). New York, NY: Cambridge University Press.

Ericsson, K. A. (Ed.). (2009). *Development of professional expertise: Toward measurement of expert performance and design of optimal learning environments.* New York, NY: Cambridge University Press.

Ericsson, K. A., Charness, N., Feltovich, P. J., & Hoffman, R. R. (Eds.). (2006). *The Cambridge handbook of expertise and expert performance.* New York, NY: Cambridge University Press.

Ericsson, K. A., & Kintsch, W. (1995). Long-term working memory. *Psychological Review, 102,* 211-245.

Facione, P. (1990). *Critical thinking: A statement of expert consensus for purposes of educational assessment and instruction. Executive summary: The Delphi report.* Millbrae, CA: Academic Press.

Ferrara, S., & DeMauro, G. E. (2006). Standardized assessment of individual achievement in K-12. In R. L. Brennan (Ed.), *Educational measurement* (4th ed., pp. 579-621). Westport, CT: National Council on Measurement in Education and American Council on Education.

Fitzpatrick, R., & Morrison, E. J. (1971). Performance and product evaluation. In R.L. Thorndike (Ed.), *Educational Measurement* (2nd ed., pp. 237-270). Washington, DC: American Council on Education.

Giancarlo-Gittens, C. (2009). Assessing critical dispositions in an ear of high stakes standardized testing. In J. Sobocan, L. Groarke, R. Johnson, & F. Ellet Jr. (Eds.), *Critical thinking education and assessment: Can higher order thinking be tested?* (pp. 17-34). London: The Althouse Press.

Gierl, M. J. (1997). Comparing the cognitive representations of test developers and students on a mathematics achievement test using Bloom's taxonomy. *Journal of Educational Research, 91,* 26-32.

Gobet, F. (2005). Chunking models of expertise: Implications for education. *Applied Cognitive Psychology, 19,* 183–204.

Gobet, F., & Lane, P. (2007). How do order effects arise in a cognitive model? In T. O'Shea, E. Lehtinen, F. E. Ritter, & P. Langley (Eds.), *Order effects in learning* (pp. 107-118). New York, NY: Oxford University Press.

Haladyna, T. M. (1997). *Writing test items to evaluate higher order thinking.* Boston, MA: Allyn and Bacon.

Haladyna, T. M. (2004). *Developing and validating multiple-choice test items* (3rd ed.). Mahwah, NJ: Erlbaum.

Hanushek, E. A. (2003). The failure of input-based schooling policies. *The Economic Journal, 113,* 64-98.

Holyoak, K. J., & Morrison, R. G. (Eds.). (2005). *The Cambridge handbook of thinking and reasoning.* New York, NY: Cambridge University Press.

Johnson-Laird, P. N. (2004). Mental models and reasoning. In J. P. Leighton & R. J. Sternberg's (Eds.), *Nature of reasoning* (pp. 169-204). New York, NY: Cambridge University Press.

Kane, M. T. (2006). Validation. In R. L. Brennan (Ed.), *Educational measurement* (4th ed., pp. 17-64). Westport, CT: National Council on Measurement in Education and American Council on Education.

Kilpatrick, J., Swafford, J., & Findell, B. (Ed.). (2001). *Adding It Up: Helping Children Learn Mathematics.* Washington, DC: National Academies Press.

Kintsch, W., & Kintsch, E. (2005). Comprehension. In S. G. Paris & S. A. Stahl (Eds.), *Children's reading comprehension and assessment* (pp. 71-92). Mahwah, NJ: Erlbaum.

Klahr, D. (2000). *Exploring science: The cognition and development of discovery processes.* Cambridge, MA: MIT Press.

Koretz, D. M., & Hamilton, L. S. (2006). Testing for accountability in K-12. In R. Brennan (Ed.), *Educational Measurement* (4th ed., pp. 531-578). Washington, DC: American Council on Education.

Krathwohl, D. R. (2002). A revision of Bloom's taxonomy: An overview. *Theory into Practice, 41,* 212-218.

Kuhn, D. (1992). Piaget's child as scientist. In H. Beilin & P. B. Pufall (Eds.), *Piaget's theory: Prospects and possibilities* (pp. 185-208) Hillsdale, NJ: Erlbaum.

Kuhn, D. (2001). How do people know? *Psychological Science, 12,* 1–8.

Kuhn, D. (2005). *Education for thinking.* Cambridge, MA: Harvard University Press.

Kuhn, D., & Dean, D. (2004). Connecting scientific reasoning and causal inference. *Journal of Cognition & Development, 5,* 261–288.

Kuhn, D., Iordanou, K., Pease, M., & Wirkala, C. (2008). Beyond control of variables: What needs to develop to achieve skilled scientific thinking? *Cognitive Development, 23,* 435-451.

Lane, S., & Stone, C.A. (2006). Performance assessment. In R. Brennan (Ed.), *Educational Measurement* (4th ed., pp. 387-431). Washington, DC: American Council on Education

Leighton, J. P., & Gierl, M. J. (Eds.). (2007). *Cognitive diagnostic assessment for education. Theories and applications.* Cambridge, MA: Cambridge University Press.

Lewis, A., & Smith, D. (1993). Defining higher order thinking. *Theory into Practice, 32,* 131-137.

Leighton, J. P., & Gierl, M. J. (2011). *The learning sciences in educational assessment.* Cambridge, MA: Cambridge University Press.

McIntire, S. A., & Miller, L. A. (2007). *Foundations of psychological testing: A practical approach* (2nd ed.). Thousand Oaks, CA: SAGE.

Murphy, P. K., & Alexander, P. A. (2002). What Counts? The predictive powers of subject-matter knowledge, strategic processing, and interest in domain-specific performance. *Journal of Experimental Education, 70,* 197-214.

National Research Council. (2001). *Knowing what students know: The science and design of educational assessment.* J. Pellegrino, N. Chudowsky, & R. Glaser (Eds.), *Committee on the foundations of assessment.* Washington, DC: National Academy Press, Board on Testing and Assessment, Center for Education.

Newell, A., & Simon, H. A. (1972). *Human problem solving.* Princeton, NJ: Prentice-Hall.

Nitko, A. J., & Brookhart, S. M. (2007). Educational Assessment of Students (5th ed.). Upper Saddle River, NJ: Pearson Education.

No Child Left Behind Act of 2002, Pub Law No. 107-110 (2002, January). Retrieved from http://www.ed.gov/policy/elsec/leg/esea02/107-110.pdf

Organization for Economic Cooperation and Development (2007, February). PISA—the OECD Programme for International Student Assessment. Retrieved from http://www.oecd.org/dataoecd/51/27/37474503.pdf

Pintrich, P. R., & Schrauben, B. (1992). Students' motivational beliefs and their cognitive engagement in classroom academic tasks. In D. H. Schunk & J. Meece (Eds.), *Student perceptions in the classroom* (pp. 149-179). Hillsdale, NJ: Erlbaum.

Quilici, J. H., & Mayer, R. E. (2002). Teaching students to recognize structural similarities between statistics word problems. *Applied Cognitive Psychology, 16*, 325-342.

Resnick, L. B. (1987). *Education and learning to think.* Washington, DC: National Academy Press.

Schmeiser, C. B., & Welch, C. J. (2006). Test development. In R. L. Brennan (Ed.), *Educational measurement* (4th ed., pp. 307-353). Westport, CT: National Council on Measurement in Education and American Council on Education.

Schommer, M., & Walker, K. (1995). Are epistemological beliefs similar across domains? *Journal of Educational Psychology, 87*, 424-432.

Schraw, G. (1998). Promoting general metacognitive awareness. *Instructional Science, 26*, 113-125.

Shrager, J., & Siegler, R. S. (1998). SCADS: A model of children's strategy choices and strategy discoveries. *Psychological Science, 9*, 405-410.

Sheppard, L.A. (2006). Classroom assessment. In R. L. Brennan (Ed.), *Educational measurement* (4th ed., pp. 623-646). Westport, CT: National Council on Measurement in Education and American Council on Education.

Sobocan, J., Groarke, L., Johnson, R. H., & Ellet, F. S., Jr. (Eds.). (2009). *Critical thinking education and assessment: Can higher order thinking be tested?* London: The Althouse Press.

Stanovich, K. E. (2009). *What intelligence tests miss: The psychology of rational thought.* New Haven, CT: Yale University Press.

Stanovich, K. E., Sá, W. C., & West, R.F. (2004). Individual differences in thinking, reasoning, and decision making. In J. P. Leighton & R. J. Sternberg's (Eds.), *Nature of reasoning* (pp. 375-409). New York, NY: Cambridge University Press.

Sternberg, R. J. (1999). The theory of successful intelligence. *Review of General Psychology, 3*, 292-316.

Stiggins, R. J. (2004). New assessment beliefs for a new school mission. *Phi Delta Kappan, 86*, 22-27.

Stiggins, R. J., Griswold, M. M., & Wikelund, K. R. (1989). Measuring thinking skills through classroom assessment. *Journal of Educational Measurement, 26*, 233-246.

Wiggins, G. (1989). Teaching to the (authentic) test. *Educational Leadership, 76*, 41-47.

Williams, R. B. (2003). *Higher order thinking skills: Challenging all students to achieve.* Chicago, IL: Robin Fogarty.

Winne, P. H. (1996). A metacognitive view of individual differences in self regulated learning. *Learning and Individual Differences, 8*, 327–353.

Zimmerman, C. (2007). The development of scientific thinking skills in elementary and middle school. *Development Review, 27*, 172-223.

Zohar, A. (2004). *Higher order thinking in science classrooms: Students' learning and teacher' professional development.* Dordrecht, The Netherlands: Kluwer.

Zohar, A. (2006). The nature and development of teachers' metastrategic knowledge in the context of teaching higher order thinking. *The Journal of the Learning Sciences, 15*, 331-377.

Zohar, A., Degani A., & Vaaknin, E. (2001). Teachers' beliefs about low achieving students and higher order thinking, *Teaching and Teachers' Education, 17*, 469-485.

PART III

HIGHER ORDER THINKING IN CONTENT DOMAINS

CHAPTER 7

THE ASSESSMENT OF HIGHER ORDER THINKING IN READING

Peter Afflerbach, Byeong-Young Cho, and Jong-Yun Kim

Assessment of higher order thinking in reading has several important uses. When used formatively, the assessment can inform teachers' understanding of students, reading instruction and reader development. When summative, assessment can report on the accomplishments of student readers, the value of instructional programs, and teacher efficacy. This chapter examines higher order thinking in reading, and describes the attributes of assessments that suitably measure it. The first section of the chapter focuses on how reading can be conceptualized as higher order thinking. We overview the development of theories that describe the complexity of reading, the most recent definition of reading from the National Assessment of Educational Progress (NAEP) and research on higher order thinking in general. We compare an amended version of Bloom's Taxonomy with state-of-the-art knowledge about reading strategies with the intent of demonstrating what aspects of reading engage reliably higher order thinking.

The second section of the chapter presents an array of assessments that allow us to examine and evaluate the nature of higher order thinking, its development in student readers, and the suitability of assessments for

Assessment of Higher Order Thinking Skills, pp. 185–217
Copyright © 2011 by Information Age Publishing

measuring particular aspects of higher order thinking. We situate these assessments in an eighth grade science classroom, where students are required to demonstrate higher order thinking while reading, and in relation to the meanings they construct from varied science texts.

Theoretical Background: Reading as Higher Order Thinking

How do we understand reading? Thorndike (1917) characterized the reading of a complex paragraph as follows:

> It (the mind) must select, repress, soften, emphasize, correlate, and organize, all under the influence of the right mental set ... reading an explanatory or argumentative paragraph ... involves the same sort of organization and analytic action of ideas as occur in thinking of supposedly higher orders. (p. 329)

Twenty years later, Rosenblatt (1938) characterized reading as a transaction between the reader and text, providing a similarly complex and dynamic description:

> The special meaning, and more particularly, the submerged associations that these words and images have for the individual reader will largely determine what the work communicates to him. The reader brings to the work personality traits, memories of past events, present needs and preoccupations, a particular mood of the moment, and a particular physical condition. These and many other elements in a never-to-be-duplicated combination determine his response to the peculiar contribution of the text. (p. 30)

These two accounts emanate from different traditions of inquiry, and they represent different perspectives on reading. Yet, both describe reading as a complex undertaking that involves higher order thinking.

In the ensuing century, research and theory have contributed fine-grained descriptions of reading and related phenomena. Under the umbrella of cognitive processes, the activity of the reader and the interaction of reader and text have been described as a series of strategies and skills, used in concert with a reader's prior knowledge. The interactions vary in nature from simple to complex, and range from letter and word identification (Goswami, 2003) to default instantiations of schema for simple inferences (Anderson & Pearson, 1984), to identifying and remembering important information in text (Van Dijk & Kintsch, 1983), and to the highly strategic monitoring and evaluation of reading (Pressley & Afflerbach, 1995).

That reading is a situated and social act of cognition adds to the variation in readers' strategies, stances and knowledge use, based on the context of reading (Brown, Collins, & Duguid, 1989). As our knowledge of reading evolves, accounts of the use of cognitive skill and strategy are enhanced by the understanding that reading in content areas demands specific sets of domain knowledge and strategies. For example, as readers become strategic and skillful in reading history, they may emulate historians and their domain-specific approaches to reading (VanSledright, 2002; Wineburg, 1997). As well, we understand that strategies and skills are used in relation to a reader's goals for reading (Afflerbach, Pearson, & Paris, 2008; Van den Broek, Young, Tzeng, & Linderholm, 1999), and that the interactivity of reader and text is subject to influence by variables that include readers' motivations (Guthrie & Wigfield, 2000), self-concepts (Chapman & Tunmer, 1995) and sense of agency and volition (Corno, 1993). That such diverse factors coalesce for successful reading strongly suggests the presence of higher order thinking in reading.

Adding to the implication of higher order thinking in reading is the idea that acts of reading are not restricted to the construction of meaning. For example, consider how the National Assessment of Educational Progress (NAEP) Reading Framework for 2009 defines reading:

Reading is an active and complex process that involves

- Understanding written text
- Developing and interpreting meaning
- Using meaning as appropriate to type of text, purpose and situation. (National Assessment Governing Board [NAGB], 2008, p. 51)

This definition represents a reconceptualization of reading, maintaining the focus on *learning and remembering text* but adding the *use of that which is learned and remembered from reading*. It also broadens the parameters in which higher order thinking may be used in *constructing* meaning, and then in *using* the constructed meaning.

Further, the recent Common Core Standards (Council of Chief State School Officers and National Governors Association, 2010) proposes reading benchmark performances that include higher order thinking. For example, the Common Core State Standards for English Language Arts and Literacy in History/Social Studies and Science describes the following student reading performances in eighth grade:

Cite a wide range of evidence throughout the text when useful to support analysis of what the text says explicitly as well as inferences drawn from the text. (p. 34)

Following is a standard for 12th grade reading:

> Synthesize explanations and arguments from diverse sources to provide a
> coherent account of events or ideas, including resolving conflicting informa-
> tion. (p. 35) (Reading Standards for Informational Text, Grades 6-12,
> retrieved March 17, 2010, from: htp://www.corestandards.org/Files/
> K12ELAStandards.pdf)

Each of the above sample standards demands of students the ability to
read and to demonstrate higher order thinking.

Higher Order Thinking Skills, Higher Order Thinking Strategies, and Higher Order Thinking: Terminology and an Observation

Before continuing, we want to provide a perspective on higher order
thinking in reading. It is common to encounter the term "higher order
thinking skills" in the literatures related to cognitive processes, learning
and teaching. We are concerned with this use of "skills" in the above term
for several reasons. First, the distinction between reading skills and reading strategies (and "skills" and "strategies" in general) is important
because while they are related terms, they are distinctly different. According to Afflerbach, Pearson, and Paris (2008),

> *Reading strategies* are *deliberate, goal-directed attempts to control and modify* the
> reader's efforts to decode text, understand words, and construct meanings
> of text whereas *reading skills* are *automatic actions* that result in decoding and
> comprehension with speed, efficiency, and fluency, usually without aware-
> ness of the components or control involved. (p. 368, italics added)

Second, accomplished reading requires a combination of reading skills
and reading strategies:

> At the heart of accomplished reading is ... automatic application and use of
> reading skills, and intentional, effortful employment of reading strategies—
> accompanied by the ability to shift seamlessly between the two when the sit-
> uation calls for it. The difficulty of the reading task, influenced by text, task,
> reader and contextual variables, will determine this shifting balance. When
> their knowledge is strong and they are given easy text and goals, students
> can apply their usual skills. In contrast, when their knowledge is sketchy,
> texts are difficult, and reading tasks are complex, more strategic reading is
> required. (p. 371)

Higher order thinking in reading most often demands a combination of
skill and strategy, and when reading is demanding we may expect many

readers to exhibit increased use of strategies. Thus, we believe that it is judicious to refer to "higher order thinking," as opposed to "higher order thinking skills" or "higher order thinking strategies," because accomplished reading regularly combines skill and strategy.

Conceptual Frames for Higher Order Thinking in Reading

Since Thorndike's (1917) suggestion that reading can involve higher order thinking, there has been intermittent focus on the relationship between higher order thinking and reading skills and strategies. There is not universal agreement on what, exactly, qualifies as higher order thinking and higher order thinking in reading. We note that this chapter presents a somewhat arbitrary, but what we hope is a principled decision about higher order thinking in reading. A subset of all the skills and strategies that successful readers use may be reliably characterized as higher order thinking. Thus, one of our goals (for a chapter that hopes to define higher order thinking in reading and then suggest appropriate assessments) is comparing recent, detailed characterizations of accomplished reading with general models of thinking. This helps us determine acts of reading and aspects of reading that involve higher order thinking, and those that do not. To do so, we focus on Bloom's (as cited in Anderson & Krathwoahl, 2001) Taxonomy of Educational Objectives, the definition of reading included in the NAEP 2009 Reading Framework, and contemporary theory and research related to higher order thinking.

Bloom's Taxonomy of Educational Objectives

Bloom's Taxonomy provides a framework for conceptualizing thinking, and the differences (and varying complexity) in the types of thinking in which human beings engage. Table 7.1 presents skills and strategies, identified through reading research, that are iterations of the types of thinking that are included in Bloom's Taxonomy. The table was constructed through a constant comparison of reading strategies with Bloom's conceptualizations of thinking. Specifically, we used reviews of reading strategy research developed by Pressley and Afflerbach (1995) and Afflerbach and Cho (2009a, 2009b) to infer reading strategy membership in particular categories of Bloom's Taxonomy. For example, we examined the notion of "synthesis" proposed by Bloom and found counterparts in reading, including strategies for constructing intertextual meaning when reading several texts (Hartmann, 1995) and for creating a coherent summary of a complex text (Johnston & Afflerbach, 1985; Bratenetal, 2009). We add the category *metacognition*, a relatively recent addition to conceptualizations of reading and human performance (Flavell, 1979) that postdates Bloom's work. Accomplished reading has a strong core of metacognition, and much of metacognitive thinking is higher order in nature (Veenman, van Hout Woulters, & Afflerbach, 2006). For example, monitoring one's progress towards the goal of synthesizing information from across multiple texts, while concurrently vetting the information for accuracy and trustworthiness, demands metacognition.

The hierarchical nature of the taxonomy also offers the means for delineating the rough boundary between higher order thinking and non-higher order thinking in reading. We propose that the distinction between higher order thinking in reading and basic thinking in reading is situated between the first two categories (knowledge and comprehension) and the remaining categories (application, analysis, synthesis and evaluation, and metacognition). We choose not to use the label "lower order thinking," preferring to use "basic" in the sense that basic thinking contributes to a literal understanding of text, and is requisite for more complex, higher order thinking.

Another perspective on the meaningful differences between higher order and basic thinking in reading is provided by Paris (2005), who proposes that particular reading skills and strategies are constrained or unconstrained in relation to students' reading development. In general, skills and strategies related to decoding and oral reading (e.g., letter knowledge, phonics, concepts of print, phonemic awareness, fluency) are constrained. They are relatively easy to learn, teach, and assess; and they are mastered quickly by a majority of developing readers. In contrast, skills and strategies related to meaning construction (e.g., comprehension, vocabulary) are least constrained. These skills and strategies require relatively more time and effort to learn, teach, and assess. While constrained skills and strategies contribute to decoding and accessing text meaning, higher order thinking involves more unconstrained skills and strategies that contribute to reading for understanding.

We make several assumptions about the boundary between basic and higher order thinking in reading, and the nature of related reading that is higher order or other. First, while being able to read represents extraordinary human accomplishment, there are particular aspects of reading that are clearly more sophisticated than others. The first two categories of Bloom's taxonomy, knowledge and comprehension, represent important thinking. A reader working in this area is able to use resources that include decoding strategies, sight word recognition, and prior knowledge to identify ideas in text and to construct literal meaning from text. For example, the application of sound-symbol correspondences to decode a printed word to sound, sound out and blend the discreet sounds back to a whole word and then attempt to match the spoken (or "sounded out") word with one in long term memory is a laudable accomplishment for a

Table 7.1.   A Comparison of Bloom's Taxonomy of Educational Objectives With Reading Skills and Strategies

	Bloom's Taxonomy and Levels of THINKING, Including Original Subcategories	Reading Skills and Strategies Related With the Particular Level of Bloom's Taxonomy
Basic thinking	*Knowledge:* • Knowledge of specifics • Knowledge of ways and means of dealing with specifics • Knowledge of universals and abstractions in a field	• Sounding out words encountered in print • Perceiving linguistic characteristics of text, including lexical/morphological/syntactic/cohesive/topic/ punctuation/typographical characteristics/type or style of language (Graves & Frederiksen, 1991). • Determining word meanings by accessing prior vocabulary knowledge (McKeown, 1985).
	Comprehension: • Translation • Interpretation • Extrapolation	• Inferring the referent of a pronoun when it is vague (Magliano & Graesser, 1993) • Paraphrasing part of text (Graves & Frederiksen, 1991). • Searching for related words, concepts, or ideas in text to assign importance (van Dijk & Kintsch, 1983).
Higher order thinking	*Application:**	• Applying the understanding of complex relationships among concepts of survival emphasizing interdependence among organisms, learned from science text, in the investigation of a local ecosystem (Guthrie et al., 2004). • Critically judging validity and reliability of texts by criteria of text contents, author's point of view, text types, and context, using a cumulative representation of a whole document set (Wineburg, 1991).
	Analysis: • Analysis of elements • Analyses of relationships • Analysis of organizational principles	• Relating a particular part of text to larger themes in the text (Graves & Frederiksen, 1991) • Deciding which information in text is important in relation to the goal for reading the text and to anticipated future use of text information (Afflerbach, 1990).

(Table continues on next page)

Table 7.1.   Continued

Bloom's Taxonomy and Levels of THINKING, Including Original Subcategories	Reading Skills and Strategies Related With the Particular Level of Bloom's Taxonomy
Higher order thinking	
Synthesis: • Production of a unique communication • Production of a plan, or proposed set of operations • Derivation of a set of abstract relations	• Developing a written account of the theme of an essay, based on information read and understood across the essay (Johnston & Afflerbach, 1985) • Using gist information from multiple texts to develop a coherent account of cross-textual contents and creating new texts by selecting, organizing, and connecting content from diverse texts (Hartman, 1995; Strømsø, Braten, & Samuelstuen, 2003).
Evaluation: • Judgments in terms of internal evidence • Judgments in terms of external evidence	• Evaluating the validity of an author's argument, claims and evidence (Bazerman, 1985). • Evaluating the trustworthiness of text based on justifications of various aspects of text, such as content, author, document types, and opinions (Rouet, Britt, Mason, & Perfetti, 1996; Wineburg, 1991). • Assessing the relevance of Internet sources that are determined to have related information (Tabatabai & Shore, 2005).
Metacognition:** • Use of metacognitive knowledge (text, task, goal, and context, and one's knowledge and strategies) • Metacognitive controls (comprehension monitoring and applying fix-it strategies)	• Resetting goals for reading at a different level of understanding because the unfolding reading experience suggests that there might be a more appropriate goal (Guthrie, Britten, & Barker, 1991). • Sensing inconsistency between hypothesized macrostructure active at the end of a reading and some of the information in the text, reader continues search for meaning: (a) material may be skimmed to "put it together"; (b) material in text may be systematically reviewed to firm up meaning, short of rereading (Johnston & Afflerbach, 1985; Kintgen, 1983). • Changing strategic processing foci from understanding within-text meaning to integrating across-text meaning by utilizing domain knowledge increased due to previous readings, during the sequential readings (Hartman, 1995) • In an Internet reading task, managing disorientation by increasing memory allocation to solve the problem of disorientation and refocusing original search plan and goal(s) (Balcytiene, 1999).

* There are no subcategories of application in Bloom's Taxonomy.
** We note that Bloom's Taxonomy did not include metacognition as a category or subcategory. In effect, metacognition and metacognitive processes had not been "named" in 1956. However, metacognition appears in later iterations of the Taxonomy (Anderson & Krathwohl, 2001).

developing student reader. Yet, the process is algorithmic and straightforward, as it is learned, practiced and mastered by the majority of developing readers. Bloom's portrayal of thinking becoming complex at subsequent levels of the taxonomy (the areas of application, analysis, synthesis and evaluation) allows for the inference that, at some point of relative complexity of text and task, reading involves higher order thinking. For example, reading behavior that includes reading several texts to determine common and opposing points of view, synthesizing the intertext information and applying rules of argumentation to make critical judgments of the texts involves combinations of strategy and skill, and reflects a more complex enterprise.

A second and related point is that the apparent difficulty of a reading text and task for a particular reader does not necessarily signal the reading as involving higher order thinking. Higher order thinking in reading is referenced to the work required of specific text/task combinations, and not to the relative challenge that reading presents to readers of differing proficiency. Consider, again, the reader who is sounding out words. The reader's working memory may be stretched to the limit, as the reader engages in the effortful use of declarative and procedural knowledge to determine a letter's sound and then to blend individual letter sounds. Successful coordination leads to fluent word recognition. Yet, at the end of the process, it is simply (relative to other reading processes and products) a word that has been decoded. Given these two points, we determined that Bloom's first two levels, Knowledge and Comprehension, represent classes of basic thinking that are critical for reading success, but constrained in nature.

Third, while we signify the division of higher order and basic thinking (the "basic" thinking that is requisite for processing and establishing a literal understanding of text) in reading, higher order thinking in reading depends on the successful application of this constrained thinking. Evaluating an author's style, synthesizing an article's main points and comparing them with previously learned material, and applying the knowledge learned from reading are always accompanied by basic thinking. Thus, the two types of thinking, basic and higher order (or constrained and unconstrained, Paris, 2005), are best regarded as essential partners in successful reading.

The National Assessment of Educational Progress 2009 Definition of Reading

The NAEP 2009 Reading Framework (NAGB, 2008) supports the idea that reading includes different levels of thinking. It also describes broadened parameters of higher order thinking: the NAEP reading definition that reading involves using that which is learned from reading. The 2009

NAEP Reading Framework includes cognitive targets, which refer to "the mental processes or kinds of thinking that underlie reading comprehension" (p. 35) The Framework focuses on three particular cognitive targets: locate/recall, integrate/interpret, and critique/evaluate, that reside on a simple-to-complex continuum. The Framework portrays reading as a multistage process in which the reader establishes literal understanding of text, develops and interprets meaning, and then uses the constructed meaning in tasks. The distinction of each of the three cognitive targets depends on the particular skills and strategies demanded of the reader by the text and task. While higher order thinking may operate across all three, it is increasingly needed as a reader, text and task are engaged in more complex reading (Figure 7.1).

The descriptions of the three cognitive targets, as provided in the NAEP Framework (NAGB, 2008), indicate this movement from relatively simple to increasingly complex reading. The following excerpts illustrate how reading varies in complexity and how more complex reading requires higher order thinking: *Understanding written text* requires that readers

> attend to ideas and content in a text by locating and recalling information and by making inferences needed for literal comprehension of the text. In doing so, readers draw on their fundamental skills for decoding printed words and accessing their vocabulary knowledge. (pp. 2-3)

The second stage, *developing and interpreting meaning*, builds upon the outcomes of the previous basic text processing and demands that readers

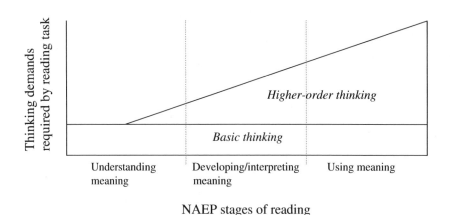

Figure 7.1.   Higher order and basic thinking processes in reading in relation to NAEP reading categories.

integrate the sense they have made of the text with their knowledge of other texts and with their outside experience. They use increasingly more complex inferencing skills to comprehend information implied by a text. As appropriate, readers revise their sense of the text as they encounter additional information or ideas. (p. 3)

The third stage, *using meaning as appropriate to type of text, purpose and situation*, requires that readers

draw on the ideas and information they have acquired from text to meet a particular purpose or situational need. The use of text may be as straightforward as knowing the time when a train will leave a particular station or may involve more complex behaviors such as analyzing how an author developed a character's motivation or evaluating the quality of evidence presented in an argument. (p. 3)

In essence, these three NAEP reading categories represent increasingly accomplished reading, reading that requires higher order thinking.

Theory and Research Related to Higher Order Thinking

A third source of support for the idea of reading involving higher order thinking is theory and related research in cognition and situated cognition. For example, Resnick (1987) characterizes higher order thinking as nonalgorithmic and complex, and suggests that the solution path from beginning to end of complex tasks is often not known in advance. Higher order thinking can involve uncertainty, in that the learner must improvise to progress. Higher order thinking may yield multiple solutions, as opposed to unique solutions, as when learners interrelate or rearrange new information to solve problems (Lewis & Smith, 1993). Higher order thinking can involve nuanced judgments and interpretations, as when the learner must apply multiple criteria to make determinations of the acceptability of work and the degree of progress towards goals. Higher order thinking is deployed when the learner is challenged to interpret, analyze, or manipulate information (Newman, 1990). Higher order thinking requires self-regulation, as complex tasks demand active management of information and cognitive action, problem-solving and fix-up strategies, and intentional learning procedures (Scardamalia & Bereiter, 1987), and higher order thinking can involve imposing meaning and finding structure where none may be initially apparent.

Higher order thinking is further implicated in Kintsch's (1998) construction-integration model of reading comprehension. A prerequisite task for comprehending text is to build propositional relationships among text information across micro- and macroprocessing levels. On the one hand, at the microprocessing level, readers put together segments of word-

and sentence-level information mostly using linguistic knowledge. On the other hand, readers build a larger, discourse-level structure of text meaning interrelating different microstructures of meaning. On this macrolevel processing, higher order thinkers analyze and synthesize different part of texts to build text-base representation.

While the process of construction affords readers an understanding of text information, the meaning constructed is not necessarily coherent unless readers impose their goals for reading on the comprehension process. Here, readers employ goal-relevant criteria (e.g., What do I want to get out of the text?) and discourse knowledge (e.g., Why am I reading this text?), in higher order thinking. This higher order thinking helps the reader to eliminate irrelevant information from the text-base model, which contributes to building a situation model. The situation model does not represent the simply sum of text information, but rather the readers' understanding of gist ideas, abstract themes distilled from the text, and interrelationships, all aided by higher order thinking.

A synthesis of the information related to higher order thinking in reading allows us to characterize such reading as *strategic, flexible*, and *self-regulated*. higher order thinking has at the core *strategic* procedures, which require a reader's deliberate control (Afflerbach, Pearson, & Paris, 2008; Alexander, Graham, & Harris, 1998; Pressley & Afflerbach, 1995; van Dijk & Kintsch, 1983). Strategic readers adjust their reading in relation to the text, task, and context (van den Broek, Rapp, & Kendeou, 2005). When reading a challenging text, accomplished readers constructively respond to the text by using an array of intentional strategies (Pressley & Afflerbach, 1995). Readers are strategic in identifying and interpreting ideas; hypothesizing about the text meaning and testing the hypothesis. They continually monitor their reading and evaluate what they read. Most, if not all acts of reading, involve strategies and higher order thinking in reading is marked by strategies beyond the level of making simple inferences.

Readers' higher order thinking is *flexible*. van Dijk and Kintsch (1983) note the following:

> Strategic processes contrast with algorithmic, rule-governed processes.... In a strategic process, there is no such guaranteed success and no unique representation of the text. The strategies applied are like effective working hypotheses about the correct structure and meaning of a text fragment, and these may be disconfirmed by further processing. (p. 11)

This statement reminds us that reading is a situated act, performed by the reader who has particular purposes, and who is operating in a particular reading context. Readers must actively respond to their reading situations, making use of their skills and strategies in optimal combination, toward achieving their goal(s). This flexibility, gauged to the reading situation, marks higher order thinking.

Higher order thinking in reading reflects (and is enhanced by) readers' *self-regulation*, as text is processed and meaning constructed (Alexander, 2003; Baker & Brown, 1984; Garner, 1987; Palincsar & Brown, 1984; Paris, Lipson, & Wixson, 1983; Pressley & Afflerbach, 1995). This metacognition contributes to the management of the entire process of reading, and to the successful outcome of reading. Accomplished readers use higher order thinking, in the form of metacognitive routines, to be cognizant of their goal for reading and available resources, and to determine what they know (prior knowledge) and can do (skills and strategies) in the midst of reading. When they encounter difficulty, they diagnose the situation and deploy fix-it strategies. They know why, when, and where to use their mental resources, reflecting their conditional knowledge of strategy use. They evaluate texts, their progress towards reading goals, and their ongoing performance.

Given our increased understanding of reading, the determination that particular acts of reading require higher order thinking may seem straightforward. Yet, the complexity of the reading process, the personalization that marks each and every act of reading, and the developmental nature of student reading often act to challenge assumptions of what is higher order thinking, and what is not. A developing reader will find complexity in many acts of reading, but complexity is relative. Higher order thinking in reading is most evident when accomplished readers engage with challenging texts, in order to meet complex goals. Part of the developing reader's challenge is to learn and practice skill and strategy, however complex, and increasingly apply them in fluid manner, contributing to the possible use of higher order thinking. From this perspective, the idea of higher order thinking in reading attains some consistency, reliable in the nature of the cognition needed to successfully undertake it.

Reading is always an act of situated cognition, and it is critical to acknowledge that higher order thinking in reading is accompanied by particular affective reader characteristics. Higher order reading is most often accomplished by readers who possess positive motivation to read, appropriate self-concept as a talented reader and a sense of agency. These readers are able to progress to such levels of accomplishment because, in part, they can conceptualize themselves as successful readers. In addition, readers who successfully engage in higher order thinking take stances towards texts, tasks and knowledge in which they must apply learning, question the author, or refute the authority of text. Thus, readers' epistemologies figure in certain acts of higher order thinking: readers who are capable of questioning the truthfulness of a text, the motive of an author or the provenance of textual information (all requiring higher order thinking) are readers who place themselves in the position to do so.

To summarize this section, much is known about the skills and strategies that are involved in successful reading. Our understanding of reading skills and strategies continually evolves, and the conceptualization of reading changes. Some subset of these skills and strategies indicates higher order thinking in reading, and conforms to the modes of higher order thinking proposed by Bloom (1956). Examination of Bloom's categories of thinking, the current NAEP Reading definition and research on higher order thinking suggests that higher order thinking in reading is strategic, self-regulated and flexible. In all cases, reading is a notable accomplishment, and higher order thinking in reading represents extraordinary achievement.

Assessment of Higher Order Thinking in Reading

This section begins with an overview of characteristics of effective assessment, focusing on the purposes of assessment, and the formative or summative nature of assessment. Then, we describe a classroom in which reading and reading-related tasks regularly require students' higher order thinking. Examination of curriculum and instruction in the classroom allows us to describe reading assessments that have construct validity, in relation to the higher order thinking demanded by the curriculum. We then provide examples of how particular assessments measure higher order thinking in reading.

Pellegrino, Chudowsky, and Glaser's (2001) model of assessment includes three key features: *cognition, observation* and *interpretation*. For the purpose of this chapter, *cognition* represents important aspects of higher order thinking in reading that we would measure. These include a reader's synthesis of text information, the critical evaluation of text and author, the analysis of a text's argument structure, the metacognitive management of a complex meaning-construction episode, and the application and use of knowledge gained through reading. *Observation* represents the assessment materials and procedures that are developed in accordance with our understanding of the things to be assessed. Given the range and potential complexity of the higher order thinking that can be measured, it is crucial to determine the types of tasks and procedures that are best suited to providing assessment information. *Interpretation* represents how assessment information is understood, and the reasoning and judgments that are made with assessment information. Following the accurate description of the higher order thinking to be assessed and the related development of assessment materials and procedures, we can gather and analyze assessment information, and then ascertain evidence that contributes to assessment decision making. In essence, attention to the alignment between cognition and observation informs construct validity.

Further, task analyses of both learning goals and assessment items help clarify what, exactly, a reader must do to demonstrate higher order thinking. It is imperative that assessment efforts are first informed by a detailed and accurate portrayal of the thing to be assessed. The assessment materials and procedures must then honor the complexity of the construct. A major expectation of any assessment is that it possesses construct validity: in this case, assessment must reflect a detailed and accurate understanding of reading that involves higher order thinking (Afflerbach, 2007).

The validity of assessment also relates to the purpose of reading assessment; that is, while construct validity is imperative, we should also consider the quality of the information yielded by an assessment, and the usefulness of the information to serve a particular purpose. There is general agreement that assessment can serve the following purposes: monitoring student progress, informing instructional decision making, and evaluating student achievement. In addition, assessment can serve the purpose of helping students learn self-assessment and increase their metacognitive involvement with reading (Black & Wiliam, 1998). Choosing one purpose over another (or choosing several) should influence the selection of a specific type of assessment. For example, if we want assessment to serve the purpose of informing instructional decision making, regular, ongoing assessment is the logical choice because it can provide detailed information on what students can and can't do in relation to near-term learning goals. A student who is expected to learn to conduct critical evaluation of texts through the examination of claim-evidence structure may benefit from instruction that is informed by assessment of this higher order thinking. In contrast, if we are evaluating student achievement over a marking period, assessment that provides a valid summary account of learning is needed.

The purpose of assessment is closely tied to the formative or summative nature of assessment. Formative assessment of higher order thinking in reading serves a primary purpose of informing teachers and students of their progress towards instructional goals. Formative assessment provides information that can be used strategically as teachers plan and provide instruction. Consider the student who is required to learn strategies that help identify the claim-evidence text structure in an argumentative text, and then critically assess the effectiveness of the author's use of this structure. The student who lacks even rudimentary knowledge of claim-evidence structure will benefit from detailed instruction on the components of claim-evidence structure, how to use knowledge of these components to guide reading of texts and then render evaluative judgments about these texts. The learning required here is considerable, as is the need for detailed and regularly updated assessment information that can guide the teacher's work with the student. Formative assessment informs the teacher's understanding of the student's progress, the student's needs, and the nature of ongoing instruction. Informing instruction and identifying teachable moments contributes to work in the student's zone of proximal development (Vygotsky, 1978)—the place where higher thinking strategies may be introduced, modeled, explained, discussed, practiced and learned. Formative assessment of higher order thinking can serve as a gauge of how students are developing in relation to curriculum goals and standards benchmarks.

Summative assessment can be used to certify that particular learning goals have been met. For example, if we are interested in helping students learn to synthesize information from across diverse texts and set this as a year-long goal, then a summative assessment focusing on student synthesis of information from traditional and Internet texts, and providing information on the extent of student learning at the end of the school year, is appropriate. As higher order thinking in reading depends on the establishment of literal understanding of text, summative assessment can be used to determine that students have comprehended what they have read, as a precursor to higher order thinking assessment. In all cases, as assessment purpose is established, assessment materials and procedures, representing a mix of formative and summative approaches, should then be tailored to best fit the purpose.

Situating Basic and Higher Order Thinking in the Classroom: Reading and Assessment

We next focus on a classroom in which students regularly engage in higher order thinking in reading. The curriculum in this classroom assumes students' competence with basic reading skills and strategies. As well, the curriculum and assessment are designed in anticipation of the teaching and learning of higher order thinking. We note that while the focus is on science and eighth grade, higher order thinking is a worthy focus and goal of reading instruction earlier in school, and should assume a more prominent role in school reading throughout high school.

Eighth-grade students in a middle school science unit on global warming read a variety of traditional and online texts and evaluate opposing arguments on whether or not global warming is due to human activity, and whether or not it represents a risk to the health of humans and the planet. The students read three assigned, common texts: a newspaper editorial, a science article from a news magazine, and a chapter from their science textbook. Students must also identify, locate and read a series of science texts on the Internet. To do so, students must conduct searches and vet the Internet texts, applying criteria of relevance, trustworthiness and currency; this before-reading work is an initial invocation of higher order thinking.

Students must construct an accurate, literal meaning of each Internet and traditional text. In this case, accuracy reflects the idea that when reading expository or informational text, the reader's goal is first tied to a reconstruction of the text model. The accomplished reader applies strategies with intention, and skills automatically, to construct meaning. At a minimum, the construction of literal meaning demands that students successfully use their basic reading skills and strategies. Based on the information load in the text, the syntactic complexity of the text, and the familiarity of the subject matter, the reader engages in thinking that is basic to literal understanding, and that may involve higher order thinking skills.

Analysis of this episode of reading reveals that the reader must bring appropriate prior knowledge with which to interpret text information. Words are, by and large, recognized automatically or with minimal attention, except those words that are notably unfamiliar. In this case, several science content words and terms, the focus of pre-reading instruction, include "greenhouse gas," "ozone," and "deforestation." As text is processed, meaning is constructed, low level inferences are generated to make connections between different text components and sections, and between the text contents and the reader's prior knowledge. Construction of meaning is occurring without much apparent effort on the part of the eighth grade readers.

The basic thinking is followed by higher order thinking strategies that allow the reader to hold syntheses of different articles in attention, while comparing their contents, similarities and differences. The students' work is aided by notes taken as they read, and their attention is on common elements across the texts, as well as points of contention between texts. In addition, the students are searching for information and analyzing the texts to identify particular text structures, including cause and effect, and claim and evidence, used by authors to forward their arguments. They will analyze each text to try to ascertain the assumed purpose of the article, its author, the dates of publication, and the sources of information cited. The readers must comprehend text and analyze opposing information to make determination of the text that is reliable and trustworthy.

Students are also expected to make evaluations as they read—the usefulness of the information contained, the talent of the author, and the trustworthiness of the sources. Students also evaluate, through metacognition, the availability of prior knowledge for the text topic, and their progress towards reading goals. They note the citations and references within the different texts they read to try to make determinations of the accuracy of the information. Students are also expected to apply that which they learn from reading. Through examination of well-written or poorly-structured texts, they compile a list of text features of compelling arguments. Based on their understanding of the causes of global warming, they design a public transportation system that minimizes greenhouse gases. Throughout, students are responsible for monitoring their progress from the start to finish of the reading assignment. This means that they are regularly applying metacognitive skills and strategies to set goals, gauge progress towards the goals, and determine if the goals are met.

The Eighth Grade Science Classroom

In this section we present assessment that is capable of providing information on students' higher order thinking in reading. The assessment includes measures of basic comprehension, or literal understanding, of each text. From this baseline assumption of literal understanding, the assessment will be capable of describing how (and how well) students work in the different areas of higher order thinking in reading. We focus on performance assessments, and describe how these assessments can tap students' higher order thinking in relation to the particular thinking described in our revision of Bloom's (1956) Taxonomy (Table 7.1). Figure 7.2 illustrates the connection between basic and higher levels of thinking, and contains a series of questions whose foci represent related, and increasingly higher order, thinking. This example, an "arc of questions" (Wolf, 1987), focuses on prompts that demand simple to complex thinking. The arc of questions is important in that it allows us to sample student learning not only at different levels, but at related levels. It also allows for consideration of strategic combinations of assessment, in this case questions and performance assessment.

Assessing Basic Thinking in Reading

Assessing knowledge with multiple choice questions. As noted earlier, a basic task for all readers is learning from text. There are many ways to measure this learning, and multiple-choice items are widespread in use and familiar to all students. They are often well-suited to assessing basic levels of thinking. While the students in the global warming unit are challenged by a series of performance assessments, the ability to perform competently on the performance assessments of higher order thinking requires that literal understanding of text has taken place. One important cognitive outcome of reading about global warming is learning facts, as these facts are essential for effective higher order thinking. Students reading the science texts learn that there are several different greenhouse gases, and that water vapor is the most prominent of the greenhouse gases. To assess

Scenario: Students are reading and learning about different perspectives on global warming from a textbook chapter, a magazine article, and an Internet document. Goals include literal and inferential comprehension of texts, determination of trustworthiness of the texts, identification of the argument structure of the texts, and using text information to decide personal stance on global warming.

Bloom's level: Knowledge; recalling information.

Assessment question: What is the most prominent greenhouse gas?

Bloom's level: Comprehension; or understanding the meaning of text

Assessment question: How does global warming occur?

Bloom's level: Application; using a concept in a new situation

Assessment question: What might happen with global warming as the number of automobiles increases?

Bloom's level: Analysis; separating concepts into component parts to understand their organizational structure

Assessment question: What proof of global warming is given by those who claim it is a potentially deadly problem?

Bloom's level: Synthesis; building a structure or pattern from diverse elements

Assessment question: What would you include in a comprehensive plan to reduce global warming?

Bloom's level: Evaluation; making judgments about the value of ideas or materials

Assessment question: Are the alternative explanations for global warming that are given by those who are opposed to taking action against global warming credible? Why?

Figure 7.2.   A simple to complex "arc" of reading assessment questions coordinated with Bloom's Taxonomy

students' knowledge of this fact, a multiple-choice item can be constructed:

The most abundant greenhouse gas is:

(a) water vapor
(b) methane
(c) carbon dioxide
(d) ozone

As illustrated by this item, particular types of knowledge can be effectively assessed in multiple-choice format. Here, there is only one correct answer, the answer is selected rather than constructed.

Assessing comprehension with brief constructed response items. Students read a science textbook chapter that provides detailed information about the process that creates global warming. For the students to construct an understanding of this process, they must identify and remember important parts of text and make a series of simple inferences while reading. Use of these cognitive skills and strategies yields an accurate mental model of the text. To assess if students have comprehended the process by which global warming occurs, a brief constructed response item is used:

> Based on your understanding of the textbook chapter, describe how global warming occurs.

Students construct a written response that suitably describes the phenomenon of global warming, as related to their comprehension of text. The response includes literal information from the texts, and low level inferences.

As we progress from multiple-choice items and brief constructed response items to complex items and tasks that assess higher order thinking, we have two observations. First, the majority of tests and high stakes assessments in the United States are comprised of multiple choice and brief constructed response items that focus on basic, or lower levels of reading. The dependence on multiple choice items in particular is related to the costs of assessment—while options exist for valid assessment of higher order thinking, these assessments are relatively expensive to administer and score. The practice of frequent testing in United States' schools is expensive, and the sheer cost of tests subverts attempts at appropriately complex assessments of complex reading. This creates the situation in which highly consequential reading assessment fairly ignores higher order thinking in reading, or provides only a very "thin" (Davis, 1998) account of it. The second point is that many assessments suitably describe students' development in relation to the knowledge and comprehension levels of thinking, because reading tests are comprised of simple, short texts, and they demand the relatively simple cognitive tasks of learning, remembering and giving back information.

Higher Order Thinking in Reading: Performance Assessments

Basic thinking in reading provides the basis for undertaking more complex actions and performances. Assessment that can describe these increasingly complex performances will focus on higher order thinking, and performance assessments have considerable potential for use as formative and summative measures of higher order thinking in reading (Baxter & Glaser, 1998; Linn, Baker, & Dunbar, 1991).

Assesssing analysis of argumentative structures in science texts. This assessment of higher order thinking in reading involves the analysis of components of the argumentative text structure. Students read a news magazine article, in which the author describes a possible solution to global warming, through the reduction of gases. Students must first construct an accurate understanding of the text to conduct the analysis. They use skills and strategies to develop their understanding of text, as this is a prerequisite to performing the high-level thinking involved in examining claims and evidence in text. Building upon this literal understanding, students analyze the structure of the text to determine the interrelationships between ideas in the text. They identify the author's claims, that global warming may be reduced. They then consider the evidence that the author provides, which includes data on how reduction in greenhouse gases contributes to diminished global warming. The students must demonstrate understanding of the underlying reasoning that holds the claim and evidence together. They are required to identify this "logical glue" (i.e., warrants), if present in the text, and they must infer warrants if they are implicit in the argument design. Finally, the students analyze and determine the text structure, assigning roles of argument components and integrating all these components into a coherent argument.

Assessing analysis with student-created graphics. Students graphically represent the structure of the text and the relationship of ideas contained within the text (see Figure 7.3), which demonstrates their understanding of argument structure in the text. Prior to student performance, the teacher introduces the task and then explains and models how to make a text graphic. The teacher shares assessment criteria with students, using the performance rubric to communicate what is included in a successful performance (Table 7.2). The rubric communicates the expectations of student performance in terms of the required components of argument structure (e.g., claims, evidence, and warrants); relationships among the components (how the claims, warrants, and evidence are interconnected); and overall coherence and clearness of graphical representation. The students' performance is graded in relation to the rubric. This performance assessment serves both formative and summative purposes it guides and assesses students' analytical thinking in reading a text with a complex structure to convey ideas, perspectives, and information.

Assessing metacognition and evaluation with identification and reading of useful websites. Students are required to search for, locate and evaluate diverse Internet texts related to global warming. Navigating the Internet hypertext structure, students locate what they believe to be three useful websites to learn more about global warming. Through the entire course of Internet reading, students employ three evaluative criteria to judge the usefulness of websites: information value, comprehensibility, and credibility. Students overview and conduct anticipatory evaluation of hyperlinks leading to particular websites before "clicking through" to the website. After accessing a particular website, students evaluate website content and

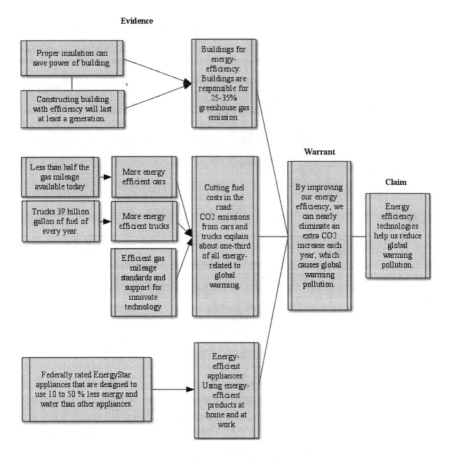

Figure 7.3.   Assessment using student created graphic representations.

structure, by examining the comprehensiveness of the website and how the information is accessed and organized. The students also check the website's credibility, investigating who created and/or managed the website (Is website public or private? Are there special interest groups involved in managing the website? Is there a profit motive operating?) and the extent to which the information is trustworthy in terms of biased perspectives (Does website content have balanced approaches to claiming an argument for/against global warming?) or unreliable facts (Does website content rely on scientific evidence or other information?). Finally, students must determine the usefulness of the websites based on their evaluations.

**Table 7.2.   Performance Assessment Rubric for
Claim-Evidence Text Analysis**

Grading	Student performance to create claim-evidence text analysis graphic
Exemplary	Student correctly identifies and clearly states all major components of the author's argument. The components include claims and/or counterclaims, supporting evidence, and warrants both stated and implicit.
	Student determines interrelationships of the argument components and recognizes overall argumentative text structure. The components are logically and coherently interconnected to one another in the graphic that represents the text structure.
	Student edits or revises the text graphic, excluding unnecessary and/or redundant information.
Satisfactory	Student identifies and states the author's claim and evidence. However, student does not identify all crucial evidence provided in the text and/or fails to find implicit warrants.
	Student makes logical and coherent interrelationships of the author's ideas. However, the graphic demonstrates only partial understanding of the argument structure.
	Student organizes the text graphic, minimizing unnecessary and redundant information.
Unsatisfactory	Student fails to identify and state correct information on the author's argument, including claim, evidence and warrant.
	Student portrays inaccurate relationships of the ideas that represent a weak understanding of the text structure.
	Student presents unnecessary, incoherent, and redundant information in the graphic.

**Table 7.3.   A Metacognitive Self-Assessment Checklist For
Internet Reading Processes**

Internet reading process	Aspects of Internet reading process to monitor
Website searching	_____ I am aware of my goals for Internet reading
	_____ I plan website searching to achieve the reading goals
	_____ I generate adequate search terms to use web search engines.
	_____ I anticipate the relevance and usefulness among the resulting entries
	_____ I conduct an additional search to find different Internet texts
Website reading	_____ I overview the website and integrate different parts of the website
	_____ I use website structures to better understand the website
	_____ I identify and learn about critical ideas and concepts in the website
	_____ I use online sources (e.g., online dictionary) to clarify unclear concepts
	_____ I compare and contrast information from different websites

(Table continues on next page)

Table 7.3.   Continued

Website evaluation	I evaluate the value of websites' information, asking:
	_____ How relevant is the information to my task?
	_____ What is the quality of the information that the website provides?
	_____ Does the website present diverse information?
	I evaluate websites' comprehensibility, asking as following:
	_____ How accessible is the website's information?
	_____ How effectively is the website designed and organized?
	_____ What is the relative ease of reading on the website?
	I evaluate website's credibility, asking:
	_____ Who created and/or manages the website?
	_____ How current is the information provided by the website?
	_____ How reliable and trustworthy is the information provided by the website?
	Finally,
	_____ I determine website usefulness by integrating the evaluation results

As students conduct their evaluations of Internet texts and websites, they engage in metacognitive monitoring of their reading processes and evaluative mindsets. Strategies for monitoring reading and navigation in a complex hypertext structure are necessary for successful Internet reading. The sheer numbers of Internet texts connected by hyperlinks present challenges to Internet readers, and readers must simultaneously perform a two-layered reading task: meaning construction and information management. Readers should invest their cognition in achieving a basic goal of reading—that is, meaning construction. They also must pay attention to the management of information sources that are hypertextually connected. When readers fail to manage numbers of hyperlinks and Internet sources, their reading may be ineffective and misled, and Internet readers may become disoriented. These problems may consume readers' attention and cognition. Thus, metacognitive monitoring on hypertext reading processes is crucial to successful reading on the Internet.

Students' higher order thinking in evaluation and metacognition is assessed through two related but different assessments. First, students use a rubric that also serves as a checklist, presented in Table 7.3, directing their attention to the relevant topics and problems. The checklist serves as both a reminder and a means to conduct self-assessment. It provides a model of good questions to ask of one's own reading performance, and offers the opportunity to practice self-assessment. The checklist helps

Table 7.4.   A Performance Assessment Rubric for Website Evaluation: Student Annotated Bibliography

Website Usefulness	*Levels of Student Evaluation Performance*			
	Not Apparent *(1)*	*Developing* *(2)*	*Proficient* *(3)*	*Exemplary* *(4)*
Information value	No apparent means for identifying and using cues to determine website's informativeness.	Identification and use of one or more cues to correctly determine websites' informativeness with insufficient evidence. For example, student evaluates websites' goal-relevance to judge the informativeness. However, identification of type of cue is inaccurate and/or determination of informativeness is erroneous.	Identification and use of one or several cues to correctly determine websites' informativeness with sufficient and detailed evidence. For example, student evaluates website' goal-relevance and breath and depth to correctly determine the informativeness.	Identification and use of all possible cues to correctly determine websites' informativeness with sufficient and detailed evidence. For example, a student evaluates websites' goal-relevance, breath and depth, and diversity in information presentation.
Comprehensibility	No apparent means for identifying and using cues to determine website's comprehensibility.	Identification and use of one or more cues to correctly determine websites' comprehensibility with insufficient evidence. For example, student evaluates websites' structure to judge the comprehensibility. However, identification of type of cue is inaccurate and/or determination of comprehensibility is erroneous.	Identification and use of one or several cues to correctly determine websites' comprehensibility with sufficient and detailed evidence. For example, a student evaluates websites' information accessibility and website structure to correctly determine the comprehensibility.	Identification and use of all possible cues to correctly determine websites' comprehensibility with sufficient and detailed evidence. For example, a student evaluates websites' information accessibility, website structure and design, and reader-consideration

(Table continues on next page)

Table 7.4.   Continued

Website Usefulness	Levels of student evaluation performance			
	Not Apparent (1)	Developing (2)	Proficient (3)	Exemplary (4)
Credibility	No apparent means for identifying and using cues to determine website's credibility.	Identification and use of one or more cues to correctly determine websites' credibility with insufficient evidence. For example, student identifies websites' author information to judge the credibility. However, identification of type of cue is inaccurate and/or determination of credibility is erroneous.	Identification and use of one or several cues to correctly determine websites' credibility with sufficient and detailed evidence. For example, a student evaluates websites' authority and types of publishing, to correctly determine the credibility.	Identification and use of all possible cues to correctly determine websites' credibility with sufficient and detailed evidence. For example, a student evaluates websites' authority, currency of information, types of publishing, and reliability of content.

students' metacognitive strategy use in evaluating multiple texts that are intertextually connected in Internet hypertext structure. Second, students participate in a performance assessment that requires the creation of an annotated bibliography of the websites deemed useful to learn about the global warming. Prior to student performance, the teacher uses think-alouds of her evaluation strategies as she scrutinizes Internet sources, using the checklist. This teacher modeling, enhanced by visualization and verbalization, helps students understand better the actual strategy use. Following teacher modeling, students access the Internet and perform website evaluation. Teachers observe students' evaluation processes which demonstrate whether they are keep checking the usefulness of Internet sources based on its three criteria. Students' annotated bibliographies must reflect their website evaluation results, and be supported by evidence. This performance assessment rubric is presented in Table 7.4. It is used to guide students' learning to use evaluation strategies on the Internet. Students' final products are graded with the scoring rubric, and the teacher provides feedback on students' performance based on their interpretation of the scores.

Synthesis and application in the science project. Students read the science texts to plan and deliver oral presentations that focus on a comprehensive plan to reduce global warming. In this task, students must use higher order thinking to: (1) synthesize their understanding of global warming from across texts, and (2) apply this understanding to perform the presentation. The series of texts that focus on global warming include the textbook chapter, the newspaper editorial, the science article, and student-located Internet texts. With these texts, students must build between- and cross-textual understanding, representing comprehension of each text and synthesis of what is comprehended across the different texts. Students compare and contrast the different perspectives contained in the texts, and they determine the reliability of information and validity of arguments. Throughout the process of juxtaposing different texts and different perspectives, students must construct a coherent intertextual model in which the contents of the texts that are deemed necessary are commingled to build the larger and more complex metarepresentation.

Based on the synthesis of texts they read, students must devise a plan to apply their understanding of the texts in the oral presentation on global warming. To do so, student must assess the task demands and available resources, conceptualize the oral presentation as a problem to solve, determine the appropriate problem-solving path, and the requirements for a successful outcome. The students must continually reference the goals as they propose a comprehensive plan to respond to global warming. They do so as they are synthesizing information from across different texts. They use their intertextual understanding to shape their concepts and theories related to global warming. This understanding is transformed into solutions and tactics that citizens, governments, and international associations can use to reduce global warming. Students must devise a persuasive plan in which they use their knowledge to inform audiences about issues in global warming and to convince the audiences of the need for swift and decisive action.

The performance assessment serves to both guide and gauge students' higher order thinking in reading. That is, this performance assessment serves both formative and summative purposes. As it is embedded in inquiry-based science classes, the performance assessment guides students' learning related to controversial issues in science. It provides students a goal for learning the theme of this science unit and helps them engage in the thematic project. As students jointly read and plan their final presentation, teachers give support and feedback to encourage students' higher order thinking related to integrating and synthesizing multiple texts that include crucial concepts and data, and different perspectives and arguments. Also, this performance assessment serves as summative evaluation, and is included as part of students' report card grades. The performance assessment rubric (Figure 7.5) provides expectations that students must meet at the end of the thematic inquiry-based science unit. Students' final projects are interpreted how they effectively and comprehensively use their constructed understandings of multiple texts. higher order thinking involved in applying outcomes of reading is evoked by this performance assessment.

To summarize this section, the assessment of higher order thinking in reading can be accomplished by performance assessments that allow students to demonstrate application, synthesis, analysis, evaluation and metacognition. The series of performance assessments demonstrates that while gathering detailed and useful information from students is possible, it is also a complex undertaking. Contrasting with performance assessments are more simple measures of students' knowledge and comprehension. These are assessable with what are widely used forms of reading assessment: multiple choice items and brief, constructed responses. A successful reading assessment program will include suitable measure of both higher order thinking strategies, and the basic thinking on which their success is dependent.

For those interested in guidelines for considering assessment of higher order thinking, we provide a series of questions in Table 7.6. The questions, informed by Pellegrino, Chudowsky, and Glaser's (2001) tripartite model of assessment, may be used to inform a process of developing assessments that focus on higher order thinking in reading.

CONCLUSIONS

Particular acts of reading require higher order thinking. The comparison of accomplished readers' strategies with research-based and theory-based characterizations of higher order thinking allows for the examination of when reading requires higher order thinking, and what strategies and skills readers use to meet the challenge. Readers' higher order thinking is related not only to what is comprehended, but also to what the reader does with what is comprehended. The examples of higher order thinking are situated in reading in the eighth grade science classroom, and related assessments demonstrate that higher order thinking may be operating in both the construction of meaning and the use of that constructed meaning.

The presence of higher order thinking in acts of reading requires that valid assessment be designed to adequately describe such thinking. The knowledge and means for developing valid assessments are continually updated, just as our understanding of reading evolves. The knowledge needed to meet the challenge of developing valid assessments of higher order thinking in reading is available. However, the intellectual and tech-

Table 7.6.   Principles and Guiding Questions for Developing Reading Assessment for Higher Order Thinking

1. Cognition: Identify and define the specific higher order thinking in reading.

    a. What is the nature of the higher order thinking?

    b. Is the higher order thinking isolable? If not, what other types of thinking are involved?

    c. Do the definition and description fully represent or under-represent the higher order thinking?

    d. What is the context or situation in which the higher order thinking in reading is occurring?

2. Observation: Develop assessment materials and procedures in relation to higher order thinking in reading.

    a. What assessment materials and procedures, related to text(s)-task(s)-reader inter-actions, are best suited to eliciting and describing the higher order thinking?

    b. Does the text(s)-task(s)-reader interaction yield higher order thinking in terms of observable performances and products?

3. Interpretation: Develop and use interpretive tools to infer higher-order thinking from student assessment performance.

    a. Given the efforts to carefully match Cognition and Observation (above), what are evidence-based inferences about higher order thinking in reading?

    b. How does the assessment result inform an understanding of the reader's higher order thinking?

    c. How will the interpreted assessment information be applied to foster continued higher order thinking in reading?

nical prowess that can be used in establishing suitably complex instruction and assessment is in contrast with assessment traditions, habits of mind and constrained resources. Many assessments, including high stakes reading tests, use multiple choice and short constructed response items exclusively to measure and describe reading. This continuing practice illustrates that there is considerable work to be done to develop assessments that honor the complexity of higher order thinking in reading.

Development of suitable assessments must occur simultaneously for formative and summative assessment. Teachers and students need formative assessments that help to identify higher order learning needs and teaching opportunities, in students' zones of proximal development. As well, formative assessment can provide models for student readers who are learning to conduct self-assessment—because metacognition is itself a class of high order thinking, student readers must learn to "do assessment" for themselves. Performance assessments, as described in this chapter, can serve both the traditional role of gathering assessment data, and helping students learn to do assessment. The performance assessments described in this chapter may serve both formative and summative functions, and given the limits on school time and resources, assessments that serve these dual purposes are sorely needed. Valid assessment of readers' higher order thinking can demonstrate, in detail, the accomplishments of students, the successes of teachers and the value of educational programs in relation to higher order thinking.

The assessment of higher order thinking in reading is critical, as demonstrated by current practice and rhetoric around high-stakes reading tests (Council of Cheif State School Officers & National Governors Association, 2010). While such tests are used to determine student achievement and school accountability, they fall short of the valid and comprehensive measure of higher order thinking in reading, the very type of reading that is essential for success in school, and in life. Reading assessment practice must develop to accurately reflect what is known about both higher order thinking in reading, and effective assessment practice. There is a substantial research literature to inform the conceptualization of such reading, just as there is ample research on the development of suitable assessments. The task of developing appropriate assessments for the measure of students' higher order thinking in reading could not be more urgent.

REFERENCES

Afflerbach, P. (2007). *Understanding and using reading assessment: K-12*. Newark, DE: International Reading Association.

Afflerbach, P., & Cho, B. (2009a). Reading strategies and reading strategy instruction. In W. Schneider & H. Waters (Eds.), *Metacognition, strategy use, and instruction: A festschrift for Michael Pressley*. New York, NY: Guilford Press.

Afflerbach, P., & Cho, B. (2009b). Identifying and describing constructively responsive comprehension strategies in new and traditional forms of reading. In S. Israel & G. Duffy (Eds.), *Handbook of reading comprehension research* (pp. 69-90). Mahwah, NJ: Erlbaum.

Afflerbach, P., Pearson, P. D., & Paris, S. (2008). Clarifying differences between reading skills and reading strategies. *The Reading Teacher, 61*, 364-373.

Alexander, P. (2003). The development of expertise: The journey from acclimation to proficiency. *Educational Researcher, 32*, 10-14.

Alexander, P. A., Graham, S., & Harris, K. R. (1998). A perspective on strategy research: Progress and prospects. *Educational Psychology Review, 10*, 129-154.

Anderson, L., & Krathwohl, D. (2001). *A taxonomy for learning, teaching, and assessing: A revision of Bloom's Taxonomy of Educational Objectives*. New York, NY: Longman.

Anderson, R., & Pearson, P. (1984). A schema-theoretic view of basic processes in reading comprehension. In P. Pearson, M. Kamil, R. Barr, & P Mosenthal (Eds.), *Handbook of Reading Research*. New York, NY: Longman.

Baker, L., & Brown, A. L. (1984). Metacognitive skills and reading. In P. D. Pearson, R. Barr, M. L. Kamil & P. Mosenthal (Eds.), *Handbook of Reading Research* (Vol. 1, pp. 353-394). New York, NY: Longman.

Balcytiene, A. (1999). Exploring individual processes of knowledge construction with hypertext. *Instructional Science, 27*, 303-328.

Baxter, G., & Glaser, R. (1998). Investigating the cognitive complexity of science assessments. *Educational Measurement: Issues and Practice, 17*, 37-45.

Bazerman, C. (1985). Physicists reading physics: Schema-laden purpose and purpose-laden scheme. *Written Communication, 2*, 3-24.

Black, P., & Wiliam, D. (1998). Inside the black box: Raising standards through classroom assessment. *Phi Delta Kappan, 80*, 139-148.

Bloom, B. S. (1956). Taxonomy of educational objectives. *Handbook 1: Cognitive Domain*. New York, NY: McKay.

Braten, I., Stromso, H., & Britt, M. (2009). Trust matters: Examing the role of source evaluatiion in students' construction of meaning within and across multiple texts. *Reading Research Quarterly, 44*, 6-28.

Brown, J. S., Collins, A., & Duguid, P. (1989). Situated cognition and the culture of learning. *Educational Researcher, 18*, 32-42.

Chapman, J., & Tunmer, W. (1995). Development of young childrens' reading self-concepts: An examination of emerging subcomponents and their relationship with reading achievement. *Journal of Educational Psychology, 87*, 154-167.

Corno, L. (1993). The best-laid plans: Modern conceptions of volition and educational research." *Educational Researcher, 22*, 14–22.

Davis, A. (1998). *The limits of educational assessment*. Oxford, England: Blackwell.

Flavell, J. H. (1979). Metacognition and cognitive monitoring: A new area of cognitive-developmental inquiry. *American Psychologist, 34*, 906-911.

Garner, R. (1987). *Metacognition and reading comprehension*. Norwood, NJ: Ablex.

Goswami, U. (2003). Orthography, phonology and reading development: A cross-linguistic perspective. In M. Joshi (Ed.), *Linguistic relativity of orthographic and phonological structures*. Dordrecht, NL: Kluwer.

Graves, B., & Frederiksen, C. H. (1991). Literacy expertise in the description of fictional narrative. *Poetics, 20*, 1-26.

Guthrie, J., Britten, T., & Barker, K. (1991). Roles of document structure, cognitive strategy, and awareness in searching for information. *Reading Research Quarterly, 26*, 300-324.

Guthrie, J. T., & Wigfield, A. (2000). Engagement and motivation in reading. In M. L. Kamil, P. B. Mosenthal, P. D. Pearson, & R. Barr (Eds.), *Handbook of Reading Research* (Vol. 3, pp. 403–422). Mahwah, NJ: Erlbaum.

Guthrie, J., Wigfield, A., Barbosa, P., Perencevich, K. C., Taboada, A., Davis, M. H., et al. (2004). Increasing reading comprehension and engagement through concept-oriented reading instruction. *Journal of Educational Psychology, 96*, 403-423.

Hartman, D. K. (1995). Eight readers reading: The intertextual links of proficient readers reading multiple passages. *Reading Research Quarterly, 30*, 520-261.

Johnston, P., & Afflerbach, P. (1985). The process of constructing main idea from text. *Cognition and Instruction, 2*, 207-232.

Kintgen, E. R. (1988). *The perception of poetry*. Bloomington, IN: Indiana University Press.

Kintsch, W. (1998) *Comprehension: A paradigm for cognition*. New York, NY: Cambridge University Press.

Lewis, A., & Smith, D. (1993). Defining higher order thinking. *Theory Into Practice,* *32,* 131-137.

Linn, R., Baker, E., & Dunbar, S. (1991). Complex, performance-based assessment: Expectations and validation criteria. *Educational Researcher, 20,* 15-21.

Magliano, J. P., & Glaesser, A. C. (1993). A three-pronged method for studying inference generation in literary text. *Poetics, 20,* 193-232.

McKeown, M. G. (1985). The acquisition of word meaning from context by children of high and low ability. *Reading Research Quarterly, 20,* 482-496.

National Assessment Governing Board. (2008). *Reading framework for the 2009 National Assessment of Educational Progress.* Washington, DC: Author.

Newman, F. M. (1990). Higher order thinking in teaching social studies: A rationale for the assessment of classroom thoughtfulness. *Journal of Curriculum Studies, 22,* 41-56.

Palincsar, A. S., & Brown, A. L. (1984). Reciprocal teaching of comprehension-fostering and comprehension-monitoring activities. *Cognition and Instruction, 1,* 117-175.

Paris, S. (2005). Reinterpreting the development of reading skills. *Reading Research Quarterly, 40,* 184-202.

Paris, S. G., Lipson, M. Y., & Wixson, K. K. (1983). Becoming a strategic reader. *Contemporary Educational Psychology, 8,* 293-316.

Pellegrino, J. W., Chudowsky, N., & Glaser, R. (2001). *Knowing what students know: The science and design of educational assessment.* Washington, DC: National Academy Press.

Pressley, M., & Afflerbach, P. (1995). *Verbal protocols of reading: The nature of constructively responsive reading.* Hillsdale, NJ: Erlbaum.

Resnick, L. (1987). *Education and learning to think.* Washington, DC: National Academy Press.

Rosenblatt, L. (1938). *The reader, the text, the poem: The transactional theory of the literary work.* Carbondale, IL: Southern Illinois Press.

Rouet, J-F., Britt, M. A., Mason, R. A., & Perfetti, C. A. (1996). Using multiple sources of evidence to reason about history. *Journal of Educational Psychology, 88,* 478-493.

Scardamalia, M., & Bereiter, C. (1987). Knowledge telling and knowledge transforming in written composition. In S. Rosenberg (Ed.), *Advances in applied psycholinguistics: Reading, writing and language learning* (Vol. 2, pp. 142-175). Cambridge, England: Cambridge University Press.

Strømsø, H. I., Bråten, I., & Samuelstuen, M. S. (2003). Students? strategic use of multiple sources during expository text reading: A longitudinal think-aloud study. *Cognition and Instruction, 21,* 113-147.

Tabatabai, D., & Shore, B. M. (2005). How experts and novices search the Web. *Library & Information Science Research, 27,* 222-248.

Thorndike, E. L. (1917). Reading as reasoning: A study of mistakes in paragraph reading. *Journal of Educational Psychology, 8,* 323-332.

van den Broek, P., Rapp, D. N., & Kendeou, P. (2005). Integrating memory-based and constructionist processes in accounts of reading comprehension. *Discourse Processes, 39,* 299-316.

van den Broek, P., Young, M., Tzeng, Y., & Linderholm, T. (1999). The landscape model of reading. In H. van Oostendorp & S. R. Goldman (Eds.), *The construction of mental representations during reading* (pp. 71-98). Mahwah, NJ: Erlbaum.

van Dijk, T. A., & Kintsch, W. (1983). *Strategies of discourse comprehension*. New York, NY: Academic Press.

VanSledright, B. (2002). *In search of America's past: Learning to read history in elementary school*. New York, NY: Teachers College Press.

Veenman, M., van Hout-Wolters, B., & Afflerbach, P. (2006). Metacognition and learning: Conceptual and methodological issues. *Metacognition and Learning, 1*, 3-14.

Vygotsky, L. (1978). *Mind in society: The development of higher psychological processes*. Cambridge, MA: Harvard University Press.

Wineburg, S. (1991). Historical problem solving: A study of the cognitive processes used in the evaluation of documentary and pictorial evidences. *Journal of Educational Psychology, 83*, 73-87.

Wineburg, S. (1997). Beyond breadth and depth: Subject matter knowledge and assessment. *Theory Into Practice, 36*, 255-263.

Wolf, D. (1987). The art of questioning. *Academic Connections*, 1-7. Retrieved from www.exploratorium.edu/IFI/resources/workshops/artofquestioning.html

CHAPTER 8

ASSESSING LEARNING FROM INQUIRY SCIENCE INSTRUCTION

Stephanie B. Corliss and Marcia C. Linn

Measuring learning from science inquiry instruction has benefitted from the development of powerful technology-enhanced curriculum materials that feature scientific visualizations and embedded assessments. We review current assessment practices to measure students' higher order thinking in science and discuss promising approaches. We describe how the knowledge integration framework can inform the design of curriculum, assessments, and professional development to support complex scientific thinking. We conclude with recommendations for effective assessment practices and implications for future research.

RATIONALE AND RESEARCH QUESTIONS

Reforms in science education emphasize the importance of teaching and learning through scientific inquiry, where students engage in complex thinking as they construct their own understanding. Assessing this form of learning requires new measures aligned with instruction (American Association for the Advancement of Science [AAAS], 1993; National

Assessment of Higher Order Thinking Skills, pp. 219–243
Copyright © 2011 by Information Age Publishing
All rights of reproduction in any form reserved.

Research Council [NRC], 1996, 2001) and consistent with advances in understanding of student learning (Bransford, Brown, & Cocking, 2000). Assessments need to measure students' deep understanding of complex science topics and their ability to use the scientific inquiry processes in support of their learning.

Learning through inquiry requires students to utilize problem solving, analytical, and science process skills, as well as to understand the nature of science (Zachos, Hick, Doane, & Sargent 2000). Students have to develop research questions, form hypotheses, design investigations, analyze and interpret data, and form and evaluate scientific explanations (Kuhn, Black, Keselman, & Kaplan, 2000). These advanced skills are essential for functioning in an increasingly complex and scientifically sophisticated society (NRC, 1996, 2001) where one must think critically about often-persuasive messages and grapple with issues such as global climate change, energy conservation, and health decision making.

Implementing inquiry in the classroom can be challenging for both students and teachers. In an inquiry classroom students engage in scientific investigations while working together to solve open and complex problems. This student-centered approach puts the teacher into the role of facilitator rather than presenter of knowledge. Teachers must find ways to deal with students' multiple and sometimes conflicting ideas about science, and they need strategies for eliciting prior knowledge, adding new ideas, and assisting students in distinguishing between and reconciling their ideas about science in order to build a more coherent and cohesive understanding (Davis & Varma, 2008). Students are active in the learning process as they construct their knowledge. Research shows that inquiry instruction, combined with effective pedagogical practices and technology supports, can lead to improved student learning of science concepts (Krajcik et al., 1998; Linn, Davis, & Bell, 2004; Reiser et al., 2001; Sandholtz & Reilly, 2004; Scardamalia & Bereiter, 1996; Songer, Lee, & Kam, 2002). However, not all assessments are sensitive to inquiry instruction (Clark & Linn, 2003).

Traditional science assessments do not measure the type of complex thinking that is promoted in inquiry instruction; they mainly focus on recall of scientific facts (Lederman & Niess, 2000). More authentic assessments that emphasize complex thinking in science are needed to assess inquiry instruction (NRC, 1996, 2000; Pellegrino, Chudowsky, & Glaser, 2001). Furthermore, assessments need to align with innovative curricular materials and professional development opportunities to support inquiry teaching in the classroom (Linn, Lee, Tinker, Husic, & Chiu, 2006).

In this chapter, we discuss assessment of inquiry in the context of research projects that investigate technology-enhanced inquiry instruction and employ professional development that emphasizes inquiry learning.

Table 8.1.   Lower Order and Higher Order Science Skills

Science Skills		Learning Activities and/or Assessments
Lower order	Demonstrating knowledge of scientific concepts, laws, theory, procedures, and instruments	Recall
		Define
		Describe
		List
		Identify
Higher order	Applying scientific knowledge and procedures to solve complex problems	Formulate questions
		Hypothesize/Predict
		Design investigations
		Use models
		Compare/Contrast/Classify
		Analyze
		Find solutions
		Interpret
		Integrate/Synthesize
		Relate
		Evaluate

The assessment, curricular materials, and professional development are all aligned using the knowledge integration framework (Linn, 1995; Linn, Davis, Bell, 2004). This work draws on findings from the Technology-Enhanced Learning in Science (TELS; http://www.telscenter.org) Center for Teaching and Learning and the Mentored and Online Development of Educational Leaders in Science (MODELS; http://models.berkeley.edu) project. We consider the following research questions:

1. What are valid assessments of complex scientific thinking?
2. How can assessments capture students' ability to reuse complex thinking strategies in new settings?
3. How can assessment support teachers' as they promote complex thinking in science?

ASSESSMENT OF COMPLEX THINKING IN SCIENCE

Both national and international science assessment efforts recognize the importance of assessment of complex thinking in science. The NAEP (National Assessment of Educational Progress) science framework includes a section on practical reasoning, described as "the ability to apply appropriate scientific knowledge, problem-solving skills, and thinking processes to the solution of real problems." The assessment items are designed to probe students to think abstractly and consider hypothetical situations; consider several factors simultaneously; take an objective view of situations; and realize the importance of practical reasoning and experience (Grigg, Lauko, & Brockway, 2006). TIMSS (Trends in International Mathematics and Science Study) assessment framework also has a focus on advanced cognitive skills, such as knowing, applying and reasoning. Key skills of the reasoning domain include: analyzing problems to determine the relevant relationships, concepts, and problem-solving steps; making connections between concepts in different areas of science; combining knowledge of science concepts with information from experience or observation to formulate questions that can be answered by investigation; formulating hypotheses; making predictions; designing or planning investigations; making valid inferences based on evidence; applying conclusions to new situations; and constructing arguments to support the reasonableness of solutions to problems (Gonzales et al., 2008).

Efforts have been made to include open-ended items that measure complex thinking on these assessments, but these items are scored with a "right-or-wrong" or "right, partial, wrong" approach. These dichotomous scoring procedures fail to capture the nuances of students thinking (Liu, Lee, Hofstetter, & Linn, 2008). Scoring methods with additional categories that emphasize links between relevant ideas about the scientific phenomena can provide more information about how students integrate their knowledge. We have investigated and refined the knowledge integration framework to design and score items that measure complex thinking in science.

KNOWLEDGE INTEGRATION FRAMEWORK

Knowledge integration focuses on how learners struggle with multiple and conflicting ideas in science, how they develop new ideas, and how they sort out connections between new and existing ideas to reach a more coherent understanding (Linn, 1995; Linn, Davis, & Bell, 2004). Students bring existing ideas to any learning situation. They come to science class with a repertoire of conflicting and often confusing ideas. These ideas evolve as students are presented with new ideas in science instruction. Students compare ideas, identify links and connections among their ideas, and gather evidence to support their ideas. Research shows that effective science instruction uses students' ideas as the starting point for investigating scientific phenomena and guides learners as they add new ideas, sort out these ides in a variety of contexts, make connections among ideas at multiple levels of analysis, develop a more nuanced criteria for evaluating ideas, and formulate linked views about the scientific phenomena (Linn, 2006; Linn et al., 2004).

The knowledge integration framework identifies four main categories of design principles to support meaningful learning: (1) making science accessible, (2) making thinking visible, (3) helping students learn from each other, and (4) promoting lifelong learning (Kali, 2006; Linn & Hsi, 2000; Linn, Clark, & Slotta, 2003). These principles guide the development of assessments to measure students' complex thinking in science, and also the design of curriculum, professional development, and instruction to promote complex thinking.

Designing Knowledge Integration Curriculum Materials

The curricular projects used in the research reported here were collaboratively designed by researchers and teachers at the TELS Center for Teaching and Learning. The projects guide students in scientific inquiry of real world issues through collaborative activities that emphasize investigation and the use of complex visualizations (Linn et al., 2006). Projects are used in 6th through 12th grade classrooms and cover topics in earth science, life science, physical science, biology, chemistry, and physics (see examples in Figures 8.1 and 8.2). Students and teachers access the projects through the Web-based Inquiry Science Environment (WISE; http://

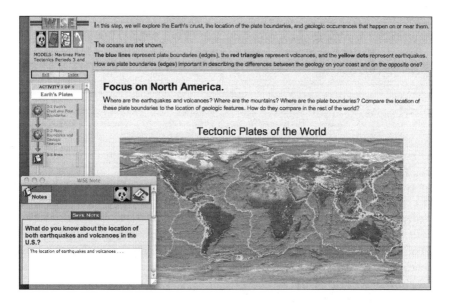

Figure 8.1.   Screenshot of TELS project, *Plate Tectonics: What's on Your Plate?,* and embedded assessment item.

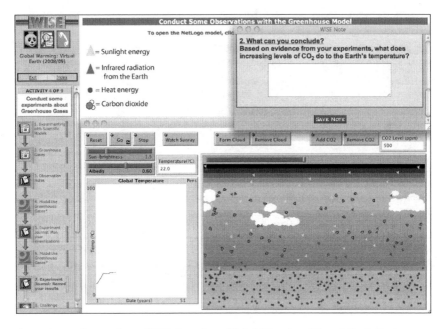

Figure 8.2.   Screenshot of TELS project, *Global Warming: Virtual Earth Project,* and embedded assessment item.

www.wise.berkeley.edu/). Each project takes approximately 7 to 10 fifty-minute science class periods to complete.

The activity structures in TELS projects are designed to engage students in the four interrelated processes of knowledge integration: eliciting ideas, introducing new ideas, developing criteria for evaluating ideas, and sorting and reorganizing ideas (Clark, Varma, McElhaney, & Chiu, 2008; Linn & Eylon, 2006). *Science is made accessible* in TELS projects by engaging students in inquiry investigations that connect to their everyday knowledge and reflect current scientific dilemmas such as interpreting claims about global warming, choosing appropriate treatments for cancer, or choosing an energy-efficient car. TELS projects *make thinking visible* by providing opportunities for students to interact with dynamic visualizations and to construct scientific explanations and visual models to represent their thinking. *Collaborative learning* is promoted throughout the projects with peer collaboration tools such as structured debates, online discussions, and share and critique activities. Finally, TELS projects encourage *lifelong science learning* by engaging students in reflecting on their own ideas and understanding in science, in critiquing diverse science information, and in developing inquiry skills useful for future science learning (Linn & Hsi, 2000).

Measuring Knowledge Integration

Knowledge integration assessments stimulate learning as well as evaluate learning. Like TELS curricular projects, the assessments engage students in complex thinking in various scientific contexts in everyday life. Items pose a dilemma and require students to generate an argument. Students must establish connections between new knowledge and existing knowledge, integrate knowledge gained from various sources, and warrant these ideas with evidence.

In TELS research studies, we use three types of assessments to evaluate how students integrate their knowledge of complex science topics: items embedded within TELS curricular projects; instruction sensitive pre/post tests, and annual benchmark tests including instruction sensitive items, standardized items, and questions about science learning. Items embedded within TELS curricular projects elicit students' ideas and explanations and encourage them to reflect on their understanding of the science concepts (see examples in Figures 8.1 and 8.2). This allows teachers to formatively evaluate students' thinking as they progress through the projects, which gives them opportunities to provide feedback to their students and to make changes to their teaching if necessary. Embedded assessments also provide researchers with information about how the project's cognitive and social supports contribute to students' learning.

Pre/posttest are given immediately preceding and following the enactment of TELS curricular projects. They are short four to six item tests that are instruction sensitive. They measure students' knowledge of the scientific concepts covered in the project. Pretests inform teachers and researchers of students' existing ideas while the posttests measure students' understanding at the end of the project.

Benchmark tests, completed at the end of each school year, serve as a delayed posttest that measures students' long-term understanding. These tests were designed to calibrate students' knowledge integration abilities, track students' development of knowledge integration over time, and compare student achievement with national norms on standardized science learning measures. TELS benchmark assessments include multiple choice items and explanation items. Students are often asked to explain their reasoning for their multiple-choice answer. Along with items developed by researchers, open-ended NAEP and TIMSS items are included in TELS assessments. Pre/posttest items and benchmark items are developed to measure students' learning of the science concepts both inside and outside of the context of the TELS projects.

All items are scored using a 5-point knowledge integration rubric that emphasizes students' links between relevant ideas about the scientific phenomena. Using a knowledge integration rubric, no answer is scored as a 0, and off task responses are scored as 1. Responses that show no links between normative ideas are scored as 2. A score of 3 represents a "partial link" where relevant ideas are expressed but not elaborated on to demonstrate how two ideas are connected. Responses that demonstrate a "full link" between two normative and relative ideas are scored a 4. Scores of 5 represent a "complex link" where two or more scientifically valid links are expressed. Figure 8.3 shows an example of an assessment item from the earth science benchmark test and the rubric used to score student responses.

A sophisticated study using the Rasch PCM item response theory (IRT) technique was conducted to gather reliability and validity data on the six TELS subject-specific (Earth Science, Life Science, Physical Science, Biology, Chemistry, Physics) benchmark tests (Liu et al., 2008). Over 3000 students took the TELS assessments at the end of the academic year. The number of items ranged from 16 to 27, depending on the test. Results provided using item response theory (IRT) provide satisfactory evidence for reliability and validity of knowledge integration assessments (Liu et al., 2008). They measure students' ability to sort, link, distinguish, and evaluate ideas and evidence. Explanation items are better at differentiating student science performance than multiple choice items, and using a knowledge integration scoring rubric on NAEP and TIMSS items greatly improves their psychometric properties. These assessments require students to think deeply about science content, which can promote an atmosphere of critical thinking in the classroom. In the following sections we report results from classroom studies where TELS curricular projects and knowledge integration assessments were used to engage both students and teachers in complex scientific thinking. In the following sections we report results from various classroom studies using knowledge integration assessments to measure complex scientific thinking. In the first study, students' knowledge integration of complex topics in earth science were examined after completing two TELS curricular projects. Next, we discuss the results of a study that assessed students' science concept knowledge integration and their ability to transfer general inquiry skills to novel tasks after completing a TELS curricular project. In the last study, we discuss the MODELS professional development program to facilitate teacher use of knowledge integration assessment and the effects on change in teacher practice. These studies combine TELS curricular projects and knowledge integration assessments to engage both students and teachers in complex scientific thinking.

Picture "A " shows a real greenhouse where light from the sun passes through the glass panels and heats the inside. The glass panels of the greenhouse keep the heat energy from escaping.

Picture A   Picture B

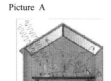

Picture "B" shows the greenhouse effect that happens on Earth. Which part of the picture is like the glass of the greenhouse? **Circle One.**

SUN   SPACE   ATMOSPHERE   EARTH

Explain your answer.

Level	Criteria	Student responses
No Answer		
Offtask Irrelevant or "I don't know."		
Irrelevant/Incorrect Have relevant ideas but fail to recognize links between them. Make links between relevant and irrelevant ideas. Have incorrect/irrelevant ideas.	-Scientifically incorrect statements, e.g. -Incorrect description of pictures, e.g. -Inaccurate connections between greenhouse and earth's atmosphere. -Says greenhouse is atmosphere, sun, earth, etc without further explanation.	-It is sent back to the sun -These pictures show about sun -Arrows are pointing out -Atmosphere is like magnifying glass -Ozone layer is like glass on the greenhouse.
Partial Have relevant ideas but do not fully elaborate links between them in a given context.	-Matches similar elements in two pictures but does not specify why/how they are similar. -Describe one picture as presented (usually focuses on how different arrows are pointing) -Mentions that atmosphere reflects, absorbs, or receives sunlight and does not relate one another.	-Because the sun reflects onto the plants and then goes back into space. -Because the earth suck some of the radiation into the earth lets it go slowly. -The dotted lines seem to show the glass and the dotted lines look like the atmosphere.
Basic Elaborate a scientifically valid link between two ideas relevant to a given context.	Mentions atmosphere is like the glass on a greenhouse and provides one of the following: -lets heat in and traps it there -keeping most of heat inside	- Earth is like the picture because the sunrays come from the sun heat up the Earth and sometimes reflect back.
Complex Elaborate two or more scientifically valid links among ideas relevant to a given context.	Mentions atmosphere is like the glass on a greenhouse and says "receive sunlight energy and blocks earth's (radiation) energy (or IR) from escaping to the space"	The glass is like the atmosphere. When solar energy hits the Earth, it turns into infrared energy (IR). If there are enough greenhouse gases the IR stays in Earth's atmosphere, heating up the Earth.

Figure 8.3.   Earth science assessment item and knowledge integration rubric.

ASSESSING COMPLEX SCIENTIFIC THINKING IN EARTH SCIENCE

In the following study, we examined how two TELS curricular projects facilitate student knowledge integration of complex topics in earth science. We report results from knowledge integration assessments to evaluate the effectiveness of the curriculum and instruction and to demonstrate gains in students learning.

Participants and Procedures

Participants were 145 mixed-ability sixth grade science students from an ethnically and economically diverse school. All students were enrolled in a science class taught by the same teacher. The teacher had 33 years teaching experience. He taught science for 20 of the 33 years, and participated in the MODELS (Mentored and Online Development of Educational Leaders for Science) professional development program for 3 years. Students completed the *Global Warming: Virtual Earth* and *Plate Tectonics: What's on Your Plate?* projects during the 2007/2008 school year.

In both TELS projects, students interacted with complex scientific visualizations and then created their own model to demonstrate understanding of the scientific content. In *Global Warming*, students constructed a model of the Greenhouse Effect to show how global warming occurs and in *Plate Tectonics*, students created their own model to explain how a geological feature, such as a volcano or mountain, is formed. Students individually completed instruction sensitive pre/post tests for each project, and spent approximately 8 days working in pairs through each project during their science class time.

Data Sources and Analysis

The pre/posttests for each project consisted of four free response questions. Each item related to a main scientific concept to be learned in the unit (e.g., How does the Greenhouse Effect work to make sure that the temperature of the Earth's surface is just right?, List two causes you think contribute to global climate change. Why are most of the active volcanoes and earthquakes in the United States located on or near the West Coast?, What is the difference between a convergent and a collisional boundary?). Other questions required students to transfer their knowledge to a new context (e.g., According to the information in the table [surface temperature, composition of atmosphere], which planet has the greatest greenhouse effect? Explain your choice using evidence from the table., What evidence do scientists have for the movement of plates? How does this evidence support their ideas?). Responses to each item were coded using a 5-point knowledge integration rubric (see Figure 8.3).

Results

Results of paired t-tests revealed significant learning gains in students' complex thinking about the topics covered in the *Global Warming* (t (125) $= -11.04$, $p < .001$) and the *Plate Tectonics* (t $(130) = -10.44$, $p < .001$) projects. Table 8.2 shows students' learning gains. For *Global Warming*, mean composite scores increased from 4.71 on the pretest to 7.14 on the post-test. Mean composite scores increased from 5.70 on the pretest to 8.10 on the posttest for *Plate Tectonics*.

Results revealed that the TELS curricular projects were successful at helping students to develop a deep understanding of complex earth science concepts. Students demonstrated their ability to apply what they learned in the projects to both similar and novel questions on the posttest. Additionally, students were able to retain and apply their knowledge on end of year assessments; benchmark analyses revealed significant student learning gains in students' understanding of complex earth science concepts from the beginning to the end of the school year (Gerard, Spitulnik, & Linn, 2009). Results show that knowledge integration assessments measure students' ability to transfer their understanding of complex science concepts to contexts outside of the TELS curricular projects and that knowledge integration rubrics can capture progressively more sophisticated levels of students' reasoning in novel settings (Liu et al., 2008).

ASSESSING TRANSFER OF COMPLEX INQUIRY SKILLS

The goal of inquiry-based science instruction, like all education, is to promote the development of skills that students can transfer across disciplines and domains and use throughout their lifetime. The following study investigated how the guided inquiry experience presented in TELS projects facilitated the development of general inquiry skills that students could apply in a new learning context.

Table 8.2.   Student Learning Gains From Pre- to Posttest

	Pretest Mean (SD)	Posttest Mean (SD)	N
Global Warming	4.71 (5.41)	7.14 (2.08)	126
Plate Tectonics	5.70 (5.01)	8.10 (5.64)	131

To study transfer of general inquiry skills, researchers determined whether and when students could transfer the inquiry skills they engaged in during the TELS *Global Warming* project to a novel task (Corliss & Varma, 2008). Inquiry skills were defined as: (1) interpreting visual data, (2) using evidence to draw conclusions, (3) designing experiments, and (4) evaluating experimental results. These were the inquiry processes students must engage in to succeed in the TELS project. The transfer tasks required students to engage in these same processes in a context other than global warming.

Participants and Procedures

Fifty sixth grade science students at an ethnically diverse public school participated in this study. Students spent approximately 1.5 weeks working in pairs through the *Global Warming* project during their science class time. Within the project, students conducted experiments with a Greenhouse Effect visualization by manipulating levels of solar energy, atmospheric carbon dioxide, albedo, sunlight, and cloud cover. Following their investigations, students drew conclusions about the role of the different factors involved in the Greenhouse Effect. Students individually completed a 20-minute pretest and posttest measuring students' content knowledge and inquiry skills.

Data Sources and Analysis

Two items on the pre/posttests measured content knowledge (e.g., Describe how the Greenhouse Effect happens. What is the difference between the greenhouse effect and global warming?) and six items measured inquiry skills. The inquiry questions were designed to present students with visual data, allow students to draw conclusions based on evidence gathered from the visualization, have students design experiments to answer research questions, and evaluate conclusions based on experimental data (see Figure 8.4 for sample items). The inquiry questions differed from pre to posttest by context; students either answered questions about the survival of California fruit crops or California ocean species based on environmental factors. To account for any order effects, approximately half of the students received the fruit crops questions on the pretest and ocean species questions on the posttest, while the order was reversed for the remaining students. These items measured transfer of inquiry skills by requiring students to engage in the inquiry process outside of the context of the *Global Warming* project.

Two content and five inquiry questions from the pre/posttests were scored using 5-point knowledge integration rubrics. Separate composite

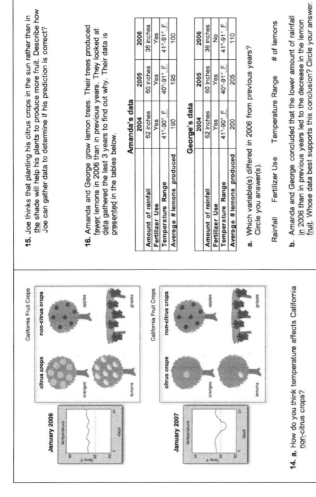

14. a. How do you think temperature affects California non-citrus crops?

b. Explain your answer using evidence from the diagram.

15. Joe thinks that planting his citrus crops in the sun rather than in the shade will help his plants to produce more fruit. Describe how Joe can gather data to determine if his prediction is correct?

16. Amanda and George grow lemon trees. Their trees produced fewer lemons in 2006 than in previous years. They looked at data gathered the last 3 years to find out why. Their data is presented in the tables below.

Amanda's data

	2004	2005	2006
Amount of rainfall	62 inches	60 inches	36 inches
Fertilizer Use	Yes	Yes	Yes
Temperature Range	41°-90° F.	40°-91° F.	41°-91° F.
Average # lemons produced	190	195	100

George's data

	2004	2005	2006
Amount of rainfall	62 inches	60 inches	36 inches
Fertilizer Use	Yes	Yes	No
Temperature Range	41°-90° F.	40°-91° F.	41°-91° F.
Average # lemons produced	200	205	110

a. Which variable(s) differed in 2006 from previous years? Circle you answer(s).

Rainfall   Fertilizer Use   Temperature Range   # of lemons

b. Amanda and George concluded that the lower amount of rainfall in 2006 than in previous years led to the decrease in the lemon fruit. Whose data best supports this conclusion? Circle your answer.

Amanda's   George's   Both

c. Explain your answer using evidence from the data tables.

Figure 8.4.   Items to measure students inquiry skills.

scores were calculated for content knowledge and inquiry items. Table 8.3 provides details of the items included in the analyses and Table 8.4 contains a sample rubric.

Results

Results of a paired t-test revealed a significant difference between content items composite scores from pretest to posttest (t (50) = -4.46, p < .01) and inquiry items composite scores from pretest to posttest (t (49) = -3.77, p < .01.). Mean composite scores on the content items increased from 4.2 to 5.2, and inquiry item composite scores increased from 8.8 to 10.8. Students were able to transfer inquiry skills (e.g. interpreting visual data, using visual data as evidence to draw conclusions, designing experiments, and evaluating experimental results) to the novel tasks represented on the posttest. The *Global Warming* Project was effective in helping students to learn these skills as they were guided to manipulate the interactive Greenhouse Effect visualization and evaluate the results of their experiments to determine how particular variables affected global temperature.

Results of these studies revealed that as teachers and curriculum engage students in inquiry, students learn to integrate their ideas. Students not only gain content knowledge, but also valuable reasoning skills, both of which can be applied to novel contexts.

KNOWLEDGE INTEGRATION PROFESSIONAL DEVELOPMENT

The various types of knowledge integration assessments used in this research provide information about students' thinking before, during, and after their interactions with TELS projects. We have discussed how researchers use and interpret data gathered through knowledge integration assessments. However, the assessments were also designed to be used by teachers, but many may not know how to take advantage of these assessment opportunities to inform their instructional practices.

Professional development support can be a mediating factor to improve teachers' practices and enactment of inquiry-based science learning materials (Davis & Varma, 2008; Fishman et al., 2003; Schneider, Krajcik, & Blumefeld, 2005; Varma, Husic, & Linn, 2008). Professional development designed around analyzing student data reveal that teachers learn by improving their understanding of their own students' thinking (Fishman et al., 2003; Kazemi & Franke, 2004). TELS designed professional development to enable teachers to use knowledge integration inquiry assessments to improve their teaching.

**Table 8.3.   Pretest and Posttest Items
Measuring Global Warming and Inquiry**

Item	Item Type	Skill Measured	Scoring Range
Q1	Explanation	Knowledge of Greenhouse Effect	0-5
Q2	Explanation	Knowledge of global warming	0-5
	Content Knowledge Composite Score (Q1+Q2)		0-10
Q13	Explanation	Interpreting visual data; Using evidence to draw conclusions	0-5
Q14	Explanation	Interpreting visual data; Using evidence to draw conclusions	0-5
Q15	Explanation	Designing experiment to gather data	0-5
Q16b	Multiple Choice	Evaluate experimental results	0-1
Q16c	Explanation	Evaluate experimental results	0-5
	Inquiry Skills Composite Score (Q13+Q14+Q15+Q16b+Q16c)		0-21

**Table 8.4.   Knowledge Integration Scoring Rubric for
Experimentation Item**

Q15: Joe thinks that planting his citrus crops in the sun rather than in the shade will help his plants to produce more fruit. Describe how Joe can gather data to determine if his prediction is correct?

Score	Level	Criteria
0	No Answer	
1	Off Task	
2	Irrelevant/Incorrect	
3	Partial Have relevant ideas but do not fully elaborate links between them.	• Plant some crops in the shade and others in the sun (Independent Variable) and compare amount of fruit produced (Dependant Variable).
4	Full Elaborate a scientifically valid link between two relevant ideas.	• Plant some crops in the shade and others in the sun (Independent Variable) and compare amount of fruit produced (Dependant Variable). AND one of the following: • Discuss measurement technique of fruit crop and/or amount of crops planted • Discuss holding all other variables constant (water, fertilizer, soil type, …)
5	Complex Elaborate two or more scientifically valid links among relevant ideas.	• Plant some crops in the shade and others in the sun (Independent Variable) and compare amount of fruit produced (Dependant Variable). AND both of the following: • Discuss measurement technique of fruit crops and/or amount of crops planted • Discuss holding all other variables constant (water, fertilizer, soil type, …)

The knowledge integration perspective informed the design of professional development to support teachers in using technology-enhanced inquiry projects in their classrooms and aligning assessment practices with instruction. Teachers have a repertoire of ideas about science instruction, ideas about the content they teach, students' reasoning, pedagogical methods, and curriculum materials (Davis, 2004). Teachers acquire new ideas from many sources such as professional development opportunities, classroom experiences, teacher colleagues, or from examining their own students' ideas. When new ideas were encountered appropriate scaffolding can support teachers to reflect on their understanding, develop criteria to distinguish among ideas, and reorganize their knowledge to include the new ideas (Davis, 2004; Davis & Varma, 2008; Slotta, 2004).

We discuss professional development conducted by the MODELS program. MODELS is a 5-year National Science Foundation Teacher Professional Continuum project to support middle and high school science teachers as they plan, enact, and reflect on their experiences integrating TELS projects into their science curriculum. MODELS professional development activities are linked to the four principles of knowledge integration (Higgins, 2008). Activities are designed to make learning *accessible* and relevant to teachers by building on teacher' beliefs about science, technology, and their everyday practices. Students' *thinking is made visible* to teachers as they analyzed their students' work within the TELS projects and teachers' thinking is made visible as they responded to reflection questions following the professional development activities. MODELS provided teachers access to a supportive professional community, and activities were designed for teachers to *work collaboratively* so they could learn from each other. Professional development activities promoted *lifelong learning* by supporting teachers in continuously reflecting on their practice and planning modifications to their teaching.

MODELS PROFESSIONAL DEVELOPMENT

Approximately 20 middle school science teachers from two diverse school districts participated in the MODELS professional development. Teachers attended yearly summer professional development workshops and used at least one TELS project in the classroom each year. A goal of the professional development program was to support teachers in using evidence of students learning, measured by knowledge integration rubrics, to inform and refine their instruction and assessment practices. The professional development evolved over time as teachers' ideas about assessment become more sophisticated. In the following section, we discuss

MODELS professional development activities and present evidence of changes in teachers' assessment practices and gains in their students' learning over time. A timeline of MODELS professional development and data collection is presented in Figure 8.5.

Workshop 1: Creating and Using Knowledge Integration Rubrics

At MODELS summer workshops, professional developers provided teachers with random samples of their students' worked from key embedded assessments within TELS projects. Teachers work collaboratively with others who used the same projects in their classrooms. At Workshop 1, teachers developed 5-point knowledge integration rubrics for the embedded assessment item and scored their student data. As students' thinking became visible to the teachers, they discovered gaps in their students understanding and made plans to address these challenging concepts the following year. Table 8.5 shows an example of one earth science teacher's data sheet from the professional development activity.

Following the professional development activity, one teacher commented, "It was very helpful to look through my students work using a very critical eye. I will need to consider if students need to have more direct instruction and class discussion to influence better comprehension of challenging information." Teachers used this evidence of student understanding to base changes to their teaching methods, assessment practices, and the technology projects.

Workshop 2: Formative Assessment and Feedback for Knowledge Integration

During Year 1, teachers reported using knowledge integration rubrics to formatively evaluate students' thinking, but complained of little time to provide individual feedback to each student about the quality of all of

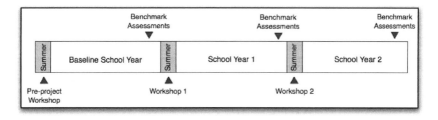

Figure 8.5.   MODELS professional development and data collection timeline.

Table 8.5.   Teacher Data Sheet From Summer Workshop 1

Project Title: Plate Tectonics: What's On Your Plate?
Activity: 3 Step: 2

Question: What do you know about the location of both earthquakes and volcanoes in the U. S.?

Categories of Student Responses	*Examples of Student Responses*	*Number of Students in Group Percentage*
1.Off-task Students give no response, or give a response that does not answer the question.	The location of earthquakes are in the United States and the location of volcanoes are in the United States. (re-stated question = no answer)	1 %
2. Irrelevant Link Student has misconceptions or makes invalid connections between ideas.	The location of earthquakes happen along the coast lines. The locations of volcanoes happen where the coastlines meet. The location of earthquakes are in flat areas and the location of volcanoes are in mountains.	14%
3. Partial Link Student needs to elaborate, or student's response is insufficient to solve the problem.	The location of earthquakes is where the plates meet. The location of volcanoes is where the magma pushes out of the ground. The locations of the earthquakes are on the west side of the U.S. The location of volcanoes are on the West Coast of the United States.	39%
4. Single Link Student makes one complete, correct connection.	Locations of earthquakes is on or near plate boundaries. The location of volcanoes is near plate boundaries. The location of earthquakes is normally on a plate boundary or fault line. The location of volcanoes is usually on a plate boundaries.	42%
5. Multiple Links Student makes 2 or more correct connections.	The location of earthquakes and volcanoes is at the plate boundaries. There is a plate boundary on the West Coast and that's why they are both there.	4%

their work within TELS projects. The online environment allowed teachers to respond to students work by typing in specific comments or inserting premade comments that were viewable to the students. The assessment tool retained a list of these premade comments that could be used repeatedly by the teachers with multiple students or over multiple years using the TELS projects. Professional development activities that emphasized more efficient use of the assessment tool to provide effective feedback to students were implemented at Workshop 2.

Teachers collaboratively scored random samples of their students work again and compared the results to those from the previous year. The teachers then reviewed their projects and selected one or two key questions they would grade during project enactments the following year. They created knowledge integration rubrics for these specific questions. As they created the rubrics, they also created generic comments that related to each knowledge integration category and would be applicable to students' work in multiple TELS projects. Table 8.6 shows examples of comments created during the workshop activity. Individual teachers then entered the comments they planned to use during the upcoming school year into the TELS teacher portal.

Following the workshop activity, one teacher commented, "Working on the comments was extremely helpful. They are generic enough to work for all projects, yet specific enough to encourage 'better' answers. I hope that overall I will see more evidence of understanding." Teachers felt the professional development activity was worthwhile and were excited about using the new assessment technique in the upcoming school year to support students thinking about the science concepts.

Table 8.6.   Examples of Teacher Comments Created During Professional Development Activity at Workshop

Teacher Comments
Needs work: Reread the question/prompt. This step needs corrections! Check for accuracy of writing/data. Try again!
Wrong-Redo: Your information is incorrect. Redo this step using better information/data. Do more research/discussion with your partner.
Evidence: You need to state facts or information based on reading or experiment data. Be specific with examples and/or real world connections.
Wow: This is great! You're providing complete answers using scientific vocabulary and evidence!
Partial link: Good start! Add more information or connections.
Evidence: Good answer. Now include specific evidence to support your statements.

Changes in Teachers' Assessment Practices

To examine how teachers' assessment practices changed after engaging in professional development, researchers reviewed records of all electronic comments given to their students through the teacher assessment tool during Year 1 and Year 2. Six teachers, one from each grade level at each school, were chosen for analysis. Each teacher attended both Workshop 1 and Workshop 2, and enacted one or more TELS projects during Year 1 and Year 2. We found that all 6 teachers graded more student work and provided more comments to their students in Year 2. The total comments given by all 6 teachers increased from 2,220 to 4,641 (see Table 8.7).

Results of the MODELS project revealed that by aligning curriculum, professional development, and assessment we saw changes in teachers' assessment practices to support students' higher order thinking. Professional development that engages teachers in the process of creating and using knowledge integration rubrics provided insight into students' thinking and evidence to base changes to the teaching and assessment practices. Further professional development on formative assessment techniques with the TELS teacher tools led to more efficient and effect strategies for examining students' thinking and providing feedback to students in the classroom. The result is better instructional practices and advances in students' higher order thinking about the science concepts presented in TELS projects over time (Gerard, Spitulnik, & Linn, 2009).

DISCUSSION

Valid assessments of inquiry learning in science are emerging in several research programs. These assessments ask students to make links among

Table 8.7.   Teacher Electronic Feedback to Students in TELS Projects

School, Grade Level	TELS Project	Number of Comments Year 1	Number of Comments Year 2
Midvale, 8th	Velocity	149	319
Alta Vista, 8th	Velocity	260	346
Midvale, 7th	Mitosis	298	1367
Alta Vista, 7th	Mitosis	857	1371
Midvale, 6th	Plate Tectonics	422	472
	Global Warming	21	278
Alta Vista, 6th	Plate Tectonics	213	488
Total Comments		2220	4641

their ideas and to buttress their conclusions with evidence, and require students to apply their knowledge and skills to novel contexts.

These innovative assessments need to align with inquiry instruction and professional development. Such alignment can change the interactions among students, teachers, and the curriculum. For schools to successfully integrate science inquiry learning, these elements need to change together. The research reported here provides evidence for the value of aligning curriculum, professional development, and assessment using the knowledge integration framework. When these practices support students to think more critically about complex science topics, we see improvement in student outcomes (Gerard et al., 2009).

Design of valid assessment requires more complex items than are typically used in state and national assessments. Assessment needs to move away from mostly multiple-choice items that do not make students thinking visible or measure students' deep understanding of scientific reasoning. Our research reveals that assessments designed for knowledge integration can accurately measure complex thinking in science inquiry. Multiple-choice assessments alone are not sensitive enough to measure deep understanding in science. Open-ended explanation items have the potential to tap into complex thinking as long as they are scored with an effective rubric that distinguishes between responses. For example, the 5-point knowledge integration rubrics successfully distinguish among students and are sensitive to inquiry teaching. Knowledge integration assessments have been used successfully to evaluate the effectiveness of TELS projects, to examine how students reuse complex thinking skills in new contexts, and to engage teachers in analyses of their students' thinking to inform changes to instructional and assessment practices.

Innovative assessments that measure inquiry learning can help teachers learn new practices by validly measuring student progress. Effective assessments help teachers identify and deal with students' multiple and sometimes conflicting ideas about science. Such assessments also encourage teachers to use the knowledge integration instructional pattern by revealing the multiple ideas that students hold and the limits of their ability to make links among ideas. The pattern calls for eliciting the prior knowledge of students in order to guide students to make links between their existing and new ideas. Second, the pattern calls for adding new, normative ideas that allow students to examine their own ideas. Third, the pattern calls for assisting students in distinguishing between the new ideas and their own views. When students develop scientific criteria for distinguishing ideas they are also able to apply these ideas to new situations. Fourth, the pattern calls for helping students sort out the repertoire of ideas that they hold and encouraging them to build a more coherent and cohesive understanding.

Professional development activities that engage teachers in using and creating knowledge integration rubrics give them better insight into their students' understanding and contribute to effective inquiry instruction. By analyzing student responses, teachers gain a deeper understanding of how students struggle to understand complex topics. Insights into student responses can help teachers improve their own assessment practices.

The studies reported here illustrate how assessment can shape learning and instruction. First, by giving knowledge integration pretests, the inquiry curriculum helps students understand the goals of inquiry instruction. Second, by embedding additional knowledge integration prompts in the instruction, the inquiry projects reinforce the importance of knowledge integration. Third, by giving teachers the opportunity to score student responses we contribute to teacher learning about the nature of inquiry and enable them to set realistic goals for their students. This activity can motivate teachers to consider ways to improve their own instructional strategies. Fourth, by using knowledge integration assessments to assign student grades, teachers elevate inquiry to a major goal of the course. Finally, by asking students to generalize their reasoning to novel problems, the assessments communicate that inquiry skills have multiple uses.

Future Research

The findings reported here show the benefit of aligning professional development, curriculum, and assessment to improve inquiry outcomes using the knowledge integration framework. We need a more nuanced understanding of how each of these aspects of science instruction contributes to student learning.

The value of knowledge integration assessments is clear but many questions remain. We know that knowledge integration measures are more sensitive than traditional multiple-choice outcome measures, but they are also more costly to score. In addition, teachers benefit from continuous information about student progress that can be gathered from embedded assessment. We need to understand how assessments can be used as learning events to improve teaching and learning over time. Research could help identify ways to design embedded assessments to replace current standardized tests and provide more informative and timely information for teachers.

We have glimmers of insight into how to promote and measure transfer of inquiry skills to new learning situations. We need more systematic and detailed studies of this question. Finally, we need more information about the long-term impact of inquiry versus traditional teaching. Additionally, as technology-enhanced instruction becomes more sophisticated, unique assessment opportunities will become available for teachers and researchers.

ACKNOWLEDGMENTS

This work was conducted in collaboration with others at the Center for Technology Enhanced Learning in Science (TELS) and researchers involved in the Mentored and Online Development of Educational Leaders in Science (MODELS) project, both of which are supported by the National Science Foundation under grant numbers 0334199 and 0455877. Any opinions, findings, and conclusions or recommendations expressed in this material are those of the authors and do not necessarily reflect the views of the National Science Foundation.

The authors wish to thank the members of the Technology-Enhanced Learning in Science (TELS) center, the Mentored and Online Development of Educational Leaders in Science (MODELS) project, and the teachers and students who participated in this work. Special thanks go to Michele Spitunik, the leader of the MODELS project, and Hee Sun Lee, the Director of Assessment for TELS.

REFERENCES

American Association for the Advancement of Science. (1993). *Benchmarks for science literacy.* New York, NY: Oxford University Press.

Bransford, J. D., Brown, A. L., & Cocking, R. R. (Eds.). (2000). *How people learn: Brain, mind, experience, and school.* Committee on Developments in the Science of Learning. National Research Council. Washington, DC: National Academy Press.

Clark, D., & Linn, M. C. (2003). Designing for knowledge integration: The impact of instructional time. *The Journal of the Learning Sciences, 12*(4), 451-494.

Clark, D. B., Varma, K., McElhaney, K., & Chiu, J. (2008). Design rationale within TELS projects to support knowledge integration. In D. H. Robinson & G. Schraw (Eds.), *Recent Innovations in educational technology that facilitate student learning* (pp. 157-193). Charlotte, NC: Information Age Publishing.

Corliss, S. B., & Varma, K. (2008, March). *Supporting the Development of Inquiry Skills in Technology-enhanced Science Curricula.* Paper presented at the annual meeting of the American Educational Research Association, New York, NY.

Davis, E. A. (2004). Knowledge integration in science teaching: Analyzing teachers' knowledge development. *Research in Science Education, 34*(1), 21-53.

Davis, E. A., & Varma, K. (2008) Supporting teachers in productive adaptation. In Y. Kali, M. C. Linn, & J. E. Roseman (Eds.), *Designing coherent science education.* New York, NY: Teachers College Press.

Fishman, B. J., Marx, R. W., Best, S., & Tal, R. T. (2003). Linking teacher and student learning to improve professional development in systemic reform. *Teaching and Teacher Education, 19,* 643-658.

Gerard, L. F, Spitulnik, M., & Linn, M. C. (2010). Teacher use of evidence to customize inquiry science instruction. *Journal of Research in Science Teaching, 47*(9), 1037-1063.

Gonzales, P., Williams, T., Jocelyn, L., Roey, S., Kastberg, D., & Brenwald, S. (2008). *Highlights From TIMSS 2007: Mathematics and Science Achievement of U.S. Fourth- and Eighth-Grade Students in an International Context* (NCES 2009–001). National Center for Education Statistics, Institute of Education Sciences, U.S. Department of Education. Washington, DC.

Grigg, W. S., Lauko, M. A., & Brockway, D. M. (2006). *The Nation's Report Card: Science 2005* (NCES 2006–466). Washington, DC: U.S. Department of Education, National Center for Education Statistics.

Higgins, T. E. (2008). *Through the eyes of professional developers: Understanding the design of learning experiences for science teachers.* Unpublished doctoral dissertation, University of California, Berkeley.

Kali, Y. (2006). Collaborative knowledge building using the Design Principles Database. *International Journal of Computer Support for Collaborative Learning, 1*(2), 187-201.

Kazemi, E., & Franke, M. L. (2004). Teacher learning in mathematics: using student work to promote collective inquiry. *Journal of Mathematics Teacher Education, 7*(3), 203-235.

Krajcik, J. S., Blumenfeld, P. C., Marx, R. W., Bass, K. M., Fredricks, J., & Soloway, E. (1998). Inquiry in project-based science classrooms: Initial attempts by middle school students. *Journal of the Learning Sciences, 7*(3 and 4), 313-350.

Kuhn, D., Black, J., Keselman, A., & Kaplan, D. (2000). The development of cognitive skills to support inquiry learning. *Cognition and Instruction, 18*(4), 495-523.

Lederman, N. G., & Niess, M. L. (2000). Problem solving and solving problems: Inquiry about inquiry. *School Science and Mathematics, 100*(3). 113-116.

Linn, M. C. (1995). Designing computer learning environments for engineering and computer science: The scaffolded knowledge integration framework. *Journal of Science Education and Technology, 4,* 103-126.

Linn, M. C. (2006). The knowledge integration perspective on learning and instruction. In R. K. Sawyer (Ed.), *The Cambridge handbook of the learning sciences* (pp.243–264). New York, NY: Cambridge University Press.

Linn, M. C., Clark, D., & Slotta, J. D. (2003). WISE design for knowledge integration. *Science Education, 87*(4), 517-538.

Linn M. C., Davis E. A. & Bell P. (2004) Inquiry and technology. In M.C. Linn, E. A. Davis & P. Bell (Eds.), *Internet environments for science education* (pp. 3-28). Mahwah, NJ: Erlbaum.

Linn, M. C., & Eylon, B. -S. (2006). Science Education: Integrating Views of Learning and Instruction. In P. A. Alexander & P. H. Winne (Eds.), *Handbook of Educational Psychology* (2nd ed., pp. 511-544). Mahwah, NJ: Erlbaum.

Linn, M. C., & Hsi, S. (2000). *Computers, teachers, peers: Science learning partners.* Mahwah, NJ: Erlbaum.

Linn, M. C., Lee, H. S., Tinker, R., Husic, F., & Chiu, J. L. (2006). Teaching and assessing knowledge integration in science. *Science, 313*, 1049-1050.

Liu, O. L., Lee, H.S., Hofstetter, C., & Linn, M. C. (2008). Assessing knowledge integration in science: Construct, measures, and evidence. *Educational Assessment, 13*, 33-55.

National Research Council. (1996). *The National Science Education Standards*. Washington, DC: National Academy Press.

National Research Council. (2001). *Inquiry and the National Science Education Standards*. Washington, DC: National Academy Press.

Pellegrino, J. W., Chudowsky, N., & Glaser, R.(Eds.).(2001). *Knowing what students know: The science and design of educational assessment*. Washington, DC: National Research Council.

Reiser, B. J., Tabak, I., Sandoval, W. A., Smith, B. K., Steinmuller, F., & Leone, A. J. (2001). BUGILE: Strategic and conceptual scaffolds for scientific inquiry in biology classrooms. In S. Carver & D. Klahr (Eds.), *Cognition and instruction: Twenty-five years of progress* (pp. 263-305). Mahwah, NJ: Erlbaum.

Sandholtz, J. H., & Reilly, B. (2004). Teachers, not technicians: Rethinking technical expectations for teachers. *Teachers College Record, 106*(3), 487-512.

Scardamalia, M., & Bereiter, C. (1996). Adaptation and understanding: A case for new cultures of schooling. In S. Vosniadou, E. DeCorte, R. Glaser, & H. Mandl (Eds.), International perspectives on the design of technology-supported learning *environments* (pp. 149-163). Mahwah, NJ: Erlbaum.

Schneider, R. M., Krajcik, J., & Blumenfeld, P. (2005). Enacting reform-based science materials: The range of enactments in reform classrooms. *Journal of Research in Science Teaching, 42*(3), 283-312.

Slotta, J. D (2004). The Web-based Inquiry Science Environment (WISE): Scaffolding teachers to adopt inquiry and technology. In M. C. Linn, P. Bell, & E. Davis (Eds.), *Internet Environments for Science Education* (pp. 203-232). Mahwah, NJ: Erlbaum.

Songer, N. B., Lee, H. S., & Kam, R. (2002). Technology-rich inquiry science in urban classrooms: What are the barriers to inquiry pedagogy? *Journal of Research in Science Teaching, 39*(2), 128-150.

Zachos, P. A., Hick, T. L., Doane, W. E. J., & Sargent, C. (2000). Setting theoretical and empirical foundations for assessing scientific inquiry and discovery in educational programs. *Journal of Research in Science Teaching, 37*(9), 938-962.

CHAPTER 9

ASSESSMENT OF HIGHER ORDER THINKING

The Case of Historical Thinking

Kadriye Ercikan and Peter Seixas

Disciplinary expertise requires mastery over both domain-specific declarative and procedural knowledge: understanding the fundamental concepts of a discipline, their organization and relationships with each other, and the means by which claims are tested and new knowledge is generated.[1] In this chapter, we use "higher order thinking" to capture the complex interaction of these various components of disciplinary expertise. Progression *towards* disciplinary expertise that involves these interactions, even at relatively novice levels, is thus a complex matter. Assessment of this progression, that is, learning, is similarly complex. In mathematics, testing students' memory of a specific formula does not capture their knowledge of when and where the application of the formula is appropriate. In history, students' recall of the date of the Dred Scott decision does not indicate their understanding of its historical significance, much less how interpretations of its significance have changed over time.

Assessment of Higher Order Thinking Skills, pp. 245–261
Copyright © 2011 by Information Age Publishing

Educational assessments play an important role in development and promotion of higher order thinking in school contexts, as well as in providing meaningful data about student learning in relation to these goals. This chapter describes and discusses (1) the important interconnections between assessment and development of higher order thinking, (2) why designing assessments for higher order thinking is more challenging than the all-too-common practice of assessing domain-specific declarative knowledge, (3) designing assessments for such constructs, (4) assessment design for historical thinking as an example, and (5) the role assessment can play in developing and refining learning and progression models of higher order thinking.

Assessment and the Development of Higher Order Thinking

The connections between assessment and learning have been researched and highlighted by many researchers during the last two decades (Black & Wiliam, 1998; Chudowsky & Pellegrino, 2003; Ercikan, 2006; Gipps, 1999; National Research Council (NRC), 2001; Pellegrino, Baxter, & Glaser, 1999; Seixas, 2009; Shepard, 2000; Stiggins, 1997). This research provided clear evidence that in order for assessments to inform and support learning, there needs to be close alignment between assessments and (1) learning goals and (2) development of learning progressions of students.

First, the clarity of definitions of learning goals are essential for developing assessments that provide meaningful information about student learning (Ercikan, 2006; NRC, 2001; Seixas, 2009). In history education, implicit or poorly articulated learning goals have had consequences for learning at both secondary and postsecondary levels. In the university context, faced with the task of writing the research essays and examination answers which are used for their evaluation, some students divine what counts as a demonstration of deep historical understanding—and many do not. In the high school context, too frequently, assessment becomes multiple-choice testing which tend to fail to capture the competencies that require students to engage in complex cognitive processes (Reich, 2009). Clearly articulated learning goals are essential for developing assessments that capture and promote these valued learning outcomes and communicate to students the kinds of learning they should be focusing on. Consider, for example, the goal, "Students will understand the causes of World War I." Without a rich prior conception of the term, "understanding," this is likely to communicate simply that students should be able to remember a list of causes. Contrast the following: "Students will be able to assess the relative strength of political, economic and ideological causes of World War I." This demands not only that students know some lists, but also that they can engage in reasoning about causes and consequences, perhaps using counterfactuals.

Other research emphasized the clear, detailed, empirically based definitions of student learning progressions in order for assessments to provide information about students' levels in relation to the progression and provide guidance about how to improve learning (Chudowsky & Pellegrino, 2003; Ercikan, 2006; NRC, 2001). Chudowsky and Pellegrino highlighted three aspects of students' learning progressions for assessments to support learning. They should (1) be based on empirical studies of learners in the domain; (2) identify performances that differentiate competent and less competent performance in the domain; and (3) provide a developmental perspective, laying out typical progressions from novice levels toward competence and then expertise, and noting landmark performances along the way.

During the last 2 decades, there has been tremendous research in learning areas such as mathematics, science, history and reading on how students learn, the progression of knowledge and competencies, and higher order thinking in these areas (NRC, 2001; Seixas, 2009). Developing learning progression models that provide empirical evidence about students' development requires years' worth of research on every topic in a subject area for each grade. In fact even when such models of learning progressions are developed, they are only hypotheses that need to be confirmed and revised based on further research. Briggs and Alonzo (2009) describe this need as follows:

> The learning progressions represent a hypothesis—both about the ways in which students actually progress through identified ideas and about the ways in which ideas about different phenomena "hang together" as students move towards the targeted level of understanding. This hypothesis must be tested with further evidence, such that the development of a learning progression and its associated assessment items is an iterative process—the learning progression informs the development of assessment items; the items are used to collect data which provides information about student thinking, leading to revisions in both the items and the learning progression itself. (p. 4)

In the context of history education, what we mean by learning progression is best conveyed with a specific example. British researchers Lee and Ashby (2000) gave elementary school students two cartoon-strip stories about (or, in their terminology, "accounts of") the end of the Roman Empire divided into three "chapters" each. The two stories present very different interpretations. The first emphasized the barbarian incursions and claimed the "real end of the Roman Empire" was in 476, with the overthrow of the last Emperor. The second said that the "real end" was in

1453, when Constantinople was taken by the Turks. Lee and Ashby (2000, pp. 204-205) asked students to explain the differences between the accounts, how there could be two accounts of the same set of events, and how one might decide which account to believe.

Students' responses to the questions provided the basis for a map of progression in their ideas about conflicting accounts. At a fairly basic level were responses like "You don't know, we wasn't there when it happened. It might have been passed down but it could have been changed or forgotten" (Lee & Ashby, 2000, p. 206) said one student. At the top of the progression, students understood, as Lee and Ashby (2000) put it, that "Stories are not just copies of the past, truthful or distorted. Authors construct stories and in doing so have to make decisions about what counts as an empire" (p. 207). Their progression orders children's understanding of the relationship between the *account* of the past and the *past itself*, a fundamental aspect of historical epistemology. The diagram in Figure 9.1 summarizes an abbreviated version of Lee and Ashby's (p. 212) scheme of progression in understanding historical accounts:

In the British context, the strong history education research tradition allowed the exploration of far more advanced classroom assessment schemes than those that predominate in North America (see, e.g., Freeman & Philpott, 2009). In fact, the quality of assessments and what they assess is as critically dependent on research on learning areas, as learning is dependent on what is assessed and how assessments are conducted. In order for assessments to serve learning, they need to be linked to an

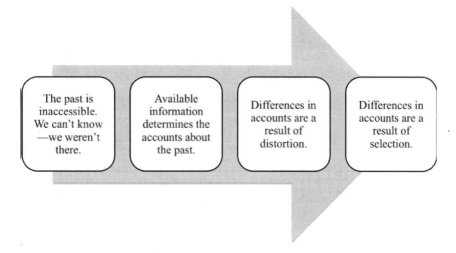

Figure 9.1.   Progression in understanding historical accounts.

empirically based learning progression. On the other hand, a cognition and learning progression model without associated assessment items and a model for linking item responses back to the progression is not useful in practical education contexts. Therefore assessment can play two critical functions that connect it to cognition: (1) an estimation of student level in relation to a hypothesized model of student cognition and learning; and (2) providing data to test and refine the hypothesized model of cognition and learning. Both of these functions are discussed in this chapter.

The Complexities of Assessment of Higher Order Thinking

As described in the previous section, an empirically based learning progression model is essential for development of assessments that capture and promote higher order thinking. Learning progression in scientific inquiry, mathematical problem solving or historical thinking have some key characteristics that make designing assessments of higher order thinking complex. First are the interconnections between domain-specific declarative and procedural knowledge. For example, assessment of scientific inquiry cannot be considered separate from the declarative knowledge in key science learning areas such as physical sciences or earth science. Similarly, procedural competence in various aspects of historical thinking (the analysis of primary sources, reasoning about causation, assessing the pace of historical change, for example) cannot be assessed independent of declarative knowledge of major topics in twentieth century European history, the American Revolution or the history of civil rights movements (see Figure 9.2). The interconnectedness of procedural knowledge with domain-specific declarative knowledge creates both assessment design and assessment data interpretation challenges.

The second factor that makes the assessment of higher order thinking challenging is cognitive complexity required by the higher order thinking that needs to be captured by the assessment tasks. Previous research has shown that surface characteristics of tasks, such as performance tasks or tasks that require students to explain their reasoning, do not necessarily engage students in the intended complex cognitive processes (Baxter & Glaser, 1998). These researchers developed a framework, a content-process space of assessment tasks, that described tasks according to their degree of content knowledge and the degree of complexity of process skills tapped by the tasks (see Figure 9.3). Some items could be identified as rich in content knowledge requirements but poor in the level of process skills required, while others required complex process skills without a requirement for previous knowledge in the content area.

Scientific inquiry	Mathematical problem solving	Historical thinking
Physical science	Algebra	20th Century European History
Life science	Geometry	American Revolution
Earth science	Statistics	Civil Rights Movements

Figure 9.2   Procedural and domain-specific declarative knowledge in science, mathematics and history

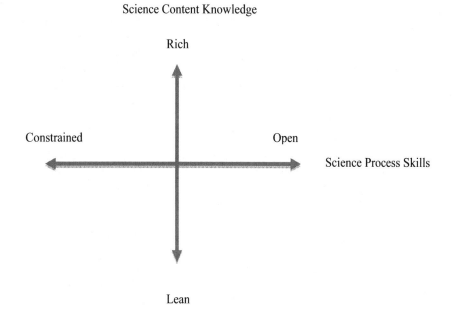

Figure 9.3.   Baxter and Glaser's content and process framework for assessment tasks.

These researchers found that some tasks they analyzed indeed matched their targeted goals of content-process complexity while others did not. For example, one task they examined, to "design and carry out experiments with a maple seed to explain its flight to a friend who has not studied physics" (Baron, Carlyon, Greig, & Lomash, 1992), was identified as content rich and process open. For this task, the researchers explained that the task required substantial physics knowledge as well as the ability to design and carry out an experiment and the employment of model-based reasoning (Baxter & Glaser, 1998). A Grade 12 task, to "describe the possible forms of energy and types of materials involved in the digestion of a piece of bread and explain fully how they are related" (Lomask, Baron, Greig, & Harrison, 1992), was analyzed as being content rich but process constrained. The process aspects of this task are constrained to explanation and the task provided fewer opportunities for other process knowledge such as planning, selecting and implementing appropriate strategies, or monitoring problem-solving procedures. In summary, two aspects of assessment of higher order thinking make it especially challenging. The first is the interconnectedness of higher order thinking with domain-specific declarative knowledge and the second is cognitive complexity required by the tasks.

Evidence Centered Assessment Design

One of the key developments in assessment design that has guided assessment of complex constructs, such as higher order thinking, has been the formulation of evidence centered assessment design (ECD) (Ercikan, 2006; Mislevy, Steinberg, & Almond, 2002; Mislevy, Wilson, Ercikan, & Chudowky, 2002; NRC, 2001). This framework was originally developed by Robert Mislevy and his colleagues at the Educational Testing Service (ETS) (Mislevy, Steinberg, & Almond, 2002). In the National Research Council book *Knowing What Students Know: The science and design of educational assessments* (NRC, 2001), ECD was further elaborated for designing assessments that support learning. ECD is a model-based approach to assessment design that requires a clear and empirically based definition of a learning progression in the target construct (*cognition and learning model*), a description of how tasks need to be designed to assess different components and progression of the construct (including domain-specific declarative as well as procedural knowledge) (*task model*), and finally, specification of the interpretation and evaluation of student performances in relation to the targeted construct (*evidence model*). Making the specific task requirements explicit in the task model provides opportunities for designing tasks and assessments that are coherent with intended target inferences that involve complex interrelated construct components, such as domain-specific declarative and procedural knowledge, and complex cognitive processes, such as scientific inquiry, problem solving and historical thinking. For example, specifying tasks in relation to its content and process demands, similar to the framework presented by Baxter and Glaser (1998), provides a framework for designing tasks with the intended cognitive requirements.

The *cognition and learning model* consists of elements of knowledge, competencies and higher order thinking that are the targets for the assessment. The aspects of this model are chosen according to reporting or instructional requirements that are tied to the purpose of the assessment such as the progression of knowledge, competencies, and skills in substantive areas. In assessments of historical thinking, this model consists of a variety of elements, such as the use of primary source evidence, the establishment of historical significance, and the analysis of cause and consequence.[2] In addition, the cognition and learning model defines a conception of progression for each of these elements. Thus, a very basic level of analysis of cause and consequence might be labeled "the billiard ball" model, where a single event (one billiard ball knocking a second) causes a single consequence (the second rolling into the pocket). More advanced analyses of causation incorporate underlying conditions (the level smoothness of the billiards table) and the active agents (the players) and their intentions. Still more advanced would incorporate the understanding that what we identify as "cause" depends on a larger framework of purposes (is our account of "causes" intended to demonstrate a law of physics, improve a shot, design a better table?). This type of information about what students are expected to do and the expected progression of these skills, knowledge and competencies is different from the test blueprints, test objectives, or learning outcomes that are typically used for developing assessments. In particular, the key component of the cognition and learning models, the progression, is not typically included in test blue-prints. Inclusion of the progression model guides both the complexity of the task development as well as the domain-specific declarative and procedural knowledge that need to be targeted by tasks.

Based on the cognition and learning model, the *task model* describes key features of tasks that can evoke student responses and products that can provide evidence of students' levels in the learning progression. These features include the characteristics of tasks that engage students in the intended cognitive processes and are directly derived from the cognition and learning model. In assessing historical thinking, the task model may focus on one of the elements in the cognition model (e.g., cause and consequence), but more likely will integrate two or more. Thus, the task of analysis of a passage from a slave narrative collected by the Depression-era Federal Writers' Project might be directed towards understanding students' use of evidence as well as their ability to take historical perspectives alien to contemporary sensibilities. Key features of the task model include the duration of the task or tasks, the materials supplied to students and the nature of the performances required.

The *evidence model* is closely tied to the cognition and learning and task models and describes how the observations we make on students' performance on tasks that are designed to elicit information about their competencies are related to the levels of the learning progression. This model presents rules for interpretation that relate observations to different levels of the learning progression.

The evidence model has two components, the *scoring model* which presents rules, such as those in scoring rubrics, to identify and characterize the essential features of the student product that are relevant to the competencies in the learning progression and assigns student responses or products into ordered scores or categories. The second component, *measurement model* accumulates evidence across student responses and products. Examples of measurement models include classical test theory-based simple sum of ordered scores, or item response theory-based models, among many others. In ECD, the cognition and learning model determines both the task model (what assessment tasks should focus on) and the evidence model (how responses to tasks should be interpreted in relation to the competencies identified in the cognition and learning model). Weaknesses in coherence between any two models are expected to impact the validity of inferences about what is being measured. For example, even if tasks are expected to elicit construct-related evidence, if scoring rubrics, and the measurement model are not consistent with this relationship, inferences based on the assessment results will be jeopardized. In other words, interrelationships among the three models in ECD are essential for making valid inferences based on assessment results (see Figure 9.4).

Assessing Historical Thinking

In this section, we describe and discuss designing assessments of historical thinking as a target learning outcome in history education. A number of developments over the past decade and a half have made the idea of "historical thinking" more central to school history curricula throughout the English-speaking world. In the United States, this includes the impact of the much contested U.S. National History Standards project, massive federal funding for the "Teaching American History" project, and the development of a cadre of researchers in history education (Stearns,

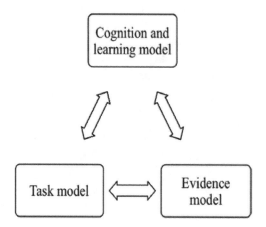

Figure 9.4.   Assessing historical thinking.

Seixas, & Wineburg, 2000; VanSledright & Limon, 2006). Activities in the United States, the United Kingdom, Australia and Canada have resulted in a rough consensus on the elements of historical thinking. In Canada, the Benchmarks of Historical Thinking (BHT) Project, combines efforts by researchers on history learning and educators to create resources and tools to promote teaching and learning of historical thinking in classroom settings (Seixas, 2009; Peck & Seixas, 2008). The Benchmarks project defines elements of historical thinking as students' ability to: (1) establish historical significance; (2) use primary source evidence; (3) identify continuity and change; (4) analyze cause and consequence; (5) take historical perspective; and (6) understand the ethical dimension of historical interpretations (see Figure 9.5). Within the ECD framework, these, along with their respective models of progression, constitute the broad components of the BHT's cognition and learning model. It is not meaningful, however, to assess these components separate from declarative historical knowledge. Therefore, in practice, these components are integrated with historical content.

In addition to defining components of each of the historical thinking concepts and features of assessment tasks for assessing these components, the BHT describes what the students are expected to do at the most sophisticated level and makes suggestions for assessment tasks. For *continuity and change*, these are presented in Figure 9.6. The first column describes the historical thinking element the assessment tasks may focus on.

The task model for assessing continuity and change describes tasks and features of tasks that will elicit evidence regarding students' reasoning in identifying continuity and change. The descriptions of tasks such as *place in chronological order* and *explain why* pictures are placed in the order they

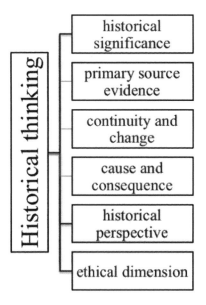

Figure 9.5.   Elements of historical thinking.

are in the historical time line, *compare* two (or more) documents from different time periods and *explain* what changed and what remained the same over time, and *assess progress and decline* from the standpoint of various groups form the basis of the task model.

In ECD, the evidence model is derived directly from the cognition and learning model which defines the typical performance at different levels of progression. Instead of a series of progression levels, BHT identifies the expected highest level of performance based on the definition of the construct component. The other levels of the progression are implicitly identified as different levels of deviations from this highest level of progression.[3] At the highest level of progression, student is expected to (1) explain how some things continue and others change, in any period of history; (2) identify changes over time in aspects of life that we ordinarily assume to be continuous; and to identify continuities in aspects of life we ordinarily assume to have changed over time; and (3) understand that periodization and judgments of progress and decline can vary depending upon purpose and perspective. The scoring rubric that identifies evidence of student's level in the learning progression follows directly from these expected performances.

At the lowest level (level 1), the student is not able to demonstrate any evidence of identifying continuity and change. At the next level (level 2),

Learning and cognition components for continuity and change	Tasks	Evidence: Scoring rubric
Continuity and change are *interrelated* Processes of change are usually continuous, not isolated into a series of discrete events Some aspects of life change more quickly in some periods than others. *Turning points* help to locate change *Progress and decline* are fundamental ways of evaluating change over time *Chronology* and *periodization* can help to organize our understanding of continuity and change	Place a series of pictures in chronological order, explaining why they are placed in the order they are. Compare two (or more) documents from different time periods and explain what changed and what remained the same over time. Assess progress and decline from the standpoint of various groups since a certain point in time.	Level 1: Fails to identify any changes. Level 2: Student makes basic observations about both continuity and change. Level 3: Supports accurate claims of continuity and change with specific historical events from a variety of sources. Level 4: All of (3) plus: presents insightful arguments and incorporates different perspectives. Recognizes power relations associated with continuity and change.

Figure 9.6. Continuity and change

the student is able to demonstrate the most basic understanding of continuity and change by explaining how some things continue and others change. At the next level (level 3), in addition to explaining how some things continue and others change, the student is expected to support their claims with specific historical events. At level 4, in addition to demonstrating evidence of levels 2 and 3, the student is expected to present insightful arguments and incorporate different perspectives, and recognize power relations associated with continuity and change.

This subsection described how definitions of components of the cognition and learning progression model, in particular what the students are expected to be able to do, are related to the task model, and how the expectations for students at the highest level can be used to develop scoring rubrics. We focused on only one component of historical thinking to demonstrate these interrelationships. This approach to assessment design addresses two challenges of designing assessments for higher order thinking. First, the design focuses on developing tasks in which domain-specific declarative and procedural knowledge requirements are integrated. The tasks described here can be used as models for developing assessments of the same historical thinking components in another history era or history education topic. Second, the tasks for assessing higher order thinking are not add-on to test items that are primarily intended to assess domain-specific declarative knowledge only. In fact, the procedural knowledge requirements are the focus of these tasks with domain-specific declarative knowledge as a context for applying these cognitive competencies.

The two aspects of assessment design described in this section address (1) interrelationships between domain-specific declarative and procedural knowledge and (2) incorporation of complex cognitive processes in task design. Currently, the tasks developed as part of the BHT are intended to be used as integral parts of classroom learning in history education. The prioritization of higher order as primary targets of assessment, as opposed to as add-ons to assessments of domain-specific declarative knowledge, plays an important role in communicating the importance of such procedural knowledge to educators and students, and promotes teaching and learning of historical thinking.

The Role of Assessment in Investigating and Refining Models of Development of Cognition and Learning

In the first section of this chapter, we highlighted the importance of assessment in developing and refining theories of student learning and progression. We also emphasized the critical dependence of meaningful assessment of learning on accurate descriptions of the learning progression, supported by empirical research. In this section, we use historical thinking as an example and discuss how assessments can be used to examine key aspects of models of student learning and cognition. We focus on two key issues related to the learning and cognition model in historical thinking: (1) how levels of historical thinking vary across different history education topics; and (2) how progression in different components of historical thinking varies. These two issues are essential for understanding how historical thinking develops, for designing instruction and for teaching.

To address these issues, tasks that are targeted to assess different components of historical thinking across different history education topics can be used as data collection tools. The variability of levels of historical thinking across different history education topics can be addressed by examining properties of assessment tasks which require students to complete the same task when applied to different history topics. As an example we focus on the degree of variability of *identifying continuity and change* across different history education topics. One of the suggested tasks for assessing *continuity and change* presented in Figure 9.6 is "Assess progress and decline from the standpoint of various groups since a certain point in time." This same task can be used to assess students' levels of identifying *continuity and change* in different eras, periods, and phenomena that are part of the history curriculum. Examining properties of assessment tasks, such as difficulty levels of an assessment task that is targeted to assess continuity and change in different eras, can provide systematic evidence of the degree of variability of sophistication of students' levels of understanding and applying continuity and change concepts to different topics in history.

The second research issue is related to student development with regards to different components of historical thinking. For example, can students have high levels of understanding and awareness in interpreting continuity and change in history but low levels of sophistication in examining historical significance? The extent to which the learning progression varies for different components of historical thinking can be addressed by examining correlational relationships among performance on assessment tasks that are targeted to assess different historical thinking components.

The data collection methods and statistical analyses for examining learning and cognition models are identical to those used in investigations of construct validity of assessments. In construct validation research, the focus is on whether the assessment tasks are assessing the targeted cognition and learning model, which is accepted as accurate, and the focus is on examining consistency of assessment data with the construct definition. In such research, inconsistencies between the assessment data and the cognition and learning model are interpreted as lack of construct-related validity evidence *for the assessment*. In contrast, in research that is intended to test hypothesized models of cognition and learning, assessment data are used to *test such hypotheses*, and typically data from assessments are accepted as capturing students' construct-related competencies accurately. In both types of research, validity research and research on learning and cognition, it should be noted that neither the learning model nor the assessment tasks can be assumed to be free of error and uncertainty. The tentativeness of learning models needs to be acknowledged and taken into account in assessment validity research and measurement error needs to be considered in research on learning when testing hypotheses of learning models.

Final Note

This chapter described and discussed assessment of higher order thinking in five connected sections that focused on: (1) the interconnections between assessment and development of higher order thinking; (2) complexities of designing assessments of higher order thinking; (3) evidence centered assessment design; (4) assessment design for historical thinking, and (5) the role assessment can play in investigating and refining models of cognition and learning. We highlighted the critical connection between assessment and learning in multiple ways. First, assessments can play a critical role in promoting higher order thinking as well as in providing insights about students' development in higher order thinking. For both of these functions, the close alignment of assessments with learning goals and the student learning progressions were identified as critical. Second, we described the mutual dependence between research on learning and assessment, that is assessments are necessary as data collection tools for understanding and describing students' cognitive processes and these definitions are needed for designing assessments. Third, for designing assessments, the cognition and learning model is the starting place for designing tasks, developing scoring rubrics and interpreting scores. The coherence between the cognition and learning model and all aspects of assessments is identified as being at the core of validity of interpretations from assessments. Finally, we demonstrated how assessments can be used to promote student development in historical thinking while providing data for research on historical thinking.

NOTES

1. This division is somewhat contested. Schraw (2006) divides knowledge into declarative and procedural. In another chapter in the same volume, VanSledright and Limon (2006) divide knowledge into substantive and procedural, with the first divided into "first-order" and "second-order." Our use of declarative and procedural, from Schraw, maps onto VanSledright and Limon's "first-order" and "second-order," which is, in turn, based on British history education research of Lee and Ashby (2000) and others.
2. While there is some degree of overlap among history educators about these elements, there is by no means one universally accepted set of elements. See, e.g., Levesque, 2008; Seixas, 1996; Taylor, 2000; VanSledright and Limon, 2006; Wineburg, 2001.
3. See the tasks, assessment rubrics and student work at www .historybenchmarks.ca . On "continuity and change," including rubrics and sample student work, see "Aboriginal Rights and Title in British Columbia," http://www.histori.ca/benchmarks/tasks/view.php?taskId=35 .

REFERENCES

Baron, J. B., Carlyon, E., Greig, J., & Lomask, M. (1992, March). *What do our students know? Assessing students' ability to think and act like scientists through performance assessment.* Paper presented at the annual meeting of the National Science Teachers Association, Boston, MA.

Baxter, G. P., & Glaser, R. (1998). Investigating the cognitive complexity of science assessments. *Educational Measurement: Issues and Practice, 17*, 37-45.

Black, P., & Wiliam, D. (1998). Inside the black box: Raising standards through classroom assessment. *Phi Delta Kappan, 80*, 139-148.

Briggs, D., & Alonzo, A. (2009, April). *Building a learning progression as a cognitive model.* Paper presented at the annual meeting of the National Council on Measurement in Education, San Diego, CA.

Chudowsky, N., & Pellegrino, J. W. (2003). Large-scale assessments that support Learning: What will it take. *Theory Intro Practice, 42*, 75-84.

Ercikan, K. (2006). Developments in assessment of student learning and achievement. In P. A. Alexander and P. H. Winne (Eds.), *American Psychological Association, Division 15, Handbook of educational psychology* (2nd ed. pp. 929-953). Mahwah, NJ: Erlbaum.

Gipps, C. (1999). Socio-cultural aspects of assessment. *Review of Research in Education, 24*, 355-392.

Freeman, J., & Philpott, J. (2009). Assessing pupil progress: transforming teacher assessment in Key Stage 3 history. *Teaching History, 137*, 4-13.

Lee, P., & Ashby, R. (2000). Progression in historical understanding ages 7-14. In P. Stearns, P. Seixas & S. S. Wineburg (Eds.), *Knowing, teaching, and learning history: National and international perspectives* (pp. 199-222). New York, NY: New York University Press.

Levesque, S. (2008). *Thinking historically: Educating students in the 21st century.* Toronto: University of Toronto Press. Symposium conducted at the annual meeting of the National Association of Research in Science Teaching, Cambridge, MA.

Lomask, M., Baron, J., Greig, J., & Harrison, C. (1992, March). *ConnMap: Connecticut's use of concept mapping to assess the structure of students' knowledge of science.* Symposium conducted at the annual meeting of the National Association of Research in Science Teaching, Cambridge, MA.

Mislevy, R. J., Steinberg, L. S., & Almond, R. G. (2002). On the structure of educational assessments. *Measurement: Interdisciplinary Research and Perspectives, 1*, 3-63.

Mislevy, R., Wilson, M., Ercikan, K., & Chudowsky, N. (2002). Psychometric principles in student evaluation. In D. Nevo & D. Stufflebeam (Eds.), *International Handbook of Educational Evaluation* (pp. 478-520). Dordrecht, the Netherlands: Kluwer Academic Press.

National Research Council. (2001). *Knowing what students know: The science and design of educational assessment.* J. W. Pellegrino, N. Chudowsky, & R. Glaser (Eds.). Washington, DC: National Academy Press.

Peck, C., & Seixas, P. (2008). Benchmarks of historical thinking: First steps. *Canadian Journal of Education, 31*(4), 1015-1038.

Pellegrino, J. W., Baxter, G. P., & Glaser, R. (1999). Addressing the "two disciplines" problem: Linking theories of cognition and learning with assessment and instructional practice. *Review of Research in Education, 24*, 307-353.

Reich, G. A. (2009). *Testing history: Standards, multiple-choice questions and student reasoning.* Paper presented at the annual meeting of the American Educational Research Association, San Diego, CA.

Schraw, G. (2006). Knowledge: Structures and processes. In P. A. Alexander & P. H. Winne (Eds.), *American Psychological Association, Division 15, Handbook of educational psychology* (2nd ed. pp. 245-264). Mahwah, NJ: Erlbaum.

Seixas, P. (1996). Conceptualizing the growth of historical understanding. In D. Olson & N. Torrance (Eds.), *Handbook of Education and Human Development: New Models of Learning, Teaching, and Schooling* (pp. 765-783). Oxford, England: Blackwell.

Seixas, P. (2009). A modest proposal for change in Canadian history education. *Teaching History, 137,* 26-31.

Shepard, L. A. (2000). The role of assessment in a learning culture. *Educational Researcher, 29,* 4-14.

Stearns, P., Seixas, P., & Wineburg, S. S. (2000). Introduction. In P. Stearns, P. Seixas, & S. S. Wineburg, (Eds.). *Knowing, teaching, and learning history: National and International perspectives* (pp. 1-13). New York & London: New York University Press.

Stiggins, R. J. (1997). *Student-centered classroom assessment.* Old Tappan, NJ: Prenctice-Hall.

Taylor, T. (2000). *The future of the past: The final report of the national inquiry into school history.* Churchill, Australia: Monash University.

VanSledright, B., & Limon, M. (2006). Learning and teaching social studies: A review of cognitive research in history and geography. In P. A. Alexander & P. H. Winne (Eds.), *Handbook of Educational Psychology* (pp. 545-571). Mahwah, NJ: Erlbaum.

Wineburg, S. S. (2001). *Historical thinking and other unnatural acts: Charting the future of teaching the past.* Philadelphia, PA: Temple University Press.

PART IV

PRACTICAL ISSUES IN THE ASSESSMENT OF HIGHER ORDER THINKING SKILLS

CHAPTER 10

ISSUES IN THE DESIGN AND SCORING OF PERFORMANCE ASSESSMENTS THAT ASSESS COMPLEX THINKING SKILLS

Suzanne Lane

The educational reform in the 1980s was based on the premise that too many students knew how to repeat facts and concepts, but were unable to apply those facts and concepts to solve realistic problems that required complex thinking skills. Proponents of the educational reform contended that assessments needed to better reflect students' competencies in applying their knowledge and cognitive skills to solve meaningful tasks. Promising advances in the study of both cognition and learning in achievement domains and of educational measurement also prompted individuals to think differently about how students process and reason with information and how assessments can be designed to capture meaningful aspects of students' cognition and learning. Performance assessments that assess complex cognitive skills were also considered to be valuable tools for educational reform by policymakers and advocates for curriculum reform (Linn, 1993; Resnick & Resnick, 1982). They were thought of as vehicles that could help shape sound instructional practice by modeling to teach-

Assessment of Higher Order Thinking Skills, pp. 265–302
Copyright © 2011 by Information Age Publishing
All rights of reproduction in any form reserved.

ers what is important to teach and to students what is important to learn. Performance assessments that measure complex thinking skills such as problem-solving and reasoning can not only serve as indicators of learning, but also serve as exemplars of assessments that stimulate and enrich learning (Bennett & Gitomer, 2009; Black & William, 1998).

This chapter focuses on issues in the design of performance assessments that measure complex thinking skills. The first section provides a brief introduction and background to performance assessments. The second section calls for continued research on the integration of cognitive theories of learning and of measurement models so as to improve the design of assessments, including performance assessments that measure complex thinking and reasoning skills. Although there has been some promising work in merging cognitive models of learning and measurement models, it has not been fully realized in the design of assessments. The third section discusses the design of performance assessments with a focus on issues that need to be considered to ensure that performance assessments are capable of eliciting the cognitive processes and skills that they are intended to measure. Issues related to the design of computer-based simulations as well as issues related to using learning progressions in assessment design are also addressed. The fourth section addresses issues related to scoring student performance, including the design of scoring rubrics and automated scoring procedures. The fifth section addresses issues related to the validity and fairness of the use and interpretation of scores derived from performance assessments. In this section, the type of evidence needed to support the validity of score interpretations and use, such as content representation, cognitive complexity, fairness, generalizability and consequential evidence, is discussed. The last section summarizes the important design and validation considerations to that will help improve assessment practice.

INTRODUCTION AND BACKGROUND

Performance assessments can measure students' cognitive thinking and reasoning skills and their ability to apply knowledge to solve realistic, meaningful problems. The close similarity between the performance that is assessed and the performance of interest is the defining characteristic of a performance assessment (Kane, Crooks, & Cohen, 1999, pp. 6-7). Performance assessments attempt to "emulate the context or conditions in which the intended knowledge or skills are actually applied" (AERA, APA, & NCME, 1999, p. 137). As this definition implies performance assessments do not have to assess higher order thinking skills. As an example, if the targeted domain is the speed at which a student can run a mile, then a measure that captures how fast a student can run a mile would be considered a performance assessment. This chapter, however, focuses on performance assessments that are designed to assess complex thinking and problem-solving skills in achievement domains.

In the design of performance assessments various frameworks can be used to ensure that the intended high level thinking skills are being assessed. A framework that is well suited for performance assessments includes the assessment standards proposed by Marzano, Pikering, and McTighe (1993). Their proposed complex thinking standards include a range of skills such as comparing, classifying, induction, deduction, error analysis, constructing support, decision making, investigation, experimental inquiry, problem solving, and analyzing perspectives. Their information processing standards includes skills such as interpreting and synthesizing information, assessing the value of information, and identifying additional information that is needed when solving a problem. Standards are also proposed for skills related to effective communication (e.g., communicates clearly, with diverse audiences, in a variety of ways and for a variety of purposes), collaboration (e.g., works toward achievement of group goals and effectively performs a variety of roles), and habits of mind (e.g., self-regulation, critical thinking and creative thinking). The design of a performance assessment that is guided by these standards would result in an assessment of higher order thinking skills that would most likely be valued by educators.

The use of performance assessments that measure complex cognitive skills in large-scale assessments has declined with the requirements of the No Child Left Behind (NCLB) Act of 2001 (U.S. Department of Education, 2005). Under the NCLB Act, states are required to test all students from Grades 3 through 8 annually in reading and mathematics and students in high school at one grade level. They are also required to test students in science at one grade level in elementary, middle and high school. Prior to NCLB Maryland had a state performance assessment program (MSPAP) for Grades 3, 5, and 8 that measured school performance and provided information for school accountability and improvement (Maryland State Board of Education, 1995). These assessments were designed to promote performance-based instruction and classroom assessment in an integrated manner in reading, writing, mathematics, science and social studies. The performance assessment tasks were interdisciplinary, required students to produce both short and extended written responses, and some required hands-on activities and collaboration. They embodied similar skills that were proposed by Marzano and his colleagues (1993). However, under NCLB, all states have been required to provide student level scores to accurately measure proficiency so Maryland's performance-based assessment was no longer tenable given the constraints involved in the design and implementation of large scale assessments. Instead of using solely multiple-choice items as some states have done, Maryland now uses an assessment system that includes multiple choice items as well as some brief and extended constructed-response items in mathematics, reading and science. Some of the reasons why a state like Maryland could not rely solely on performance assessments that assess complex thinking skills to provide individuals scores for use in a high-stakes accountability system will be discussed in this chapter.

NEED FOR THE INTEGRATION OF COGNITIVE THEORIES OF LEARNING AND PSYCHOMETRICS

The need for models of cognition and learning and quantitative psychometric models to be used together to develop and interpret achievement measures has been widely recognized (Embretson, 1985; Glaser, Lesgold, & Lajoie, 1987; National Research Council [NRC], 2001). The deeper our understanding of how individuals acquire and structure knowledge and cognitive skills, and how they perform cognitive tasks, the better able we will be to assess students' cognitive thinking and reasoning and obtain information that will lead to improved student learning. Substantial theories of knowledge acquisition are needed in order to design assessments that can be used in meaningful ways to guide instruction and monitor student learning. Several early research programs that have had implications for the measurement of achievement studied the difference between experts' and novices' knowledge structures (e.g., Chi, Feltovich, & Glaser, 1981; Simon & Chase, 1973). Chi and her colleagues demonstrated that an expert's knowledge in physics is organized around central principals of physics, whereas a novice's knowledge is organized around the surface features represented in the problem description. Other early approaches to link cognitive models of learning and psychometrics have drawn upon work in the area of artificial intelligence (e.g., Brown & Burton, 1978). Brown and Burton as an example represented the complex procedures underlying addition and subtraction as a set of component procedural skills. Using artificial intelligence, they were able to uncover procedural errors or bugs in students' performance that represented misconceptions in their understanding. The results from these types of studies that uncover how students process and organize knowledge and skills can be used in the design of more meaningful assessments.

Theories and models of cognition and learning can be used to assess the progress of individual students or groups of students, and provide information for guiding instruction. An empirically validated model of cognition and learning can be used to design assessments that can monitor students' learning as they develop expertise in the content domain. Assessments that are designed to reflect learning progressions that describe successively more sophisticated ways of problem solving and reasoning in a content domain (NRC, 2006) will further improve the meaningfulness and usefulness of assessment results for enhancing the instructional process and monitoring student learning.

While there is the recognition that theories of cognition and learning should serve as the foundation for the design and interpretation of assessments, there is not widespread use of cognitive models of learning in assessment design. As summarized by Bennett and Gitomer (2009), there are three primary reasons for this: (1) the disciplines of psychometrics and of cognition and learning have developed separately, (2) theories of the nature of proficiency and learning progressions are not fully developed and have not been utilized in assessments, and (3) there are both economic and practical constraints. There are promising assessment design efforts however that are taking advantage of what has been learned about the acquisition of student proficiency and learning. Some of these design efforts will be discussed below.

ISSUES IN THE DESIGN AND SCORING OF PERFORMANCE ASSESSMENTS AND TASKS

Performance assessments are designed to more closely reflect the performance of interest, allow students to construct or perform an original response, and use predetermined criteria to evaluate student work. Consequently, they are well-suited to measuring students' problem solving and reasoning skills and the ability to apply knowledge to solve meaningful problems. The design of performance assessments begins with the delineation of the conceptual framework that includes a description of the construct to be assessed, the purpose of the assessment, and the intended inferences to be drawn from the assessment results (Lane & Stone, 2006). The extent to which the design of a performance assessment considers cognitive theories of student proficiency in an academic domain will affect the validity of score interpretations. The conceptual framework for an assessment therefore needs to clearly articulate the cognitive demands of the tasks, problem-solving skills and strategies that can be employed, and criteria to judge performance. The cognitive demands of a science inquiry task may require students to formulate hypotheses, conduct an investigation, interpret results, and formulate and justify conclusions. The framework needs to include knowledge and strategies that are not only linked closely to the content domain, but also those that are content domain independent (Baker, 2007). The scoring criteria should reflect the cognitive demands of the task and the problem-solving skills and strategies that the student employs. The conceptual framework guides the development of the test specifications that reflect the content, cognitive processes and skills, and psychometric characteristics of the tasks. The performance tasks and scoring rubrics are then developed iteratively based on a well delineated conceptual framework and test specifications.

Assessment Design

The use of conceptual frameworks in designing performance assessments leads to assessments that are linked to educational outcomes and provide meaningful information that can guide curriculum and instructional reform. As an example, a construct-centered approach was taken in the design of a mathematics performance assessment that required students to show their solution processes and explain their reasoning (Lane, 1993; Lane et al., 1995). The conceptual framework that Lane and her colleagues proposed then guided the design of the performance tasks and scoring rubrics. Cognitive theories of student mathematical proficiency provided a foundation for defining the construct domain of mathematics. Four components were specified for the assessment design and further delineated: cognitive processes, mathematical content, mode of representation and task context. As an example, to reflect the complex construct domain of mathematical problem solving, reasoning and communication, a range of cognitive processes were specified including discerning mathematical relations, using and discovering strategies and heuristics, formulating conjectures, and evaluating the reasonableness of answers.

Carefully crafted and detailed test specifications are even more important for performance assessments than selected-response tests because there are fewer performance tasks and typically each is designed to measure something that is unique (Haertel & Linn, 1996). Test specifications indicate the content, cognitive processes and skills, and statistical characteristics of the assessment tasks. The design of assessment tasks is then guided by the test specifications, purpose of the assessment, population of examinees and the intended score interpretations. The degree of structure for the problem posed and the response expected should be considered in the design of performance tasks. One framework for designing assessment tasks is provided by Baxter and Glazer's (1998) characterization of performance assessments along two continuums with respect to their task demands. One continuum represents the task demand for cognitive processes ranging from open to constrained and the other continuum represents the task demand for content knowledge from rich to lean.

A task is process open if it promotes opportunities for students to develop their own procedures and strategies, and a task is content rich if it requires substantial content knowledge for successful performance. These two continuums are crossed to form four quadrants so that tasks can be designed to fit one or more of these quadrants. Tasks can then be designed with clearly articulated cognitive and content targets, and can be evaluated in terms of the alignment with these targets (Baxter & Glazer, 1998). In the design of performance assessments that assess complex cognitive thinking skills, task design may be target primarily in the quadrant that reflects tasks that are process open and content rich.

Another model-based assessment approach that is of particular use in the design of performance assessments has been proposed by Baker (2007). The major components of the model are the cognitive demands of the task, criteria to judge performance derived by expert performance, and a content map that describes the subject matter, including the interrelationships among concepts and the most salient features of the content. The cognitive demands of the tasks can be represented in terms of families of tasks such as reasoning, problem solving, and knowledge representation tasks (Baker, 2007). As an example, the explanation task template requires students to read one or more texts that require some prior knowledge of the subject domain, including concepts, principles and declarative knowledge, in order to understand them, and to evaluate and explain important issues introduced in the text material (Neimi, Baker, & Sylvester, 2007). The model not only addresses strategies and skills that are specific to the subject matter, but also domain-independent skills such as data collection strategies. The use of templates within particular families of tasks in the design of performance assessments can improve the generalizability of the score inferences.

An example of a task from the explanation family that was developed for assessing student proficiency in Hawaii is provided below (Neimi, Baker, & Sylvester, 2007, p. 199).

Imagine you are in a class that has been studying Hawaiian history. One of your friends, who is a new student in the class has missed all the classes. Recently, your class began studying the Bayonet Constitution. Your friend is very interested in this topic and asks you to write an essay to explain everything that you have learned about it.

Write an essay explaining the most important ideas you want your friend to understand. Include what you have already learned in class about Hawaiian history and what you have learned from the texts you have just read. While you write, think about what Thurston and Liliuokalani said about the Bayonet Constitution, and what is shown in the other materials.

Your essay should be based on two major sources:

1. The general concepts and specific facts you know about Hawaiian history, and especially what you know about the period of Bayonet Constitution.
2. What you have learned from the readings yesterday.

Prior to receiving this task, students were required to read the primary source documents that were referred to in the prompt. This task requires students to not only make sense of the material from multiple sources, but to integrate material from more than one source in their explanations.

The National Assessment of Educational Progress (NAEP) includes hands-on performance tasks in their science assessment (U.S. Department of Education, 2005) so as to better measure complex problem-solving and reasoning skills. These tasks require students to conduct experiments, and to record their observations and conclusions by answering both multiple-choice and constructed-response items. As an example, a public release fourth grade task, named Floating Pencil, provides students with a set of materials, including bottles of freshwater, salt water and "mystery" water. Students are required to perform a series of investigations to determine the properties of salt and freshwater, and to determine whether the bottle of mystery water is salt water or freshwater. After responding to a number of questions throughout their investigation, the students are asked (U.S. Department of Education, 2005, p. 10):

Is the mystery water fresh water or is it salt water?
How can you tell what the mystery water is?

When people are swimming, is it easier for them to stay afloat in the ocean or in a freshwater lake?
Explain your answer.

The use of these hands-on performance tasks and constructed-response items better allows NAEP to assess scientific inquiry skills.

Analyses of expert's thinking and reasoning when problem solving in a content domain can elucidate key features of knowledge structures that should be considered in the design of performance assessments. Features of expert's thinking, knowledge, procedures, and problem posing are considered to be indicators of developing expertise in the domain (Glaser, Lesgold, & Lajoie, 1987) and can be used systematically in the design of performance tasks. To build the link between what is assessed and intended score interpretations, these features should also be an integral aspect in the design of scoring rubrics by the systematic representation of them in the scoring criteria at each of the score levels of rubrics. The assessment programs like the ones discussed above draw on studies of expert thinking to better inform their assessment design procedures.

Design of Computer-Based Simulation Tasks

Computer-based simulations have made it possible to assess complex thinking skills that cannot be measured well by more traditional assessment methods. Using extended, integrated tasks, a large problem-solving space with various levels of complexity is provided (Vendlinski, Baker, & Niemi, 2008). Computer-based simulation tasks can assess student competency in formulating and testing hypotheses, selecting an appropriate solution strategy, and when necessary, adapting strategies based on the degree of success to solution. They may also include some form of immediate feedback to the student according to the course of actions taken by the student. Other important features of computer-based simulations are the nature of the interactions that a student has with tools in the problem solving space and the recording of how student use these tools (Vendlinski et al., 2008). Technology used in computer-based simulations allow assessments to provide more meaningful information by capturing students' processes and strategies, as well as their products. Information on how a student arrived at an answer or conclusion can be valuable in guiding instruction and monitoring the progression of student learning (Bennett, Persky, Weiss, & Jenkins, 2007). The use of automated scoring procedures for evaluating student performances to computer-based simulations tasks can provide an answer to the cost and time demands of human scoring.

Several issues arise in the design of computer-based simulations such as the examinee's familiarity with the navigation rules and controls imposed by the computer interface and testing network requirements, the potential requirement of examinee's to record their answers in an unusual manner, and the large amount of data that needs to be summarized in a meaningful way (Bennett et al., 2007; DeVore, 2002). If the assessment is measuring factors which are irrelevant to the construct that is intended to be assessed, the validity of the score interpretations can be affected. Therefore, it is important to ensure that the computer interface is one in which examinees are familiar with and that examinees have had the opportunity to practice with the computer interface and navigation system. It is also possible that the range of cognitive skills and knowledge assessed may be narrowed to those that are more easily assessed using computer technology. Further, the scores generated from computer automated scoring procedures may be somewhat inaccurate if the scoring procedures do not reflect important features of proficiency (Bennett, 2006;

Bennett & Gitomer, 2009). The use of test specifications that specify the cognitive skills and knowledge that are intended to be assessed by the computer based simulations will help ensure representation of the assessed content domain.

The advancements of computer technology have made it possible to use performance-based simulations that assess problem solving and reasoning skills in large scale, high-stakes assessment programs. The most prominent large-scale assessments that use computer-based simulations are in the areas of licensure examinations in medicine, architecture and accountancy. As an example, computer-based case simulations have been designed to measure physicians' patient-management skills, providing a dynamic interaction simulation of the patient-care environment (Clyman, Melnick, & Clauser, 1995). In this examination, the examinee is first presented with a description of the patient and then the examinee must manage the patient case by selecting history and physical examination options or by making entries into the patient's chart to request tests, treatments, and/or consultations. The condition of the patient changes in real time based on the patient's disease and the examinee's course of actions. The computer-based system generates a report that displays each action taken by the examinee and the time that the action was ordered. The examinee performance is then scored by a computer automated scoring system according to the appropriateness of the sequence of the ordered actions. It is apparent that this licensure examination captures some relevant problem-solving skills that is required of physicians

Using evidence-centered design (Mislevy, Steinberg, & Almond, 2003), a method for designing assessments and for using the evidence observed in student performances on complex problem-solving tasks to make inferences about proficiency, computer simulations tasks in the physics domain were developed in the context of the NAEP Problem-Solving in Technology-rich Environments (TRE) study (Bennett, Persky, Weiss, & Jenkins, 2007). The goal of this project was to examine the feasibility of including computer-based simulations on the NAEP science assessment. The computer simulation tasks were designed to represent exploration features of real-world problem solving, and incorporated "what-if" tools that students used to uncover underlying scientific relationships. To assess scientific inquiry students were required to design and conduct experiments, interpret results, and formulate conclusions. As part of the simulations, students needed to select values for independent variables and to make predictions as they designed their experiments. To interpret their results they needed to develop tables, graphs or formulate conclusions. In addition to these scientific inquiry tasks, tasks were also developed to assess students search capabilities on a computer. One eighth grade inquiry computer-based simulation task required students to investigate why scientists use helium gas balloons to explore out of space and the atmosphere (Bennett et al., 2007). An example of an item within this task that required students to search a simulated World Wide Web is provided below:

> Some scientists study space with large helium gas balloons. These balloons are usually launched from the ground into space but can also be launched from spacecraft near other planets.
>
> Why do scientists use these gas balloons to explore outer space and the atmosphere instead of using satellites, rockets, or other tools? Be sure to explain at least three advantages of using gas balloons.
>
> Base your answer on more than one web page or site. Be sure to write your answer in your own words. (Bennett et al., 2007, p. 14)

An example of a related scientific inquiry task that required students to form conclusions and provide rationales after designing and conducting an experiment is provided below:

> How do different amounts of helium affect the altitude of a helium balloon?
>
> Support your answer with what you saw when you experimented. (Bennett et al., 2007, p. 46)

These simulation tasks were based on models of student cognition and learning and allowed for the assessment of problem-solving and reasoning skills that are valued by experts within the scientific discipline.

Computer-based simulation tasks in the reading, mathematics and writing domains are being designed and evaluated for their potential inclusion in an integrated accountability and formative assessment system (Bennett & Gitomer, 2009; O'Reilly & Sheehan, 2009). As an example, in the reading domain, a cognitive model of reading competency serves at the basis for both assessing learning and advancing learning. Three assessment design features that are aimed at assessing deeper processing by requiring students to actively construct meaning from text and that are based on a cognitive model of reading are described by O'Reilly and Sheehan. First, in the assessment a scenario is provided that describes the purpose of reading. The purpose of reading is clearly articulated since students engage in the reading process in meaningfully different ways dependent on the purpose of reading. Second, students are required to read multiple texts so as to encourage students to integrate and synthesize information across texts. Last, to assess students' evaluation skills texts of varying quality are provided.

One of the four important components assessed in their reading competency model is the student's ability to extract discourse structure (the other three are understanding vocabulary, drawing necessary inferences, and identifying important details). As O'Reilly and Sheehan (2009) point out, requiring students to construct a lengthy written summary may be more appropriate in the assessment of writing since the quality of students' response to a reading task can be affected by their writing ability. Instead they use graphical representations for students to map out the structure of the text, including graphic hierarchical organizers and construct maps. The use of graphical representations instead of written summaries helps ensure that a student's writing ability does not affect their performance on the reading tasks. Further, the use of graphical representations will more easily allow for computer automated scoring procedures to be used in the scoring of students' competency in organizing and summarizing information that they have read from one or more texts. This research program draws on models of cognition and learning and advances in technology and measurement to design assessments that capture students' complex thinking skills and thus will provide meaningful information to guide instruction. As the researchers have indicated there are numerous issues that need to be addressed in the design of these computer-based simulation tasks, such as issues related to the format of response, content and cognitive skill representativeness, and scoring of student performances.

Design Of Assessments That Measure Learning Progressions

There have been some recent advances in assessment design efforts that reflect learning progressions or sometimes referred to as construct maps. The goal for these assessments is to identify where a student is on the continuum of the underlying construct so as to better inform instruction and monitor student learning (NRC, 2006). Learning progressions indicate what it means to acquire more expert understanding within a content domain. The intention is for the specification of learning progressions to be based on theories and models of cognition and learning, but for many subject domains cognitive theories of how competency develops have not been fully realized. Therefore, the design of learning progressions may need to be supplemented by what expert teachers and other educators know about student learning within a content domain. Another complexity in the design of learning progressions is that there may be multiple paths to proficiency; however some paths typically are followed by students more often than others (Bennett & Gitomer, 2009; NRC, 2006). The use of these common paths to define learning progressions and the ways in which students gain a deep understanding of the content domain can be used as the foundation for designing assessments that monitor student learning. Learning progressions that are based on cognitive models of learning and are supplemented by expert knowledge of student learning within content domains can inform the design of assessments that will elicit evidence to support inferences about student achievement at different points along the learning progression (NRC, 2006.

Wilson and his colleagues have designed an assessment system that incorporates information from learning progressions and advances in both technology and measurement referred to as the BEAR Assessment System (Wilson, 2005; Wilson & Sloane, 2000). One application of this assessment system is for measuring student's progression for one of the three "big ideas" in the domain of chemistry, namely *matter*. As indicated by Wilson (2005), *Matter* is concerned with describing molecular and atomic views of matter. The two other "big ideas are *change* and *stability*, the former is concerned with kinetic views of change and the conservation of matter during chemical change, and the latter is concerned with the system of relationships in conservation of energy. Table 10.1 illustrates the construct map for the *matter* big idea for two of its substrands, visualizing and measuring.

Level 1 in Table 10.1 is the lowest level of proficiency and reflects students' lack of understanding of atomic views of matter and reflects only their ability to describe some characteristics of matter, such as differentiating between a solid and a gas (Wilson, 2005). At level 2, students begin to use a definition or simple representation to interpret chemical phenomena, and at level 3 students begin to combine and relate patterns to

Table 10.1.   BEAR Assessment System Construct Map for the Matter Strand in Chemistry

Levels of Success	Matter Substrands	
	Visualizing Matter: Atomic and Molecular Views	*Measuring Matter: Measurement and Model Refinement*
5 - Integrating	bonding and relative reactivity	models and evidence
4 - Predicting	phase and composition	limitations of models
3 - Relating	properties and atomic views	measured amounts of models
2 - Representing	matter with chemical symbols	mass with a particulate view
1 - Describing	properties of matter	amounts of matter

Source: Adapted from Wilson (2005)

account for chemical phenomena. Items are designed to reflect the differing levels of the learning progression, or construct map, and empirical evidence is then collected to validate the construct map. An example of a task designed to assess the lower levels of the construct map depicted in Table 10.1 asks students to explain why two solutions with the same molecular formula have two very different smells. The task presents students with the two solutions, butyric acid and ethyl acetate, and their common molecular formula, $C_4H_8O_4$, and a pictorial representation depicting that one smells good and the other bad. The students are required to respond in writing to the following prompt,

> Both of the solutions have the <u>same molecular formulas,</u> but <u>butyric acid smells bad and putrid while ethyl acetate smells good and sweet.</u> Explain why these two solutions smell differently. (Wilson, 2005, p. 11, emphasis in original)

By delineating the learning progressions within each of the "big ideas" of chemistry based on models of cognition and learning and supplemented with experts' understandings of how students' progress to competency, assessments can be designed so as to provide evidence to support inferences about student competency at different points along learning progressions. Performance assessments are well-suited for capturing student understanding and thinking along these learning progressions.

ISSUES IN SCORING STUDENT PERFORMANCE

This section addresses issues in the design of scoring rubrics so as to ensure a coherent link between the performance assessment and the score inferences. Automated scoring procedures that support the use of performance assessments including writing assessments and computer-based simulation tasks will also be discussed. Automated scoring procedures can be used in conjunction with human scoring. The quality of these scoring procedures depends on the extent to which they can capture important features of student performances to complex tasks.

Design of Scoring Rubrics

In the development of performance assessments that are intended to assess problem solving and reasoning skills, it is critical to design scoring rubrics that include criteria that are aligned to the processes skills that are intended to be measured by the assessment. Unfortunately, some performance assessments are accompanied by scoring rubrics that focus on lower levels of thinking rather than the more complex reasoning and thinking skills that the tasks are intended to measure. Thus, the benefits of the performance task are not fully achieved. If the cognitive skills are articulated clearly in the design of the performance tasks, it will allow for well-specified scoring rubrics. As an example, Marzano and his colleagues (1993) provide scoring rubrics that can be adopted and modified to assess their complex thinking standards, communication standards, collaboration/cooperation standards, and habits of mind standards which were described earlier. As an example, for the complex thinking skill, induction, they have proposed a rubric for interpreting the information from which inductions are made. At the lowest level, a 1, the criteria are:

> Significantly misinterprets the information. Makes interpretations that have no bearing on the area or are clearly illogical (p. 70)

At the highest level, a 4, the criteria are

> Provides accurate interpretations that illustrate insight into the information from which they were made. The interpretations reflect a study of or a familiarity with the particulars of the topic. (p. 70)

Typically, scoring rubrics should not be developed to be unique to specific tasks nor generic to the entire construct domain, but should be reflective of the "classes of tasks that the construct empirically generalizes or transfers to" (Messick, 1994, p. 17). In the design of performance assessments, Baker and her colleagues (Baker, 2007; Neimi, Baker, & Sylvester, 2007) have represented the cognitive demands of the tasks in terms of classes or families of tasks such as reasoning, problem solving, and knowledge representation tasks (Baker, 2007). To ensure a coherent link between the tasks and the score inferences, they have designed a scoring rubric for each of these families of tasks. An important issue that needs to be considered in the design of scoring rubrics is the number of score levels that best reflects the various levels of student understanding. The number of score levels used depends on the degree to which the criteria across score levels can distinguish among various levels of performance and therefore performance reflected at each score level should differ distinctively form those at other levels (Lane & Stone, 2006).

In the adoption of a construct-driven approach to the design of a mathematics performance assessment, Lane and her colleagues (Lane, 1993; Lane et al., 1995) used this approach to the design of their holistic scoring rubric. They first developed a generic rubric, as shown in Table 10.2 that reflects the conceptual framework used in the design of the assessment, including mathematical knowledge, strategic knowledge and communica-

Table 10.2. Holistic General Scoring Rubric for Mathematics Constructed-Response Items

Performance Criteria

4 *Mathematical Knowledge.* Shows understanding of the problem's mathematical concepts and principles; uses appropriate mathematical terminology and notations; executes algorithms completely and correctly.

Strategic Knowledge. Identifies all the important elements of the problem and shows understanding of the relationships among them; reflects an appropriate and systematic strategy for solving the problem; gives clear evidence of a solution process, and solution process is complete and systematic.

Communication. Gives a complete response with a clear, unambiguous explanation and/ or description; may include an appropriate and complete diagram; communicates effectively to the identified audience; presents strong supporting arguments which are logically sound and complete; may include examples and counter-examples.

3 *Mathematical Knowledge.* Shows nearly complete understanding of the problem's mathematical concepts and principles; uses nearly correct mathematical terminology and notations; executes algorithms completely; and computations are generally correct but may contain minor errors.

Strategic Knowledge. Identifies the most important elements of the problem and shows general understanding of the relationships among them; and gives clear evidence of a solution process, and solution process is complete or nearly complete, and systematic.

Communication. Gives a fairly complete response with reasonably clear explanations or descriptions; may include a nearly complete, appropriate diagram; generally communicates effectively to the identified audience; presents strong supporting arguments which are logically sound but may contain some minor gaps.

2 *Mathematical Knowledge.* Shows understanding of some of the problem's mathematical concepts and principles; and may contain computational errors.

Strategic Knowledge. Identifies some important elements of the problem but shows only limited understanding of the relationships among them; and gives some evidence of a solution process, but solution process may be incomplete or somewhat unsystematic.

Communication. Makes significant progress towards completion of the problem, but the explanation or description may be somewhat ambiguous or unclear; may include a diagram which is flawed or unclear; communication may be somewhat vague or difficult to interpret; and arguments may be incomplete or may be based on a logically unsound premise.

1 *Mathematical Knowledge.* Shows very limited understanding of some of the problem's mathematical concepts and principles; may misuse or fail to use mathematical terms; and may make major computational errors.

Strategic Knowledge. Fails to identify important elements or places too much emphasis on unimportant elements; may reflect an inappropriate strategy for solving the problem; gives incomplete evidence of a solution process; solution process may be missing, difficult to identify, or completely unsystematic.

Communication. Has some satisfactory elements but may fail to complete or may omit significant parts of the problem; explanation or description may be missing or difficult to follow; may include a diagram, which incorrectly represents the problem situation, or diagram may be unclear and difficult to interpret.

0 Shows no understanding of the problem's mathematical concepts and principles.

Source: Adapted from Lane (1993)

tion (i.e., explanations) as overarching features. These features guided the design of families of tasks: tasks that assessed strategic knowledge, tasks that assessed reasoning, and tasks that assessed both strategic knowledge and reasoning. Of course, these families of tasks all assessed mathematical knowledge. The generic rubrics guided the design of each task specific rubric that reflected one of these three families. The use of task specific rubrics helped ensure the consistency in which raters applied the scoring rubric and the generalizability of the score inferences to the broader construct domain of mathematics. Another important issue in the design of scoring rubrics is that each of the score levels addressed each of the important scoring criteria. As can be seen in Table 10.2, at each of the score levels criteria are specified for each of the overarching features: mathematical knowledge, strategic knowledge, and communication.

The scoring rubric for the tasks that assess students learning in the matter strand in the chemistry domain (Wilson, 2005) that was discussed previously is presented in Table 10.3. The scoring rubric is reflective of the construct map depicted in Table 10.1, with students progressing from the lowest level of describe to the highest level of explain. Score levels 1 (describe) and 2 (represent) in the rubric further differentiate students into 3 levels. A constructed-response that reflects level 2 (represent) is:

> They smell differently b/c even though they have the <u>same molecular formula</u>, they have <u>different structural formulas</u> with different arrangements and patterns. (Wilson, 2005, p. 16, emphasis in original)

This example response is at the level 2 because it "appropriately cites the principle that molecules with the same formula can have different arrangements of atoms. But the answer stops short of examining structure-property relationships (a relational, level 3 characteristic)" (Wilson, 2005, p. 16). A major goal of the assessment system is to be able to estimate, with a certain level of probability, where a student is on the construct map. Students and items are located on the same construct map which allows for student proficiency to have substantive interpretation in terms of what the student knows and can do (Wilson, 2005). The maps can then be used to monitor the progress of an individual student as well as groups of students. Thus, valid interpretations of a student's learning or progression require a carefully designed assessment system that has well-conceived items and scoring rubrics that represent the various levels of the construct continuum as well as the empirical validation of the construct map, or learning progression. As previously indicated, students do not necessarily follow the same progression in becoming proficient within a subject domain. Thus, as indicated by Wilson, in the design of assess-

**Table 10.3.   Bear Assessment System Scoring Guide for
the Matter Strand in Chemistry**

Level	Descriptor	Criteria
0	Irrelevant or Blank Response	Response contains no relevant information
1	Describe the properties of matter	Rely on macroscopic observation and logic skills. No use of atomic model. Uses common sense and no correct chemistry concepts.
		1- makes one or more macroscopic observation and/or lists chemical terms without meaning
		1 uses macroscopic observation AND comparative logic skills to get a classification, BUT shows no indication of using chemistry concepts
		1+ makes simple microscopic observations and provides supporting examples, BUT chemical principle/rule cited incorrectly
2	Represent changes in matter with chemical symbols	Beginning to use definitions of chemistry to describe, label, and represent matter in terms of chemical composition. Use correct chemical symbols and terminology
		2- Cites definitions/rules about matter somewhat correctly
		2 Cites definition/rules about chemical composition
		2+ Cites and uses definitions/rules about chemical composition of matter and its transformation
3	Relate	Relates one concept to another and develops models of explanation
4	Predicts how the properties of matter can be changed	Apply behavioral models of chemistry to predict transformation of matter
5	Explains the interactions between atoms and molecules	Integrates models of chemistry to understand empirical observations of matter

Source: Adapted from Wilson (2005)

ments that measure cognition and learning, considerations should be given to identifying the range of strategies used for solving problems in a content domain, with an emphasis on those strategies that are more typical of the student population. This assessment design effort provides an interesting example of the integration of models of cognition and learning, and of measurement models in the design of an assessment system that can monitor student learning. A measurement model called the saltus (Latin for leap) model developed by Wilson (1989) can incorporate developmental changes as well as the incremental increases in skill in estimating proficiency and monitoring learning.

In an effort to assess complex science reasoning in middle and high school grades, a systematic assessment design procedure was adopted by Liu, Lee, Hofstetter, and Linn (2008). First, they delineated the construct, science knowledge integration. An integrated system of inquiry-based science curriculum modules, assessment tasks and scoring rubric were then developed based on this construct. A scoring rubric was designed so that the different levels captured qualitatively different kinds of scientific cognition and reasoning that focused on elaborated links rather than individual concepts. Their assessment design is similar to the modeling of construct maps, or stages in learning progressions, described by Wilson and his colleagues (Wilson, 2005; Wilson & Sloane, 2000). The knowledge integration scoring rubric is shown in Table 10.4. The examples in the rubric are for a task that requires students to determine whether the amount of light energy is more than, less than, or the same as the amount of electrical energy needed to power a lamp. Students also need to provide a rationale for their answer. The rubric is applied to all the tasks that represent the family of knowledge integration tasks, allowing for score comparisons across different items (Liu et al., 2008). As they indicate, having one scoring rubric that can be applied to the set of items that measure knowledge integration makes it more accessible for teachers to use and provides coherency in the score interpretations. The authors also provided validity evidence for the learning progression reflected in the scoring rubric.

Table 10.4.   Knowledge Integration Scoring Rubric

Link Levels	Description
Complex	Elaborate 2 or more scientifically valid links among relevant ideas (e.g., energy turns into heat and light energies under the conservation of energy framework)
Full	Elaborate 1 scientifically valid link between 2 relevant ideas (e.g., energy is transformed to heat; energy is needed to warm up the lamp)
Partial	State relevant ideas but do not fully elaborate the link between relevant ideas (e.g., energy is lost to surroundings; electrical energy is used as light energy)
No links and incorrect	Make invalid ideas or have non-normative ideas (e.g., electricity is just flowing into the lamp)

Source: Liu, Lee, Hofstetter, and Linn (2008).

Automated Scoring Procedures

Automated scoring procedures have supported the use of computer-based performance assessments such as computer-delivered writing assessments and computer-based simulations. For some assessment programs automated scoring procedures are being used to score student responses instead of human raters. Regardless if they are used in conjunction with human raters or as the sole mechanism for assigning scores, validation studies are needed. Yang, Buckendahl, Juszkiewicz, and Bhola (2002) identified three categories of validation approaches for automated scoring procedures, including approaches focusing on the relationship among scores given by different scorers (human and computer), approaches focusing on the relationship between test scores produced by automated scoring procedures and external measures of writing such as instructor scores on written assignments, and approaches focusing on the scoring process including what the automated scoring procedures are programmed to focus on in assigning scores. Most studies have examined the relationship between human and computer generated scores, typically indicating that the relationship between the scores produced by computer and humans is similar to the relationship between the scores produced by two humans. There have been few studies however that focus on the latter two categories. In particular, validation studies focusing on the scoring process for automated scoring procedures are very limited. As Bennett (2006) has argued, automated scoring procedures should be grounded in a theory of domain proficiency, using experts to delineate proficiency in a domain rather than having them as a criterion to be predicted. The credibility and meaningfulness of the scoring models therefore needs to be further examined.

Studies are needed that have experts evaluate the relevance of the computer-generated features of the target construct, identify extraneous and missing features, and evaluate the appropriateness of the weights assigned to the features (Ben-Simon & Bennett, 2007). One such study conducted by Ben-Simon and Bennett found that the dimensions that experts in writing believe are most important in the assessment of writing are not necessarily the same as those obtained by automated procedures that statistically optimize weights of the dimensions. As an example, experts indicated that approximately 65% of the essay scores in this study should be based on organization, development and topical analysis, while empirical weights gave approximately 21% of the emphasis to these dimensions. The opposite pattern occurred for the dimensions related to grammar, usage, mechanics, style and essay length, with a much lower emphasis assigned by experts and a higher emphasis given by the automated scoring procedure. Other results indicated that the parameters of automated scoring procedures can be adjusted to be more consistent with those that experts believe are features of good writing; however these adjustments may not be based on the criteria specified in the scoring rubric implemented in the study but rather the criteria used by the scorers in assigning scores. The authors indicated that the rubric employed was missing key features of good writing, leaving experts to apply some of their own criteria in the scoring process. This further highlights the importance of linking the cognitive demands of the tasks to the design of scoring rubrics. The authors further suggest that current theories of writing cognition can be used in assessment design so as to ensure that a more theoretical, coherent model for identifying scoring dimensions and features is used when designing scoring rubrics.

Typically, the agreement between the scores that are assigned by human raters and those assigned by automated scoring procedure is very high. There is some research however that has indicated that scores assigned by human raters and by automatic scoring procedures may differ to some extent depending upon student demographics. Bridgeman, Trapani, and Attali (2009) examined whether there were systematic differences in the performance of subgroups using an automated scoring procedure versus human scoring for an eleventh grade English state assessment. The essay prompt required students to support an opinion on a proposed topic within a 45-minute class period. The essays were scored holistically using a 6-point scale. The results indicated that on average, both Asian American and Hispanic students received higher scores from the automated scoring procedure than from human raters, whereas African American students scored similarly across the two scoring methods. Under the assumption that Asian American and Hispanic subgroups have a higher proportion of students with English as a second language, the authors suggested that this finding may not be due to minority status, but instead it may be related to having English as a second language. This may be reasonable given that the African American subgroup performed similarly across the two scoring methods. In their conclusions, they state "although we treat human scores at the gold standard, we are reluctant to label discrepancies from the human score as bias because it is not necessarily the case that the human score is a better indicator of writing ability than the e-rater score (Bennett & Bejar, 1997)" (Bridgeman, Trapani, & Attali, 2009, p. 17). As suggested by the authors, additional research needs to examine features that contribute to differential subgroup results for human and automated scores. It is important to note that scores assigned by automated scoring procedures and those assigned by human raters are typically very high.

Automated scoring procedures have also been developed to score short constructed-response items. In the NAEP study that designed physics computer-based simulations, c-rater was used to score the items that required students to use search queries (Bennett et al., 2007). The c-rater models were built using student queries and then cross-validated using a sample of queries that were independently hand-scored. The agreement between human raters and c-rater for the cross-validation study was 96%. These studies highlight the need for both human and computer components of the scoring process to be evaluated routinely.

EVALUATING THE VALIDITY AND FAIRNESS OF PERFORMANCE ASSESSMENT

Assessments are used in conjunction with other information to make important inferences about proficiency at the student, school, and state level, and therefore it is essential to obtain evidence about the appropriateness of those inferences and any resulting decisions. In evaluating the worth and quality of any assessment, including performance assessments, evidence to support the validity of the score inferences is at the forefront. Validity pertains to the meaningfulness, appropriateness, and usefulness of test scores (Kane, 2006; Messick, 1989). The *Standards for Educational and Psychological Testing* (AERA, APA, & NCME, 1999) state that "validity refers to the degree to which evidence and theory support the interpretations of test scores entailed by proposed uses of tests" (p. 9). This requires specifying the purposes and the uses of the assessment, designing the assessment to fit these intentions, and providing evidence to support the proposed uses of the assessment and the intended score inferences. As an example, if the purpose of a performance assessment is to assess complex thinking skills so as to make inferences about students' problem solving and reasoning one of the important validity studies would be to examine the cognitive skills and processes underlying task performance for support of those intended score inferences. The alignment between the content knowledge and cognitive skills underlying task responses and those underlying the targeted construct domain needs to be made explicit because typically the goal is to generalize assessment score interpretations to the broader construct domain (Messick, 1989). Fundamental to the validation of test use and score interpretation is also the evaluation of both intended and unintended consequences of an assessment (Kane, 2006; Messick, 1989). Because performance assessments are intended to improve teaching and student learning it is essential to obtain evidence of such positive consequences as well as any evidence of negative consequences (Messick, 1994).

There are two sources of potential threats to the validity of score inferences—construct underrepresentation and construct irrelevant variance

(Messick, 1989). Construct underrepresentation occurs when the assessment does not fully capture the targeted construct, and therefore the score inferences may not be generalizable to the larger domain of interest. Issues related to whether the content of the assessment is representative of the targeted domain will be discussed later in this section.

Construct-irrelevant variance occurs when one or more irrelevant constructs is being assessed in addition to the intended construct. Sources of construct irrelevant variance for performance assessments may include, but are not limited to, task wording and context, response mode, and raters' attention to irrelevant features of responses or performances. In designing a performance assessment that measures students' mathematical problem solving and reasoning problems should be set in contexts that are familiar to the population of students. If one or more subgroups of students are unfamiliar with a particular problem context and it affects their performance, the validity of the score interpretations for those students is hindered. Similarly, if a mathematics performance assessment requires a high level of reading ability and students who have very similar mathematical proficiency perform differently due to differences in their reading ability, the assessment is measuring in part a construct that is not the target, namely, reading proficiency. Construct-irrelevant variance may also occur when raters score student responses to performance tasks according to features that do not reflect the scoring criteria and are irrelevant to the construct being assessed (Messick, 1994). The linking of the design of performance assessments to models of cognition and learning illuminates the importance of an important principle in test design - assessments should measure the attributes that are relevant to the construct being assessed and not irrelevant features (AERA, APA, & NCME, 1999).

Validity criteria that have been suggested for examining the quality of performance assessments include, but is not limited to, content representation, cognitive complexity, transfer and generalizability, fairness, and consequences (Linn, Baker, & Dunbar, 1991; Messick, 1994). The discussion that follows is organized around these validity criteria. These criteria are closely intertwined to some of the sources of validity evidence proposed by the *Standards for Educational and Psychological Measurement*. (AERA, APA, & NCME, 1999): evidence based on test content, response processes, internal structure, relations to other variables, and consequences of testing.

Content Representativeness

An analysis between the content of the assessment and the construct it is intended to measure provides important validity evidence (AERA, APA,

& NCME, 1999). Test content refers to the skills, knowledge and processes that are intended to be assessed by tasks as well as the task formats and scoring procedures. Performance tasks that measure complex thinking skills can be designed so as to emulate the skills and processes reflected in the targeted construct; however the ability to generalize from a student's score on a performance assessment to the broader domain of interest may be limited because performance assessments typically consist of a small number of tasks. Although the performance tasks may be assessing students understanding of some concepts or set of concepts at a deeper level, the content of the domain may not be well represented by a relatively small subset of performance tasks. For some large scale assessments, including state assessments, performance tasks are used in conjunction with multiple-choice items to ensure that the assessment represents the content domain and to allow for inferences about student performance to the broader domain.

The coherency among the assessment tasks, scoring rubrics and procedures, and the target domain is another aspect of validity evidence for score interpretations. It is important to ensure that the cognitive skills and content of the target domain is systematically represented in the tasks and scoring procedures. The method used to transform performance to a score provides evidence of the validity of the score interpretation. Both logical and empirical evidence can support the accuracy of this conversion.

Cognitive Complexity

One of the most beneficial aspects of performance assessments is that they can assess complex thinking skills and problem solving; however as Linn et al. (1991) has cautioned it should not be assumed that a performance assessment measures complex thinking skills. Evidence is needed to examine the extent to which tasks and scoring rubrics are capturing the intended cognitive skills and processes. The alignment between the cognitive processes underlying task responses and the construct domain needs to be made explicit because the goal is to generalize scores interpretations to the broader construct domain (Messick, 1989).

Several methods have been used to examine whether tasks are assessing the intended cognitive skills and processes (Messick, 1989). These methods include *protocol analysis, analysis of reasons,* and *analysis of errors.* In *protocol analysis,* students are asked to think aloud as they solve a problem or describe retrospectively how they solve the problem. In the method of *analysis of reasons,* students are asked to provide rationales, typically written, to their responses to the tasks. The method of *analysis of errors* requires an examination of procedures, concepts or representations of the problems in order to make inferences about students' misconceptions or errors in their understanding. As an example, in the design of a science performance assessment Shavelson, Ruiz-Primo, and Wiley (1999) used Baxter and Glaser's (1998) analytic framework reflects a content-process space depicting the necessary content knowledge and process skills for successful performance. Using protocol analysis Shavelson, Ruiz-Primo, and Wiley compared expert and novice reasoning on the science performance tasks that were content-rich and process-open. Their results from the protocol analysis confirmed some of their hypotheses regarding the different reasoning skills that tasks were intended to elicit from examinees. Further, the results elucidated that complexity of experts' reasoning as compared to the novices and informed the design of the tasks and interpretation of the scores.

Generalizability of Score Inferences

A major threat to the validity of score interpretations of performance assessments is the extent to which the scores from the performance assessments can be generalized to the broader construct domain (Lane & Stone, 2006; Linn et al., 1991). Generalizability theory allows for the examination of the extent to which scored derived from an assessment can be generalized to the intended construct domain (Brennan, 1996, 2001; Cronbach, Gleser, Nanda, & Rajaratnam, 1972), and it is particularly relevant in evaluating performance assessments that assess complex thinking skills because it examines multiple sources of errors, such as error due to tasks, raters and occasions, that can limit the generalizability of the results. Error due to tasks occurs because there are only a small number of tasks typically included in a performance assessment. As explained by Haertel and Linn (1996), students' individual reactions to specific tasks tend to average out on multiple-choice tests because of the relatively large number of items, but such individual reactions to specific items have more of an effect on scores from performance assessments that are composed of relatively few items. Error due to raters can also affect the generalizability of the scores in that raters may differ in their evaluation of the quality of a students' response to a particular performance task. Raters may differ in their leniency resulting in rater mean differences or they may differ in their judgments about whether one student's response is better than another student's response resulting in an interaction between the student and rater facets (Hieronymus & Hoover, 1987; Lane et al., 1995, 1996; Shavelson, Baxter, & Gao, 1993). Typically, occasion is an important hidden source of error because performance assessments are only given on one occasion and is not typically included in generalizability studies.

Generalizability theory uses analysis of variance (ANOVA) procedures to estimate variance components for the object of measurement (e.g., student, class, school), each source of error in measurement such as task and rater (commonly referred to as facets), and each interaction term. Examination of the estimated variance components provides information about the relative contribution of each source of measurement error. The variance estimates are then used to design measurement procedures that allow for more accurate score interpretations. As an example, the researcher can examine the effects of increasing the number of items or number of raters, or both, on the generalizability of the score interpretations. Generalizability coefficients are estimated to examine the extent to which the scores generalize to the larger construct domain for relative or absolute decisions, or both.

Generalizability studies have shown that interrater consistency for science hands-on performance tasks (e.g., Shavelson et al., 1993) and mathematics constructed response items (Lane, Liu, Ankenmann, & Stone, 1996; Lane, Stone, Ankenmann, & Liu, 1995) tend to be higher than for writing assessments. To help achieve high interrater consistency care is needed in designing precise scoring rubrics, selecting and training raters, and rechecking rater performance (Lane & Stone, 2006; Linn, 1993; Mehrens, 1992). Researchers have shown that task-sampling variability as compared to rater-sampling variability in students' scores is a greater source of measurement error in performance assessments in science, mathematics, and writing (Baxter, Shavelson, Herman, Brown, & Valdadez, 1993; Gao, Shavelson, & Baxter, 1994; Hieronymus & Hoover, 1987; Lane et al., 1995, 1996; Shavelson et al., 1993). In other words, increasing the number of tasks has a greater effect on the generalizability of the scores than increasing the number of raters.

Shavelson and his colleagues (1993) reported that task-sampling variability was the major source of measurement error using data from 5th and sixth grade mathematics and science performance assessments. The results of person x tasks x rater (p x t x r) generalizability studies on a math assessment and two science assessments indicated that the person x task variance component accounted for the largest percent of total score variation, 49%, 48%, and 82%, respectively. The variance components that included raters (i.e., rater effect, person x rater interaction, and task x rater interaction) were either zero or negligible, indicating that sampling variability due to raters contributed little to no measurement error. They reported that to reach a .80 generalizability coefficient 15 tasks were needed for the math assessment, 8 for the state science assessment and 23 for the other hands-on science performance assessment. Lane and her colleagues (1996) found similar results with a mathematics performance assessment that consisted of constructed-response items requiring students to show their solution processes and explain their reasoning. The results indicated that error due to raters was minimal, whereas error due to tasks was more substantial indicating that here was differential student performance across tasks. Person x task x rater (p x t x r) generalizability studies for each form of the mathematics assessment indicated that between 42% and 62% of the total score variation was accounted for by the pt variance component. The variances due to the rater effect, person x rater interaction, and rater x task interaction were negligible. When the number of tasks was equal to 9 the generalizability coefficients for the p x t x r design ranged from .71 to .84. To examine the generalizability of school-level scores for each form, a person nested within a school) by task design was used. The coefficients for absolute decisions ranged from .80 to .97 when the number of tasks was equal to 36 using a matrix sampling design.

Shavelson and his colleagues (Shavelson et al., 1993; Shavelson, Ruiz-Primo, & Wiley, 1999) provided evidence that the large task sampling variability in science performance assessments was due to variability in both the person x task interaction and the person x task x occasion interaction. They conducted a person x rater x task x occasion (p x t x r x o) generalizability study, using data from a science performance assessment administered to fifth and sixth grade students (Shavelson et al., 1993). The person x task variance component accounted for 32% of the total variability whereas, the person x task x occasion variance component accounted for 59% of the total variability. In a reanalysis of sixth grade science performance assessment data from Ruiz-Primo, Baxter, and Shavelson (1993), Shavelson and his colleagues (1999) provided additional support for the large effects due to occasion. In a person x task x occasion x method generalizability study, the person x task variance component accounted for 26% of the total variability and the person x task x occasion variance component accounted for 31% of the total variability, indicating that there was a tendency for students to change their approach to each task from occasion to occasion. The variance component for the person x occasion effect was close to zero. In summary, "even though students approached the tasks differently each time they were tested, the aggregate level of their performance, averaged over the tasks, did not vary from one occasion to another (Shavelson et al., 1999, pp. 64-65). The results of these studies demonstrate that ignoring occasion in the design leads to an overestimate of the generalizability coefficient as Cronbach Linn, Brennan, and Haertel (1997) warned.

Fairness of Assessments

The evaluation of the fairness of an assessment is inherently related to all sources of validity evidence. Bias can be conceptualized "as differential validity of a given interpretation of a test score for any definable, relevant subgroup of test takers" (Cole & Moss, 1989, p. 205). A fair assessment therefore requires evidence to support the meaningfulness, appropriateness, and usefulness of the test score inferences for all relevant subgroups of examinees. Validity evidence for assessments that are intended for students from various cultural, ethnic and linguistic backgrounds needs to be collected continuously and systematically as the assessment is being developed, administered and refined.

Some proponents of performance assessments in the 1980's had hoped that subgroup differences that were exhibited on multiple-choice tests would be smaller or alleviated by using performance assessments. However, as stated by Linn and his colleagues (1991), differences among subgroups most likely occur because of differences in learning opportunities, familiarity, and motivation, and are not necessarily due to item format. Most of the research in the 1980s and 1990s that has examined subgroup differences has focused on both the impact of an assessment on subgroups by examining mean differences or differential group performance on individual items when groups are matched with respect to ability, that is, differential item functioning (Lane & Stone, 2006).

Statistical differential item functioning (DIF) methods are commonly used for examining whether individual test items are measuring a similar construct for different groups of examinees (e.g., gender and ethnic groups) of similar ability. Differential item functioning occurs when there is differential performance on an item for subgroups of students of approximately equal ability. The presence of DIF may suggest that inferences based on the test score may be less valid for a particular group or groups. Although researchers have argued that performance assessments offer the potential for more equitable assessments, performance assessments may measure construct-irrelevant features that contribute to DIF. Gender or ethnic bias could be introduced by the typical contextualized nature of performance tasks or the amount of writing and reading required. In addition, the use of raters to score responses to performance assessments could introduce another possible source of differential item functioning (see, e.g., Gyagenda & Engelhard, 2010).

Some researchers have supplemented differential item functioning methods with cognitive analyses designed to uncover reasons why items are behaving differently across subgroups of students of approximately equal ability. In a study to detect DIF in a mathematics performance assessment consisting of constructed-response items that required students to show their solution processes and explain their reasoning, using the *analyses of reasons* method, Lane, Wang, and Magone (1996) examined differences in students' solution strategies, mathematical explanations and mathematical errors as a potential source of differential item functioning. They reported that for those items that exhibited DIF and favored females, females performed better than their matched males because females tended to provide more comprehensive conceptual explanations and were more complete in displaying their solution strategies. Ericikan (2002) examined differential item response performances among different language groups. In her research, she conducted linguistic comparisons across different language test versions to identify potential sources of differential item functioning. As Wilson (2005) has suggested, the inclusion of DIF parameters into measurement models would allow for a direct measurement of different construct effects such as using different solution strategies and different types of explanations (Lane et al., 1996), or linguistic differences (Ericikan, 2002).

Research studies conducted in the 1980's and 1990's has shown both gender and ethnic mean differences on performance assessments that measure complex thinking skills (see, e.g., Lane & Stone (2006) for a summary). More recently, studies have used multilevel modeling to examine subgroup differences so as to better control for student demographic variables and school level variables. Using multilevel modeling, one study examined the extent to which potentially heavy linguistic demands of a performance assessment might interfere with the performance of students who have English as a second language (Goldschmidt, Martinez, Niemi, & Baker, 2007). The results obtained by Goldschmidt and his colleagues revealed that subgroup differences on student written essays to a writing prompt were less affected by student background variables than a language arts commercially developed test consisting of multiple choice items and some constructed-response items The performance gaps between white students, English only students and traditionally disadvantaged students (e.g., English language learners (ELLs)) were smaller for the writing performance assessment than the commercially developed test (Goldschmidt et al., 2007). Thus, the performance of students on the writing assessment used in this study was less affected by student demographic variables than their performance on the commercially developed test. As the authors indicate, although these are promising results, additional research is needed to determine if they can be replicated in other settings and with other subgroups.

Instructional Sensitivity

An assessment concept that can help inform the consequential aspect of validity is instructional sensitivity. Instructional sensitivity refers to the degree to which tasks are sensitive to improvements in instruction (Popham, 2003). Performance assessments are considered to be vehicles that can help shape sound instructional practice by modeling to teachers what is important to teach and to students what is important to learn. In this regard it is important to evaluate the extent to which improved performance on an assessment is linked with improved instructional practices. To accomplish this, the assessments need to be sensitive to improvements of instruction. Assessments that may not be sensitive to well-designed instruction may be measuring something outside of instruction such as irrelevant constructs or learning that may occur outside of the school. Two methods have been used to examine whether assessments are instructional sensitive: Studies have either examined whether students have had the opportunity to learn (OTL) the material or they have examined the extent to which differences in instruction affect performance on the assessment. Studies that examine whether students have had the OTL the material typically examine the alignment between the instruction and the test content. In a study that examined the extent to which differences in instruction affect performance using a model-based approach to assessment design (Baker, 2007), it was found that student performance on a language arts performance assessment was sensitive to different types of language instruction and were able to capture improvement in instruction (Niemi, Wang, Steinberg, Baker, & Wang, 2007). This study examined the effects of 3 different types of instruction (literary analysis, organization of writing, and teacher-selected instruction) on student responses to an essay about conflict in literary work. The results indicated that students who received instruction on literary analysis were significantly more able to analyze and describe conflict in literature that students in the other two instructional groups, and students who had direct instruction on organization of writing performed significantly better on measures of writing coherency and organization. These results provide evidence that assessments are sensitive with respect to different types of instruction.

Consequential Evidence

A major goal of performance assessments is to improve teaching and student learning; therefore it is essential to obtain evidence of such positive consequences and any potentially negative consequences (Messick, 1994). As Linn (1993) stated, the need to obtain evidence about consequences is "especially compelling for performance-based assessments ... because particular intended consequences are an explicit part of the assessment systems' rationale" (p. 6). There is evidence that large-scale performance assessments that measure complex thinking skills do have an impact on instruction and student learning (Lane, Parke, & Stone, 2002; Stecher, Barron, Chun, & Ross, 2000; Stein & Lane, 1996; Stone & Lane, 2003). In a study examining the consequences of Washington's state assessment, Stecher and his colleagues (Stecher et al., 2000) indicated that approximately two-thirds of forth and seventh grade teachers reported that the state standards and the state assessment short-answer and extended-response items were influential in promoting better instruction and student learning. An important aspect of consequential evidence for performance assessments is the examination of the relationship between changes in instructional practice and improved student performance on the assessments. One study examined the relationship between changes in instructional practice and improved performance on the Maryland state assessment, MSPAP, which comprised entirely of performance tasks that were integrated across content domains (Lane, Parke, & Stone, 2002; Stone & Lane, 2003). The results of this study revealed that teacher reported reform-oriented instructional features accounted for differences in school performance on MSPAP in reading, writing, mathematics and science, and they accounted for differences in the rate of change in MSPAP school performance in reading and writing. The former suggests that schools in which teachers reported that their instruction over the years reflected more reform-oriented problem types and learning outcomes similar to those assessed by MSPAP had higher levels of school performance on MSPAP than schools in which teachers reported that their instruction reflected less reform-oriented problem types and learning outcomes. The latter suggests that increased reported use of reform-oriented tasks in writing and reading and a focus on the reading and writing learning outcomes in instruction was associated with greater rates of change in MSPAP school performance over a 5-year period.

When using test scores to make inferences regarding the quality of education, contextual information is needed to inform the inferences and actions (Haertel, 1999). Stone and Lane (1993) indicated that a school contextual variable, percent free or reduced lunch which is typically used as a proxy for socioeconomic status (SES), was significantly related to school-level performance on MSPAP in mathematics, reading, writing, science and social studies. That is, schools with a higher percentage of free or reduced lunch tended to perform poorer on MSPAP. There was no significant relationship, however, between percentage free or reduced lunch and growth on MSPAP at the school-level in four of the five subject areas—mathematics, writing, science and social studies. This result suggests that improved school performance on performance assessments like MSPAP is not necessarily related to contextual variables such as SES (as measured by percent free or reduced lunch).

IMPROVING ASSESSMENT PRACTICE

A number of issues have been addressed in this chapter that can inform the design and validation of performance assessments that measure complex thinking skills. This section will highlight some of the important assessment design and validation considerations. The design of performance assessments should be guided by cognitive theories of knowledge acquisition so that the assessment results can be used in meaningful ways to guide instruction and monitor student learning. This will require continued research on theories and models of student cognition and learning. Assessments designed to reflect learning progressions that describe successively more sophisticated ways of problem solving and reasoning in a content domain can improve the meaningfulness and usefulness of assessment results. They allow for the assessment of the progress of individual students or groups of students, and provide useful information for guiding instruction. The development of a conceptual framework that clearly articulates the cognitive demands of the tasks and, if possible, learning progressions will help support valid score interpretations. Because performance assessments typically have a small number of tasks and each is designed to measure in part something that is unique, detailed test specifications are critical to ensure the assessment is measuring what it is intended to measure. The criteria delineated in the scoring rubrics should reflect the cognitive demands of the task and the problem solving skills and strategies that the students employ. Computer-based simulation tasks can emulate meaningful, real world problems. In the design of these tasks, issues related to response format, content and cognitive skill representativeness, and scoring needs to be considered. Automated scoring procedures are well suited to evaluating student performances to computer-based simulation tasks as well as other performance assessments such as writing assessments; however it is important to conduct validation studies that focus on the appropriateness of the scoring process.

The evaluation of the quality and value of an assessment includes evidence to support the validity and the fairness of the assessment results. An analysis of the extent to which the content of the assessment represents the construct it is intended to measure provides important validity evidence. Evidence is also needed regarding the extent to which the tasks and scoring rubrics are capturing the intended cognitive skills. Thus, examining the coherency among the tasks, scoring rubrics and procedures, and the target construct domain in terms of both content and cognitive skills provides evidence to support the score inferences. The extent to which scored derived from a performance assessment can be generalized to the intended construct domain also needs to be examined. It is also important to obtain evidence of any positive consequences as well as any potentially negative consequences of the assessment. This is of particular importance given that a major goal of performance assessments is to improve teaching and student learning. The evaluation of the fairness of an assessment is related to all sources of validity evidence. In order to ensure a fair assessment, evidence is needed to support the meaningfulness, appropriateness, and usefulness of the test score inferences for all relevant subgroups of examinees.

CONCLUSION

Assessment is a process of reasoning from evidence that should be driven by theories and data on student cognition and learning (Mislevy, Steinberg, & Almond, 2003; NRC, 2001). Cognitive theories of student proficiency and learning in subject matter domains provide a foundation for the design of performance assessments. There are some promising efforts on how to design assessments and scoring procedures to reflect theories of cognition and learning although additional research is needed so that assessments, including performance assessments, can better reflect these theories of cognition and learning and therefore better emulate the constructs of interest. Technological developments such as computer-based simulations and computer automated scoring procedures have emerged and hold promise for improvements in the design and use of performance assessment. The positive effects of the integration of cognitive theory and psychometrics may best be exemplified by the measurement models that capture the progression of student thinking and reasoning. The use of these models in assessment design can better inform the instructional process than traditional models that are used in most assessment programs. The primary goal of large scale assessment and accountability efforts in this country—to improve learning for all students— would benefit greatly if resources were made available to ensure that advances in cognitive theory, assessment design, technology and psychometrics have a pivotal role in the education and assessment of students as we begin the twenty-first century.

REFERENCES

American Educational Research Association, American Psychological Association, National Council on Measurement in Education. (1999). *Standards for educa-*

tional and psychological testing. Washington, DC: American Educational Research Association.

Baker, E. L. (2007). Model-based assessments to support learning and accountability: The evolution of CRESST's research on multiple-purpose measures. *Educational Assessment, 12*(3&4), 179-194.

Baxter, G. P., & Glaser, R. (1998). Investigating the cognitive complexity of science assessments. *Educational Measurement: Issues and Practice, 17*(3), 37-45.

Baxter, G. P., Shavelson, R. J., Herman, S. J., Brown, K. A., & Valdadez J. R. (1993). Mathematics performance assessment: Technical quality and diverse student impact. *Journal for Research in Mathematics Education, 24*, 190-216.

Ben-Simon, A., & Bennett, R.E. (2007). Toward more substantively meaningful essay scoring. *Journal of Technology, Learning and Assessment 6*(1). Retrieved from http://escholarship.bc.edu/jtla/

Bennett, R., & Bejar, I. (1997). *Validity and automated scoring: It's not only the scoring* (ETS RR-97-13). Princeton, NJ: Educational Testing Service.

Bennett, R. E. (2006). Moving the field forward: Some thoughts on validity and automated scoring. In D. M. Williamson, R. J. Mislevy, & I. I. Behar (Eds.), *Automated scoring of complex tasks in computer-based testing* (pp. 403-412). Hillside, NJ: Erlbaum.

Bennett, R. E., & Gitomer, D. H. (2009). Transforming K-12 Assessment: Integrating accountability testing, formative assessment and professional support. In C. Wyatt-Smith & J. Cumming (Eds.), *Educational assessment in the 21st century* (pp. 44-61). New York, NY: Springer.

Bennett, R. E., Persky, H., Weiss, A. R., & Jenkins, F. (2007). *Problem solving in technology-rich environments: A report from the NAEP Technology-Based Assessment Project* (NCES 2007-466). Washington, DC: National Center for Education Statistics, U.S. Department of Education. Retrieved from http://nces.ed.gov/pubsearch/pubsinfo.asp?pubid=2007466

Black, P., & William, D. (1998). Inside the black box: Raising standards through classroom assessment. *Phi Delta Kappan, 80*, 139-148.

Brennan, R. L. (1996). Generalizability of performance assessments. In G. W. Phillips (Ed.), *Technical issues in large-scale performance assessment.* Washington, DC: National Center for Education Statistics (NCES 96-802).

Brennan, R. L. (2001). *Generalizability theory.* New York, NY: Springer-Verlag.

Bridgeman, B., Trapani, C., & Attali, Y. (2009, April). *Considering fairness and validity in evaluating automated scoring.* Paper presented at the annual meeting of the National Council on Measurement in Education, San Diego, CA.

Brown, J. S., & Burton, R. R. (1978). Diagnostic models for procedural bugs in basic mathematical skills. *Cognitive Science, 2*, 155-192.

Chi, M. T. H., Feltovich, P. J., & Glaser, R. (1981). Categorization and representation of physics problems of experts and novices. *Cognitive Science, 5*, 121-152.

Cole, N. S., & Moss, P. A. (1989). Bias in test use. In R. L. Linn (Ed.), *Educational measurement* (3rd ed., pp. 201-220). New York, NY: American Council on Education and Macmillan.

Clyman, S. G., Melnick, D. E., & Clauser, B. E. (1995). Computer-based case simulations. In E. L. Mancall & P. G. Bashook (Eds.), *Assessing clinical reasoning: The oral examination and alternative methods* (pp. 139– 149). Evanston, IL: American Board of Medical Specialties.

Cronbach, L. J., Gleser, G. C., Nanda, H., & Rajaratnam, N. (1972). *The dependability of behavioral measurements: Theory of generalizability of scores and profiles.* New York, NY: Wiley.

Cronbach, L. J., Linn, R. L., Brennan, R. L., & Haertel, E. H. (1997). Generalizability analysis for performance assessments of student achievement or school effectiveness. *Educational and Psychological Measurement, 57*(3), 373-399.

DeVore, R. N. (2002). *Considerations in the development of accounting simulations.* (Technical Report 13). NJ: AICPA.

Embretson, S. E. (1985). *Test design: Developments in psychology and psychometrics.* Orlando, FL: Academic Press.

Ericikan, K. (2002) Disentangling sources of differential item functioning in multi-language assessments. *International Journal of Testing, 2,* 199-215.

Gao, X., Shavelson, R. J., & Baxter, G. P. (1994). Generalizability of large-scale performance assessments in science. Promises and problems. *Applied Measurement in Education, 7,* 323-334.

Glaser, R., Lesgold, A., & Lajoie, S. (1987). Toward a cognitive theory for the measurement of achievement. In R. R. Ronning, J. A., Glover, J. C., Conoley, & J. C. Witt (Eds.), *The influence of cognitive psychology on testing* (pp. 41-85). Hillsdale, NJ: Erlbaum.

Goldschmidt, P., Martinez, J. F., Niemi, D., & Baker, E. L. (2007). Relationships among measures as empirical evidence of validity: Incorporating multiple indicators of achievement and school context. *Educational Assessment, 12*(3 & 4), 239-266.

Gyagenda, I. S., & Engelhard, G. (2010). Rater, domain, and gender influences on the assessed quality of student writing. In M., Garner, G., Engelhard, M., Wilson, & W. Fisher (Eds.). *Advances in Rasch Measurement* (Vol. 1). Maple Grove, MN: JAM Press.

Haertel, E. H. (1999). Performance assessment and education reform. *Phi Delta Kappan, 80*(9), 662-667.

Haertel, E. H., & Linn, R. L. (1996). Comparability. In G.W. Phillips (Ed.), *Technical Issues in Large-Scale Performance Assessment* (NCES 96-802). Washington, DC: U.S. Department of Education.

Hieronymous, A. N., & Hoover, H. D. (1987). *Iowa tests of basic skills: Writing supplement teacher's guide.* Chicago, IL: Riverside.

Kane, M. T. (2006). Validation. In B. Brennan (Ed.), *Educational measurement.* American Council on Education & Praeger: Westport, CT.

Kane, M., Crooks, T., & Cohen, A. (1999). Validating measures of performance. *Educational Measurement: Issues and Practice, 18*(2), 5-17.

Lane, S. (1993). The conceptual framework for the development of a mathematics performance assessment instrument. *Educational Measurement: Issues and Practice, 12*(3), 16-23.

Lane, S., Liu, M., Ankenmann, R. D., & Stone, C.A. (1996). Generalizability and validity of a mathematics performance assessment. *Journal of Educational Measurement, 33*(1), 71-92.

Lane, S., Parke, C. S., & Stone, C. A. (2002). The impact of a state performance-based assessment and accountability program on mathematics instruction and student learning: evidence from survey data and school performance. *Educational Assessment, 8*(4), 279-315.

Lane, S., Silver, E. A., Ankenmann, R. D., Cai, J., Finseth, C., Liu, M., et al. (1995). *QUASAR Cognitive Assessment Instrument (QCAI)*. Pittsburgh, PA: University of Pittsburgh, Learning Research and Development Center.

Lane, S., & Stone, C.A. (2006). Performance assessments. In B. Brennan (Ed.), *Educational measurement*. Westport, CT: American Council on Education & Praeger:

Lane, S., Stone, C. A., Ankenmann, R. D., & Liu, M. (1995). Examination of the assumptions and properties of the graded item response model: An example using a mathematics performance assessment. *Applied Measurement in Education, 8*, 313-340.

Lane, S., Wang, N., & Magone, M. (1996). Gender related DIF on a middle school mathematics performance assessment. *Educational Measurement: Issues and Practice, 15*, 21-27, 31.

Linn, R. L. (1993). Educational assessment: Expanded expectations and challenges. *Educational Evaluation and Policy Analysis, 15*, 1-16.

Linn, R. L., Baker, E. L., & Dunbar, S.B. (1991). Complex performance assessment: Expectations and validation criteria. *Educational Researcher, 20*(8), 15-21.

Liu, O. L., Lee, H. Hofstetter, C., & Linn, M.C. (2008). Assessing knowledge integration in science: Constructs, measures, and evidence. *Educational Assessment, 13*(1), 33-55.

Maryland State Board of Education. (1995). *Maryland school performance report: State and school systems*. Baltimore, MD: Author.

Marzano, R. J., Pickering, D. J., & McTighe, J. (1993). *Assessing student outcomes: Performance assessment using the dimensions of learning model*. Alexandria, VA: Association for Supervision and Curriculum Development.

Mehrens, W. A. (1992). Using performance assessment for accountability purposes. *Educational Measurement: Issues and Practice, 11*(20), 3-9.

Messick, S. (1994). The interplay of evidence and consequences in the validation of performance assessments. *Educational Researcher, 23*(2), 13-23.

Messick, S. (1989) Validity. In R. L. Linn (Ed.), *Educational Measurement* (3rd ed., pp. 13-104). New York, NY: American Council on Education and Macmillan.

Mislevy, R. J., Steinberg, L. S., & Almond, R. G. (2003). On the structure of educational assessments. *Measurement: Interdisciplinary Research and Perspectives, 1*(1), 3-62.

National Research Council. (2001). *Knowing what students know: The science and design of educational assessment*. J. Pellegrino, N. Chudowsky, & R. Glaser (Eds), Board on Testing and Assessment, Center for Education. Division of Behavioral and Social Sciences and Education. Washington, DC: National Academy Press.

National Research Council. (2006). *Systems for state science assessment*. M.R. Wilson & M.W. Bertenthal (Eds.), Board on Testing and Assessment, Center for Education, Division of Behavioral and Social Sciences and Education. Washington, DC: National Academy Press.

Niemi, D, Baker, E. L., & Sylvester, R. M. (2007). Scaling up, scaling down: Seven years of performance assessment development in the nation's second largest school district. *Educational Assessment, 12*(3&4), 195-214.

Niemi, D., Wang, J., Steinberg, D. H., Baker, E. L., & Wang, H. (2007). Instructional sensitivity of a complex language arts performance assessment. *Educational Assessment, 12*(3 & 4), 215-238.

O'Reilly, T., & Sheehan, K. M. (2009). *Cognitively based assessment of, for and as learning: a framework for assessing reading competency* (ETS-RR-09-26). Princeton, NJ: ETS.

Popham, W. J. (2003). Living (or dying) with your NCLB tests. *School Administrator, 60*(11), 10-14.

Resnick, L. B., & Resnick, D. P. (1982). Assessing the thinking curriculum: New tools for educational reform. In B. G. Gifford & M.C. O'Conner (Eds.), *Changing assessment: Alternative views of aptitude, achievement and instruction* (pp. 37-55), Boston, MA: Kluwer Academics.

Ruiz-Primo, M. A., Baxter, G. P., & Shavelson, R. J. (1993). On the stability of performance assessments. *Journal of Educational Measurement, 30*(1), 41-53.

Shavelson, R. J., Baxter, G. P., & Gao, X. (1993). Sampling variability of performance assessments. *Journal of Educational Measurement, 30*(3), 215-232.

Shavelson, R. J., Ruiz-Primo, M. A., & Wiley, E. W. (1999). Note on sources of sampling variability. *Journal of Educational Measurement, 36*(1), 61-71.

Simon, H. A., & Chase, W. G. (1973). Skill in chess. *American Scientist, 61*, 394-403.

Stecher, B., Barron, S., Chun, T., & Ross, K. (2000, August). *The effects of the Washington state education reform in schools and classrooms* (CSE Tech. Rep. NO. 525). Los Angeles: University of California, National Center for Research on Evaluation, Standards and Student Testing.

Stein, M. K., & Lane, S. (1996). Instructional tasks and the development of student capacity to think and reason: An analysis of the relationship between teaching and learning in a reform mathematics project. *Educational Research and Evaluation, 2*(1), 50-80.

Stone, C. A., & Lane, S. (2003). Consequences of a sate accountability program: Examining relationships between school performance gains and teacher, student and school variables. *Applied Measurement in Education, 16*(1), 1-26.

U.S. Department of Education (2005). The Nation's Report Card. Washington, DC: Author Retrieved from http://nationsreportcard.gov/science_2005/s0116.asp

Vendlinski, T. P., Baker, E. L., & Niemi, D. (2008). *Templates and objects in authoring problem-solving assessments.* (CRESST Tech. Rep. No. 735). Los Angeles: University of California, National Center Research on Evaluation, Standards, and Student Testing (CRESST).

Wilson, M. (2005). *Constructing measures: An item response modeling approach.* Mahwah, NJ: Erlbaum.

Wilson, M. (1989). Saltus: A psychometric model for discontinuity in cognitive development. *Psychological Bulletin, 105*, 276-289.

Wilson, M., & Sloane, K. (2000). From principles to practice: An embedded assessment system. *Applied Measurement in Education, 13,* 181-208.

Yang, Y., Buchendahl, C. W., Juszkiewicz, P. J., & Bhola, D. S. (2002) A review of strategies for validating computer-automated scoring. *Applied Measurement in Education, 15*(4), 391-412.

CHAPTER 11

INCORPORATING COGNITIVE DEMAND IN CREDENTIALING EXAMINATIONS

Susan L. Davis and Chad W. Buckendahl

Considering cognitive demand as a dimension of educational and psychological exam development and validation has been recommended for decades (e.g., Anastasi, 1988; Bloom, 1956). These recommended best practices have also been more recently validated as important to state educational assessments through expectations of federal peer review in the No Child Left Behind (U.S. Congress, 2002) legislation. Specifically, expectations about alignment in the federal regulations necessitate at a minimum, an explicit consideration of content and cognitive demand (Bhola, Impara, & Buckendahl, 2003; Webb, 1997). Moving beyond just the content domain representation of an exam, cognitive demand specifies the depth to which areas of content should be measured. For most examination programs, the goal of incorporating cognitive demand is to target the appropriate level of higher order thinking skills. In this chapter, we focused our interpretation of cognitive demand on the level of cognitive processing identified by an exam objective or required to answer an exam question.

Assessment of Higher Order Thinking Skills, pp. 303–325

By including cognitive demand as a part of the exam development and validation process, educational programs have successfully created exams that reflect the mental processing that is expected of students based on state-defined content expectations and match classroom activities. It also helps to characterize the range of cognitive demand that students may exhibit within a given content domain. Because students have a range of abilities, developing assessments with differing levels of cognitive demand also provides multiple opportunities for students to access the content and demonstrate their understanding.

Explicit consideration of cognitive demand can also be very beneficial to exam development and validation within credentialing programs. The necessity to apply this concept is readily apparent in the purpose of credentialing. Credentialing requirements, specifically licensure, exist to ensure public safety by regulating the persons who are permitted to do a job or assume a professional responsibility. Given the stakes that are involved in some of these credentials (e.g., potential harm to the public), the associated exams should serve as a proper screening tool for ensuring qualifications. Exam developers must go beyond just representing content areas to target the requirements of the higher order thinking skills that are required by those possessing the credential.

Credentialing examinations generally focus on a narrower range of the ability continuum compared with educational assessments (e.g., the distinction between the unqualified and minimally qualified candidate). Therefore, the need to measure the full range of candidate abilities may not be as important in the credentialing context. Rather, the challenge with developing credentialing exams is to ensure that exam questions represent the job-related knowledge, skills, abilities, or judgments, as appropriate. Because a credential (e.g., license, certification, registration) has a specific meaning, it is important to align the meaning to the expectations that are measured. Although difficult, this part of the process is a necessary component to the validity of the interpretation and use of exam scores for differentiating those who are minimally qualified from those who are not. In this chapter we describe steps in the exam development and validation process where cognitive demand can be considered and practical strategies for infusing cognitive demand in credentialing examination programs.

In the first section we provide a conceptual description of cognitive demand and some current models for understanding and using cognitive demand in exam development. The second section discusses reasons for why cognitive demand should be integral in the development of credentialing exams. The final section provides some specific suggestions for how cognitive demand can be incorporated in such exam development.

A graphical illustration of a validity-centered test development cycle is illustrated in Figure 11.1. The process begins with defining the intended use and interpretation of scores (design program and design test) and then moves into analyzing the content domain, creating the exam blueprint, developing and reviewing the exam content (i.e., exam items, prompts, stimuli), pretesting and analyzing the exam content, creating test forms, setting standards, and continues with ongoing exam maintenance. This process is shown as a lifecycle rather than strictly linear because it is continuous during the life of the examination program without a defined endpoint. Exam developers and users must continue to monitor, evaluate, and improve the quality of exam results.

At the center of this representation of the exam development cycle is the concept of validity as the fundamental consideration at each step. According to the *Standards for Educational and Psychological Testing* (AERA, APA, NCME, 1999), validity refers to the appropriate interpretation and use of exam scores based on its defined, intended purpose(s). Because interpreting validity is a matter of degree, practitioners continually evaluate validity evidence collected across the exam development cycle. It is important for exam developers to evaluate evidence of domain representation including the appropriateness of the content and cognitive demand. Again, the goal is to match the requirements set forth by job-related knowledge, skills, abilities, and judgments that can vary across a given field/profession. In the subsequent sections of this chapter, we present strategies for integrating cognitive demand at several of these development steps.

The Nature of Cognitive Demand

Cognitive demand can be conceptualized as a continuum. At the lower end are cognitive processes such as recall, memorization or any type of rote response. We might characterize the continuum as then moving through more moderate levels of cognitive demand that include understanding and applying knowledge and skills to common and then more complex problems. At the highest end of the continuum are the types of cognitive processes that require generating one's own ideas and formulating opinions that can be supported with evidence.

Numerous frameworks have been conceptualized for organizing, understanding, and evaluating cognitive demand. Perhaps the most notable one was developed by Bloom (1956) and has been a crucial component in training for many educators. Bloom's taxonomy organized the cognitive domain into six areas:

Figure 11.1.   Illustrative validity-centered test development cycle.

1. Knowledge: Information retrieval

2. Comprehension: Understanding the meaning of information

3. Application: Using information to solve problems that have a best answer

4. Analysis: Understanding parts of a whole and the organization of the parts to make inferences or draw conclusions

5. Synthesis: Applying knowledge and skills to produce new ideas or representation of material

6. Evaluation: Using information and knowledge to make judgments

Since this initial conceptualization, several groups have revised and reorganized Bloom's conceptualization. For example, Marzanno and Kendall (2007) identified over 20 revisions to the taxonomy. Other researchers have taken a different approach and created unique frameworks (e.g., Frisbie, 2003; Webb, 1997).

There is no one commonly accepted conceptualization, organization, or framework of cognitive demand. Rather one can focus on the common features of each of taxonomy. The first feature is that each framework divides the conceptual continuum of cognitive demand into comparable and relatable parts (e.g., levels, dimensions, components, types). The second feature is that each framework should be understandable and feasible for use in exam development, validation and evaluation. Specifically, the "levels" or "dimensions" of cognitive demand should be operationally defined such that they include one distinct type of cognitive processing yet large enough that the framework is understandable and transferable to subject matter experts (SMEs) who are often not familiar with the concept.

It is important to distinguish cognitive demand from content or empirical difficulty as these characteristics can be easily confounded. Difficulty refers to the *amount* of knowledge or processing required whereas demand refers to the *type* of knowledge or processing required. If we think of difficulty and demand as intersecting characteristics of an exam item it important to realize that an item high in difficulty does not necessarily mean the item is high in cognitive demand. As an example, let us say that we are developing a credentialing program to certify entry-level psychometricians. Within this hypothetical program, we have developed the following items that were judged to match the content of a predetermined objective:

1. What is the conceptual formula for an observed score in classical test theory?

2. What is the formula for calculating the probability of a correct response given a specific ability level using a 3PL model in IRT?

3. Using the 3PL IRT model and the following parameters, $a = 0.20$, $b = -0.50$, and $c = 0.15$, what is the probability of a correct response for a candidate whose ability is 0.05?

The first example item would likely be considered low in difficulty and low in cognitive demand as it requires only memorization of three elements (observed score, true score, and error). The second item is of the same cognitive demand (also memorization) but likely represents a higher level of empirical difficulty because it requires memorization of a more complex framework for entry-level practitioners (e.g., theta, difficulty parameter, discrimination parameter). The third item represents a different level of cognitive demand (an application of knowledge, more complex formula) as the candidate must first recall the formula for the 3PL IRT model and then use this recalled information to solve the problem. The first two items (and the recall portion of the third) represent knowledge that either the examinee will either know or not know—this is not the type of question an examinee can "figure out" in the exam setting. Solving the problem in the third item clearly involves different cognitive processes and it is important to recognize that the examinee must perform a process (that is likely familiar) that is required to derive the correct answer. Although this example is somewhat artificial, it illustrates the importance of defining the intended interpretation and use of scores as part of the design process.

Although conceptually different, it is worthy to note that in most settings cognitive demand and difficulty are related. For example, most exam items written that are of higher cognitive demand are quite difficult (e.g., analyzing, making a judgment supported by evidence, organizing one's own ideas). The distinction is important because without this additional dimension it is possible to create an exam that is difficult but not accessing the intended level(s) of cognitive challenge. Such exams often require extensive memorization of terms, facts, or details. This type of content is very appropriate for some professional exams (e.g., memorization of drug interactions for those in the pharmaceutical field). However, as is discussed in this chapter, many credentialing exams are designed to focus on assessing higher order thinking skills (e.g., application of knowledge, diagnosis, evaluation) and the recall of information is a subsumed ability, but not the critical part of the job requirements that define the intent of the certification process.

Cognitive Demand Considerations for Credentialing Exams

The purpose of credentialing programs makes cognitive demand an important consideration. A credential is an acknowledgement of a professional's knowledge, skills, or abilities within a particular domain. As described above, credentials are sometimes awarded following participation in an educational or training program and then successful completion of some measure of competency (e.g., written or performance exam). There are two distinct areas within credentialing: licensure and certification. Licensure is a requirement for entering practice and its purpose is narrowly defined to be protection of the public. Professionals must demonstrate that they have minimally sufficient abilities to safely function within the domain. Alternatively, certification is generally voluntary with a purpose to acknowledge specialized knowledge and skills within a given domain. Although specific credentials may be required by some employers, using these scores for a dual purpose as personnel selection instruments (e.g., higher scores are predictive of on-the-job performance) likely goes beyond the intended uses supported by the validity evidence collected by these programs.

Despite this difference in purpose, the shared goal for these examination programs is to determine if candidates have met expectations defined for a minimally qualified candidate (MQC). Credentials are sometimes mislabeled in practice (e.g., initial teacher certification), but the most notable difference between the two is that licensure is mandatory and state-controlled. Conversely, certification is a voluntary program established by an organization or within a professional field.

Hamm (2000) noted that one critical step in building a certification program is to establish the value of the credential to relevant stakeholder groups. This can be accomplished by following several important steps, one of which is to engage in systematic exam development and collect the necessary validity evidence during the development process to support the intended interpretation of the exam scores. To make the credential valuable within the profession, the exam format and expectations must reflect the nature of the profession to the greatest extent feasible. To do so, programs have targeted assessment of the knowledge, skills, abilities, or judgments required for entry-level practice. Such exams are typically carefully scrutinized by various stakeholder groups: current professionals, recently credentialed professionals, educators, employers, and perhaps the public. A common criticism of credentialing exams that is often raised by practitioners is that they appear to lack face validity (i.e., knowledge and skills do not appear to measure job-related skills) and focus too much on trivial knowledge. A similar common criticism is that they lack perceived "rigor" or do not challenge examinees at a level that they will be challenged on the job. Typically, such concerns arise when the level of cognitive demand is below that of the job requirements (e.g., job requires employees to troubleshoot software application, but the exam items focus on recall of technical specifications). This then raises validity concerns as to whether the exam scores are appropriate for their intended uses.

Often, these criticisms are likely indirectly reflecting an intuitive need to integrate the cognitive demand dimension into the exam development process. From a conceptual perspective, attending to the issue of cognitive demand means that the level of challenge required by the credentialing exam should match entry-level practice. To implement this practically, exam developers must identify, exemplify, and integrate cognitive demand in the exam development process. The result is an exam that reflects at least the minimum the level of cognitive processing within the content required for entry level practice within a credentialing field.

Although several credentialing programs have successfully used such processes for exam development, some researchers have suggested that differentiating cognitive demand beyond two levels for exam items should not be a concern for these types of exams (Clauser, Margolis, & Case, 2006). Specifically, Clauser et al. suggested that the level of cognition required to answer an exam item correctly varies across individual candidates, and therefore, cannot be accurately identified or classified in credentialing exams. Although job domains can be quite large, exam development within credentialing should be focused on the target knowledge, skills, and abilities that are necessary for candidates to demonstrate. With this position, we argue that cognitive demand can be identified and classified for items on credentialing exams. Although such estimations may vary across individuals, for the purposes of exam development classifications can be made by focusing on the intended use of the exam scores and the characteristics of the intended population. Specifically, because the purpose of the exam is to determine who is at least minimally qualified, judgments about cognitive demand can be made by focusing on the MQC. As the critical decision point for the exam, this point of focus provides supportive validity evidence for the intended use of exam scores.

APPLYING COGNITIVE DEMAND TO EXAM DEVELOPMENT

There are four steps within our representation of the exam development process (Figure 11.1) where consideration of cognitive demand is important for supporting the intended use of exam scores. These four areas are domain analysis, content development, content review, and standard setting. The ability to integrate the consideration for cognitive demand in each of these four steps is dependent on how the prior steps in the process were completed. In other words, this process starts by setting expectations for the exam and the MQC at the beginning of the process and the subsequent steps build up on those expectations by making them operational in the exam. Before starting the exam development process, one must select an appropriate cognitive demand taxonomy/framework. As an example, we elaborate here on a modification of Anderson et al.'s (2001) cognitive demand framework. Anderson et al.'s revised Bloom's taxonomy of cognitive demand is characterized with the following levels:

1. Remember: Recalling, retrieving, recognizing.
2. Understand: Interpreting, summarizing, inferring, comparing and explaining.
3. Apply: Executing or implementing a procedure.
4. Analyze: Differentiating, relating parts of a system, organizing, distinguishing between parts of a system.
5. Evaluate: Making judgments based on criteria, critiquing, making recommendations.

6.   Create: Creating new patterns, generating ideas, planning, synthesize information in a new way.

This organization of cognitive demand represents several significant changes from Bloom's original framework including renaming levels, reordering two categories, and moving away from the theory that this hierarchy is cumulative—one does not have to master each lower level to achieve cognitive processing in the higher levels. For example, one does not have to memorize a mathematical formula to be able to apply it to problem solving.

The complexity of this taxonomy presents a problem for developers of credentialing exams. Developers typically have a very limited amount of time to orient and train SMEs in the exam development process and necessary terminology. One solution to this problem is to consolidate the framework that Anderson et al. proposes. As part of their argument that classification by cognitive demand is subjective, Clauser et al. (2006) suggest that it is appropriate to make a simple dichotomous classification of cognitive demand (recall of information, application of knowledge). Our suggestion is that the six-level framework of Anderson et al. (2001) can be synthesized for practical use but with more specificity than the dichotomized structure that Clauser et al. (2006) suggests. We believe this a reasonable compromise because the number of ability levels needed to differentiate among candidates for a credentialing exam (e.g., "met" or "not met") is not as great as the multiple ability levels often required within educational settings (e.g., below basic, basic, proficient, advanced). Given that the measurement goals of credentialing exams are narrower than those of educational exams, we have created the following consolidation of the Anderson et al. framework for use with credentialing programs:

1.   Remember: Recalling, retrieving, recognizing.

2.   Understand/Apply: interpreting, summarizing, inferring, comparing, explaining, executing or implementing a procedure.

3.   Analyze/Evaluate: differentiating, relating parts of a system, organizing, distinguishing between parts of a system, making judgments based on criteria, critiquing, making recommendations.

4.   Create: creating new patterns, generating ideas, planning, synthesize information in a new way

In our work applying cognitive demand in exam development, this consolidated version of Anderson et al.'s (2001) framework has appeared to be understandable and feasible for use with SMEs from a variety of professional fields including healthcare and technology. Although this framework may not fully align with theoretical conceptualizations of how information is stored and accessed, this framework was designed to be practical with respect to thinking about how knowledge, skills, and abilities are applied in the work place and communicated to a lay audience. In these settings, SMEs receive an overview of the cognitive demand framework that would be used throughout the exam development.[1] Such training usually includes (1) an overview of how cognitive demand can be operationally defined, (2) a description of how and where cognitive demand will be used at different stages of the exam development process, (3) a description of each level of cognitive demand, and (4) examples of how each level of cognitive demand can be targeted to a given context that is applicable to the participants. In this section we outline how cognitive demand can be incorporated in several major steps in exam development. It is important to remember that the stages of the exam development processes build on the efforts taken in previous steps and may iterate. Therefore, successfully integrating cognitive demand into a examination program requires the consideration of the concept at each of these steps.

Domain Analysis

One of the most important aspects of credentialing exam development is the specification of the elements of the domain that will constitute the exam. This is typically conducted through a practice analysis (e.g., job task analysis, occupational analysis, process analysis) or other systematic process using the input of qualified SMEs (e.g., focus groups, survey of practitioners). Knapp and Knapp (1995) describe this step in the exam development process as "the systematic collection of data describing the responsibilities required of a professional and the skills and knowledge needed to perform these responsibilities" (p. 94). This process is important for creating a meaningful exam that is representative of the domain, aiding the sponsoring organization determine who should receive the associated credential, and laying a foundation for legal defensibility of the program. Typically, a practice analysis focuses on identifying the areas of content (i.e., knowledge, skills, abilities, judgments) that are part of entry level practice[2] in the job or certification field which later become the framework for an exam blueprint.

In a basic definition of job responsibilities we can think about at least two dimensions: content and cognitive demand. The first dimension of content is usually the primary focus when designing an exam framework. Content includes facets such as facts, concepts, principles, or procedures

(Haladyna, 1997). As a second, important dimension, cognitive demand is often not consciously addressed in such designs but may occur as a by-product of the content design. Specifically, during the domain analysis process, the SMEs and facilitators will document knowledge, skills, abilities, and judgments that are required by the job and though documentation they will include an implied level of cognitive demand. For example, consider the following hypothetical exam objectives that might be developed for a teacher licensure exam designed to measure candidates' knowledge of reading development in elementary students:

1. The candidate will know different instructional strategies that can be used with elementary students to develop reading skills.
2. Given a student's reading ability history, classroom assessment information, and related parent feedback, the candidate will recommend appropriate instructional strategies that are likely to foster the student's reading skill development.

In general, both of these objectives cover the content area of understanding and using instructional strategies to help promote reading skills. The difference between the two is the level of cognitive processing that is implied by the way the objective is written. In the first example, the wording is somewhat vague and could be interpreted to mean the examinee would only need to recall what different strategies exist. It does not specifically describe what the examinee is expected to do with this knowledge. In the second objective, the candidate expectations are more clearly stated to incorporate information from multiple sources (history with reading instruction, parent report, performance ratings) to make an informed judgment in a job-related context.

By making a conscious effort to clearly define job responsibilities as objectives in terms of both content and the cognitive demand associated with a particular area of knowledge or skill, the content specification process can produce a more targeted set of expectations for an MQC in a field. It is important that these expectations be clearly specified through use of verbs that guide the expectations. For example, consider the verb in each of the two example objectives above. The first objective (*know*) suggests a knowledge-level understanding of the content specified in the objective. It does not specify the examinee using this knowledge in any way or taking actions based on it. In contrast, the verb in the second objective (*recommend*) suggests the examinee will have to make some type of judgment. Most published cognitive demand frameworks also include lists of verbs typically associated with each particular level of cognitive demand. It is important to caution that a given verb alone does NOT dictate the level of cognitive demand. Carrying over the same theme from above, consider the following variations of the example exam objectives presented previously:

1. Identify different instructional strategies that can be used to assist students with reading skills development.
2. Given a student's reading ability history, classroom assessment information, and related parent feedback, the candidate will identify which instructional strategies are appropriate for assisting the student develop his or her reading skills.

Typically, the verb *identify* is associated with an expectation of a lower cognitive demand as it represents locating a match to recalled information. However, in this second example objective, we are illustrating that this same verb can suggest a different type of cognitive demand.

In crafting each objective, the exam development facilitator should guide SMEs to effectively phrase the objective to reflect the intended level of cognitive demand that is required of the typical MQC in the targeted population. Because the SMEs' task in the domain analysis process is to document the expectations for the job, it is important that this information is clearly communicated to the item writing team. Depending on the size of the credentialing program and the intended interpretation and use of the scores, this may be the same group of SMEs, a different group of SMEs, or a group of professional item writers. Therefore, to ensure the item writing panel comprehends the expectations defined by the content specification panel, it is suggested to document examples of skills or tasks within an objective that reflect the cognitive demand of the objective.

Raymond and Neustel (2006) also propose a way for integrating evaluation of cognitive demand in the practice analysis conducted through a survey of professionals. They suggest that for each task that is part of a job, one could provide SMEs with a range of behaviors ranging from low to high in cognitive demand. The SMEs would be asked to identify two points on the scale: the first would be the level of skill expected of the average entry level practitioner. The second would be the minimum acceptable level of skills expected for an entry level practitioner. This approach may be particularly useful when trying to identify candidates who have higher abilities in contrast to the expectations of the MQC.

After going through the domain analysis process, the drafted job requirements are then often utilized in weighting activities where SMEs have the opportunity to indicate the relative importance of each requirement to entry-level practice. These judgments are then used to determine how much of the final exam content will be dedicated to assessing each area of the job. This information including the final phrasing of the job requirements (e.g., objectives) and associated weightings are used to create the exam blueprint. The exam blueprint then serves as the roadmap for creating the exam content in the item writing and forms assembly portions of the exam development processes. Utilizing such a structured process for creating the exam blueprint will provide needed validity evidence to support the use of exam scores based on content that reflects the job requirements.

Content Development

The process of developing examinations for credentialing programs all starts with an articulation of the intended use and interpretation of scores. These intended uses then drive the domain specification and prioritization process. From there, the important elements of the domain are then translated into the exam content (e.g., items, stimuli, supporting materials). Although exam developers in credentialing programs often follow this path with respect to content, they have often overlooked specific consideration of cognitive demand.

Consider the following hypothetical exam objective and two questions from a clinical examination that may be used to evaluate competency of entry-level dental hygienists:

Objective X: Use patient health information to develop appropriate treatment plans.

1. What patient health information would a dental hygienist need to develop an appropriate treatment for a patient whose chief complaint is sensitivity to cold drinks?
2. Review this patient's chief complaint, medical history, oral history, and radiographs. What is the appropriate treatment plan for this patient?

Both illustrative exam items clearly match the example objective in terms of content because both are related to information that is needed to develop a treatment plan based on a patient's health information. However, the first question only requires the recall of memorized information whereas the second question requires the examinee to first recall what information they need for such an assessment, filter pertinent information from the patient's medical and oral health histories, and radiographs, and then interpret and apply that information to develop an appropriate treatment plan for this patient.

An SME could argue that the first question is part of the skills and cognitive processes outlined in the example objective but from a cognitive demand perspective, the first question does not reach the intended cognitive demand level of the objective. Items such as the first are often written when creating exams simply because these items are easier to create. Typically they can be drawn from textbooks or other reference materials. Professional item writers who are not SMEs also find it easier to write lower-level questions because they do not have the depth of content knowledge necessary to understand the subtleties of the material. The problem can then be compounded when a disproportionate number of items like the first example are represented on an exam. When this lack of alignment occurs, the concern noted earlier about effectively representing the domain is often raised. Specifically, stakeholders may express concerns that the exam does not reflect an appropriate level of rigor or demand given the intended inferences they want to make about candidates' abilities.

Many programs use SMEs who have been trained to serve as item writers because a greater depth of understanding of the content is often required to complete such tasks. We contend that it is possible to train SMEs with relevant content expertise to create items to meet higher levels of cognitive demand. This process begins by dedicating time to training on effective item writing guidelines (e.g., Downing & Haladyna, 1989) and the cognitive demand framework being used by the examination program. As part of training, SMEs should review the exam framework and discuss the specific level of cognitive demand of each objective so they have a clear target as they begin writing items. It is usually advantageous to have a representative from the domain analysis process to communicate the targeted depth of knowledge. As mentioned above, many published cognitive frameworks also provide associated verb lists and such aids can be helpful to new item writers. However, using such words does not guarantee that an item will target the intended level. An example list is included in Appendix A.

Generic item templates can also serve as an aid to item writers. Some examples include:

1. Understand/Apply

    (a) What is the difference between _____?
    (b) What is an example of _____?
    (c) Use the _____ procedure to solve this problem.

2. Analyze/Evaluate

    All examples below would follow a scenario, situation, or given information that provides a job-related context

    (a) What is the most likely cause of _____?

    (b) What would happen if _____ ?

    (c) What information is needed to solve this problem?

    (d) What is the most cost effective solution to this problem?

    (d) What is the next step in the process?

These are very generic examples that can be used as a starting point that also require well-crafted contextual information to elicit the intended level of cognitive demand. More domain-specific illustrations might be appropriate for training of items writers. After the item writing process begins it is important to closely monitor the draft items, encourage peer review, and mentor SMEs to create items that meet the content and cognitive demand match.

A second strategy for writing items to higher levels of cognitive demand is to incorporate different item types that are sometimes viewed as more conducive to these levels of measurement. Many credentialing exams use single response multiple-choice items that include a stem and a set of response options. As shown with some of the simplistic item templates above, these types of items can be used to test memorization, understanding, and some critical thinking when presented in the context of a stimulus or scenario. By including this contextual information, an item requires the examinee to process the information, determine what is relevant to the problem presented in the stem, and solve the problem.

However, some credentialing exams are going farther and creating stimulus material or scenarios that are then used to solve multiple problems (see, e.g., Parshall & Harmes, 2009). These types of items typically require more cognitive processing as the examinee must sort through more information, much of which may not be relevant to any of the questions they are answering. From a credentialing exam perspective, these types of problems may more closely approximate typical job-related tasks. Beyond items with additional material, other credentialing programs have incorporated computer-based simulation items that require an examinee to perform a procedure or process in a simulated environment. Exam developers have been given more flexibility to use these items that more closely resemble the job as the examinee is required to do something rather than answer questions about how they might do it (e.g., the steps, the order of the process). Sireci and Zenisky (2006) also describe many of the innovative item types that are afforded when exams use a computer-based format and how these item types can be used to enhance authenticity of exam and reduce construct-irrelevant variance.

Exam developers have acknowledged that because of an expected performance demand, one cannot write multiple-choice items at some of the highest levels of cognitive demand. For example, in the framework we adapted from Anderson et al. (2001) the highest level *Create* represents the examinee creating their own work or their own representation of material. Obviously if an examinee must create something new they cannot select it from a set of options. Exams that include oral responses, essay or short answers, or other types of performance can be used to test an examinee's ability to design, organize, present, and support their own ideas.

Overall, training and use of different item types can help create items that are at higher levels of cognitive demand. However, it is important to acknowledge that the goal is not to make items as cognitively, conceptually, or empirically challenging as possible but rather to reflect the job-related demands. When determining the cognitive demand of items one has to consider the target population for the exam. As discussed in the first section of this chapter, Clauser et al. (2006) suggest that cognitive demand (in terms of the level of processing required) is subjective and different for each examinee. Although the speed of processing for candidates will be influenced by their education and experiences, we argue that for credentialing programs, the target population would be the MQCs defined in the performance standard.

Content Review

Most content review processes in credentialing exam development include evaluating the content match between each item and the exam objectives and a review of the technical accuracy of the item (e.g., only one correct answer, proper terminology, distracters that reflect common errors). As part of these important quality control checks, we recommend evaluating the match between the cognitive demand of the item and the intended objective.

An *independent* process is the most credible form of item review. To conduct this process independently, SMEs, who do not have prior knowledge of the items, would be asked to judge the level of cognitive demand of the set of exam objectives, exam items, and the content match between items and objectives. Post-hoc analysis would then evaluate the match in cognitive level. Although less ideal, a *confirmatory* process can also be used to review items. In a confirmatory process, SMEs, who may or may not have prior knowledge of the items, would be shown the intended objective to which the items should be aligned and ask whether the content and/or cognitive level matches the objective. The required level of independence of the raters should be informed by factors such as the stakes of the exam and the representativeness and availability of SMEs within the eligible population.

In addition to selecting a content review process, exam developers must also determine the extent to which items match the targeted cognitive demand. We find some guidance for this issue in the literature that state educational assessment programs have used to evaluate this validity evidence in their programs. Specifically, under the No Child Left Behind (U.S. Congress, 2002) peer review guidance regulations, states must have an independent (i.e., SMEs who did not write the items) panel conduct such a process. Webb's (1997) criteria that many states use for these studies suggests that at least 50% of the items matched by content to each objective must have a cognitive demand level at or above the cognitive demand level of the objective. This may be a reasonable target for educational assessment programs that often use multiple cut scores and have objectives that may be broadly described. However, for credentialing programs that typically target measurement around a single cut score, including information that does not contribute to the intended decision may not be useful and may waste valuable measurement capital.

Therefore, in the development of credentialing exams, we recommend that exam developers target 100% of items be at or above the level of cognitive demand suggested by the associated exam objective. This criterion sounds very strict—any flexibility in this rule should be considered in the context of the purpose of the exam. Whereas educational assessments are often designed to evaluate proficiency at multiple levels, credentialing exams are designed to determine whether someone is ready to independently perform a job or responsibility. The nature of the job or responsibilities dictates the true stakes associated with the exam. Therefore, exam developers should consider the validity evidence needed to support decision making associated with these particular stakes and make the final decision about how stringent the item review process should be.

Conducting an item review with this higher criterion will likely add more time to the process and require additional training. Facilitators and exam developers conducting the item review must acknowledge that some items will have to be rejected or heavily edited during this process to ensure the item bank represents a sufficient level of cognitive demand.

Standard Setting

Finally, considerations of cognitive demand should also be made during the standard setting process. Standard setting literature cites the importance of including a discussion of the qualifications of the MQC during the training and relevant, operational components of the study (Giraud, 2005; Raymond & Reid, 2001). Specifically, it is helpful to review the expected knowledge, skills, and abilities of the MQC in relation to the exam content (blueprint, objectives). This discussion is often documented so the SMEs can refer to this information while making judgments about expected performance of the MQC on specific exam items.

In conducting this discussion it is important to not only specify the content areas that are necessary for the MQC to be familiar with but also the level of cognitive demand. For example, in a given content area, should the MQC be familiar with the terms, understand the concepts, be able to provide judgments integrating information, or even create a novel representation of the material? This additional point of clarification will help target the expectations for this hypothetical candidate and allow the panelists to parallel one another in how they translate their expectations to the standard setting process.

Most test-based standard setting processes also include some type of practice activity or opportunity for SMEs to discuss specific items and how they expect an MQC to perform on each item. By using the language of cognitive demand, SMEs can discuss how an MQC would process an item and what steps they would have to take to answer the item. By relating these conversations to the description of the MCQ with similar language, the expectations defined earlier in the process can be confirmed through example ratings.

EVALUATING COGNITIVE DEMAND OF CREDENTIALING EXAMS

In addition to incorporating these considerations in new programs, exam owners can also integrate these ideas into existing programs. If exam forms or content were created without considering cognitive demand, it is still possible that the exam, or parts of the exam meet the professional expectations for depth of processing. As outlined in this chapter, there are numerous elements that should be systematically evaluated for cognitive demand. Exam developers or users can enlist SMEs to conduct a systematic review of existing exam characteristics. Specifically, the goal of this needs analysis would be to evaluate which parts of the existing examination program would need to be modified or redeveloped to match the expected level of cognitive demand. There are four areas that should be considered in the analysis: (1) the description of the MQC, (2) the exam blueprint, (3) the existing items, and (4) the process used for recommending the cut score. The processes for reviewing each of these elements are described below.

The first step in such a review would be to orient the SMEs to working with cognitive demand. Similar to the process described in the previous section, this training should include an orientation to the concept of cognitive demand as well as a thorough familiarization with the organizational framework or taxonomy. The SMEs could then begin with the MQC description and provide any edits necessary to clarify the expectations for cognitive processing. The final description should clearly specify the content areas that are to be mastered for entry-level practice and to what level the profession expects the MQC be able to process the material. The second step would be to review the content framework for the exam, or exam blueprint. The same group of SMEs could engage in a systematic review of all exam objectives (e.g., standards, claims) to ensure they all include the appropriate expectations for cognitive processing. This may require rewriting or refining some exam specifications to narrow their breadth to the important areas of work for entry-level practice. The third step in this process is to review the actual exam content. The review process could employ the strategies that many educational examination programs use to evaluate how well items align with content specifications (Porter, 2002; Rothman, Slattery, Vranek, & Resnick, 2002; Webb, 1997). Such processes require SMEs to review each item, explicitly identify the cognitive level of the item and the match between the item and the exam blueprint. This review process provides validity evidence that all items included in assessments match the content intended to be measured by the exam. It also ensures that content is covered well enough to support interpretation of exam scores. Most importantly for the purposes discussed here, this type of review allows for analysis of how the cognitive level of the items matches that of the exam objectives to which they are aligned. Finally, if any of the aforementioned aspects of the exam have been modified in any way (expectations of MQC, exam blueprint, exam items), it will be important to review the previously set passing standard. The best way to approach aligning the passing standard with the new exam content and expectations will be to have the SMEs engage in a standard setting process using a structured examinee- or test-based standard setting approach. All four of these review elements are important to provide validity evidence about whether or not the actual exam content reflects the specified job requirements and the intended use of exam scores.

CONCLUSIONS AND RECOMMENDATIONS

Although the use of cognitive demand has been more extensively incorporated into exam development and validation in the educational sector, its application to credentialing exam development is equally relevant. The purpose of this chapter was to describe the steps in the exam development and validation process where opportunities exist to explicitly include cognitive demand models in the discussion. Programs must start the exam development process with the intent to integrate cognitive demand in the exam development process. This process begins with selecting or creating an organizational framework for considering cognitive demand and then using the framework to exemplify the cognitive demand required for entry-level practice. The subsequent parts of this process then require exam developers to integrate cognitive demand in the processes used in content specification, item writing, item review, and standard setting. In addition, guidance was provided on conducting a postdevelopment review for existing programs that are interesting in reviewing the cognitive expectations of their program.

Ultimately, considerations of cognitive demand must be aligned with the intended use and interpretations of scores from the exam. The goal is not to make the exam content as cognitively challenging as possible, but rather to represent the level of demand required by entry-level practice within the professional domain. In any case, it is important that each program determine whether such considerations are needed for their programs while concurrently considering the psychometric and policy factors.

ACKNOWLEDGMENTS

The authors wish to thank the editor and anonymous reviewer for their feedback and comments on the draft version of this chapter.

NOTES

1. Note that a given program may have already adopted a particular cognitive framework or taxonomy for use. We are not suggesting that there is only one approach when considering integration of cognitive demand into the development process.
2. Certification programs often specify expertise beyond minimal qualifications (e.g., board certified surgeon, geriatric specialty physical therapists).

REFERENCES

American Educational Research Association, American Psychological Association, & National Council on Measurement in Education. (1999). *Standards for educational and psychological testing*. Washington, DC: American Educational Research Association.

Anastasi, A. (1988). *Psychological testing*. New York, NY: McMillan.

Appendix A: Example Verb List for Cognitive Taxonomy

Cognitive Level	Description	Associated Verbs
Remember	Retrieve relevant knowledge from long-term memory	define, describe, find, identify, label, list, match, name, recall, recognize, record, repeat, reproduce, state, tell, underline
Understand/ Apply	Construct meaning from information, demonstrate comprehension of concepts or processes, apply processes or procedures in familiar or unfamiliar situations.	apply, arrange, calculate, classify, compare, complete, compute, contrast, convert, demonstrate, discuss, distinguish, estimate, execute, explain, extend, extrapolate, generalize, give examples, illustrate, infer, interpolate, interpret, locate, manipulate, measure, modify, operate, outline, paraphrase, predict, prepare, report, restate, schedule, score, show, show, sketch, solve, sort, summarize, translate, use, utilize
Analyze/ Evaluate	Break material into parts, determine how parts relate to one another or overall structure, make judgments based on criteria.	analyze, appraise, argue, assess, attack, breakdown, conclude, criticize, critique, debate, decide, deduce, defend, determine, diagram, differentiate, discriminate, discuss, distinguish, evaluate, examine, experiment, investigate, judge, justify, prioritize, question, rate, reason, recommend, reconcile, separate, subdivide, support, survey, take apart, test, transform, value, verify
Create	Put elements or material together to form a new representation or product, reorganize material in a new pattern.	assemble, combine, compile, compose, construct, create, design, devise, edit, formulate, generate, invent, modify, organize, plan, predict, present, propose, rearrange, reconstruct, reorganize, revise, rewrite, set up, synthesize and create a new representation

This illustrative list is based on a synthesis of similar efforts by Bloom (1956), Webb (1997), Anderson et al. (2001) and Frisbie (2003).

Anderson, L., Krathwohl, D., Airasian, P., Cruikshank, K., Mayer, R., Pintrich, et al. (2001). *A taxonomy for learning, teaching, and assessing: A revision of Bloom's taxonomy of educational objectives.* New York, NY: Longman.

Bhola, D. S., Impara, J. C., & Buckendahl, C. W. (2003). Aligning tests with state content standards: Methods and issues. *Educational Measurement: Issues and Practice, 22*(3), 21-29.

Bloom, B. S. (Ed.) (1956). *Taxonomy of educational objectives, the classification of educational goals – Handbook I: Cognitive Domain.* New York, NY: McKay.

Clauser, B., Margolis, M., & Case, S. (2006). Testing for licensure and certification in the profession. In R. Brennan (Ed.), *Educational Measurement* (4th ed., pp. 701-732). Westport, CT: American Council on Education and Praeger Publishers.

Downing, S., & Haladyna, T. (1989). A taxonomy of multiple choice item writing rules. *Applied Measurement in Education, 2*(1), 37-50.

Frisbie, D. A. (2003). *Checking the alignment of an assessment tool and a set of content standards* (Iowa Technical Adequacy Project (ITAP)). Iowa City, IA: University of Iowa.

Giraud, G. (2005). Teachers' conceptions of the target examinee in Angoff standard setting. *Applied Measurement in Education, 18*(3), 223-232.

Haladyna, T. (1997). *Writing test items to evaluate higher order thinking.* Needham Heights, MA: Allyn & Bacon.

Hamm, M. (2000). Establishing and demonstrating the value of a credential. In C. Schoon & I. Smith (Eds.), *The licensure and certification mission: Legal, social, and political foundations* (pp. 31-52). New York, NY: Professional Examination Service.

Knapp, J. & Knapp, L. (1995). Practice analysis. In J. C. Impara (Ed.), *Licensure testing: Purposes, procedures and practices* (pp. 93-116). Lincoln, NE: Buros Institute of Mental Measurements.

Marzanno, R., & Kendall, J. (2007). *The new taxonomy of educational objectives* (2nd ed.). Thousand Oaks, CA: Corwin Press.

Parshall, C., & Harmes, J. C. (2009). Improving the quality of innovative item types: Four tasks for design and development. *Journal of Applied Testing Technology.* Retrieved from http://www.testpublishers.org/JATT

Porter, A. C. (2002). Measuring the content of instruction: Uses in research and practice. *Educational Researcher, 31*(7), 3-14.

Raymond, M., & Neustel, S. (2006). Determining the content of credentialing examinations. In S. Downing and T. Haladyna (Eds.), *Handbook of Test Development* (pp. 181-224), Mahwah, NJ: Erlbaum.

Raymond, M. R., & Reid, J. B. (2001). Who made thee a judge? Selecting and training participants for standard setting. In G. J. Cizek (Ed.), *Setting performance standards: Concepts, methods, and perspectives* (pp. 119-157). Mahwah, NJ: Erlbaum.

Rothman, R., Slattery, J. B., Vranek, J. L., & Resnick, L. B. (2002). *Benchmarking and alignment of standards and testing.* Los Angeles, CA: National Center for Research on Evaluation, Standards, and Student Testing.

Sireci, S., & Zenisky, A.(2006). Innovative Item Formats in Computer-Based Testing: In Pursuit of Improved Construct Representation. In S. Downing and T.

Haladyna (Eds.), *Handbook of Test Development* (pp. 329-348). Mahwah, NJ: Lawrence Erlbaum Associates.

U.S. Congress. (2002). *Public Law 107-110: No Child Left Behind Act of 2001.* Retrieved from http://www.ed.gov/policy/elsec/leg/esea02/index.html

Webb, N. L. (1997). Criteria for alignment of expectations and assessments in mathematics and science education. Council of Chief State School Officers and National Institute for Science Education. Madison, WI: Wisconsin Center for Educational Research, University of Wisconsin

CHAPTER 12

STRATEGIES FOR CONSTRUCTING ASSESSMENTS OF HIGHER ORDER THINKING SKILLS

Susan M. Brookhart and Anthony J. Nitko

In this chapter, we present some specific, practical advice for constructing assessment items or tasks that tap higher order thinking skills. We also consider how to construct appropriate scoring schemes. A complex task requiring higher order thinking can be subverted by a scoring scheme that only gives points for facts reported. Conversely, scoring the quality of students' reasoning on even some very simple tasks can assess higher order thinking.

A general first principle for assessing higher order thinking is to think about the assessment item or task from the point of view of the person assessed. "How would that person have to think to answer the question?" should help ascertain the thinking skills required. "What would that person have to think about to answer the question?" should help ascertain the content required. Both should match the knowledge and skills the assessment is intended to tap. This chapter focuses on the first question,

Assessment of Higher Order Thinking Skills, pp. 327–359
Copyright © 2011 by Information Age Publishing
All rights of reproduction in any form reserved.

the question about thinking, but it is worth mentioning that both are important and must be considered together in assessment design.

There are several different definitions of higher order thinking. Anderson and Krathwohl (2001) divide learning into learning for recall and learning for transfer:

> Two of the most important educational goals are to promote retention and to promote transfer (which, when it occurs, indicates meaningful learning) ... retention requires that students remember what they have learned, whereas transfer requires students not only to remember but also to make sense of and be able to use what they have learned. (p. 63)

Recall certainly requires a type of thinking, but it is learning for transfer which Anderson, Krathwohl, and their colleagues consider "meaningful learning." This approach has informed their construction of the Cognitive Dimension of the revised Bloom's taxonomy. Items or tasks that ask students to actually apply, analyze, evaluate, or create, must present students with tasks that require conceptual grouping or categorizing, logical reasoning, using judgment, and/or generating original theses or solutions. "Originality" in this context means a combination of ideas that the student has not thought of before, not necessarily something universally new.

Leighton has discussed in more detail the nature of these cognitive activities. In particular, her working definition of higher order thinking for the purpose of assessment includes four components. They are summarized as follows (see Leighton, this volume, for more detail):

1. inquiring or investigating questions, assumptions, or issues;
2. applying multiple appropriate criteria and tools to collect, analyze, and interpret evidence;
3. making inferences, predictions, explanations, or evaluations based on logic and evidence; and
4. self-regulating the cognitive effort required to do these things.

Other terms that are sometimes invoked in discussions of higher order thinking are "critical thinking" and "problem solving." Norris and Ennis (1989, p. 3) define critical thinking: "Critical thinking is reasonable, reflective thinking that is focused on deciding what to believe or do." (p. 3). Nitko and Brookhart (2011) define problem solving:

> Students incur a problem when they want to reach a specific outcome or goal but do not automatically recognize the proper path or solution to use to reach it. The problem to solve is how to reach the desired goal. When stu-

dents cannot automatically recognize the proper way to reach the desired goal, they must use one or more higher-order thinking processes. These thinking processes are called *problem-solving*. (p. 231)

In this chapter, we focus on how to design assessments that require those who are assessed to do these kinds of thinking in an explicit enough form that the thinking becomes visible for appraisal, feedback and discussion. In basic and higher education, assessment of higher order thinking assumes teaching of higher order thinking; while teaching these skills is not the subject of this chapter, it is worth noting that working through similar strategies with lots of feedback could be part of such instruction. In some other contexts (for example, assessments for selection or placement), it is assumed that the examinees will already have learned higher order thinking skills. In either case, the ultimate goal is for people to learn to do more of this kind of thinking, and do it better.

The next section presents general advice about how to assess higher order thinking of all types. The following section gives examples of strategies for constructing items and tasks to assess various specific kinds of higher order thinking. The examples are not exhaustive; they have been selected to represent common kinds of higher order thinking. A third section describes strategies for constructing criteria or scoring schemes for higher order thinking tasks. Criteria are needed for both giving feedback (if the assessment is formative) and scoring (if the assessment is summative) assessments of higher order thinking. An item or task without criteria for evaluating it is just an activity, not an assessment. A final section discusses the use of different formats to assess higher order thinking.

HOW WOULD YOU GET EVIDENCE THAT STUDENTS ARE DOING HIGHER ORDER THINKING?

Three general principles apply to all assessment design, including assessment of higher order thinking. (a) Begin by specifying clearly and exactly the kind of thinking, about what content, for which you wish to see evidence. (b) Design a task or test item that requires the use of this kind of thinking and content knowledge. (c) Decide what you will take as evidence that the person assessed has, in fact, exhibited this kind of thinking about the appropriate content, and design a scheme for scoring or interpreting performance. These common assessment design principles should be familiar to readers of this chapter. More details can be found in Nitko and Brookhart (2011).

Assessing higher order thinking almost always involves three additional principles. First, present something for those who are assessed to think *about*, usually in the form of introductory text, visuals, scenarios, problems, or choices of some sort. This makes higher order thinking the primary construct assessed and removes "recall," as much as possible, to the realm of construct-irrelevant variance. (Of course there is always some "recall" involved in any task, knowing the words one reads, for instance.) For more extended tasks in basic or higher education, like term papers or projects, you might ask students to look up their own information but still, you don't ask them to memorize it.

Second, make sure the material you present is novel material, not already familiar and thus subject to recall. It is this principle which causes the most problems for basic or higher education instructors in regard to higher order thinking. Many assessment tasks and questions look like they require higher order thinking when, in fact, they do not. For example, consider this question, which might be an essay test question in a high school or college Social Studies class or a take-home essay or a research paper, depending on the scope of the project (which should also be provided in directions to students, as well as the criteria by which answers will be evaluated).

- In his Bank Veto speech (July 10, 1832), President Andrew Jackson said, "It is to be regretted that the rich and powerful too often bend the acts of government to their selfish purposes." Do you think this is still the case in the post-World War II United States? Support your position with evidence from this period.

To answer this question, it seems that students would have to analyze post-World War II U.S. events they have studied—or that they look up, if this were expanded to a research paper—categorize them into those that might be examples of abuse of government by the rich and powerful, and present them in the form of details that support a thesis that Jackson's observation still holds. Alternatively, students might analyze events they have studied, categorize them into those that might be examples of times when the rich and powerful were not able to use government for their own purposes, and present them in the form of details that support a thesis that the post-World War II U.S. government is more egalitarian than in Jackson's day. However, if this very question had been the basis of a class discussion, then to answer the question, all students would have to do is recall what they and their classmates had said. Looking at this question in a textbook test, there is no way to know whether it would require higher order thinking on the part of the students who would actually take the test.

Teachers should avoid short-circuiting assessments that are meant to assess higher order thinking by using in class the same questions or ideas that they know will be on the test. Sometimes this is easier said than done, as students may complain—and rightly so—"we never did that before." Students should be assessed on things they were taught to do, not surprised on a test or performance assessment with tasks for which they have had no practice. The obvious conclusion is that teachers who want their students to be able to demonstrate higher order thinking should teach it. Dealing with novel ideas, solving problems, and thinking critically should not be something students feel they "never did before." By the time students arrive at a summative assessment that requires higher order thinking in the content domain of instruction, they should have had many opportunities to learn and practice, using other novel material.

A third point to keep in mind when designing assessments of higher order thinking is that level of difficulty (easy vs. hard) is *not* the same thing as level of thinking (recall vs. higher order thinking). There can be "easy" and "hard" higher order thinking tasks, just like there can be "easy" and "hard" recall-level tasks. If you doubt that, consider these examples.

	Easier	*More Difficult*
Recall	1 + 1 = ?	What is the value of pi to the first 24 significant digits?
	Who was the first president of the United States?	Name Virginia's 7 delegates to the Constitutional Convention of 1787.
Higher order thinking	Write your own story problem for 3 + 2 .	Write your own story problem for –8 < x < –2 .
	How did George Washington's experience as commander of the Continental Army help him when he became president of the United States?	Explain the major differences between the Articles of Confederation and the Constitution of the United States in regard to the relationship between states and the federal government. In what way(s) were these changes an improvement? Support your thesis with historical evidence.

The misconception that recall is "easy" and higher order thinking is "hard" leads to bad results. The two most insidious ones, in our opinion, happen in basic education: shortchanging young students and shortchanging low achievers of any age, by offering them only recall and drill worksheets, thinking they are not "ready" to do higher order thinking. In either case, while they are waiting to be ready, they will also learn that school is boring—with all that means, including misbehaving and dropping out—and they will not develop good thinking skills.

STRATEGIES FOR DESIGNING TASKS
ASSESSING HIGHER ORDER THINKING

Each section below presents a general strategy, a description of the kind of higher order thinking assessed, and examples. We have annotated each strategy with the component of Leighton's (this volume) working definition of higher order thinking for the purpose of assessment design that is most closely aligned with the strategy. A complex task may contain elements of several of these components, however. Categorizing our strategies according to Leighton's components is intended to illustrate the range of these practical strategies and, conversely, the comprehensiveness of Leighton's components, and is not meant to limit the strategies or claims about the thinking they require of those assessed.

We attempted to vary the examples. Readers are encouraged to do some "transfer" thinking of their own and envision examples of each strategy in their own content areas. It is important to remember, however, that the content domain does make a difference. Some of these strategies will be more appropriate for some content areas than others.

This is not an exhaustive set of strategies. Others could be listed. We selected these sixteen because they tap aspects of reasoning, problem-solving, and judgment that are common in academic learning tasks and in transfer of learning to real-world reasoning, problem solving, and judgment. Table 12.1 summarizes these strategies.

Focus on a Question

Educated people who encounter a text, a speech, a documentary, a policy statement, a situation, or pretty much anything, for that matter, should be able to critically review it to determine its main points, thesis, or argument (Leighton component 1). They also should be able to formulate or select appropriate criteria by which to evaluate this main point, thesis, or argument. To assess how examinees focus on a question, give them a statement of a problem or policy, a political address or cartoon, or an experiment and results. Then ask what the main issue or problem is. You could also ask what criteria they would use to evaluate the quality, goodness, or truth of the argument or conclusions. Here is an example.

**Table 12.1.   Summary of Strategies for
Assessing Higher Order Thinking**

Strategy	Description	Assessment Criteria
Focus on a question	Identify the main idea, question, or point in a text	Soundness of thesis Quality of reasoning Appropriateness of evidence
Analyze arguments	Describe the structure of an argument, identify assumptions, support, and/or irrelevancies (if any)	Soundness of analysis Quality of reasoning Appropriateness of evidence
Evaluate the credibility of a source	Judge the degree of confidence one should have in the information from a particular resource	Soundness of evaluative judgment Quality of reasoning Appropriateness of evidence
Make or evaluate deductive conclusions	Reason from a principle to an instance of the principle, or judge the quality of such reasoning	Appropriateness of instance Quality of reasoning Appropriateness of evidence
Make or evaluate inductive conclusions	Reason from an instance(s) to a generalization, or judge the quality of such reasoning	Appropriateness of generalization Quality of reasoning Appropriateness of evidence
Identify implicit assumptions	Identify premises that must be true in order for an argument to be sound	Accuracy of assumptions noted Quality of reasoning Appropriateness of evidence
Identify rhetorical mechanisms and tactics	Describe the persuasive strategies used in a message, text, or other communication	Accuracy of strategy identification Quality of reasoning Appropriateness of evidence
Identify a problem	Define a problem to be solved	Appropriateness of problem identification Quality of reasoning Appropriateness of evidence
Identify irrelevancies to solving a problem	Identify unnecessary information	Accuracy of identified irrelevancies Quality of reasoning Appropriateness of evidence
Describe and evaluate multiple solution strategies	Describe several different ways to solve the same problem, and prioritize them according to appropriate criteria	Appropriateness of solution strategies Quality of reasoning Appropriateness of evidence

(Table continues on next page.)

Table 12.1.   Continued

Strategy	Description	Assessment Criteria
Evaluate the quality of a solution	Judge the effectiveness or appropriateness of solutions to a problem	Soundness of evaluative judgment Quality of reasoning Appropriateness of evidence
Model a problem	Diagram, draw, or represent a problem visually	Appropriateness of model Quality of reasoning Appropriateness of evidence
Identify obstacles to solving a problem	Describe additional information needed to solve a problem	Appropriateness of identified obstacles Quality of reasoning Appropriateness of evidence
Reason with data	Solve a problem using data in graphs, tables, charts, or other displays	Soundness of conclusion(s) Quality of reasoning Appropriateness of evidence
Use analogies	Apply a lesson or principle from one situation in another, similar situation	Soundness of application of principle to new situation Quality of reasoning Appropriateness of evidence
Solve a problem backward	Work backward from a desired end point	Appropriateness of solution strategies Quality of reasoning Appropriateness of evidence

The United States Environmental Protection Agency put this text on their website. Why do you think they did that: What question is the text excerpt intended to answer, and why is that question important?

The term climate change is often used interchangeably with the term global warming, but according to the National Academy of Sciences, "the phrase 'climate change' is growing in preferred use to 'global warming' because it helps convey that there are [other] changes in addition to rising temperatures."

Climate change refers to any significant change in measures of climate (such as temperature, precipitation, or wind) lasting for an extended period (decades or longer). Climate change may result from:

- natural factors, such as changes in the sun's intensity or slow changes in the Earth's orbit around the sun;
- natural processes within the climate system (e.g. changes in ocean circulation);

- human activities that change the atmosphere's composition (e.g. through burning fossil fuels) and the land surface (e.g., deforestation, reforestation, urbanization, desertification, etc.)

Global warming is an average increase in the temperature of the atmosphere near the Earth's surface and in the troposphere, which can contribute to changes in global climate patterns. Global warming can occur from a variety of causes, both natural and human induced. In common usage, "global warming" often refers to the warming that can occur as a result of increased emissions of greenhouse gases from human activities. (United States Environmental Protection Agency. Retrieved from http://www.epa.gov/climatechange/basicinfo.html)

Analyze Arguments

Once an argument is identified, it can be analyzed. Identifying underlying assumptions (stated or unstated), representing the logic or structure of the argument, finding irrelevancies if there are any, judging the similarities or differences in two or more arguments, are all analysis skills (Leighton component 2). Identifying what is relevant and irrelevant to particular arguments or concepts is an important reasoning skill, sometimes called the logic of class inclusion. Reasoning about what points support what arguments, what details are related to what concepts, and so on, is important to a number of the strategies discussed in this chapter.

To assess how students analyze arguments, give students an argument, a text or a speech, for example. Then ask students one or more of the following questions.

- What conclusions are logically appropriate?
- What evidence is presented that genuinely supports the argument(s)?
- What evidence is presented that genuinely contradicts the argument(s)?
- What are the unstated assumptions that need to hold for the argument(s) to be valid?
- What part(s) of the statement is irrelevant to the argument(s)?
- Outline the logical structure of the argument(s).
- Summarize the main parts of the argument(s).

We once observed in a freshman composition class, where the students were struggling with an assignment to analyze the structure of Jefferson's argument for democracy in the Declaration of Independence. Some of the students were having trouble with the concept that the Declaration of Independence *was* an argument, much less something they could analyze. They had all been taught that this document was an important event in history, and some had even memorized parts of it. Years of "recall-level" interaction with the Declaration had left some of them so stuck in lower-order thinking about it that they had trouble approaching the assignment.

As an aside, this is also a good time to reiterate our earlier caution that higher order thinking only happens if the student does the analysis himself or herself. In looking for a copy of the text of the Declaration, we found that there is an analysis of the structure of its argument in Wikipedia. Beware: A less than comprehensive, but original, analysis by a student is still an example of analysis; an elegant rendition of someone else's argument is merely evidence of comprehension.

Practice analyzing arguments should start way before freshman English class. Consider the following example. Item 9 is from the National Assessment of Educational Progress (NAEP), and it asks students for the main idea (focus on a question skill, above). We added item 10 to ask for an explanation of how students reached their conclusion for item 9, which amounts to a simple argument analysis, in this case explaining Lincoln's argument by analogy.

> A house divided against itself cannot stand. I believe this government cannot endure permanently half slave and half free. I do not expect the Union to be dissolved—I do not expect the house to fall—but I do expect it will cease to be divide.
>
> —Abraham Lincoln, 1858

9. What did Abraham Lincoln mean in this speech?

    (a) The South should be allowed to separate from the United States.

    (b) The government should support slavery in the South.

    *(c) Sometime in the future slavery would disappear from the United States.

    (d) Americans would not be willing to fight a war over slavery.

10. Explain how you decided what Abraham Lincoln meant in this speech. (National Assessment of Educational Progress, History Grade: 4   Block: 2006-4H7   No.: 9. Retrieved from http://nces.ed.gov/nationsreportcard/itmrls/)

Evaluate the Credibility of a Source

This critical thinking skill has received a lot of attention since students began using the Internet extensively. The explosion of available information means people need to be able to judge the credibility of an ever-widening array of sources (Leighton component 2). To assess judging the credibility of a source, present material to think about (texts of arguments, advertisements, and so on). Then ask which parts, if any, of the material are credible, which parts are not, and why.

A computer teacher we work with recently did a lesson on evaluating the credibility of electronic resources in a ninth grade class. In groups of three or four, students were given three websites and asked to discuss whether they believed these websites would be good sources of information for school projects. After the discussion, each group was asked to create a list of five questions they could use to evaluate any website, apply them to one of the websites they had discussed, and write a paragraph explaining why they would or would not choose that website for use in a school project.

Prior to the discussion, the teacher had reviewed with students how to ask good questions. The teacher also modeled asking evaluative questions about websites as he circulated among the groups doing their work. The level of scaffolding could be adjusted, increased for more novice classes and decreased for classes of more expert website credibility judgers. One successful group came up with these five questions: When was the website last updated? Who is the author? How do the pictures relate to the topic? When is the copyright date? Who sponsors the website? Based on their answers to these questions, they decided not to recommend the website they wrote about.

Make or Evaluate Deductive Conclusion

In logic, deduction is reasoning from a general principle or truth to particular conclusions (Leighton component 3). The character Sherlock Holmes is famous for his powers of deduction. For example, in "The Adventure of the Speckled Band," Holmes reasoned that if the murder weapon was poisonous snake venom from India, the murderer must be someone who had a connection with India. To assess how people make or evaluate deductive conclusions, give a statement that they are to assume is true and one or more logically correct and/or incorrect conclusions. Then ask which conclusions follow. Or, ask directly for a deduction from a theory or principle.

We generally think of empirical science as an inductive process, but along the way deduction has an important place in experimental design. The theory to be tested is the principle from which research hypotheses are generated. So, for example, a doctoral student designing dissertation research might theorize that, according to the principles of social cognitive theory, a certain type of instructional intervention might be more effective than a comparison intervention. The hypothesis that the experimental group's mean performance gains will be greater than the comparison group's mean performance gains is a deduction from the theory.

Here is an example of an assessment task requiring knowledge of economic principles and demonstration of deductive reasoning (Nitko & Brookhart, 2011, p. 230).

> Supposing the federal government increased the prime lending rate by one-half percent tomorrow. What would you expect to happen? Explain your reasoning.

As written, this question requires both deductive reasoning and extended content knowledge, both about economic principles and the current-day economic context. The question could be amended by stating the principles as introductory material, by allowing reference to a textbook or other source material, and/or by creating a fictional economic context to simplify the deductive reasoning required.

Make or Evaluate Inductive Conclusions

In logic, induction is drawing an empirical generalization from particular instances of it (Leighton component 3). This thinking skill is an important basis of empirical science, but induction is also a powerful logic for many other disciplines. To assess how people make or evaluated inductive conclusions, present a situation statement and information (data). Then ask examinees to draw the proper conclusion from the data and explain why the conclusion is correct. For multiple choice items, have them select from among alternative conclusions.

A ninth grade science teacher we work with used this strategy to evaluate students' understanding of chemical and physical changes. Students had observed demonstrations about ice floating in water, then melting, and had drawn diagrams of the molecular structure. Then, pairs of students were given cards with everyday events. They were to sort them into two categories, physical change and chemical change, and explain why they put them where they did. Then, they were to write what they learned about physical and chemical changes. We'll come back to this example in the scoring section below, and describe how the teacher evaluated these. In passing, we should mention that this exercise sparked some interesting student higher order thinking beyond simple categorizing and inductive thinking. For example, one student asked, "Is cutting the grass a chemical or physical change if you consider that the cut part of the grass dies?"

Identify Implicit Assumptions

Identifying what is assumed (Leighton component 1) is an important skill in itself, and examining assumptions also helps students judge the soundness of arguments. To use a multiple-choice item to assess how people identify implicit assumptions, give students an argument or explanation with some of its bases not included and choices: one option that is the correct implicit assumption and two or more options that are not the implicit assumption *and* that are not conclusions. Ask which option is probably assumed or taken for granted. To use a constructed response item, present the material and ask those assessed to identify implicit assumptions directly and explain their reasoning.

Consider these examples, two versions of a question about assumptions from a speech by Marcellus in Act I, Scene I of William Shakespeare's *Hamlet*.

In Act I, Scene I of *Hamlet*, Marcellus speaks the following lines to Francisco, Bernardo, and Horatio:

Horatio says 'tis but our fantasy,
And will not let belief take hold of him
Touching this dreaded sight, twice seen of us:
Therefore I have entreated him along
With us to watch the minutes of this night;
That if again this apparition come,
He may approve our eyes and speak to it.

(Multiple choice question) What must we assume in order for this speech to make sense?

   (a) Horatio has seen a ghost.

  *(b) Both Marcellus and Horatio have seen a ghost.

   (c) Horatio is hoping to see a ghost.

   (d) Both Marcellus and Horatio are hoping to see a ghost.

(Constructed response question) What must we assume in order for this speech to make sense? Explain your reasoning and support it with evidence from the lines.

The multiple choice version of the question requires higher order thinking for the simple identification of the assumption. Shakespeare counts on some in the play's audience to be able to do this; this is the first reference in the play to the ghost of Hamlet's father, the late King of Denmark. For playgoers who cannot do this, the references get successively clearer until the ghost himself appears on the stage. At that point, those who understood at first have as their reward a confirmation that they figured it out, and presumably all the more enjoyment of the scene.

The constructed response version of the question requires both identifying assumptions and explanation of reasoning. A successful answer will explain the reader's analysis and give appropriate evidence from the lines. Presumably a person who successfully answered the multiple choice version would have also done this analysis, but this is an inference. Success with the multiple choice item is also subject to guessing, while the constructed response format eliminates the possibility of guessing.

Identifying assumptions is a useful skill in many disciplines. In Social Studies, students can identify assumptions behind newspaper articles covering local or national events, political speeches and commentary, and the like. In English, students can identify assumptions characters in novels or short stories make about the world or their situation, motivating their actions.

Identify Rhetorical Mechanisms and Tactics

Identifying rhetorical tactics is not only important for literary analysis, but also for interpreting communications of all sorts, from news media, advertisers, political campaigns, and historical accounts (Leighton component 2). One of the authors remembers a high school Social Studies unit titled "Developing a Crap Detector." Advertisements—memorably, the Marlboro Man—were the vehicle, and we were encouraged to ask what the advertisers meant to communicate and what their motives might have been. The goal, of course, was to make our class of teenagers a little less gullible and susceptible to glossy ads suggesting that we would be cool, sexy, or popular if we only bought some product or other.

To assess how people identify rhetorical mechanisms, give them persuasive writing, a political campaign speech, or an advertisement in any medium (print or video, for example). Then ask what statements or strategies are used to persuade, what their expected effects would be, and which if any of the statements or strategies are deceptive or misleading. In multiple choice exercises, examinees select answers, and in constructed response exercises, they can explain their reasoning.

Here is an example from recent current events, which might be used in a high school or college civics class but also underscores the relevance of higher order thinking skills for everyday life.

> On September 9, 2009, President Obama addressed a Joint Session of Congress on the topic of health care reform. Here is the first part of the text of his speech:
>
>> Madam Speaker, Vice President Biden, members of Congress, and the American people:
>> When I spoke here last winter, this nation was facing the worst economic crisis since the Great Depression. We were losing an average of 700,000 jobs per month. Credit was frozen. And our financial system was on the verge of collapse.
>> As any American who is still looking for work or a way to pay their bills will tell you, we are by no means out of the woods. A full and vibrant recovery is still many months away. And I will not let up until those Americans who seek jobs can find them, until those businesses that seek capital and credit can thrive; until all responsible homeowners can stay in their homes. That is our ultimate goal. But thanks to the bold and decisive action we've taken since January, I can stand here with confidence and say that we have pulled this economy back from the brink.
>
> In this introduction, how does President Obama appeal to his listeners, both those in Congress and those who were watching the speech on television? Why do you think he chose to begin a speech on health care reform with this kind of appeal: What might have been his rhetorical purpose in doing so? Support your ideas with evidence from the speech and from the historical context.

Identify a Problem to be Solved

Identifying or defining a problem is the first step toward solving it (Leighton component 1). To assess how people identify a problem to be solved, present a scenario or problem description. Ask them to identify the problem to be solved. Or, present a statement that contains the problem and ask respondents to pose the question(s), using the language and concepts of the discipline, that need(s) to be answered to solve the problem. Of course to say "problem" makes many people think of mathematics, but there are other kinds of problems, too. We'll give a mathematics example and an economics example.

An eighth grade mathematics teacher we work with was familiarizing his students with the kind of open-ended math problems that might appear on the Pennsylvania System of School Assessment (PSSA) test. Open-ended PSSA items include phrases like, "Show all your work" and "Explain why you did each step." In order to do that, students need first to be able to identify the problem. Here is one part of one of the sample problems he used.

> The Gomez family is taking a trip from Kittanning [PA] to Atlanta, Georgia. The trip is 744 miles. They are leaving at 6 a.m. and would like to arrive at 6 p.m. How fast would they have to drive in order to arrive on time? Show and explain your work.

The teacher gave students feedback on both the correctness of their answers and the quality of their explanations. While it may seem automatic to the adults reading this chapter, identifying the problem in part 1 as a distance problem that requires division is an important skill. We will return to this problem and discuss scoring student answers in the section below on scoring.

Students should be able to identify problems in all disciplines, not just mathematics. Here is an example of an economics assessment that requires first identifying the problem.

> After a festival, food vendors leave behind a great deal of garbage. Other than telling the vendors to clean up the garbage, what is one policy the city can adopt to reduce the amount of garbage left by food vendors at future festivals? How will this policy affect both the supply of foods offered during future festivals and the price of these foods? (National Assessment of Educational Progress, Economics Grade: 12 Block: 2006-12E4 No.: Retrieved from http://nces.ed.gov/ nationsreportcard/itmrls/)

Before students can identify a policy, they need to define the problem as asking for a description of an economic incentives or sanctions (rewards or punishments) that a city is legally able to enact, that will have the desired effect of reducing garbage. Then any of the potential solutions (fines, taxes, registration limits, security deposits, and so on) are defined in, and other inappropriate solutions (using force, for example) are defined out. Once a solution has been named, answering the second part of the question becomes a matter of deduction.

Identify Irrelevancies

Real-life problems often present themselves as a context or situation within which people have to figure out what information is important or relevant and what is not in order to identify and solve a problem (Leighton components 1 through 4). To assess how they identify what is and is not relevant to a particular problem, present interpretive materials and a problem statement and ask respondents to identify all the irrelevant information.

Identifying irrelevancies can be simple and fairly concrete. For example, elementary mathematics students are taught to identify relevant and irrelevant information in word problems. Consider this problem.

> Mr. Smith bought 12 cookies. He gave Ryan two cookies and Sarah four cookies. How many more cookies did Sarah have than Ryan?

Elementary word-problem solvers need to figure out that the fact that there were a dozen cookies in all is irrelevant to solving the problem, which involves subtracting two from four. This skill is important to solving classroom based academic problems. To see if students can identify the irrelevancy, you could simply ask them to solve the problem. You could also explicitly ask what information they would use and what information they would not use.

In the larger critical thinking context, the broader skill of identifying irrelevancies during library and information searching is a very difficult thing. Students and other researchers need not just a topic but a research question, and they need to stay with it long enough to verify findings and draw concepts from the findings (Kuhlthau, 2005), instead of being distracted by interesting irrelevant information they run across along the way – or worse, not realizing the information is irrelevant. We have all read those term papers that are "dumps" of everything found in the library, without any sense of what is relevant and what is not.

McClymer and Knoles (1992) have identified at least two (they do not claim their categories are exhaustive) ways in which college students cope with assignments rather than learn from them, or to use their term, exhibit ersatz learning: *clumps* and *shapes*. "By *clumps*, we mean those acritical responses to assignments that entail the amassing of elements found in critical analyses minus their underlying logic" (p. 38). Students can clump data, reproducing lots of information with little or no thinking; they can clump jargon, using technical language without really understanding it; and they can clump assertions, for example by making thesis statements surrounded by lots of "stuff" that doesn't really support the thesis. "By *shapes*, we mean simulations of the logical forms of critical analysis without the substance" (p. 39). Some common "shapes" students employ to mimic critical thinking without actually doing it include borrowing the analysis of another author, analyzing only surface meanings, and analyzing a single thread or issue as if it represented the topic.

For both of these, especially for the clumps, the critical thinking skills listed here as "focus on a question" and "identify irrelevancies" are lacking. Students who cannot do these things are often overwhelmed by college assignments. A college information technology specialist who works in the library at one of our universities, in fact, says that secondary teachers often ask him what they should teach their students about new information technologies. They usually are thinking about things like how to use electronic card catalogs, how to find journal articles online, and the like. He always counters that what secondary teachers should do is teach their students how to ask questions, and how to judge what information is relevant to answering the question and what is not. If you can just teach them that, he says, they would be fine. He can show them how to use the computer, and programs change all the time anyway. But when a student goes to the library with the agenda "to look up" something (e.g., "to look up the French Revolution"), without knowing what information will be relevant to their assignment and what will not, they are doomed.

We agree with our information technology friend, Bob, that identifying what information is relevant, and what is irrelevant, to a particular assignment, question, or theme is perhaps the most important critical skill that students can develop in their basic education. By the way, can you identify an irrelevant fact in the previous sentence? (Sorry, we could not help ourselves.)

To assess whether students can identify irrelevancies to a larger "problem" like what information should go into a paper or thesis, we recommend an assignment that proceeds in stages. First, ask students to pick topics and read enough in the topic that they can write a single sentence, either a research question or a thesis statement. Use self-, peer-, and/or teacher assessment to evaluate the usefulness of these questions or theses. Is the question important enough in the discipline to warrant basing a whole project on it? Will the student be likely to locate enough relevant information? Then, ask students to proceed with research and prepare a brief essay, or an outline, organizing their work to date, and assess that. Is the information listed relevant to the question or thesis, and can the student explain how? Finally, after these opportunities for formative and corrective feedback, students can proceed to finish the project. Scoring of the final project should include an appraisal of the relevance and coherence of the information students have put together to answer their research question or support their thesis.

Describe and Evaluate Multiple Strategies That Could Be Used to Solve a Problem

Thinking through several different ways to solve a problem, evaluating and choosing the best (according to some criterion appropriate to the problem, for example the most efficient, most effective, least expensive, and so on), and then solving the problem, is a real-world skill as well as an important higher order thinking skill (Leighton components 3 and 4). To assess how people describe multiple problem-solving strategies, state a problem and ask them to (a) solve the problem in two or more ways and (b) show their solutions using pictures, diagrams, or graphs. Or, state a problem and two or more strategies for solving it, and ask respondents to explain why both strategies are correct. Be certain both strategies yield the correct solution. In writing an item you might, for example, state that these were different ways that two fictional people solved the problem.

Here is an example asking for two solutions and an evaluation of which one was better. This example would require generating and using one's own criteria for a "better" solution. For example, one person might prefer a longer solution with easier steps, while another might prefer a shorter solution. You would evaluate the response about preference according to the criteria the examinee described, not your own preferences.

> The box office manager of a theater printed a set of tickets to sell for a concert. If one-tenth of the tickets were for box seats, one-fourth of the tickets were for orchestra seats, one-half of the tickets were for seats in the main part of the auditorium, and the remaining 45 tickets were for seats in the balcony, how many tickets were for seats in the main part of the auditorium?
>
> (a) Solve this problem in two different ways. Show your work.
>
> (b) Which solution do you prefer, and why?

The example about vendors leaving garbage, presented in the section above on identifying problems, is a problem open to multiple solution strategies. Any one of the following solutions is acceptable, in addition to specifying that the food supply will decrease and food prices will increase if such measures are taken. Examinees could specify the city should fine offending vendors, limit number of vendors, tax the vendors' profits, require a registration or cleanup fee, require a security deposit, require a refundable fee or deposit, or rule that vendors leaving garbage will not be allowed to return to the festival the next year. A question like this one could easily be revised to require stating and evaluating more than one solution, comparing them on criteria (either specified or left to the student), evaluating and justifying which one would likely be the best.

Multiple-solution problems can be genuine problems, that is, problems where there really are multiple good solutions (and some not so good ones) and where the exact value of any given outcome is not known. Such problems offer excellent ways to demonstrate real-world problem-solving and decision-making skills. For example,

> Ms. Guarneri's eighth-grade class has two computers for students to use and one at the teacher's desk. The class would like to start a project using FaceBook or Twitter to talk with other classes around the country about school issues. They need to address both practical issues about computer use and policy issues like what kinds of questions they should ask the other classes. For example, would FaceBook or Twitter be better for this purpose? Should each student get an account on the chosen platform, or should they get one account for the class? What kinds of questions are appropriate to ask eighth grade classes in other schools? Make two different plans for solving this problem, decide which one you think is best, and explain why.

An exercise requiring all four of Leighton's components of higher order thinking and prominently featuring identification of a problem to be solved, evaluating multiple solutions, and identifying irrelevancies came to our attention just recently, while listening to a National Public Radio interview of Tracy Gary, coauthor of the book *Inspired Philanthropy*. One of her points was that many people's charitable giving is reactive, responding to requests for donations as they come, without much plan or purpose. She recommended writing a personal mission statement describing what you hope to accomplish with your philanthropic work. Then use your mission statement (a) to filter requests for donations (identifying irrelevancies—declining those requests that do not fit your purpose and responding to those that do) and (b) to seek out programs, institutions, and other philanthropic venues that will further your personal mission (proposing multiple solutions, evaluating their fit, and allocating resources accordingly). A project of this sort could be adapted as a real-world, complex performance assessment for individual or group work.

Evaluate the Quality of a Solution

As the examples in the previous section has illustrated, any problem for which multiple solutions have been proposed lends itself to evaluating the quality of those solutions (Leighton components 3 and 4). To assess how people evaluate the quality of a solution, state a problem and ask examinees to evaluate several different strategies for solving the problem. Ask them to produce several different solutions, or provide several solutions and ask them to evaluate those provided. If you provide solutions to evaluate, be certain to vary their correctness and quality, so that examinees can display their ability to evaluate. For example, some may be more efficient, some may have negative consequences, and some may not work at all. Ask examinees to determine the best strategy, explain why some strategies work better than others, and why some do not work at all. Assess the students' ability to justify the hierarchical ordering of the strategies' quality.

Model a Problem

We like the anecdote below because it so clearly illustrates how important it is to be able to "wrap one's head around" the nature of a problem in order to solve it with thinking, not with plugging numbers into a formula by rote (Leighton component 1).

> A colleague of ours teaches an introductory calculus section. Early one term, he and his class were working through some standard motion problems: "A boy drops a water balloon from a window. If it takes 0.8 seconds to strike his erstwhile friend, who is 5 feet tall, how high is the window?" On the exam, the problem took this form: "Someone walking along the edge of a pit accidentally kicks into it a small stone, which falls to the bottom in 2.3 seconds. How deep is the pit?" One student was visibly upset. The question was not fair, she protested. The instructor had promised that there would not be any material on the exam that they had not gone over in class. "But we did a dozen of those problems in class," our colleague said. "Oh no," shot back the student, "we never did a single pit problem." (McClymer & Knoles, 1992, p. 33)

This freshman had been able to match class problems to formulas without ever understanding the underlying model, in this case about the relationships among distance, time, velocity and acceleration. As McClymer and Knoles (1992) put it, "This student had studied, but she had not learned—at least, not mathematics." Her instructor had encouraged his students to draw the problems each time, which she had not done. Had she been able to do that, she might have recognized the "pit problem" as just another motion problem.

To assess how people model a problem, state a problem and ask them to draw a diagram or picture showing the problem situation. Assess how they represent the problem rather than whether the problem is correctly solved. Drawings of time problems in mathematics, for example, should depict time lines, not scales. Drawings of motion problems should depict motion.

Identify Obstacles or Additional Information for Solving a Problem or Scenario

Solving problems well is sometimes as much about figuring out the right information to use as it is inventing a solution (Leighton components 1 through 4). This is another example of the usefulness of the logic of class inclusion and of the relationships among factual, conceptual, procedural, and metacognitive knowledge. What is relevant, and what is irrelevant?

To assess how people identify obstacles and/or additional information needed for solving a problem, present a difficult problem to solve, perhaps one missing a key piece of information, and ask examinees to explain (a) why it is difficult to complete the task, (b) what the obstacle(s) are, and/or (c) what additional information they need to overcome the obstacle(s). Assess whether they can identify the obstacle to solving the problem. Here is a civics example.

Teresia is a small country that has been invaded by its neighbor Corollia. The king of Teresia is a long-standing United States ally who has been living in exile since the Corollian invasion. Teresia is an important exporter of uranium; it sends most of its supply to members of the European Union. The king appeals to the United States and the United Nations for military help in driving Corollia from his country.

12.   What official argument would members of the United Nations be most likely to make for supporting military efforts against Corollia?

   (a) The stability of the international system depends on countries maintaining their current forms of government.

   (b) The United Nations and the European Union should control the mining of uranium worldwide.

   *(c) The stability of the international system depends on absolute respect for national borders and sovereignty.

   (d) Countries such as the United States should become the main judges in all international disputes.

13.   Identify two pieces of information NOT given above that you would need before you could decide whether or not the United States military should help Teresia. Explain why each piece of information would be important. (National Assessment of Educa-

tional Progress, Civics Grade: 8 Block: 2006-8C4 Nos.: 12-13. Retrieved from http://nces.ed.gov/nationsreportcard/itmrls/)

Identifying the argument in question 12 involves understanding the mission of the United Nations and applying that understanding to the scenario. Question 13 requires additional content knowledge in civics, for example about the U.S. military and its relationship with government and society, plus reasoning skills at identifying what additional information is needed to put all that together in an argument for military intervention.

Reason With Data

To assess how people reason with data (Leighton components 2 and 3), present interpretive material (story, cartoon, graph, data table) and a statement of a problem that requires using information from the interpretive material. Then ask respondents to (a) solve the problem and (b) explain the procedure they used to reach a solution. Here is an example that requires reasoning from data and also identifying assumptions (Nitko & Brookhart, 2007, p. 231).

FACTS: According to the Federal Election Commission, the percentage of the voting population who voted in the presidential election years 1932–1988 were:

Year	%	Year	%	Year	%	Year	%
1932	52.4	1948	51.1	1964	61.9	1980	54.0
1936	56.0	1952	61.6	1968	60.9	1984	53.1
1940	58.9	1956	59.3	1972	55.2	1988	50.1
1944	56.0	1960	62.8	1976	53.5		

CONCLUSION: The number of persons voting in national elections in presidential election years 1932–1988 was at its lowest in 1988.

1. For this conclusion to be true, it must be assumed that

*(a) the number of voting-age persons in 1988 was the same as or less than each of the other presidential election years in 1932–1988.

(b) the number of voting-age persons increased from 1932 to 1988.

(c) the percentage of voting-age persons who voted in each of the other presidential election years was less than 50.1%.

2. Explain the reasoning that led you to your answer in question 1.

Use Analogies

Reasoning by analogy is classic, and is sometimes considered a type of inductive reasoning (Leighton component 3). Analogical reasoning allows a person to apply a lesson learned in one situation to another situation that is like it. The trick is that the similarities between the two situations have to be on attributes that are relevant to the problem and its solution. This judgment itself requires higher order thinking, again an example of identifying and analyzing relevant and irrelevant characteristics.

To assess use of analogies, present a problem statement and a correct solution strategy, and ask examinees to (a) describe other problems that could (by analogy) be solved by using this same solution strategy and (b) explain why the solution to the problem they generated is like the solution to the problem you gave them. Assess the analogical relationship of the students' solution strategy to the solution strategy you gave them. Here is an example (Nitko & Brookhart, 2007, p. 220).

Questions 1 and 2 Refer to the Situation Below

Members of a certain congressional committee talked a lot during committee hearings. Some members talked to explain their own views, some treated a witness as hostile and tried to discredit that witness's testimony, some wanted to prevent their opponents on the committee from speaking, and some wanted to prolong the debate and the hearing to postpone or prolong a committee vote. To solve this problem rules were established to give each committee member a fixed amount of time to speak and to ask questions of a witness. Under these rules, a committee member is allowed to give another member all or part of his allotted time.

1. Describe several other problems in different situations that could be solved by using a set of rules similar to those that the congressional committee used.

2. For each of the problems you listed, explain how the rules might be modified and why this would solve the problem you listed.

When you give feedback, discuss responses with students, and/or score the results, be sure to include as criteria both the quality of students' reasoning from one situation to the other (how similar are the situations, in what ways, and are those similarities relevant to this problem) and the quality of the application of the solution from one situation to the other.

Solve a Problem Backward

Solving a problem backward can be a good learning strategy, especially in mathematics or science. That is one of the common uses for answers to exercises that appear at the back of mathematics textbooks. Students who have trouble working the problems as presented can work backward from the answer and see how to solve the problem. Often, they will then be able to tackle similar problems without first looking up the answer.

More generally, reasoning from a desired end point to work out the means by which to arrive at that end point is an important life skill (Leighton component 3). To assess how people solve a problem backward, presents a complex problem situation or a complex, multi-step task to complete, and ask them to work backwards from the desired outcome to develop a plan or a strategy for completing the task or solving the problem. For example, ask to develop the steps and time frame needed to complete a library research paper, or carry out a home improvement project, or advertise a local little theater production successfully. Assess the quality of the backward solution strategies.

STRATEGIES FOR GIVING FEEDBACK OR SCORING TASKS ASSESSING HIGHER ORDER THINKING

General examples of criteria are listed with each strategy in Table 12.1. You can adapt them as appropriate to a particular assessment. However, be sure to include criteria about the quality of thinking, as illustrated in Table 12.1. Scoring schemes that do not evaluate thinking (e.g., "one point each, up to four, for listing each of the following causes of the Civil War") do not measure thinking. Similarly, feedback that does not comment on the quality of thinking is not likely to help a person advance his or her thinking.

Assessors can give feedback on responses to items or tasks, score the responses, or both. In general, feedback is appropriate for formative assessment purposes and scoring for summative (Hattie & Timperley, 2007), although in practice these lines sometimes blur. Base both feedback and scoring criteria about the quality of thinking exhibited in the work. An activity without criteria is just an activity, not an assessment.

Observing and discussing reasoning directly can be a powerful way to assess higher order thinking. Conversations with students about their reasoning or substantive feedback interpreting the quality of thinking and suggesting ways to extend or deepen that thinking are excellent methods for formative assessment (Brookhart, 2008). This is what the eighth grade math teacher did for the Gomez family trip problem. His purpose for using this problem was to help students appraise the quality of their explanations of math problem solving, a formative purpose. These skills would help the students on the PSSA, a summative evaluation. Table 12.2 reproduces two student responses for just the portion of the Gomez family trip problem we have used as an example.

For student #1, the teacher wrote, "This is correct, but explain why you divided—what are you looking to find? Your explanations are improving—continue to include every piece of data in the explanation." The teacher noticed and named one strategy (including data in the explanation) that the student had been working on and did successfully, and gave one suggestion for improvement (provide a rationale for using division).

Table 12.2.   Examples of Student Work and Explanation of the Mr. Gomez Math Problem

Response #1

Work:

$$\underset{\text{hours}}{12}\,\overline{\smash{\big)}\,\underset{\text{miles}}{744}} \quad \underset{}{62}\ \text{mph}$$

12 hours   62 mph

Explanation: I counted how many hours they drove which is 12 then divided 12 into 744 to get my answer of 62 mph.

Response #2

Work: d = r t $\dfrac{744}{12} = r\,\dfrac{12}{12}$ 62 = r

		mph	hours
744	=	62 •	12
d		r	t
i		a	i
s		t	m
t		e	e
a			
n			
c			
e			

Explanation: In order to get the rate, I took the amount of hours and canceled it out by dividing 12 by 12 and 744 by 12 and got the rate which is 62.

Both of these would help the student make his reasoning more transparent to a reader, and would also help with the state test expectations for explaining reasoning.

For student #2, the teacher wrote next to $d = rt$, "Good use of the formula!" Next to the explanation, he wrote, "62 ? Please refer to the question to display the units! Good explanation!" The teacher noticed and named one specific (use of the formula) and made one general comment (good explanation) and one specific suggestion for improvement (specify the units).

For summative assessment of how students or other examinees use higher order thinking—for example, for graded tests and projects—a scoring scheme must be devised in such a way that higher order thinking is required to score well. Rubrics or other scoring schemes that attend mainly to surface features or count facts can turn an exercise in which students did use higher order thinking into a score that doesn't reflect the thinking students did.

The multiple choice exercises in our examples would typically be scored with one point for a correct choice and no points for an incorrect choice. The "thinking" is encoded into the choosing. It is worth reminding readers here that for the resulting scores to mean that students use higher order thinking, the questions have to be designed so that higher order thinking really is required to answer, and not just recall.

For short constructed response answers of questions designed to tap various kinds of reasoning, often a rubric with a short scale will work well. Start with the criterion, the type of thinking you intended to assess. For example, ask "Does the student reason deductively?" or "Does the student evaluate the credibility of the source?" Then use a scale that gives partial credit depending on the quality of the reasoning. Here is an example of a scoring scheme that could be used with the ninth grade science class example of physical and chemical changes. We list the scale as 2, 1, 0, but it could also be 3, 2, 1, or 6, 4, 2, or whatever weight is appropriate for other scores with which it needs to be combined for a particular test or grade composite score.

Did the student reason inductively from the examples to arrive at a clear, accurate description of physical and chemical changes?

2 = Completely and clearly – response gives clear evidence of reasoning from the examples

1 = Partially – response is accurate, but reasoning from examples isn't clear or is only partial

0 = No – response does not demonstrate reasonable conclusions from the examples

Recall that this assignment was done in pairs. Table 12.3 presents responses from three student pairs. Each pair was to list one example of physical and chemical change, and then a paragraph explaining what the pair had learned about physical and chemical changes from their inductive reasoning. Response #1 would score a 0. The teacher did not think that this student showed any evidence of having figured out differences between physical and chemical changes based on sorting the examples. Response #2 would score a 1. These students' statement about molecular structure is correct, but as the teacher commented, "Textbook response, got the concept but I'm not sure if it was from discussion." The response does not allow us to conclude much about their reasoning. Response #3 would score a 2. In fact, the teacher was very pleased: "Not an answer I would expect but they really got the concept."

For more elaborated scoring, for example for longer constructed response questions, use brief analytical rubrics with a scale for each criterion. Here is an example of a general rubric that might be used with the example of identifying the assumption behind Marcellus's speech in Act I of *Hamlet*. The criteria are that the thesis (statement of what the assumption is) is clear, that the evidence brought to bear does support the thesis, and that the reasoning process is clear and is clearly explained. This could also be a task-specific rubric (stating what the thesis should be, what the evidence is, and so on). General rubrics are more useful for instruction, and do not have to be rewritten for each task or question.

	5	3	1
Thesis	Thesis is clear, complete, and accurately reflects the main point.	Thesis is clear and at least partially reflects the main point.	Thesis is not clear and/or does not reflects the main point.
Evidence	Evidence is accurate, relevant, and complete.	Evidence is mostly clear, relevant, and complete.	Evidence is not clear, relevant, or complete.
Logic and clarity	The way in which the evidence supports the thesis is clear, logical, and well explained.	The way in which the evidence supports the thesis is mostly clear and logical. Some explanation is given.	The way in which the evidence supports the thesis is not clear, illogical, and/or not explained.

The scoring 5, 3, 1 allows for the assignment of 4 or 2 for intermediate levels of quality, and comports with the recommendation (Leighton, this

**Table 12.3.   Examples of Student Explanation of Physical and
Chemical Changes Based on Induction**

Response #1

Physical: Ripping paper   Chemical: Burning paper

I've learned that during physical changes and chemical changes there can be alot of argue-
ments and disputes. Also physical changes can be very difficult to recognize. Chemical
changes are basically just common sense.

Response #2

Physical: Cutting a banana   Chemical: Baking soda & vinegar

Chemical changes occur when there is a change in the molecular structure of an object.
Physical however the shape or form changes while molecular structure stays the same.

Response #3

Physical: Cleaning your locker   Chemical: Melting plastic

I learned that you can not base the type of change on the object. Just because it may look
like a physical doesn't mean it is. You have to figure out that if you can get it back the way
it was, if not then its chemical.

volume) to use 4 to 7 points for scales that allow for optimal distinction of
levels of quality. The scoring could also be 3, 2, 1 or 2, 1, 0, or something
else, as appropriate for the intended use for the scores (for example, to fit
within a class or school grading policy). Alternatively, the levels could be
labeled instead of numbered, for example, "Proficient," "Nearly proficient," and "Not proficient."

The state of Kentucky uses an open-ended scoring guide for mathematics, social studies, science, arts and humanities that can be defined in
more specific detail for specific assessment items or tasks. The advantage
of using such a general framework as the basis for scoring all kinds of
work is that students will come to see the types of thinking expected in the
general rubric as learning goals. They will be able to practice and work
consistently toward these achievement outcomes. Table 12.4 shows the
general scoring guide for the middle and high school levels. A very similar version of this rubric is used for the upper elementary level.

For bigger performance assessments, papers, and projects, analytical
rubrics are usually used. At least one of the rubric scales should be about
the quality of thinking demonstrated in the work. Teachers and other
assessors can write their own rubrics or select a rubric for use from among
the many that are available on the Internet or in curriculum materials. An
Internet search for "problem-solving rubrics," for example, yielded

Table 4.4. Kentucky General Scoring Guide

Score Point 4	• You complete all important components of the question and communicate ideas clearly. • You demonstrate in-depth understanding of the relevant concepts and/or processes. • Where appropriate, you choose more efficient and/or sophisticated processes. • Where appropriate, you offer insightful interpretations or extensions (generalizations, applications, analogies).
Score Point 3	• You complete most important components of the question and communicate clearly. • You demonstrate an understanding of major concepts even though you overlook or misunderstand some less-important ideas or details.
Score Point 2	• You complete some important components of the question and communicate those components clearly. • You demonstrate that there are gaps in your conceptual understanding.
Score Point 1	• You show minimal understanding of the question • You address only a small portion of the question.
Score Point 0	• Your answer is totally incorrect or irrelevant.
Blank	• You did not give any answer at all.

Source: Kentucky Department of Education. (2007). Grade 8 Kentucky Core Content Test Spring 2007 Released Items Mathematics, p. 2. Used with permission of the Kentucky Department of Education, Frankfort, Kentucky 40601.

85,500 results. Select or write rubrics that are appropriate to the content and thinking skills you intend to assess and that are appropriate for the educational development of your students. Select or write rubrics that describe qualities (e.g., "reasoning is logical and thoughtful") rather than count facts (e.g., "includes at least 3 reasons").

ASSESSMENT FORMAT

Validation research is needed to support inferences and expectations about the type of thinking elicited by any assessment format. A validity argument for the claim that a particular assessment measures higher order thinking might be supported with direct (e.g., think-aloud studies) and/or indirect (e.g., expert reviewers) evidence. The comments about assessment format in this section are not meant to substitute for validation research, but simply to present some issues with which to begin validity arguments.

Multiple Choice Items

It may have surprised some readers of this chapter that multiple choice questions can assess higher order thinking skills, especially those with introductory material. The strategies in Table 12.1 can be used with several different test item or performance assessment formats. It depends on exactly what you want the examinee to demonstrate. Context-dependent multiple choice item sets, sometimes called interpretive exercises, offer introductory material and then one or several multiple choice items based on the material. To assess higher order thinking, such multiple choice questions must be carefully constructed in such a way that one can infer with some confidence that, if the examinee selects the correct answer, he or she must have used the intended thinking processes.

Constructed Response Items

Constructed response questions with introductory material are similar to context-dependent multiple choice items, except examinees must write their own answers to the questions. Constructed response questions are therefore not subject to guessing in the same way as multiple choice items are.

If constructed response questions ask for an explanation of reasoning, the reasoning itself is available for appraisal. This is at once both a strength and a weakness. It is a strength because there is direct evidence of reasoning, so there is less inference. It is a weakness because construct-irrelevant variance, namely writing ability, is also included. This weakness is somewhat mitigated if explanation of reasoning is part of the intended construct—and, if the assessment occurs in an educational setting, if explanation of reasoning is explicitly taught.

Performance Assessments

Performance assessments—including various kinds of papers and projects—require those assessed to make or do something more extended than answering a test question, and can assess higher order thinking especially if they ask students to support their choices or thesis, explain their reasoning, or show their work. An advantage is that performance assessments can be opportunities for assessment tasks requiring complex and contextual reasoning. Another advantage is that performance assessment can include more authentic tasks than most test items can.

One drawback is that performance assessments include even more opportunity for construct-irrelevant variance, most notably in background and experience with the task and its context, than in multiple choice and constructed response questions. Person-by-item interaction variance is typically large in performance assessment, for this reason (Brennan, 2000). This means that a large number of tasks with a variety of different contexts is needed for reliable generalization about performance. A compounding drawback is that performance assessments require a lot of time; therefore, there is less opportunity to sample tasks from a domain as well as to present the variety required for reliable generalization. Thus content representativeness as well as reliability may be an issue.

CONCLUSION

Our aim in this chapter has been that readers would be able to select or construct test items or assessment tasks that tapped higher order thinking and score them meaningfully. We began with three general principles for assessing higher order thinking: (1) Disentangle recall of content from thinking processes by giving those assessed content material to think about (or having them obtain it); (2) Make sure that the material is novel; and (3) Don't confuse level of difficulty with level of thinking. Then we illustrated how this would look in strategies to assess 16 different aspects of higher order thinking. Our list was not exhaustive, but we hope it was representative enough. We also hope that the examples were comprehensive enough to illustrate how to reason back and forth from a task to the thinking skills it requires. We encourage you to assess higher order thinking in various ways and as often as possible. Education should be first and foremost, we believe, about learning to think.

REFERENCES

Anderson, L. W., & Krathwohl, D. R. (Eds.). (2001). *A taxonomy for learning, teaching, and assessing*. New York, NY: Longman.

Brennan, R. L. (2000). Performance assessments from the perspective of generalizability theory. *Applied Psychological Measurement, 24*, 339-353.

Brookhart, S. M. (2008). *How to give effective feedback to your students*. Alexandria, VA: ASCD.

Hattie, J., & Timperley, H. (2007). The power of feedback. *Review of Educational Research, 77*, 81-112.

Kentucky Department of Education. (2007). Grade 8 Kentucky Core Content Test Spring 2007 Released Items Mathematics. Retrieved from http://

www.kde.state.ky.us/NR/rdonlyres/A5DC55A7-9B73-4AF9-A29C-7B4BFB2EC5C6/0/Release_07_Grade_8MA.pdf

Kuhlthau, C. C. (2005). Towards collaboration between information seeking and information retrieval. *Information Research, 10*(2), 225. Retrieved from http://informationr.net/ir/10-2/paper225.html

McClymer, J. F., & Knoles, L. Z. (1992). Ersatz learning, inauthentic testing. *Journal on Excellence in College Teaching, 3*, 33-50.

Nitko, A. J., & Brookhart, S. M. (2007). *Educational assessment of students* (5th ed.). Upper Saddle River, NJ: Pearson Merrill Prentice Hall.

Nitko, A. J., & Brookhart, S. M. (2011). *Educational assessment of students* (6th ed.). Boston, MA: Pearson.

Norris, S. P., & Ennis, R. H. (1989). *Evaluating critical thinking*. Pacific Grove, CA: Critical Thinking Press & Software.

CHAPTER 13

CRITICAL THINKING IN THE CLASSROOM

Teachers' Beliefs and Practices in Instruction and Assessment

Bruce Torff

For what seems like time immemorial, dispute has raged between curriculum-centered educators who emphasize the memorization of a canon of valued facts (e.g., Hirsch, 1996) and educators who take a more student-centered approach in which students follow personal interests and discover information on their own (e.g., Lambert & McCombs, 1998). But these are differences in degree, not in kind. Even the most student-centered educators concede that students need to memorize such factual staples as the multiplication table. And even the most curriculum-centered agree that schooling ought not simply provide students with facts to memorize, but should also help students draw their own conclusions and solve problems.

Support is thus widespread for policies and practices in education that help students develop skills in *critical thinking*: "cognitive skills and strategies that increase the likelihood of a desired outcome ... thinking that is

Assessment of Higher Order Thinking Skills, pp. 361–394
Copyright © 2011 by Information Age Publishing
All rights of reproduction in any form reserved.

purposeful, reasoned, and goal-directed—the kind of thinking involved in solving problems, formulating inferences, calculating likelihoods, and making decisions" (Halpern, 2003, p. 6; see also Brown & Campione, 1990; Browne & Keeley, 2001; Ennis, 1987; Henderson, 2001; Kuhn, 2005; O'Tuel & Bullard, 1993; Perkins, Jay, & Tishman, 1993; Pogrow, 1990, 1994, 2006; Raths, Wasserman, Jonas, & Rothstein, 1986; Resnick, 1987). It's difficult to overestimate the importance of critical thinking (CT) in everyday life. Which career to pursue, car to buy, person to marry, and countless other life-changing decisions ultimately rest on an individual's CT skills.

In light of the crucial role played by CT in schools, it seems important to consider teachers' beliefs about CT, since it is teacher decision making that results in the implementation of one kind of instruction or another in the classroom. What do teachers believe about use of CT activities in schools? What do they believe about the assessment of students' work in these activities? In this chapter, I review the research literature on teachers' beliefs about CT in schools. The review begins with an overview of research in this area, including a framework of eight strands of research this body of work might well include. A discussion of these eight strands follows, revealing extensive gaps in the literature. The concluding section suggests directions for future research on teachers' beliefs about classroom use of, and assessment of, CT activities in schools.

RESEARCH ON CRITICAL THINKING IN SCHOOLS

A large and vibrant body of literature is focused on use of CT activities in schools. In this work, CT is typically treated as a categorical variable, with "high-CT" activities (e.g., debate, problem solving) arrayed against "low-CT" ones (e.g., lecture, note copying). (See Table 12.1; see also Appendix for high-CT and low-CT items included in the survey instrument described below). This bifurcation has proven useful in both theory and research in this area, but the extent to which a classroom activity requires students to think critically can also be measured as a continuous variable (e.g., age, income).

Theory and research in this area encompasses two distinct aspects of CT in schools, in *instruction* and *assessment*. Instruction seems the appropriate word to describe when teachers design high-CT activities, decide which students should receive them, and implement them in the classroom. Assessment is the term that describes the processes by which teachers evaluate students' work once high-CT activities have been initiated in the classroom (during and after these activities). A thorough analysis of CT in schools should involve both: the design and implementation of

Table 13.1.   Examples of High-CT and Low-CT Classroom Activities

High-CT Activities	*Low-CT Activities*
Socratic discussion	Lecture
Debate	Note copying
Problem solving	Word searches
Problem finding	Fill-in-the-blank worksheets
Brainstorming	Videos
Decision making	Drill and practice
Critique	Matching
Analysis	Memorization
Imaginative writing	Writing of summaries
Classification	PowerPoint presentation by teacher

See also high-CT and low-CT prompts in CTBA instrument, in Appendix.

high-CT activities; and teachers' efforts to assess student performance in these activities.

Theory and research in this area have included an additional distinction, taking into account differences that may obtain between groups of students that vary in SES (socioeconomic status). A distinction has been drawn between high-SES populations who have a high level of resources at their disposal, and low-SES populations with comparatively fewer advantages. SES can also be treated as a continuous variable, and often is in a variety of academic disciplines.

But the high/low distinction serves a purpose in studies of CT in schools, which include a theory that endeavors to document inequities in how high-CT activities are used in high-SES and low-SES schools (Pogrow, 1990, 1994, 2006; Raudenbush Rowan, & Cheong, 2003; Torff, 2005, 2006; Torff & Sessions, 2006; Torff & Warburton, 2005; Warburton & Torff, 2005; Zohar, Degani, & Vaakin, 2001; Zohar & Dori, 2003). According to this theory, the widely decried achievement gap between the "haves" and "have nots" in our society has many causes, but high on the list is the all too common practice of providing low-SES students with a less rigorous curriculum (i.e., one that requires fewer high-CT activities but more low-CT ones), compared to the rigorous, thinking-rich curriculum typically afforded high-SES students. This "rigor gap," the theory goes, stems in part from teachers' beliefs about what kind of instruction is effective with student populations that vary in SES advantages. Teachers purportedly support high-CT activities more for high-advantage students (who are thought to be able to handle them) while favoring a remedial regimen long on low-CT activities for low-advantage students.

According to this theory, a self-fulfilling prophecy may result: high-advantage students receive a curriculum with lots of high-CT activities, which boosts their academic performance, which in turn makes additional high-CT instruction likely. But low-advantage students receive less rigorous instruction, which inhibits their academic growth, likely resulting in still more low-CT activities in the future. On this view, the rich get richer and the poor get poorer, largely because teachers' beliefs about effective instruction drive inequitable classroom practices (Zohar et al., 2001).

Of course, substantiating this theory requires researchers to examine classroom use of high-CT and low-CT activities with student populations that vary in SES. But the theory also implies that teachers' beliefs should be investigated, not just their practices. Since it's claimed that teachers' beliefs lay the heart of the rigor gap, research should be undertaken to determine the nature and development of teachers' beliefs about use of (and assessment of) high-CT and low-CT activities for different student populations. At the same time, teachers' beliefs are not always highly correlated with actual classroom practices (Fang, 1996), so studies of teachers' actual classroom practices also are vital.

In sum, studies in CT in schools might well encompass multiple strands of theory and research, including the following:

1. The nature and development of teachers' beliefs about classroom use of high-CT activities
2. Teachers' classroom practices with respect to these activities
3. The correlation of beliefs and practices with respect to classroom use of high-CT activities
4. The extent to which academic outcomes are predicted by beliefs and practices concerning classroom use of high-CT activities
5. Teachers' beliefs concerning assessment of students' work in high-CT activities
6. Teachers' classroom practices in conducting this assessment
7. The correlation of beliefs and practices with respect to assessment of high-CT activities
8. The extent to which academic outcomes are predicted by beliefs and practices concerning classroom use of high-CT activities

In what follows, I review theoretical constructs, assessment models, and research findings in these strands. The review reveals, among other things, that theory and research have yet to be developed in all but the first of the eight. The eight strands are revisited in the concluding section of this chapter.

TEACHERS' BELIEFS ABOUT CT ACTIVITIES

In recent decades a great deal of literature has been devoted to discussions of the level of rigor in school curricula, including the claim that disadvantaged students are frequently given short shrift in this regard (e.g., Kozol, 1991; Lee & Burkam, 2002). Widespread is the view that underachieving students are too often afforded a watered-down curriculum that exacerbates the achievement gap. Barton (2004) identified14 factors linked to the achievement gap (including in-school factors such as teacher experience and out-of-school factors such as birth weight) and heading the list was rigor of curriculum. Researchers interested in CT have made similar points, suggesting that high-CT activities (a central feature of rigorous curriculum) are more often directed to high-advantage students than their low-advantage peers (Pogrow, 1990, 1994, 2006; Raudenbush et al., 2003; Torff, 2005, 2006; Torff & Sessions, 2006; Torff & Warburton, 2005; Warburton & Torff, 2005; Zohar et al., 2001; Zohar & Dori, 2003).

Evidence that low-advantage students can indeed profit from high-CT activities has been published (Pogrow, 1990, 1994, 2006; Zohar & Dori, 2003). But this evidence has not been widely disseminated among teachers, given the generally weak connection of research and practice in education. It also possible that to some extent teachers are not persuaded that the evidence is compelling, holding instead to the belief that low-advantage students just can't handle the challenges of high-CT activities. If so, teachers' well-intended efforts to create lessons that are appropriately rigorous for a given group of students may result, in the long run, in fewer high-CT activities for low-advantage populations.

Such a possibility has motivated researchers to examine teachers' beliefs, in particular their beliefs about what constitutes effective instruction for different student populations. In the first study on this topic, 303 teachers of four secondary subjects (English, math, science, and social studies) in 16 schools in California and Michigan were asked to identify instructional objectives for upper-track and lower-track classes and then were given specially designed scales that assessed teachers' emphasis on high-CT activities in these classes (Raudenbush et al., 2003). Regression analysis revealed an effect of academic track: instructional objectives and emphasis on high-CT activities differed significantly across academic tracks such that teachers were more likely to focus on high-CT activities in upper-track classes.

Attempts to analyze teachers' beliefs about low-CT activities were unsuccessful due to low reliabilities produced by the researchers' low-CT scales, precluding analyses comparing beliefs about high-CT and low-CT activities. Based on the data for high-CT activities, however, the researchers concluded that teachers favored differentiation of high-CT instruction based on academic track (i.e., a tracking effect), especially in math and science. According to the researchers, differentiation of instruction based on academic track is commonplace in modern schools, due to a "transmission style of teaching that avoids challenging teacher-student interactions" in lower-track classes (Raudenbush et al., 2003, p. 546).

Obtaining similar results, Zohar et al. (2001) conducted semistructured interviews in which 40 secondary teachers in Israel discussed their instructional goals for students identified by the researchers as low-achieving or high-achieving. The researchers separated these goals into three categories—two corresponding to low-CT activities ("knowledge" and "comprehension") and one corresponding to high-CT activities ("higher-order thinking"). No attempt was made to statistically compare beliefs in these categories. Participants' levels of educational attainment and teaching experience were reported but not entered into analyses of instructional goals. Nineteen of 40 teachers (47.5%) judged high-CT activities to be inappropriate for low-achieving students—a finding interpreted by the researchers as evidence of an "achievement effect" comparable to the tracking effect found by Raudenbush et al. (2003).

The researchers interpreted these findings as reflecting teachers' construal of learning as progressing from simple, lower-order cognitive skills (e.g., comprehension) to more complex ones (e.g., analysis), with the latter being feasible only for high-achieving students. However, the finding that 21 of 40 teachers (52.5%) did not judge high-CT activities to be inappropriate for low-achieving students points to variability in teachers' beliefs about use of high-CT activities in the classroom. Moreover, since beliefs about low-CT and high-CT activities were not compared, it remains unclear what blend of high-CT and low-CT activities teachers favor for different student populations.

Results reported by Raudenbush et al. (2003) and Zohar et al. (2001) indicate that at least some teachers judged high-CT activities to be more appropriate for high-advantage students than low-advantage ones. Based on these data, these researchers have suggested that teachers may prefer low-CT activities to high-CT ones when teaching low-advantage students. However, since the researchers did not compare low-CT and high-CT ones, their results do not speak to the extent to which the reported tracking effect and achievement effect are unique to high-CT activities or obtain with low-CT activities as well. This seems a crucial issue to investigate, because it concerns the extent to which teachers hold beliefs that result in less rigorous curriculum for low-advantage students.

DEVELOPMENT OF THE CTBA

Designed to move into the breech, a new survey called the *Critical Thinking Belief Appraisal* (CTBA) was developed and its scores evaluated for validity and reliability (Torff & Warburton, 2005). (See Appendix for the instrument in its entirety.) Based on a four-factor model, the CTBA was designed to assess teachers' beliefs concerning the effectiveness of (1) high-CT activities for high-advantage students (high-CT/high-advantage), (2) high-CT activities for low-advantage students (high-CT/low-advantage), (3) low-CT activities for high-advantage students (low-CT/high-advantage), and (4) low-CT activities for low-advantage students (low-CT/low-advantage). The scale is comprised of a series of 12 prompts—vignettes describing classroom activities in English, mathematics, science, social studies, and languages other than English. The prompts are divided equally between high-CT and low-CT activities:

> *High-CT:* A social-studies class is studying the Treaty of Versailles signed at the end of World War I. The teacher assigns students to write "letters from the future" to President Wilson arguing why the United States should or should not support the treaty.
>
> *Low-CT:* A social-studies class is studying the industrial revolution. The teacher provides students with a list of inventions, explains the impact of these inventions during this period, and describes how they continue to influence the modern world.

The CTBA was designed to allow teachers' beliefs to be assessed separately for high-advantage and low-advantage students. As the instrument was being developed, it seemed clear that simply asking respondents to rate prompts for "high advantage" and "low advantage" students had potential to manifest bias caused by leading questions, since it is not socially acceptable to openly discriminate against students based on SES. An unpublished study will help to make the point: In 2008, the CTBA prompts were used in a study in which participants (in-service teachers) were asked to respond to each prompt for either "high-SES" or "low-SES" students. Results showed that such a "direct" assessment approach masked the effects obtained and consistently replicated in other CTBA work that employed the original CTBA form (including "advantage characteristics" summarized below). With "direct" assessment, respondents apparently gave socially scripted responses following social norms indicating that SES groups should be treated equally; however, in prior work using the original instrument (with advantage characteristics instead of direct references to SES), a variety of effects have been obtained and replicated. Evidently, assessment of teachers' beliefs about appropriate instruction for different populations presents an assessment challenge requiring a modicum of guile on the part of the researcher.

To circumvent this response bias, a contextualized assessment scheme was designed drawing on the characteristics that teachers have been shown to take into consideration as they judge students' SES advantages. Three such "advantage characteristics" were used: *ability* (students' capacity for academic achievement when dealing with the specific topic to which a given prompt refers); *prior knowledge* (the extent of students' knowledge about the specific topic to which a given prompt refers before students participate in additional activities); and *motivation* (how much interest and attention students demonstrate when dealing with the specific topic to which a given prompt refers) (Archer & McCarthy, 1988; Dweck, 1986; Givvin, Stipek, Salmon, & MacGyvers, 2001; Madon, Jussim, Keiper, Eccles, Smith, & Paolumbo, 1998; Moje & Wade, 1997; Pintrich & Schunk, 1996; Tollefson, 2000). These characteristics were nominated not as factors underlying use of high-CT activities, but as indications of teachers' judgments of students as high-advantage or low-advantage.

This method appears to have been effective, given that factor-analytic and internal-consistency reliability results strongly supported ability, prior knowledge, and motivation collectively as indicators of teachers' perception of student advantages—but not as independent factors. This conclusion can be drawn from Table 13.2, which shows some of the pattern/structure coefficients ("loadings") produced in validation research (Torff & Warburton, 2005). Respondents produced data with little separation between ability, prior knowledge, and motivation for each of the four factors in the CTBA's assessment model; for each factor, the selected items produced loadings that averaged .64 and ranged from .40 to .86. In contrast, none of the other loadings in Table 13.2 (i.e., loadings inconsistent with the CTBA's posited four-factor structure) exceeded .26. When evaluating the CTBA prompts, respondents appeared not to conceptualize ability, prior knowledge, and motivation as separate factors, but instead treated these variables as indications of a single underlying construct (interpreted as indicating learners' SES advantages).

The original CTBA survey uses six-point Likert-type scales, with each of the scale's 12 prompts followed by either a high-advantage item or a low-advantage one for each advantage characteristic. For example, the first prompt is followed by a low-ability item, a low prior-knowledge item, and a high-motivation item. The survey has a total of 36 items balanced as follows: it has a total of 12 prompts, six high-CT and six low-CT; it presents 18 items for high-advantage students and 18 for low-advantage ones; and it includes 12 of each of the three advantage characteristics, six for high-advantage students and six for low-advantage ones.

Table 13.2.   Pattern/Structure Coefficients and Communalities for CTBA Prompts

Prompt	Advantage Characteristic	Pattern/ Structure Coefficients				Communalities
		F1	F2	F3	F4	
High-CT/High-Advantage						
Prompt 3: A mathematics class	H_ABL	−.22	.04	.04	**.55**	.39
Prompt 5: A science class	H_PKN	−.26	.05	.23	**.40**	.38
	H_MTV	−.19	−.16	.24	**.40**	.32
Prompt 7: A social-studies class	H_ABL	.00	.07	.07	**.85**	.73
	H_PKN	−.04	−.13	.14	**.70**	.53
	H_MTV	−.01	14	.03	**.79**	.66
Prompt 8: A mathematics class	H_MTV	−.23	.01	.14	**.40**	.27
Prompt 10: A French class	H_ABL	.00	−.02	.26	.52	.39
	H_PKN	−.10	−.20	.07	.40	.27
High-CT/Low-Advantage						
Prompt 3: A mathematics class	L_PKN	.02	−.02	**.61**	.05	.40
	L_MTV	.00	−.07	**.58**	.08	.35
Prompt 5: A science class	L_ABL	.26	.12	**.40**	.05	.35
Prompt 8: A mathematics class	L_ABL	−.19	.18	**.45**	.10	.39
	L_PKN	.04	.13	**.51**	.07	.35
Prompt 4: An English class	L_MTV	.23	.09	**.40**	.05	.35
Prompt 11: A French class	L_ABL	.00	.01	**.71**	.08	.52
	L_PKN	.14	−.02	**.67**	.10	.47
	L_MTV	.09	.03	**.78**	.00	.62

(Table continues on next page.)

Table 13.2.   Continued

Prompt	Advantage Characteristic	Pattern/ Structure Coefficients				Communalities
		F1	F2	F3	F4	
Low-CT/High-Advantage						
Prompt 1: An English class	H_MTV	**.55**	.07	.08	−.09	.32
Prompt 4: An Italian class	H_ABL	**.73**	.11	.16	−.12	.59
	H_PKN	**.79**	−.01	.17	−.13	.67
Prompt 9: A Spanish class	H_ABL	**.86**	.05	−.02	−.06	.75
	H_PKN	**.86**	−.03	.01	−.06	.75
	H_MTV	**.79**	.04	.05	−.03	.63
Prompt 12: A mathematics class	H_ABL	**.80**	−.04	−.03	−.16	.67
	H_PKN	**.82**	−.10	−.05	−.13	.72
	H_MTV	**.81**	−.07	−.06	−.02	.67
Low-CT/Low-Advantage						
Prompt 1: An English class	L_ABK	−.07	**.59**	−.06	−.17	.38
	L_PKN	.05	**.58**	−.07	.05	.35
Prompt 2: A social-studies class	L_ABL	−.10	**.79**	−.17	−.13	.67
	L_PKN	−.09	**.75**	−.05	.13	.59
	L_MTV	−.04	**.67**	.12	−.26	.57
Prompt 4: An Italian class	L_MTV	.26	**.57**	−.18	.19	.48
Prompt 6: An English class	L_ABL	.16	**.69**	.26	−22	.62
	L_PKN	.09	**.60**	−.16	−.19	.40
	L_MTV	−.02	**.61**	.25	−.06	.45
Postrotation:	*Percent of variance*	16.72	11.22	10.44	9.69	
	Percent of covariancec	34.78	23.34	21.92	20.16	
	Eigenvalues	6.45	5.02	3.48	2.36	

Notes: CTBA = Critical Thinking Belief Appraisal; CT = critical thinking; H_ABL = high ability, L_ABL = low ability, H_PKN = high prior knowledge, L_PKN = low prior knowledge, H_MTV = high motivation, and L_MTV = low motivation. (Adapted from Torff and Warburton, 2005)

A series of five validation studies produced results supporting the theoretical and practical utility of the construct and measure of teachers' beliefs about classroom use of high-CT and low-CT activities for high- and low-advantage student populations (Torff & Warburton, 2005). The scale produced scores with high internal-consistency reliability, with an overall alpha level of .89. The CTBA was found to have a stable factor structure comprised of four factors that collectively accounted for 62% of the within-group variance. The instrument also produced satisfactory internal-consistency reliability results (Table 13.3). A replication study produced similar internal-consistency reliability and factor-analytic results. The scale's scores also demonstrated satisfactory discriminant validity, producing low correlations (ranging from .02 to .28, $p < .05$) between each of the four factors and measures of CT ability (the *California Critical Thinking Skills Test*; Facione, Facione, & Giancarlo, 2000), CT disposition (the *Need for Cognition* scale; Cacioppo & Petty, 1982; Cacioppo Petty, Feinstein, & Jarvis 1996), and social desirability (The *Marlowe-Crowne Social Desirability* scale; Crowne & Marlowe, 1964). Finally, the scale yielded scores with acceptable predictive validity, with an overall correlation of .72 ($p < .05$) between ratings of observed classroom use of CT activities and the subset of CTBA items that matched the student characteristics of the classroom observed (as judged by the teacher). As noted, validation research also supported the use of the three advantage characteristics: factor-analytic results and internal-consistency correlations (ranging from .74 to .96, $p < .05$) indicated that ability, prior knowledge, and motivation collectively were reliable indicators of teachers' perception of student advantages but had little effect as independent factors.

In sum, validation research showed that the scores produced by the CTBA evinced favorable psychometric characteristics. Strong dominance of the four-factor set, stable pattern/structure coefficients, and high internal-consistency reliabilities indicated that the shared variation of the

Table 13.3.   Internal Consistency Reliability Data for the CTBA

	Facto	*Alpha*
1.	High-CT activities for high-advantage learners.	.88
2.	High-CT activities for low-advantage learners.	.76
3.	Low-CT activities for high-advantage learners.	.90
4.	Low-CT activities for low-advantage learners.	.88
Overall (4 factors)		.89

Notes: CTBA = Critical Thinking Belief Appraisal; CT = critical thinking. (Adapted from Torff and Warburton, 2005.)

items reliably assessed a common set of factors. Moreover, this result was unlikely to be an artifact of response biases, since instructions and item wording were designed to minimize acquiescence and self-presentation, and correlations between CTBA scores and social desirability were weak. The empirical method of deriving the scale enhances the confidence that can be placed in the construct and content validity of obtained scores, and the CTBA produced scores with favorable discriminant and predictive validity. Taken together, the results of five validation studies support the theoretical utility of the CTBA for assessing teachers' beliefs about critical thinking.

IN-SERVICE TEACHERS' BELIEFS ABOUT CT ACTIVITIES

With the CTBA found to be an effective research tool, a series of studies were conducted to examine in-service teachers' beliefs about high-CT and low-CT activities for different student populations (Torff, 2005, 2006; Warburton & Torff, 2005). In three studies, the CTBA was administered to a total of 350 in-service secondary teachers in over 100 schools in New York State and South Carolina (N = 145, 103, and 102, respectively).

Within-participants MANCOVA procedures revealed that in-service teachers rated high-CT activities as significantly more effective for high- than low-advantage students, with large eta-squared statistics (effect sizes) of .63, .58, and .67 in the three studies. (Effect sizes less than .20 have been categorized as "small," between .20 and .40 as "moderate," and above .40 as "large;" Cohen, 1988). This sizeable "advantage effect" is similar to the tracking effect (Raudenbush et al., 2003) and achievement effect (Zohar et al., 2001) previously reported with respect to high-CT activities. However, in results not previously reported, teachers also rated low-CT activities as more effective for high-advantage students than low-advantage ones (also with large effect sizes of .53, .52, and .48, respectively in the three studies). Both low-CT activities and high-CT ones were associated with strong advantage effects.

In-service teachers also produced "pedagogical-preference effects" in which high-CT activities were rated as significantly more effective than low-CT ones for both student populations. The effects were moderate to weak for high-advantage students, with effect sizes of .24, .20, and .08 in the three studies. For low-advantage students, the effect was weaker and less consistent, with two studies yielding weak effects of .09 and .05 respectively (Warburton & Torff, 2005; Torff, 2005) and one study showing no statistically significant effect (Torff, 2006).

These findings do not unambiguously support the assertion that teachers judge low-CT activities to be preferable to high-CT ones for low-advantage students. Teachers preferred high-CT to low-CT activities for both student populations (although this effect was stronger for high-advantage than low-advantage students). But it would not be accurate to suggest that the results show teachers to support use of high-CT activities equally for both student populations. The advantage effect was stronger for high-CT than low-CT activities, and the pedagogical preference effect was stronger and more consistent for high-advantage students than low-advantage ones. Teachers may have favored high-CT activities over low-CT ones for both student populations, but they still deemed it appropriate that high-advantage students receive more high-CT activities than low-advantage students. The available research yields this conclusion: although it is apparently not true that teachers simply favor high-CT activities for high-advantage students and low-CT activities for low-advantage ones, teachers do support a pedagogy in which high-CT activities are more often used with high-advantage students than their low-advantage peers.

EXPERT TEACHERS' BELIEFS ABOUT CT ACTIVITIES

The results described above indicate that teachers supported use of high-CT activities more for high- than low-advantage student populations. But these studies do not necessarily reveal teachers' beliefs to be problematic. Perhaps educational outcomes are enhanced when high-CT activities are directed more often to high-advantage students than low-advantage ones. In that case, expert teachers (top-quality practitioners unlikely to hold beliefs that exacerbate educational problems such as the rigor gap) would produce similar CTBA responses relative to the ones produced by the randomly selected in-service teachers. But if in-service teachers' beliefs are impoverished to some extent, their CTBA responses should differ significantly from those of expert teachers.

To investigate whether in-service teachers' beliefs should be viewed as problematic, a study was conducted along the lines of expertise research in other domains (for a review see Bereiter & Scardamalia, 1993). In this study, the CTBA was administered to 92 expert teachers (from 27 different schools) and 110 randomly selected in-service teachers in New York State (Torff, 2006). Teachers in the expert group were nominated by their supervisors (a principal or assistant principal). In-service teachers were randomly selected from 30 schools similar in socioeconomic status (SES) to the schools at which the expert teachers were employed, with data on housing costs used for SES matching. In this case, *experts* are teachers with the highest level of pedagogical skill (though they are technically employed as in-service teachers) and *in-service teachers* are the group representing the range of levels of teaching skill (though it's likely that this group also includes some teachers that would have been classified as experts had their supervisors been tapped to nominate experts).

Between-participants MANCOVA procedures showed that the groups did not differ in ratings of high-CT activities for high-advantage students. This result indicates that experts and in-service teachers were similarly supportive of high-CT instruction for high-advantage students. However, experts exceeded in-service teachers in ratings of high-CT activities for low-advantage students (with a large effect size of .48). Experts were considerably more likely than in-service teachers to support use of high-CT activities in the classroom. Moreover, in-service teachers were more supportive of didactic instruction than experts were. In-service teachers produced higher ratings for low-CT activities for both student populations (with effect sizes of .36 for high-advantage students and .15 for low-advantage students).

In within-participants MANCOVA procedures, each group rated both high-CT and low-CT activities as more effective with high-advantage students than low-advantage ones, unsurprisingly. Experts as well as in-service teachers demonstrated the advantage effects yielded in other research (Raudenbush et al., 2003; Torff, 2005; Warburton & Torff, 2005; Zohar et al., 2001). At the same time, the effects produced by in-service teachers (.68 for high-CT activities and .52 for low-CT ones) were substantially stronger than those produced by expert teachers (.28 and .09). In-service teachers produced much stronger advantage effects relative to expert teachers.

For high-advantage students, both groups produced pedagogical preference effects favoring high-CT activities over low-CT ones, but with very different effect sizes. The pedagogical preference effect was vastly stronger among experts (effect size of .65) than for in-service teachers (.08). For low-advantage students, experts (but not in-service teachers) demonstrated a pedagogical-preference effect (with a large effect size of .69). In-service teachers did not produce a statistically significant pedagogical preference effects for low-advantage students.

Experts were generally more supportive of high-CT activities and less supportive of low-CT ones compared to randomly selected in-service teachers. Experts were also less inclined to differentiate use of high-CT and low-CT activities based on student advantages—a finding suggesting that experts were less likely to contribute to the rigor gap. Overall, this study's results indicate that in-service teachers' beliefs obtained in this project and other research (Torff, 2005, 2006; Warburton & Torff, 2005) can be viewed as problematic. Teacher-education initiatives designed to provide more equitable use of high-CT activities in schools would seem warranted.

THE DEVELOPMENT OF TEACHERS' BELIEFS ABOUT CT ACTIVITIES

How do in-service teachers come to hold such beliefs? To what extent are these beliefs already in place as prospective teachers self-select their careers and enroll in a teacher-education program? How does participating in these programs influence their beliefs? And what is the impact of the combination of teaching experience and in-service education? To answer these questions, research on the development of teachers' beliefs was conducted (Torff, 2005). This research has potential to inform teacher-education practices designed to promote changes in beliefs where they are most needed.

In this study, the CTBA was administered in New York State to four groups ($N = 408$): (1) *in-service teachers*—practitioners with a minimum of five years of teaching experience; (2) *preservice teachers*—undergraduates who had completed preservice teacher education but had yet to begin teaching; (3) *prospective teachers*—undergraduates who had indicated an intention to enter the teaching profession but had yet to begin preservice teacher education; and (4) nonteacher *controls*—undergraduates with no desire or intention to enter the teaching profession. This research was designed to explore differences associated with teachers' self-selection of their careers, preservice education, and the combination of teaching experience and in-service education. (See Table 13.4 for a summary of results.)

Effects associated with self-selection. Prospective teachers' self-selection of their careers was associated with increased support for high-CT activities for both high- and low-advantage students. Between-participants MANCOVA procedures showed that preservice teachers were higher that controls in ratings of high-CT activities for both high-advantage students (effect size of .11) and low-advantage students (.05). However, prospective teachers and controls showed no statistically significant differences for low-low-CT activities for either student population. Prospective teachers came to their teacher-education programs already enthusiastic about high-CT activities. But this enthusiasm did not extend to low-CT activities, indicating that the groups held didactic instruction in similar esteem.

Within-participants MANCOVA analyses also reflected this pattern. Both the prospective teachers and controls produced advantage effects for both high-CT and low-CT activities. Controls produced smaller effect sizes (.59 and .39, respectively) relative to prospective teachers (.78 and .51). Differences in pedagogical preference effects also emerged between groups, for both populations. For high-advantage students, prospective teachers favored high-CT over low-CT activities (.30), while controls produced no statistically significant effect. For low-advantage students, controls judged low-CT activities to be preferable to high-CT ones (.36),

Table 13.4.   Summary of Between-Participants Results in Teacher-Development Research

Effect	HH	HL	LH	LL
Self-selection	Cont < Pros	Cont < Pros	n.s.	n.s.
	$p < .0001$	$p < .05$		
	(.11)	(.05)		
Preservice education	Pros > Pres	n.s.	Pros > Pres	Pros > Pres
	$p < .05$		$p < .01$	$p < .05$
	(.05)		(.06)	(.06)
In-service education and teaching experience	n.s.	Pres > Ins	n.s.	n.s.
		$p < .05$		
		(.02)		

Notes: HH = high-CT activities for high-advantage learners; HL = high-CT activities for low-advantage learners; LH = low-CT activities for high-advantage learners; LL = low-CT activities for low-advantage learners; Cont = control group; Pros = prospective-teacher group; Pres = preservice-teacher group; Ins = in-service teacher group; > = significantly greater than; < = significantly less than; n.s. = not significant. Effect sizes (partial eta-square statistics) are in parentheses. (Adapted from Torff, 2005.)

while prospective teachers produced no significant effect. Overall, substantial differences were obtained between controls and prospective teachers, with prospective teachers considerably more supportive of high-CT activities and less likely to differentiate the level of CT in instruction based on students' SES advantages.

Effects of preservice education. Between-participants analyses showed that preservice and prospective teachers did not differ in ratings for high-CT activities for low-advantage students. However, the groups did differ in support for high-CT activities for high-advantage students and low-CT activities for both student populations—and in all three cases preservice teachers produced lower ratings than did prospective teachers. Preservice teachers were somewhat lower than prospective ones in ratings for high-CT activities for high-advantage students (effect size of .05), indicating a loss of support for use of high-CT activities with high-advantage students. Preservice teachers were also marginally lower than prospective ones in ratings for low-CT activities for both high- and low-advantage students (each with an effect size of .06). Preservice education evidently had the effect of encouraging students to rethink their support for low-CT instruction, for all students.

This pattern may be linked to students' experiences in preservice teacher-education programs. These programs vary in philosophy and methods, but the zeitgeist is one that supports student-centered, constructivist teaching emphasizing such methods as hands-on activities and student inquiry (e.g., Lambert & McCombs, 1998). Curriculum-centered pedagogy (e.g., lecture, note copying) is often derided as less effective in promoting students' learning and well-being in school. Given this widely held view among teacher-educators, it is unsurprising that preservice teachers in this study tended to devalue low-CT activities after they have been enrolled in a teacher-education program for an extended period.

Within-participants analyses showed that preservice education was associated with reductions in advantage-effect sizes. Preservice teachers produced weaker advantage effects (.67 for high-CT activities and .38 for low-CT ones) relative to prospective teachers (.78 and .51). The groups also differed in pedagogical-preference effect sizes. For high-advantage students, preservice teachers produced a pedagogical-preference effect size of .22, relative to .30 for prospective teachers. For low-advantage students, preservice teachers yielded a pedagogical-preference effect size of .07, while prospective teachers produced no significant effect. With the declining advantage effect for high-CT activities combined with the emerging pedagogical preference effect favoring high-CT activities for low-advantage students, the conclusion may be drawn that preservice education reduced teachers' inclination to differentiate the level of CT in instruction according to students' SES advantages.

Effects of teaching experience and in-service education. Teachers often say that classroom experience is the single most powerful influence on their work, much more so than preservice education. But this judgment is inconsistent with the findings of this study. The combination of teaching experience and in-service education was associated with very little change in teachers' beliefs. One small change was obtained: in between-participants analyses, in-service teachers were marginally lower than preservice ones in ratings for high-CT activities for low-advantage students, with a minuscule effect size of .02. Support for high-CT activities for low-advantage learners diminished following preservice education—but with an effect size this small, it can hardly be see as a meaningful shift. The groups did not differ in ratings for high-CT activities for high-advantage students. Neither were differences obtained for low-CT activities for either student population. These results suggest that teachers' beliefs about CT in the classroom are largely stable nature of during the in-service years, except for an exceedingly small reduction of support for high-CT activities for low-advantage students.

Following teachers' self-selection of their careers, development of beliefs about CT activities appeared to work by contraction rather than expansion. Among all teacher groups in the study, the highest ratings were produced by the least experienced: prospective teachers. And all the ratings that changed went down, not up. Where differences were obtained, prospective teachers exceeded preservice ones and preservice teachers exceeded in-service ones. For teacher educators who advocate use of CT in schools (e.g., Browne & Keeley, 2001; Ennis, 1987; Halpern, 2003; Henderson, 2001; King & Kitchener, 1994; Kuhn, 2005; Torff, 2003; Raths et al., 1986; Resnick, 1987), the task at hand involves countering the reduction of existing support for high-CT activities, not facilitating an increase in support for these activities where such support is weak or lacking.

Such a task might well be undertaken during preservice education, when the greatest amount of change in teachers' beliefs was recorded. Among the teacher groups in this study (prospective, preservice, and in-service), the largest group differences were associated with preservice education, which appeared to be a time of substantial belief change. Preservice education thus seems to be a favorable period for interventions that promote use of high-CT activities. However, support for high-CT activities for low-advantage students was lower among in-service teacher than preservice ones, suggesting that professional-development initiatives for in-service teachers also have potential for promoting equitable use of high-CT activities in schools.

ISSUES INFLUENCING IN-SERVICE TEACHERS' BELIEFS ABOUT CT

This research summarized above explores the nature and development of teachers' beliefs about use of high-CT and low-CT activities for student populations that vary in SES advantages. But this research has little to say about what prompts teachers to ascribe to such beliefs. To explore the specific issues that teachers take into account in deciding what kind of teaching to support for low-advantage students, a study was conducted combining qualitative and quantitative methods (Torff & Sessions, 2006).

Initially, interviews were conducted with secondary social-studies teachers ($N = 20$), who were asked to review and comment on high-CT and low-CT activities included in the CTBA, particularly with respect to how effective these activities would be for teaching low-advantage students. A set of 11 issues were mentioned as important to classroom decision-making, including *students' level of prior knowledge, time constraints, influence of parents, influence of colleagues, students' level of motivation, students' level of ability, high-stakes tests, influence of administrators, nature of the subject* (social studies), *classroom management,* and *ease of assessment.*

These 11 issues were further examined using a survey instrument that included two prompts from the original CTBA (presented above). Each prompt was followed by 11 items—6-point Likert-type scales asking respondents to rate their level of agreement with a statement describing one of the eleven issues. For example, the issue *students' level of prior knowledge* is described in the statement, "Low-advantage students have sufficient prior knowledge to participate successfully in the activity." To make their ratings, respondents used the following scale: 1 = strongly agree; 2 = agree; 3 = agree more than disagree; 4 = disagree more than agree; 5 = disagree; and 6 = strongly disagree. The instrument was administered to 120 secondary social-studies teachers in New York State. To determine the extent to which each issue was associated with a statistically significant pedagogical-preference effect (i.e., a difference between the high-CT prompt and the low-CT one for a given issue), within-subjects MANCOVA procedures were performed on the dependent variables.

The variables *classroom management* and *ease of assessment* yielded no statistically significant pedagogical preference effects. Several of the interviewees mentioned classroom-management challenges as an argument against use of high-CT activities with low-advantage students, but the survey respondents did not concur. Similarly, some interviewees pointed out that low-CT ones are easier to assess compared to high-CT activities; for example, it is more straightforward to assess students' responses to the question "Who discovered America?" than it is to assess responses to "What did the discovery of the New World mean to people on both sides of the Atlantic?" But these assessment challenges were apparently not intimidating to the survey respondents, who produced no pedagogical preference effects for the variable *ease of assessment.*

Three variables were associated with significant preferences for high-CT activities over low-CT ones when teaching low-advantage students. These include *influence of high-stakes tests* (partial eta-squared effect size of .12), *influence of administrators* (.09), and *the nature of the subject* (social studies) (.05). The issue *influence of high stakes tests* was associated with support for high-CT activities, not low-CT ones as some interviewees suggested. Apparently teachers are cognizant that testing procedures nowadays emphasize CT challenges in ways that earlier tests did not; in many cases, the multiple-choice tests of the past have been replaced by tests that combine multiple-choice items with essay writing, which to some extent involves a higher level of CT. The results also indicate that teachers regard administrators as supportive of high-CT activities and that the discipline of social studies lends itself to these activities, even for low- advantage students.

Statistically significant preferences for low-CT activities over high-CT ones (for low-advantage students) were obtained with respect to six variables. These include, in order of effect size: students' level of prior knowledge (effect size of .15); time constraints (.13); influence of parents (.08); influence of colleagues (.08); students' level of motivation (.07); and students' level of academic ability (.04). These half-dozen issues apparently prompted survey respondents to support the low-CT activity over the high-CT one for teaching low-advantage students.

The obtained effect sizes indicate that teachers were least supportive of high-CT activities when they perceive students to lack prior knowledge of the topic being taught. Such a result is consistent with the claim that teachers see a knowledge base as a necessary precondition for successful participation in high-CT activities, not something that can be gained through these activities. This "hierarchical" view of learning (in which higher order processes necessarily grow out on lower-order ones) has been suggested a root cause of beliefs that result in fewer high-CT activities for low-advantage students (Zohar et al., 2001).

It is difficult to argue with the oft-made claim that high-CT activities are more time-consuming that low-CT ones, so it is little surprise that the variable *instructional time* was associated with diminished support for using high-CT activities with low-advantage students. Also associated with reduced use of high-CT for low-advantage students: two variables involving teachers' social environment, *influence of parents* and *influence of colleagues*; and two variables involving students' characteristics, *motivation* and *academic ability*.

For advocates of equitable access to high-CT activities in schools, these six issues provide topics of relevance for preservice and in-service teacher education. This research has potential to inform teacher-education practices that encourage new teachers to rethink their beliefs about which students can handle high-CT activities.

CONCLUSION AND DIRECTIONS FOR FUTURE RESEARCH

The study of CT in schools can be viewed as encompassing at least eight strands of possible theory and research, including two units of analysis (teachers' beliefs and their classroom practices) each investigated concerning two aspects of CT-use (classroom implementation of CT activities and assessment of student work in these activities), with a pair of additional considerations: how beliefs about instruction and assessment vis-à-vis high-CT activities are associated with classroom practices; and how beliefs and practices concerning instruction and assessment predict academic outcomes. From the literature review presented above, it appears that only one of these eight strands includes a developed corpus of theory and research. And even this one occupied strand leaves work yet to be done. This concluding section offers suggestions as to how future theory and research might well proceed.

Teachers' beliefs about use of high-CT activities. In this strand, a body of theory and research is focused on teachers' beliefs about classroom use of CT activities. This research revealed, among other things, the utility of entering the variable *students' SES advantages* into the analyses. A series of studies makes the case that teachers' beliefs about the appropriate use of CT activities may be reducing low-advantage students' access to these activities. Beliefs as such appear to add to a "rigor gap" that likely contributes to the achievement gap—and motivates teacher-education practices aimed to promote equitable use of CT in schools.

But gaps in this literature persist. To begin with, there is the possibility that beliefs differ across communities that vary in SES. To what extent do teachers who actually work in disadvantaged areas have different beliefs relative to teachers who work in more affluent areas? As of yet, no research has been undertaken to compare the beliefs of teachers who work in low-SES schools with the beliefs of teachers in more affluent schools. Such a comparison seems essential. If teachers in low-SES schools do not support reduced use of high-CT activities for low-advantage students, then the research cited above would not seem problematic (and no response by teacher educators warranted). However, if teachers in low-SES schools equal or exceed their colleagues in high-SES schools in the extent to which they favor reduced use of high-CT activities for low-advantage students, such a result would highlight a problem in our nation's schools. Needed is a study that compares CTBA responses across groups of teachers who vary in the SES of the community in which they teach.

Another area of needed research involves comparisons of teachers who work in different settings (elementary education, secondary education, special education). The work reviewed in this chapter involved only secondary teachers. There is little research on elementary teachers, who comprise a large share the workforce in our nation's schools. Neither has research focused on special education teachers, who may have disproportionally frequent contact with low-advantage population. Might elementary, secondary, and special-education teachers differ in beliefs about CT?

Similarly, there remains little work comparing secondary teachers who teach different subjects. It's widely believed among secondary educators that teaching math is one thing, and teaching English is quite another. But there is no research exploring the extent to which these subject differences yield differences in belief s about CT.

To explore these possible differences, the CTBA could be administered to elementary teachers, special-education teachers, and secondary teachers in different subjects. Such an initiative could help to inform teacher-education practices by targeting belief-change initiatives where they are most needed.

Teachers' practices concerning classroom use of CT activities. It remains unclear the extent to which teachers' beliefs about CT are predictive of their actual classroom behavior. With teachers' beliefs about CT, only one type of error is likely: a teacher might espouse high-CT activities but not actually use them (a false positive). But it is unlikely that a teacher would downplay high-CT activities and then proceed to use them in the classroom, making a false negative improbable. So, when teachers express doubt that high-CT activities will be effective in a given situation (say, with low-advantage students), these activities are probably not in use in the classroom. That said, there remains a need for research on teachers' practices concerning use of high-CT activities. How do teachers actually use high-CT activities in schools?

Despite its evident urgency, this question remains unexplored in published theory and research. This research might well use a similar set of independent variables as the belief work discussed above, including community (high-SES, low-SES), teachers' gender, age, educational attainment, years of teaching experience, assignment (elementary education, secondary education, special education), and subject taught (for secondary teachers). But in this case the dependent variable, classroom use of high-CT activities, will need to be measured using classroom observations. Initially, an assessment scheme that measures the amount of CT in a lesson must be developed, perhaps one that in which classroom observers rate CT-use on a minute-to-minute basis using a 6-point scale (with low-CT on one end and high-CT on the other). Computing the mean for each observed lesson yields an overall CT score. To collect data, at least two raters should implement the assessment scheme by spending a significant amount of time (3-5 days, say) in each participating teacher's classroom—a labor-intensive effort. Inter-rater reliability must then be calculated, presumably using Cronbach's Alpha. A tuning process in classrooms or using videotape would assist in getting the raters to a suitably high level of agreement prior to data collection. Data collection is needed in both high-SES and low-SES communities.

Correlation of beliefs and practices concerning classroom use of high-CT activities. The correspondence of beliefs to behavior is among the hoariest issues in the social sciences, and research in education is no exception. At issue in this case is the extent to which teachers' beliefs about use of different kinds of classroom activities (as assessed by the CTBA) are associated with actual classroom practices. Correlations between CTBA scores and classroom-observation data can be calculated. Regression modeling might also be used, with classroom practices as the outcome measure and predictor variables including CTBA scores, community (high-SES, low-SES), teachers' gender, age, educational attainment, years of teaching experience, assignment (elementary education, secondary education, special education), and subject taught (for secondary teachers). Research as such examines the extent to which teachers' espoused beliefs are associated with their actual classroom practices, and also explores factors that may influence these associations.

Effect of beliefs and practices about use of CT activities on academic outcomes. In educational research, the bottom line is often the extent to which schooling results in valued outcomes, most (but not all) of which involve students' academic performance. At present, in research that purports to measure academic achievement, students' standardized test results are by far the most influential outcome variable. This situation is unlikely to change in the near future, so research might well determine the extent to which standardized test scores are predicted by teachers' beliefs and practices with respect to use of CT in the classroom. In this case, regression procedures could help to determine the extent to which CTBA scores, classroom-observation data, community type, and demographic variables (e.g., teaching experience, educational attainment) predict standardized test scores. There is evidence that low-advantage students can benefit from high-CT instruction (e.g., Pogrow, 1990; Zohar & Dori, 2003) but little that sheds light on the relationship between beliefs and achievement outcomes.

Such a study would examine the extent to which test scores are associated with teachers' beliefs and practices with respect to CT in the classroom. At the same time, outcome variables other the test scores can be considered, including students' grades, teacher-designed assessments, and assessments designed by researchers to tap particular performances of interest (e.g., the extent to which a pedagogy long on high-CT activities helps science students reason using the scientific method). Measures in the affective domain might also be useful, including perceived well-being in school, reported self-efficacy, and perceived rapport with the teacher.

Teachers' beliefs about assessment of high-CT activities. On the subject of teachers' beliefs about appropriate *assessment* of student work in high-CT activities, the literature is silent. The question remains unanswered: What is the nature and development of teachers' beliefs about assessment of student work in CT activities?

An analysis of students' SES advantages should be included. The findings summarized above speak to diminished expectations that teachers apparently have for low-advantage students, and these diminished expectations may obtain as well when it comes to assessing student work. If low-SES students are deemed not to be able to handle many high-CT activities, they may face low expectations in the few high-CT activities they receive.

Instrumentation is lacking in this area. There exists at present no survey, interview protocol, or other method for collecting data on teachers' beliefs about assessment of CT activities. Instrument development will precede research in this instance, and developing a new survey seems a prudent choice. Development of the survey will involve an item selection procedure informed at minimum by evaluation of face validity, factor analysis, and measurement of internal consistency reliability. Studies of the discriminant validity of the selected items are needed, especially to determine the extent to which the survey taps beliefs about assessment that differ from respondents' more general assessment views (i.e., beliefs about assessing student work in activities that are not necessarily rich in CT).

Teachers' classroom practices about assessment of high-CT activities. What do teachers' actually do in their classrooms to assess students' work in high-CT activities? With this strand in theory and research on CT unexplored, observational studies similar to those discussed above are needed. It starts with development of a coding scheme that observers use to score teachers' assessment practices. In this case, data collection will need to take place in two ways. The first occurs as students participate in high-CT activities; for example, in a debate activity, teachers need to assess students' performance during class in real time. The second takes place after the lesson has concluded—as teachers take stock of students' performance in the lesson, typically by grading their work (e.g., essays or projects). The research should be conducted in communities that vary in SES advantages, since this variable has proven useful in prior research.

This research should include a distinction between the disciplinary content a lesson entails and the CT it requires. It is possible that teachers focus more on the former than the latter, since content is easier to assess. For example, in an essay on the significance of the Magna Carta, assessing the relevant names, dates, and facts is more straightforward than assessing the quality of the essay's critical reasoning. It may prove useful to explore how teachers weigh content and CT in their grading.

Correlation of beliefs and practices with respect to teachers' assessment of CT activities. The question of the correlation of beliefs and practices applies to assessment of CT activities, of course. Do teachers assess students' work as they say they do? In this case, survey data tapping teachers' beliefs about assessment of CT activities will be compared with the classroom-practice data. As above, correlations can be computed between survey data and observation data. The latter can also serve as the outcome variable in a regression analysis in which the predictors include scores on the belief survey, community SES (high-SES, low-SES), gender, age, educational attainment, years of teaching experience, assignment (elementary, secondary, special education), and subject taught (for secondary teachers).

Effect of beliefs and practices about assessment of CT activities on academic outcomes. It is possible that teachers' beliefs and practices about the assessment of high-CT activities may account for some of the variance in students' standardized test scores (and/or other outcome variables). High-CT activities that are skillfully assessed may afford students feedback that helps develop their thinking skills and knowledge base. If so, research may unearth a positive association between the quality of teachers' CT assessments and academic outcomes (if likely a small one, considering how many variables account for the variance in test scores). Accordingly, studies are needed that explore how teachers' beliefs and practices are associated with measures of academic achievement. Here the research design calls for measures of teachers' beliefs (presumably a new survey instrument), measures of teachers' practices (presumably an observational protocol), and other variables (e.g., community SES, demographic variables) to serve as predictors in a regression analysis predicting achievement measures.

In closing, a more complete picture of CT in schools requires a great deal more theory and research than is currently present in the literature. Among the multiple strands of work in this area, only one includes a significant body of literature, and even that strand has gaps. Notably, there is no literature devoted to teachers' beliefs and practices concerning assessment of CT activities. This seems a major blind spot. Further development of theory and research on CT in schools has promise to inform teacher-education practices that promote more equitable and effective use of CT in schools.

APPENDIX

The Critical Thinking Belief Appraisal

Below are descriptions of educational activities–parts of a classroom lesson. Please rate the educational effectiveness of each activity for the learners indicated by circling the appropriate number. There are no correct or incorrect answers. Assume that each activity is well suited to the age level of the learners.

Definitions:

Ability—the learners' capacity for intellectual or academic achievement when dealing with the specific topic the class is studying.

Prior knowledge—how much the learners know about the specific topic the class is studying <u>before</u> they participate in the activity indicated.

Motivation—how much interest and attention learners typically show when dealing with the specific topic the class is studying.

1. An English class is studying the sonnet, a form of English poetry. The teacher explains its history and structure, lists prominent sonnet writers, and asks individual students to read aloud several classic sonnets. (Low-CT)
    To what extent would this activity be effective for …

    … **low**-ability learners? (circle one)

1	2	3	4	5	6
highly ineffective				highly effective	

    … learners with a **low** level of prior knowledge of the topic? (circle one)

1	2	3	4	5	6
highly ineffective				highly effective	

    … learners with **high** motivation? (circle one)

1	2	3	4	5	6
highly ineffective				highly effective	

2. A social-studies class is studying the industrial revolution. The teacher provides students with a list of inventions, explains the impact of these inventions during this period, and describes how they continue to influence the modern world. (Low-CT)
    To what extent would this activity be effective for…

    … **low**-ability learners? (circle one)

1	2	3	4	5	6
highly ineffective				highly effective	

… learners with a **low** level of prior knowledge of the topic? (circle one)

1	2	3	4	5	6
highly ineffective				highly effective	

…learners with **low** motivation? (circle one)

1	2	3	4	5	6
highly ineffective				highly effective	

3. A mathematics class is studying single-variable algebra. The teacher poses a problem requiring single-variable algebra, asks students to invent a way to write down the problem and then to compare their notations to the algebraic one written on the board. (High-CT)
    To what extent would this activity be effective for …

    … **high**-ability learners? (circle one)

1	2	3	4	5	6
highly ineffective				highly effective	

    … learners with a **low** level of prior knowledge of the topic? (circle one)

1	2	3	4	5	6
highly ineffective				highly effective	

    … learners with **low** motivation? (circle one)

1	2	3	4	5	6
highly ineffective				highly effective	

4. An Italian class is studying the vocabulary involved in ordering food in a restaurant. The teacher writes several new words on the board, defines them, asks students to repeat them, and provides a handout on which students add them to sample sentences. (Low-CT)
    To what extent would this activity be effective for …

... **high**-ability learners? (circle one)

1	2	3	4	5	6

highly ineffective   highly effective

... learners with a **high** level of prior knowledge of the topic? (circle one)

1	2	3	4	5	6

highly ineffective   highly effective

... learners with **low** motivation? (circle one)

1	2	3	4	5	6

highly ineffective   highly effective

5. A science class is studying the sun. The teacher asks students to write down several ways in which the sun influences everyday life and then to predict what would happen if the sun stopped shining. (High-CT)
    To what extent would this activity be effective for ...

    ... **low**-ability learners? (circle one)

1	2	3	4	5	6

highly ineffective   highly effective

    ... learners with a **high** level of prior knowledge of the topic? (circle one)

1	2	3	4	5	6

highly ineffective   highly effective

    ... learners with **high** motivation? (circle one)

6. An English class is studying *For Whom the Bell Tolls* by Earnest Hemingway. The teacher overviews Hemingway's life and work, explains the history and significance of the novel, and describes Hemingway's influence on contemporary authors. (Low-CT)
    To what extent would this activity be effective for ...

… **low**-ability learners? (circle one)

1	2	3	4	5	6
highly ineffective				highly effective	

… learners with a **low** level of prior knowledge of the topic? (circle one)

1	2	3	4	5	6
highly ineffective				highly effective	

… learners with **low** motivation? (circle one)

1	2	3	4	5	6
highly ineffective				highly effective	

7. A social-studies class is studying the Treaty of Versailles signed at the end of World War I. The teacher assigns students to write "letters from the future" to President Wilson arguing why the United States should or should not support the treaty. (High-CT)
    To what extent would this activity be effective for …

… **high**-ability learners? (circle one)

1	2	3	4	5	6
highly ineffective				highly effective	

… learners with a **high** level of prior knowledge of the topic? (circle one)

1	2	3	4	5	6
highly ineffective				highly effective	

… learners with **high** motivation? (circle one)

1	2	3	4	5	6
highly ineffective				highly effective	

8. A mathematics class is studying how to calculate the area of a triangle. The teacher assigns students to evaluate several possible for-

mulas for calculating the area, determine which formula is the correct one, and explain why they answered as they did. (High-CT) To what extent would this activity be effective for ...

... **low**-ability learners? (circle one)

1	2	3	4	5	6
highly ineffective				highly effective	

... learners with a **low** level of prior knowledge of the topic? (circle one)

1	2	3	4	5	6
highly ineffective				highly effective	

... learners with **high** motivation? (circle one)

1	2	3	4	5	6
highly ineffective				highly effective	

9. A Spanish class is studying the conjugation of verbs in the preterit, a form of past tense. The teacher provides a handout explaining the conjugation rules, conjugates several sample verbs on the blackboard, and then gives students a handout to practice them. (Low-CT)
    To what extent would this activity be effective for...

... **high**-ability learners? (circle one)

1	2	3	4	5	6
highly ineffective				highly effective	

... learners with a **high** level of prior knowledge of the topic? (circle one)

1	2	3	4	5	6
highly ineffective				highly effective	

... learners with **high** motivation? (circle one)

1	2	3	4	5	6
highly ineffective				highly effective	

10. An English class is studying Jack London's short story *To Build a Fire*. The teacher asks students to read all but the last section and then write their own versions of the final section. (High-CT)
To what extent would this activity be effective for ...

   ... **high**-ability learners? (circle one)

1	2	3	4	5	6
highly ineffective				highly effective	

   ... learners with a **high** level of prior knowledge of the topic? (circle one)

1	2	3	4	5	6
highly ineffective				highly effective	

   ... learners with **low** motivation? (circle one)

1	2	3	4	5	6
highly ineffective				highly effective	

11. A French class is studying adjectives used to describe clothing. The teacher provides a handout featuring advertising photos with captions that include the adjectives, and then gives a second handout with intentionally incorrect captions, asking students to make corrections. (High-CT)
To what extent would this activity be effective for ...

   ... **low**-ability learners? (circle one)

1	2	3	4	5	6
highly ineffective				highly effective	

... learners with a **low** level of prior knowledge of the topic? (circle one)

1	2	3	4	5	6
highly ineffective				highly effective	

... learners with **low** motivation? (circle one)

1	2	3	4	5	6
highly ineffective				highly effective	

12. A mathematics class is studying how to convert fractions to decimals. The teacher explains how to make this conversion, completes sample problems using an overhead projector, and then gives an in-class assignment in which students solve similar problems. (Low-CT)

To what extent would this activity be effective for ...

... **high**-ability learners? (circle one)

1	2	3	4	5	6
highly ineffective				highly effective	

... learners with a **high** level of prior knowledge of the topic? (circle one)

1	2	3	4	5	6
highly ineffective				highly effective	

... learners with **high** motivation? (circle one)

1	2	3	4	5	6
highly ineffective				highly effective	

REFERENCES

Archer, J., & McCarthy, B. (1988). Personal biases in student assessment. *Educational Research, 30,* 142-145.

Barton, P. (2004). Why does the gap persist? *Educational Leadership, 62,* 8-13.

Bereiter, C., & Scardamalia, M. (1993). *Surpassing ourselves: An inquiry into the nature and implications of expertise.* New York, NY: Open Court.

Brown, A., & Campione, J. (1990). Communities of learning and thinking, or a context by any other name. In D. Kuhn, (Ed.), Developmental perspectives on teaching and learning thinking skills. *Contributions to Child Development* (Vol. 21, pp. 108-126). Basel, Switzerland: Karger.

Browne, M., & Keeley, K. (2001*). Asking the right questions: A guide to critical thinking* (6th ed.). Upper Saddle River, NJ: Merrill/Prentice Hall.

Cacioppo, J., & Petty, R. (1982). The need for cognition. *Journal of Personality and Social Psychology, 42*, 116-131.

Cacioppo, J. T., Petty, R. E. Feinstein, J. A., & Jarvis, W. B. (1996). Dispositional differences in cognitive motivation: The life and times of individuals varying in need for cognition. *Psychological Bulletin, 119*, 197-253.

Cohen, J. (1988). *Statistical power analysis for the behavioral sciences* (2nd ed.). Hillsdale, NJ: Erlbaum.

Crowne, D., & Marlow, D. (1964). *The approval motive.* New York, NY: Wiley.

Dweck, C. (1986). Motivational processes affecting learning. *American Psychologist, 41*, 1040-1048.

Ennis, R. (1987). A taxonomy of critical-thinking dispositions and abilities. In J. Baron & R. Sternberg (Eds.), *Teaching thinking skills: Theory and practice* (pp. 9-26). New York, NY: Freeman.

Facione, P., Facione, N., & Giancarlo, C. (2000). *The California critical thinking skills test.* Millbrae, CA: California Academic Press.

Fang, Z. (1996). A review of research on teacher beliefs and practices. *Educational Research, 38*, 47-65.

Givvin, K. B., Stipek, D. J., Salmon, J. M., & MacGyvers, V. L. (2001). In the eyes of the beholder: Students' and teachers' judgments of students' motivation. *Teaching and Teacher Education, 17*, 321-331.

Halpern, D. (2003). *Thought and knowledge* (4th ed.). Mahwah, NJ: Erlbaum.

Henderson, J. (2001). (3rd Ed.). *Reflective teaching: Professional artistry through inquiry.* Upper Saddle River, NJ: Merrill/Prentice Hall.

Hirsch, E.D. (1996). *The schools we need and why we don't have them.* New York, NY: Doubleday.

King, P. M., & Kitchener, K. S. (1994). *Developing reflective judgment.* San Francisco, CA: Jossey-Bass.

Kozol, J. (1991). *Savage inequalities.* New York, NY: Crown.

Kuhn, D. (2005). *Education for thinking.* Cambridge, MA: Harvard University Press.

Lambert, N., & McCombs. B. (Eds.). (1998). *How learners learn: reforming schools through learner-centered instruction.* Washington DC: American Psychological Association.

Lee, V., & Brukam, D. (2002). *Inequality at the starting gate: Social background differences in achievement as children begin school.* Washington, DC: Economic Policy Institute.

Madon, S., Jussim, L., Keiper, S., Eccles, J., Smith, A., & Paolumbo, P. (1998). The accuracy and power of sex, social class, and ethnic stereotypes: A naturalistic study in person perception. *Personality and Social Psychology Bulletin, 24*, 1304-1318.

Moje, E. B., & Wade, S. E. (1997). What case discussions reveal about teacher thinking. *Teaching and Teacher Education, 13*, 691-712.

O'Tuel, F., & Bullard, R. (1993). *Developing higher-order thinking in the content areas.* Pacific Grove, CA: Critical Thinking Books and Software.

Perkins, D. N., Jay, E., & Tishman, S. (1993). New conceptions of thinking: From ontology to education. *Educational Psychologist, 28,* 67-85.

Pintrich, P., & Schunk, D. (1996). *Motivation in education.* Upper Saddle River, NJ: Prentice Hall.

Pogrow, S. (1990). Challenging at-risk learners: findings from the HOTS program. *Phi Delta Kappan, 71,* 389-397.

Pogrow, S. (1994). Helping learners who "just don't understand." *Educational Leadership, 52,* 62-66.

Pogrow, S. (2006). Restructuring high-poverty elementary schools for success: A description of the high-perform school design. *Phi Delta Kappan, 88,* 223-229.

Raths, L., Wasserman, S., Jonas, A., & Rothstein, A. (1986). *Teaching for thinking.* New York, NY: Teachers College Press.

Raudenbush, S. W., Rowan, B., & Cheong, Y. F. (2003). Higher order instructional goals in secondary schools: Class, teacher, and school influences. *American Educational Research Journal, 30,* 523-553

Resnick, L. (1987). *Education and learning to think.* Washington DC: National Academy Press.

Tollefson, N. (2000). Classroom applications of cognitive theories of motivation. *Educational Psychology Review, 12,* 63-83.

Torff, B. (2003). Developmental changes in teachers' use of higher-order thinking and content knowledge. *Journal of Educational Psychology, 95,* 563-569.

Torff, B. (2005). Developmental changes in teachers' beliefs about critical-thinking activities. *Journal of Educational Psychology, 97,* 13-22.

Torff, B. (2006). Expert teachers' beliefs about critical-thinking activities. *Teacher Education Quarterly, 33,* 37-52.

Torff, B., & Sessions, D. (2006). Issues influencing teachers' beliefs about use of critical-thinking activities with low-advantage learners. *Teacher Education Quarterly, 33,* 77-92.

Torff, B., & Warburton, E. (2005). Assessment of teachers' beliefs about classroom use of critical-thinking activities. *Educational and Psychological Measurement, 65,* 155-179.

Warburton, E. C., & Torff, B. (2005). The effect of perceived learner advantages on teachers' beliefs about critical-thinking activities. *Journal of Teacher Education, 56,* 24-33.

Zohar, A., & Dori, J. (2003). Higher order thinking and low-achieving students: Are they mutually exclusive? *The Journal of the Learning Sciences, 12,* 145-182.

Zohar, A., Degani, A., & Vaakin, E. (2001). Teachers' beliefs about low-achieving students and higher-order thinking. *Teaching and Teacher Education, 17,* 469-485.

CHAPTER 14

ALIGNED BY DESIGN

A Process for Systematic Alignment of Assessments to Educational Domains

William D. Schafer

INTRODUCTION

Alignment of tests to content specifications has been difficult and often elusive, as well as expensive for many states and the approaches taken to achieve it have not always been either effective or helpful to education activities in the state. Here we review the dimensions of alignment and discuss some educational implications of alignment activities.

The chapter culminates in recommendations for assessment development designed to accomplish two major goals. The first goal is that the assessments arise from carefully considered content specifications. That is, they are aligned with the stated curriculum. The second goal is that the content specifications are part of a process that may be used efficiently and effectively by both test developers in creating new forms and by teachers and other educators to promote student learning over those explicit content domains. Our overarching goal is to enable curriculum,

Assessment of Higher Order Thinking Skills, pp. 395–418
Copyright © 2011 by Information Age Publishing
All rights of reproduction in any form reserved.

instruction, and assessment to be aligned with each other, with curriculum playing the dominant role, so that every student is learning what they should be learning and is tested over that same content.

IMPORTANCE OF ALIGNMENT

Of the three domains of educational outcomes, affective (attitudes and beliefs), cognitive (intellectual understandings and skills), and psychomotor (physical skills), accountability assessments have traditionally been restricted to the cognitive domain. Although many feel schools should develop psychomotor skills, such as musical and sports outcomes, and perhaps fewer feel schools should develop positive attitudes and habits that are valued by society, such as punctuality and love of country, virtually all believe that intellectual understandings and skills are proper outcomes of schooling. School accountability assessments therefore have been exclusively cognitive in virtually all statewide programs.

Cognitive outcomes are traditionally separated along disciplinary or content-based lines. There are assessments of language arts, math, science, and social studies for example. These are sometimes divided into subcontents such as reading and writing for language arts; algebra, geometry, and statistics for math; biology, chemistry, physics, and Earth studies for science; and history, economics, and government for social studies. Each of these may be further subdivided as well, and an assessment may be written to cover material at any of these degrees of generalization in any of these contents, and at any particular grade level.

Assessment may also be performed for several purposes. For accountability assessments, the most common foci are students and schools. Virtually everyone feels that schools should be held accountable for the intellectual growth of their students; however that may be defined operationally. Teachers are commonly asked to react with programmatic adjustments when the results are less than satisfactory, and so it is also reasonable to consider teachers as an additional focus of school accountability, whether explicitly (e.g., in a merit pay context) or implicitly. Often high stakes exist for students, such as marking, promotion from grade to grade or, more and more commonly, decisions about graduation status for the granting of a diploma.

Whatever the focus, fairness demands that assessments with stakes cover explicit domains of cognitive outcomes. No matter who is held accountable (teachers, students, or others), if they do not understand the content the assessment will cover, they cannot work very effectively toward improvements in student achievement or in the school activities that promote it. The content that may appear on the assessment, often called its domain (even though that term has been used more broadly at the beginning of this section), should therefore be clarified. How that may be done is discussed within the topic of the next section.

CHARACTERISTICS OF ALIGNMENT

The results of an assessment will be used to make inferences about the achievement of the examinees over the assessment's domain. If the use of the assessment to make those inferences can be justified, then the inferences are said to be valid. One sort of evidence that can be used to justify test use is the degree to which the assessment covers the content that is contained within the domain, and that is the fundamental question in alignment.

Any assessment consists of a collection of tasks, or prompts, or items given to examinees, usually students. For a content domain, though, the items are only a sample of those that could be asked, which is conceptually an infinite universe of items. The collection of items on a test may be a good (i.e., representative) sample of the domain, or it may not. The degree to which the sample is representative is called alignment.

Alignment can only be judged when the domain of the assessment is specified. That specification is most often accomplished using an enumeration of the elements of the domain, sometimes called outcomes (different states use different terms). An example of an outcome might be "Carry out basic arithmetic operations." Clearly, that is a very broad statement. Outcomes are usually elaborated with lists of indicators (again, different states use different terms), such as "Add numbers." And indicators are often clarified using assessment limits (Schafer & Moody, 2004), such as "Any pair of positive, whole numbers with a sum less than 199 may be presented."

Through a careful description of the domain through assessment limits within indicators within outcomes, it may be possible for the teacher and student to understand exactly what is "fair game" for the assessment. But it is still necessary to be able to compare the assessment with the domain to ensure that the items do not overly represent the domain in some areas and underrepresent it in others. In order to make that comparison, a methodology of alignment has been developed. The next section describes the broad nature of the alignment and the following section describes some of the specifics.

DIMENSIONS OF ALIGNMENT

Like educational objectives, test items ask students to do something with something. Every item has these two characteristics, one a noun and the other a verb (Anderson & Krathwohl, 2001). For example, the item, "Add

5 and 8" has two numbers as the elements and addition as the task. The elements are called the content and the task is called the process, or cognition that the examinee is asked to apply to the content.

One often hears the term, "standards" in education. It is important to clarify a distinction between two uses of that term, content standards and achievement (sometimes called performance) standards. The term content standards, refers to the domain over which instruction (and hopefully testing) takes place. Achievement standards are degrees of attainment of the objectives within the content standards; for example, a content standard might be to use the Pythagorean theorem and an achievement standard might be to recognize when the theorem might and might not be useful. There is an active literature in the assessment field that investigates how to set achievement standards for a given assessment or assessment program (see Cizek, 2001). While achievement standards must be set in order to establish a basis for establishing performance levels, such as basic, proficient, and advanced, we are here focusing on the content standards and ignoring achievement standards.

Some states, notably Massachusetts, describe their assessed content domains in both these terms. Most states, however, list their domains using content, primarily, with little attention to cognition. We will advocate here a system that makes explicit both content and cognition and will result in aligned assessments along with documentation for that alignment. First, we will discuss the two dimensions separately.

Content

The content to be included in the domain of a test is determined based on disciplinary and pedagogic concerns. Often these are developed from statements of national (or international) agencies, such as the National Council of Teachers of English (see http://www.ncte.org/standards), The National Council of Teachers of Mathematics (see http://standards.nctm.org/document/), The National Science Teachers Association (see http://scienceanchors.nsta.org/), or National Council for the Social Studies (http://www.socialstudies.org/). Another source for content standards is the National Assessment of Educational Progress (NAEP; see http://nces.ed.gov/nationsreportcard/ for links to their various content frameworks), which tests state-by-state in Grades 4, 8, and 12.

While the content elements differ across disciplines, there are categories into which they fall. These are often called types of knowledge. One analysis (Anderson & Krathwohl, 2001) discusses three types: factual knowledge (vocabulary, concepts, and other basic elements in the disciplines), conceptual knowledge (interrelationships between factual knowledge elements), and procedural knowledge (skills, including how and when to use them). Another type is also discussed, called metacognitive knowledge, but because it is less clear whether or how metacognitive knowledge differs from discipline to discipline (Anderson & Krathwohl, 2001), we will not pursue that concept further. This is not to minimize the importance of metacognition. Indeed, we should not be surprised if metacognition eventually proves to be the key to a future in which students possess procedural knowledge that they can apply to problems requiring higher thinking skills across disciplines.

There is often a tension between two perspectives in specifying the domain of a test. On the one hand, many educators wish to avoid specifications that limit what a teacher (or district curriculum specialist) may instruct. Proponents of this perspective typically try to write open-ended standards that specify areas of content through examples and generally eschew assessment limits (see below). This orientation appears to be motivated by the belief that only what is in the assessment domain will be taught.

The opposite perspective, and the one that is advocated here, holds that a clear understanding of the domain of the test is useful to all educators in that it defines exactly what is fair for the assessment to include. Teachers will understand the minimum content that must be delivered and test writers will understand the limits of what they may place on the assessment. To continue with the earlier Pythagorean Theorem example, educators might decide that only integer solutions (e.g., 3-4-5 or 5-12-13) may appear in real-world applications on the test. This orientation is motivated in part by the belief that a clear goal is necessary in order for teachers to provide instruction that prepares their students to meet it, and that instruction beyond that goal is the prerogative of the teacher (or school or district curriculum specialist). Without the clarity provided by assessment limits that actually limit, teachers (and schools and district curriculum specialists) are left guessing about what may or may not appear; some will guess right and some will guess wrong, and those guesses become an irrelevant source of differences between the students, teachers, and schools whose results are used to make what are then less valid judgments about success on the basis of test scores.

In the final analysis, we advocate clear assessment limits as elaborations of the indicators (within outcomes) in the domain of the test. For some examples and links to state documents specifying assessment limits, especially for high school assessments in Maryland (see Schafer & Moody (2004). An example is given here of assessment limits from Maryland's high school assessment in algebra and data analysis for the indicator:

The student will interpret data and/or make predictions by finding and using a line of best fit and by using a given curve of best fit. The

assessment limits (see http://mdk12.org/assessments/high_school/clg/
algebra_data_analysis.html) are:

- Items should include a definition of the data and what it represents.
- Data will be given when a line of best fit is required.
- Equation or graph will be given when a curve of best fit is required.

Cognition

Cognition refers to thinking skills that students are engaged in as they
learn and are asked to engage in as they are assessed. The verb, as com-
panion to a noun in an educational task, is the task's cognitive element.

While content differs from discipline to discipline, cognition in general
does not. The same thinking skills are manifest in reading as in math as in
science, and all other disciplines (Bloom, Engelhart, Furst, Hill, & Krathwohl, 1956). Because of this principle, several investigators have developed taxonomies of cognition. The most widely know of these is that of
Bloom et al. (1956). There are six major categories in the Bloom et al.
taxonomy: knowledge, comprehension, application, analysis, synthesis,
and evaluation; they are ordered by degree of complexity.

There is a common misperception among many educators that tasks
that tap more complex cognitive levels are more difficult for students
than less complex tasks. However, easy, moderate, or difficult items may
be written for any level of cognitive functioning. Indeed, it is a useful
exercise for educators to attempt to write at all the three levels of difficulty, items for each of the cognitive processes. One way to do that is to
consider what the criteria are that should be represented in a rubric, and
then to write to elicit those characteristics. For example, if you want students to analyze, you could write an item that asks them to define the elements they use, discuss why they are important, and explain their
interrelationships. If you want students to evaluate, you could write an
item that asks them to explain their criteria, describe why those criteria
are important, and apply them. Analysis is of moderate complexity in the
taxonomy, and evaluation is at the highest, yet neither of these activities
seems more difficult inherently than the other. Indeed, students are capable of all levels of cognition (a 4-year old can justify why he or she should
be allowed to stay up another half-hour, and that's evaluation); a goal of a
teacher is to get them to think at all levels using the new content.

Anderson and Krathwohl (2001) have developed a revision of the
Bloom et al. (1956) taxonomy that alters the category names and to some
extent their meaning, but more importantly, that focuses on 19 subcategories, each of which has an implication for teaching as well as for testing.

That is, what a teacher does to help a student engage in one of the cognitive subcategories and what an item writer does to elicit the engagement, differ in explicit ways from subcategory to subcategory. This is a highly desirable property for a taxonomy to have because it helps make instruction and assessment mesh with each other. It could also facilitate the development of metacognitive tools that differ across the subcategories. Generating support for the ability of the Anderson and Krathwohl (2001) taxonomy to stand up to these claims would be a valuable line of research in education.

The six Anderson and Krathwohl (2001) categories of cognitive processes are remembering (retrieving knowledge from memory), understanding (constructing meaning), applying (using a procedure), analyzing (determining how parts form a whole), evaluating (making judgments using criteria), and creating (forming a new whole). It should be remembered, though, that the nineteen cognitive processes, themselves, are more important than the categories of them as they are the basis for how teachers teach and how test authors write.

Anderson and Krathwohl (2001) also discussed a relationship between content and cognition. They suggest that a loose association exists between the processes of remembering and understanding with the factual and conceptual types of knowledge. Similarly, the cognitive category of applying is loosely associated with procedural knowledge.

In virtually any statewide description of the outcomes and indicators in any of the disciplines at any grade level, one finds both content elements and process elements. There are several sources that are used for the content elements, notably national statements of standards and statewide educator (and perhaps other stakeholder) committees. The same sources are often used for the cognitive process elements, but one cannot help in looking at these descriptions to be struck by a comparative lack of careful analysis of the process dimension. Different terminology is used in different disciplines (making cross-discipline applications of cognitive skills difficult if not impossible for teachers) and within-disciplines, the verbs associated with content elements appear often to be there for convenience and not to imply that *un*stated processes are *not* to be part of the domain. We believe it is clear that cognition does not receive the same careful and informed attention that the content elements do.

Unfortunately, in assessing alignment, the levels of cognition implied by the state's content standards are driving characteristics. This is not surprising considering that they are the only available definitions of each state's curriculum, as it is to be translated into statewide assessments. The recommended process for state assessment development below will include a way for states to be more systematic about their content domain elements, and especially about their cognitive process domain elements, in how assessment domains are developed and disseminated.

ASSESSMENT OF ALIGNMENT

Alignment between the assessment domain (curriculum standards) and a test is normally carried out for a particular form of the test (e.g., the collection of items on a particular reading test given at the end of a particular school year). Since statewide tests are developed using field-test items as well as operational items, and the field-test items are evaluated for entry into the bank of items for eventual use in the testing program, the one-form application of alignment methodology must be viewed as an evaluation of a sample of the test forms that are developed over time. Given the current status of alignment evaluation in most states, then, alignment is implied but not formally evaluated unless it is carried out every year on every form, a very expensive undertaking. We will describe here the process usually used for evaluating alignment for the operational items, those that are used for a student's score on a single test form. Later we will propose an alternative that is more efficient than form-by-form evaluation and is also more effective in that its application can guarantee aligned forms every time, during test development, rather than using after-the-fact alignment methodology.

There are four primary aspects of alignment that are considered in a typical study (Webb, 2005). These are categorical concurrence, depth of knowledge consistency, range of knowledge correspondence, and balance of representation. Each of these is amplified next.

We note in passing that sometimes another characteristic is considered: source of challenge (Webb, 2005). This is an item-level characteristic rather than a test-level characteristic and has to do with whether the item taps the academic content that was intended as opposed to irrelevant constructs such as demographics (i.e., item bias), irrelevant demand characteristics (e.g., too much reading in a math item), or cues in the item that lead to (or away from) the answer (e.g., grammatical cues). Since these are characteristics of a flawed item rather than a flawed test, we will not consider it further here.

An alignment study of an existing test form begins with a review of the statewide content standards along with their indicators, organized into outcomes. The terminology varies considerably from state-to-state. Webb (2002), for example, uses the term standard where we are using outcome and uses objective where we are using indicator. The level of cognition implied by the statement of each indicator is also noted. Then the items are reviewed and allocated to indicators by content, and the level of cognition tapped by each item is also noted. These reviews are conducted by committees of educators who are trained as part of the study to make the judgments and their work is the raw data from which the alignment dimensions are evaluated.

Categorical Concurrence

Categorical concurrence assesses whether there are sufficient items on the assessment to support all subscales (subscales are content subdivisions for which scores are reported). We will assume that all outcomes in a content area are represented in subscales. In general, there must be at least six items for each subscale (Webb, 2005). If the state does not report subscores, then this analysis is performed for the outcomes represented, which is reasonable since if subscores were developed, they would most likely be presented (or reported) at the outcome level. So the criterion for categorical concurrence is at least six items per outcome.

Depth of Knowledge Consistency

Depth of knowledge consistency has to do with the match between the cognitive demand of the items and of the indicators they are measuring. Webb (2005) describes four levels of cognitive demand:

- Level 1 (recall). Recalling information and carrying out simple procedures.
- Level 2 (skill/concept). Some thinking beyond a simple, habitual response.
- Level 3 (strategic thinking). Reasoning, planning, drawing conclusions, and using concepts and evidence.
- Level 4 (extended thinking). Complex processing using multiple concepts.

The criterion of depth of knowledge consistency is met when at least half the items associated with an indicator are at or above the cognitive level of the indicator, both cognitive level assignments coming from the committee judgments.

Range of Knowledge Correspondence

The range of knowledge correspondence criterion is satisfied if for every outcome, there is at least one item associated with at least half of the indicators.

Balance of Representation

The balance of representation criterion evaluates the even-ness of coverage of the indicators for those that are represented within the outcomes.

Webb (2002) presents an index to assess balance of representation. Here, the index is modified to describe balance within each outcome separately.

$$\text{Balance Index} = 1 - \frac{\sum_{i=1}^{\wedge} \left| \frac{1}{k} - \frac{I_j}{N} \right|}{2}$$

$K=$ the number of indicators (with at least one item) for an outcome
$I_j =$ the number of items for indicator j
$N =$ the total number of items measuring the outcome

Webb recommended that an outcome with a Balance Index of .7 or greater is said to meet the criterion, and an outcome with a value less than .7 is said not to meet the criterion.

Evaluating Alignment

Alignment is normally evaluated measure-by-measure. The system of criteria in Table 14.1 is proposed as a way to associate a verbal statement about the alignment of a test form (or blueprint) with each of the measures.

IMPORTANCE OF ALIGNMENT

Alignment constitutes important evidence about the validity of inferences made on the basis of scores from an achievement test. In order to infer that students with higher scores have achieved more than other students, it is necessary to document that the test covers the achievement domain. That issue is precisely what is considered in evaluation of alignment. Indeed, it can be argued that for achievement tests, alignment evidence of validity is the most important type [other types of evidence are also used for statewide achievement test; see Schafer, Wang, & Wang (2009) for a study of the nature of validity evidence used in by the U.S. Department of Education in the peer review process].

Table 14.1.   Overall Alignment Conclusions for Alignment Measures

| | Alignment Measure | | | |
Overall Alignment Conclusion	Balance of Representation	Range of Knowledge	Categorical Concurrence	Depth of Knowledge
Fully Met	100% of the outcomes meet the alignment criterion			100% of indicators meet
Substantially Met	90-99% of the outcomes meet the alignment criterion			75-99% of indicators meet
Mostly Met	80-89% of the outcomes meet the alignment criterion			50-74% of indicators meet
Partially Met	70-79% of the outcomes meet the alignment criterion			25-49% of indicators meet
Not Met	Less than 70% of the outcomes meet the alignment criterion			< 25% of indicators meet

There are also educationally important reasons that argue for alignment beyond justification of the tests, themselves. Chief among them is the goal of assessment-inspired instruction, which cannot be achieved without clear communication of assessment domains. We will consider these topics next.

Assessment Inspired Instruction

There is an assumption implicit in statewide assessment programs (and other policy-driven testing) that educators will be motivated to be able to document high achievement using the results. This very reasonable assumption implies that teachers will strive to educate their students over the domains of the assessments.

Although curricula are intended to communicate the content that is to be taught, they are often either vague, overambitious or both, and are thus uninformative about the precise nature of the assessment domain. That leaves teachers and other educators guessing about what the tests will cover; they may want to instruct students over appropriate assessment domain(s), but do not know exactly what they are.

Communication of Assessment Domains

We agree with Schafer and Moody (2004), who argue for public com-munication of assessment domains. This does not mean that test items should be publicly available (except after they may have been released, of course). Rehearsing test items before the test would skew the sampling of the items away from representing assessment domains fairly; one could not infer that student performance would be consistent across different samples of items (i.e., different forms of the test). But as long as the test forms are built to specifications that are consistent from form-to-form, it is entirely reasonable and, we argue, desirable to make those specifica-tions available to all.

Some disagree with this position. Their argument seems fundamentally to be that complete specification of the domain of an assessment will nar-row instruction away from the broad curriculum to the test domain. We counter with four arguments.

First, we feel the narrowing of the curriculum may in some cases be desirable. Especially when curriculum is overbroad, it will be narrowed, anyway. The more important issue is to make the narrowing (expressed as the domain of the assessment) consistent with that which is most valuable to teach. The process of opening test domains allows more input into decisions about value of content elements (and other features, such as cognitive processes), from educators, parents, and other stakeholders. This may be a messy enterprise, but engaging in it will produce a more justified product in the end.

Second, fairness argues that teachers and their students should have an equal chance to document success. But if teachers are guessing about the coverage of an assessment, neither they nor their students are being treated fairly. Different teachers when faced with ambiguity will select content differently, and the test results will in part reflect those choices, confounding them with student achievement.

Third, only when assessment domains are visible will educators be able to capitalize on the motivation that assessments produce. Teachers can help their students reach learning targets only when the targets are understood (i.e., visible) and indeed, can discuss with their students expectations of them as communicated by the standards.

Fourth, instruction can always go beyond the assessment domains, if appropriate. That could happen by design, as when a district might broaden its own curriculum beyond the state's assessment domains, and perhaps clarify its additional expectations using its own assessments, with their own outcomes, indicators, and assessment limits. Or, a teacher might provide instruction in additional areas for his or her own class. These curricular enhancements are reasonable, especially for students who can easily master the state's assessment domains. But they should be done with a full understanding of the differences between the enhancements and the state's expectations. If the state's expectations are not sufficient for its students, the appropriate response would be to make them sufficient as opposed to hide them from public scrutiny.

ASSESSMENT BLUEPRINT

What characteristics about an assessment domain should be communicated to the public? Remembering that every item must ask a student to do something with something, certainly content and cognition are important. The relative emphases of the content and cognition subdivisions are also important. Teachers will find it helpful to know the formats that will be used, such as selected-response (SR; e.g., multiple-choice) and constructed-response (CR; e.g., essay) and there is no good reason to withhold that information. Our example blueprint to appear later will not have item types, as they are idiosyncratic to states, but they could easily be added using codes within the cells.

These features of a test, its content/cognition coverage and its format(s), are often presented in blueprints useful for test construction. Many states either already express test blueprints using these dimensions or are moving in that direction. We will discuss the content and cognition dimensions below and present a format that can be adapted by a state for internal use as well as dissemination to the public.

We should comment first, though, on a dimension that would be valuable in test construction but does not need to be communicated to the public. That dimension is item difficulty, an empirical determination (measurable as the item's mean across examinees, but also often expressed as the location on a student achievement scale where some proportion of the examinees would answer the item correctly for an SR item or achieve a certain score on a CR item). Easy or difficult items can be written for any content/cognition combination and a test development plan should specify a balance of difficulty across the combinations so that the test has appropriate coverage of domain subdivisions for students of all achievement levels.

Example of a Test Blueprint

Table 14.2 presents an example of a test blueprint. This example is taken from a state's content standards [at the indicator level, which included verbs (what students were to do) as well as nouns (what the students were to do it with)] along with the state's draft test specifications. We will comment on features of this example below.

Content Dimension

The content dimension is in the left most column in Table 14.2. Note the indicators are organized into four strands, which is a synonym for outcomes in our terminology. The state planned for the ability to report subscores for each of these strands, so that there are to be five scores reported, four strand scores and an overall score.

Many of the indicators differed only in the verbs. In those cases, we collapsed across verbs and showed the differences in the columns (discussed below).

A state might find it a useful exercise to review the types of knowledge as described by Anderson and Krathwohl (2001) with committees of educators and other stakeholders. These groups could then evaluate the content components of the indicators to make sure all factual, conceptual, and procedural elements that should be represented are there. Developing recommendations about assessment limits would be a helpful goal of these discussions, as well. The objective of the process should be to generate an organized (by strands and substrands) list of content elements to be included across the indicators that has legitimacy in the state (legitimacy is normally established through a broad-based process that culminates in state board or other authority approval).

Once the blueprint is developed, it may be verified by an independent agency to ensure that it fairly represents the content and cognition that are consistent with the state's content standards. This step need be done only once. Although it is normally done each time an alignment study is undertaken, that work seems redundant. The process recommended here seems not only to be more efficient, but also more effective than current practice in that the evaluation is done at a time when something can be done about deficiencies that may be noted.

Cognition Dimension

The columns of Table 14.2 represent the verbs, or cognition elements in the indicators. They are organized into three columns. The first is intended to include Anderson and Krathwohl's (2001) processes of remembering and understanding and deals primarily with factual knowledge; we called it Understanding Facts. The second column, called Applying Methods, is used for Anderson and Krathwohl's process of applying

Table 14.2. Blueprint for Eighth Grade Math

	Cognition Understanding Facts	Cognition Applying Methods	Reasoning	Strand Total	Difficulty Basic	Difficulty Proficient	Advanced
Strand 1: Numbers & Operations				8	2	4	2
1. Rational & Irrational Numbers	1						
2. Pairs of Real Numbers	1	1					
3. Approximate Solutions for Real Numbers		1					
4. Equivalents of Numerical Expressions		1					
5. Exponents	1	1					
6. Scientific Notation		1					
Strand 2: Algebra				24	6	12	6
1. Linear & Nonlinear Functions							
1. Definitions & Notation	1						
2. Linear Function Models		1					
3. Linear Equations	1						
4. Linear Arithmetic Sequences	1						
5. Geometric Sequences	1						
2. Use of Functions							
1. Linear Function Expressions	1						
2. Linear Function Graphs	1						
3. Properties of Linear Graphs	1						
4. Models of Arithmetic Sequences			2				
5. Models of Geometric Sequences			2				
3. Realizing Algebraic Expressions							

(Table continues on next page)

Table 14.2. Continued

	Cognition				Difficulty		
	Understanding Facts	Applying Methods	Reasoning	Strand Total	Basic	Proficient	Advanced
1. Evaluating Expressions		1					
2. Operating on Algebraic Expressions			1				
4. Equations & Inequalities							
1. Rates, Proportions, Non-Proportional Relations		1	1				
2. Multistep Linear Equations		1					
3. Linear Equation Forms		1					
4. Equations & Inequalities		1	2				
5. Relationships in Context	1						
6. Systems of Linear Equations	1						
7. Squares and Square Roots	1						
Strand 3: Geometry & Measurement				6	2	3	1
1. Right Triangles							
1. Pythagorean Theorem		1	1				
2. Distance Between Points		1					
2. Pairs of Lines on Coordinate Axes							
1. Parallel & Perpendicular Lines	1						
2. Polygons		1					
3. Finding Lines		1					
Strand 4: Data Analysis & Probability				6	1	3	2
1. Scatterplots		1	1				
2. Lines of Best Fit		1	1				
3. Predictions from Scatterplots		1	1				
TOTAL	14	18	12	44	11	22	11

and is associated primarily with procedural knowledge. Finally, we used Reasoning to include the remaining three of Anderson and Krathwohl's processes of analyzing, evaluating, and creating.

Although there are parallels between the Anderson and Krathwohl (2001) taxonomy and the Webb (2002) taxonomy, we chose to use the former. This was primarily for two reasons. First, the Anderson and Krathwohl (2001) taxonomy appears to stem from a broader knowledge base in cognitive theory and draws directly from the Bloom et al. (1956) taxonomy that is most familiar to teachers. Second, there exist implications for teaching as well as assessing in the 19 cognitive processes that are grouped within the Anderson and Krathwohl (2001) taxonomic levels. Thus, use of the Anderson and Krathwohl taxonomy has heuristic implications for both instruction and assessment, which seems to be a compelling advantage.

Another possibility for listing the cognitive processes along the columns would be to draw on the various discipline-specific analyses. We did not choose that approach for two primary reasons. First, the heuristic implications noted above would be lost. Second, a common taxonomy of processes would allow for cross-transfer of cognition from discipline to discipline and would foster research and perhaps an eventual curriculum in the area of metacognition that could be implemented in all classrooms and content areas.

The 19 individual cognitive processes can be organized into the columns of the example in Table 14.2. Once the state has determined its content elements (assessment limits) related to each of its indicators, a useful next step would be to review all the 19 cognitive processes for relevance to each of them. Those that are important enough to assess would be represented as entries in the cells of the test series' blueprint. Expressing the columns this way would best inform both teachers and test writers. Again, a broad-based committee would be best able to carry out this task.

Cells as Content-Cognition Combinations

Each of the cells in the blueprint represents a combination of a type of verb (the column) with a type of noun (the row). The verbs are typed by the cognitive processes they tap and the nouns by the content and assessment limit specifications. Together, they constitute a grouping of very specific activities that can be used to represent the cell. They should also be evaluated by a legitimizing process and once completed, the resulting blueprint can be used repeatedly for forms construction. The content-cognition cells can be used as specifications to item writers in the development of new prompts for field testing and by independent agencies in verifying that the resulting item matches its intent in both content and cognition.

Matching the Blueprint With Content Standards

One check on the quality of the blueprint would be to attempt to match it with the existing content standards. Any differences would be helpful information to process before the blueprint is finalized.

Use of the Blueprint in Forms Construction

The blueprint defines how many items, measuring what, are to be included on the test. It can also specify item types to be used within the cells as well as the spread of item difficulties to be represented. Assuming the items are available, it becomes a relatively straightforward process to assemble a test form that matches the specifications. Of course, there are always other criteria to be applied in forms development, such as making sure an item does not cue the answer to another item, but those are beyond our scope here.

An issue that can arise is that there may not be enough testing time available to cover the cells that need to be tested. One approach to that problem would be to develop multiple blueprints and to use different ones as forms are developed. This process can be open (nonsecure) as long as the information of which blueprint is to be used for a given form is held secure.

ASSESSMENT OF ALIGNMENT USING THE BLUEPRINT

Our contention is that development and use of the blueprint process as described here will result in test forms that are aligned with state content standards without further verification. Here we will test that claim using the example and the dimensions described by Webb (2002).

Categorical Concurrence

Recall that the categorical concurrence criterion is met if there are at least six items for each subscale (strand). In our example blueprint, each strand is assessed with six or more items (two with 6, one with 8 and one with 24; see the Total column). In general, when a new blueprint is completed, it must conform to the six-or-more rule. But note it is the blueprint that is evaluated, not a specific form. This is clearly so objective a judgment that it can be completed without additional verification.

Depth of Knowledge Consistency

The criterion for the measure of depth of knowledge consistency is met when at least half the items associated with an indicator are at or above the cognitive level of the indicator in the content standards, both cognitive level assignments coming from committee judgments. In our blueprint, the indicators are associated with the cells and carry cognitive level information through the columns using a different scheme than Webb proposed, but essentially parallel to his system. As long as the items represent the cell indicators, not just half, but all the items will be at the cognitive level of the indicator. Again, this is an objective determination as long as the cognitive levels of the items have been verified.

Range of Knowledge Correspondence

The range of knowledge correspondence criterion is satisfied if for every outcome, there is at least one item associated with at least half of the indicators. This criterion is clearly met in the example blueprint since every indicator row has at least one item. In practice, and especially with multiple blueprints, each blueprint will need to be evaluated as it is finalized. But again, this is a one-time judgment that is made at the blueprint level.

Balance of Representation

One hardly needs the Webb formula to note the balance in the example blueprint. But even if further justification were needed, it would again be at the blueprint level.

We note that all four criteria can be established on the basis of a sufficiently detailed and justified blueprint, as long as sufficient evidence exists that the items match the cells of the table. A process for that is suggested next.

ITEM TAGGING AND ITEM TAGS VERIFICATION

For every item, two judgments are necessary. It must be established that the item tests the specified content and that it does so using the specified cognitive process. Both these are judgments best made by trained committees, which is the method used in virtually all alignment studies. The process suggested here will involve two independent judgments per item.

The independence of the judgments is important. Since alignment evidence is perhaps the most important type for the validity of the judgments made from statewide achievement tests, it must be very credible. If judgments about the assignments of items to cells were made only by the test developers, they would be open to question since the test developers naturally have a self-serving interest in documenting high quality. Historically, the use of outside agencies to conduct alignment studies stems in part from the need for independent verification of the internal judgments.

We will assume a new blueprint has been developed for a test series (i.e., a grade-level test in one of the content areas). We will also assume that the blueprint will be used to replace an existing test development document for the test series and that a bank of items exists. We will need to describe what could be done for the existing bank and then how items could be added to the bank. Again, what needs to be verified is the cell-placement of each item.

Existing Items

For existing items, there may be content and/or cognition notations already available. If so, they can be reviewed by the state and/or the test contractor. If not, they can be created by either of these agencies. They then would need to be classified into the cells independently by another agency. Where discrepancies exist, those items could be reviewed for modification and/or deletion from the bank, and appropriate actions taken.

New Items

New items can be developed by asking item writers to represent certain specified cells. As they are developed, individually or in batches, an independent agency can be tasked with reviewing the classifications in order to verify the cell placements. This step should be done before the item is placed on a test form to be field-tested.

ITEM POOL ASSESSMENT

Every item should have two tags (labels). First, the cell should be identified, and the cell identification carries both content and cognition information. These should be verified judgments. Second, the difficulty should be established, which is done empirically after field testing (this can be done when item parameters are estimated). These are the two pieces of information that are needed to apply a blueprint like that in Table 14.2.

Counts of items in the pool can then be developed, cell-by-cell. The contractor may then determine how many items are needed in the bank to be able to develop the necessary forms and make recommendations about how many items representing which cells are needed for new item development. That will generate directions for item writers to work from.

The health of the item bank can also be evaluated according to the empirical levels of difficulty of the items in the various cells. Item writers may be given a target difficulty level, with their associated achievement level descriptions to try to fill gaps. This is the reason why the difficulties appear as columns in the example table.

SUMMARY AND RECOMMENDATIONS

We have described a process for test development that can result in an aligned form every time it is used. While there is a lot of development work up-front, doing the work pays many dividends down the road because the entire test development and verification process becomes much more efficient as well as effective compared with what most (almost all) states are currently doing. We will describe here a step-by-step list of activities for a state to undertake in order to implement the process. We assume the state has several ongoing test series; what is presented here would need to be done for each series.

1. Determine how cognition will be represented in the blueprint. This would be best carried out using a committee of educators, including curriculum developers, cognitive theorists, classroom learning specialists, and assessment experts. Coordination across test series is especially desirable.

2. Determine the content elements of the outcomes and indicators to be represented in the blueprint. This will come from the current content standards, perhaps augmented. For each indicator, develop assessments limits (the criterion for an assessment limit is that it can be used unambiguously to decide whether a particular item is or is not fair game for the assessment). This step is best done using a committee of curriculum developers, classroom learning specialists, and assessment practitioners.

3. Determine how many items will be on the test and how many will be associated with the content elements of each outcome and indicator. Distributions of item difficulty levels could conveniently be made at this time. This would best be carried out through contractor recommendation, reviewed by state department content and assessment specialists using a committee of curriculum developers and the state's technical advisory committee. One question the latter needs to address is the adequacy of item sampling for the intended uses of the scores (e.g., for individual vs. group-level interpretations).

4. Allocate the items associated with each of the content elements of the indicators across the levels of cognition. This is best accomplished using a committee of curriculum specialists and the state's technical advisory committee. The latter should be asked to apply the criteria of an alignment methodology to the result as part of the process. This step will result in the final blueprint(s) to be used.

5. Slot the existing item pool into the cells of the blueprint. This can be done by the contractor in consultation with curriculum specialists. At the same time, the contractor should determine the difficulty levels of the items using existing data.

6. Obtain independent verification of the nonempirical judgments made in the prior step using another outside contractor (perhaps called the alignment contractor). Note any problem items and generate recommendations about what to do with each.

7. Review the numbers of items needed and available in the various cells of the blueprint, including difficulty levels and make recommendations for new item development in order to make recommendations for new item development. The contractor would be best for this task.

8. Develop items for specific cells and difficulty levels. Again, the contractor should do this.

9. Obtain independent verification of the cell placements of the new items. The alignment contractor could perform this task.

10. Administer the items as field test items and review for psychometric acceptability and difficulty classifications.

This process, though detailed and requiring a great deal of up-front work, should pay dividends in more efficient assessments in the future with more information that is useful to educators in designing more effective ways achieve and to document success.

Alignment and Higher Order Thinking

In this chapter we have described a system for highlighting both content and cognition in the descriptions of each of the assessed domains in a statewide testing program. The process results in clear and publicly supportable achievement targets that can direct the work of both teachers and curriculum specialists in ensuring that instruction matches the assessments. Further, the process is flexible enough for states to include the content elements that evolve from their own curriculum development processes and the approach to cognition that they find most useful for their educators to use. Finally, the process can result in assessments that are aligned within the test design process, obviating the need for outside checks on alignment after the tests have been used.

A note about the role of higher order thinking in assessment is important here. While cognition, sometimes called processing has long been recommended in assessment courses for teachers, when states write their assessments blueprints, they often ignore everything but content considerations. This has resulted far too often in a hodgepodge of cognition that is represented on tests only in a haphazard way. The work of practitioners like Webb (2002, 2005) has gone a long way toward making sure cognition is represented adequately in assessments. We view our proposal as a next step in support of ensuring that higher order thinking becomes a regular goal in instruction through its representation as regular elements in the goal of assessment.

ACKNOWLEDGMENT

This chapter was partially funded by the Maryland State Department of Education (MSDE) through the Maryland Assessment Research Center for Education Success (MARCES) at the University of Maryland. The opinions expressed are those of the author and not necessarily those of MARCES or MSDE.

REFERENCES

Anderson, L. W., & Krathwohl, D. R. (2001). *A taxonomy for learning, teaching, and assessing*. New York, NY: Longman.

Bloom, B. S., Engelhart, M. D., Furst, E. J., Hill, W. H., & Krathwohl, D. R. (1956). *Taxonomy of educational objectives: The classification of educational goals* (Handbook I: Cognitive Domain). New York, NY: Longman.

Cizek, G. J. (2001), *Setting performance standards: Concepts, methods, and perspectives*. Mahwah, NJ: Erlbaum.

Schafer, W. D., & Moody, M. (2004). Designing accountability assessments for teaching. *Practical Assessment, Research & Evaluation, 9*(14). Retrieved from http://PAREonline.net/getvn.asp?v=9&n=14

Schafer, W. D., Wang, J., & Wang, V. (2009). Validity in action: State assessment validity evidence for compliance with NCLB. In R. W. Lissitz (Ed.), *The concept of validity* (pp. 173-193). Charlotte, NC: Information Age.

Webb, N. L. (2002). *Alignment study in language arts, mathematics, science, and social studies of state standards and assessments for four states*. Washington, DC: Council of Chief State School Officers.

Webb, N. L. (2005, April). *Issues related to judging the alignment of curriculum standards and assessment.* Paper presented at the annual meeting of the American Educational Research Association, Montreal, Canada.